Russia and the

Challenge of

Fiscal Federalism

WORLD BANK

REGIONAL AND

SECTORAL STUDIES

Russia and the

Challenge of

Fiscal Federalism

EDITED BY

CHRISTINE I. WALLICH

The World Bank
Washington, D.C.

The World Bank Regional and Sectoral Studies series provides an outlet for work
that is relatively limited in its subject matter or geographical coverage but that
contributes to the intellectual foundations of development operations and policy
formulation.

The findings, interpretations, and conclusions expressed in this publication are
those of the authors and should not be attributed in any manner to the World Bank,
to its affiliated organizations, or to the members of its Board of Executive Directors
or the countries they represent.

The material in this publication is copyrighted. Requests for permission to
reproduce portions of it should be sent to the Office of the Publisher at the address
shown in the copyright notice above. The World Bank encourages dissemination
of its work and will normally give permission promptly and, when the reproduction
is for noncommercial purposes, without asking a fee. Permission to copy portions
for classroom use is granted through the Copyright Clearance Center, Suite 910,
222 Rosewood Dr., Danvers, Massachusetts 01923, U.S.A.

The boundaries, colors, denominations, and other information shown on any map
in this volume do not imply on the part of the World Bank Group any judgment
on the legal status of any territory or the endorsement or acceptance of such
boundaries.

The complete backlist of publications from the World Bank is shown in the annual
Index of Publications, which contains an alphabetical title list and indexes of subjects,
authors, and countries and regions. The latest edition is available free of charge
from Distribution Unit, Office of the Publisher, The World Bank, 1818 H Street,
N.W., Washington, D.C. 20433, U.S.A., or from Publications, The World Bank,
66, avenue d'Iéna, 75116 Paris, France.

Christine I. Wallich is lead economist in the World Bank's Europe and Central
Asia Regional Office, Central Europe Department.

Cover design by Sam Ferro

Library of Congress Cataloging-in-Publication Data

Russia and the challenge of fiscal federalism / edited by Christine
   I. Wallich.
      p. cm.—(World Bank regional and sectoral studies)
   Includes bibliographical references and index.
   ISBN 0-8213-2683-X
   1. Intergovernmental fiscal relationships—Russia (Federation)
   2. Russia (Federation)—Economic policy—1991–   I. Wallich,
   Christine, 1952– . II. World Bank. III. Series.
   HJ1211.52.Z6R87   1994
   336.47—dc20
                                                 93-47897
                                                    CIP

Contents

Contributors

Roy Bahl is professor of economics and director of the Policy Research Center at Georgia State University.

Jennie I. Litvack is country economist for Viet Nam in the World Bank's East Asia and Pacific Region.

Jorge Martinez-Vazquez is professor of economics and associate director of the Policy Research Center at Georgia State University.

Charles E. McLure, Jr., is senior fellow at the Hoover Institution, Stanford University.

Christine I. Wallich is lead economist in the Central Europe Department of the World Bank's Europe and Central Asia Region.

Preface

History shaped this book. The work on which it is based originated in a program of technical assistance for the U.S.S.R. When the advisory team began its work in early 1991, issues of federalism in the U.S.S.R. were mainly technical. Relationships between the U.S.S.R. and its fifteen republics were still intact and, it could be argued, strong. The challenge, then, was to design a system of fiscal relationships between the Union and the republics that was market friendly and would help underpin the decentralization that the U.S.S.R. was determined would go ahead as part of *perestroika.*

Destiny then took a hand. Late in 1991, events moved quickly. The powers and activities of the U.S.S.R.'s central government were gradually eroded, culminating in the dissolution of virtually all central bodies in November 1991. These events also affected the union budget. Expenditures continued, but revenues dried up as the union republics halted fiscal transfers to the center. The union budget died, one might say, a fiscal death. Pressure for political autonomy also became irresistible, and Russia declared its independence in November 1991. When the president of the U.S.S.R. resigned in December 1991, so ended seventy-four years of soviet organization that had begun with the workers' revolution of 1917.

The focus of the authors' work then changed to Russia itself. It was clear, almost from the outset, that fiscal federalism in the Russian Federation would be as important as in the U.S.S.R. The team set out to examine fiscal decentralization and intergovernmental fiscal relations between Russia and its eighty-nine *oblasts*—Russia's second tier of government and its basic territorial units, equivalent to states. The team worked in collaboration with the Russian Ministry of Finance, Russia's oblast administrations, and the parliamentary commissions of the Supreme Soviet of the Russian Federation to understand and analyze the current intergovernmental system and make recommendations for its reform. Early on it was also apparent that the issue of potentially huge revenues from natural resource taxes could prove very divisive—who gets what share?—and would become explosive if prices rose to world levels. Obvious also was that ethnicity, regional differences, and demands for fiscal sovereignty within Russia were growing and that, as in the Union, the intergovernmental system could play an important role in increasing (or reducing) political tensions.

Fieldwork was the basic method of gathering information. Members of the team visited oblasts in both European Russia (Moscow City and Moscow, Riazanskaia, and Nizhniy Novgorod oblasts) and Asian Russia (Khanty-Mansiiskii autonomous okrug and Tyumenskaia oblast). Field visits were made to rural and urban areas, rich and poor regions, and agricultural and industrial regions. Some oblasts were prosperous and diversified, and some were in industrial decline. In each oblast we visited *rayons* (Russia's third tier of government), both rural and urban, as well as the oblast seat, or capital.

The contrasts were startling. One autonomous *okrug* (region) in Siberia, Khanty-Mansiiskii (the size of France, but with one-fiftieth of the population), produces about as much oil as Texas or Kuwait—and more than 80 percent of Russia's oil. Unlike Dallas or Kuwait City, however, its capital had only one paved street, no glitz, no glamour. Pedestrians mingled with livestock. Workers in the oil industry are among the best paid in Russia. Yet the neat wooden, blue-painted, white-gingerbreaded houses for workers had walls of bare wood and windows of paper. Many had no running water, and floors were often earthen—all this in an area where temperatures fall to minus 40°C or below. Environmental damage from exploitation of oil and gas was rife. Small wonder, perhaps, that the okrug's finance director made the impassioned plea for a fair share of Russia's resources, some ownership in the region's natural resource heritage, and the retention of enough fiscal revenues to enable the okrug to raise social service standards in Khanty-Mansiiskii—especially for schools and health facilities—to some fraction of the average for Russia.

One of the best-off regions in Russia is Moscow oblast. Its income levels, endowment of industrial investments from the planning system, and social services far exceed anything offered elsewhere in Russia. In the days of the U.S.S.R., it was said that Moscow's budget was the fifth largest in the Union, following that of the federal government, Russia itself, Ukraine, and Kazakhstan. But life is not easy here either: Moscow oblast is struggling to privatize its industrial heritage and, like other regions in Russia, is striving to find budgetary resources to replace the outlays that were previously the responsibility of enterprises but which the enterprises, once privatized, will no longer be able to maintain. It, too, wants more from the center.

We concluded that the design of a well-functioning intergovernmental fiscal system is key to Russia's macroeconomic stability, to structural adjustment, to the provision of social services and a social safety net during the difficult transition to a market economy, and, especially, to Russia's political cohesion. Outlining the nature of these center-oblast issues and tensions, and the contribution a well-designed intergovernmental system can make to reducing them, is the purpose of this book.

This book is not a political science tract, nor does it examine the centrifugal forces of center-oblast relationships from this perspective. It does not look at municipal finance per se, and it touches only lightly on the issues of intergovernmental finance *within* an oblast. Although there is significant empirical work, it is not a data-intensive or statistical study; it is still early days in Russia for that. In addition, it is not a historical treatise, and it examines the past history of intergovernmental relations in the U.S.S.R. only insofar as that history sheds light on the present. Finally, this is not an academic book. Although some of the authors are academicians and the subject matter offers much for researchers to address, our purpose is to present the importance of intergovernmental fiscal relations in Russia to a broad lay audience.

Thus, the book is policy oriented and is designed to analyze the emerging process of fiscal federalism and the effects of recent legislation on intergovernmental relations in Russia. It seeks to evaluate the strengths and weaknesses of the new structures that emerge and to outline possible directions for further reform. The book, with chapters contributed by four authors in addition to the editor, was written as a team effort and represents an integrated view of fiscal federalism in Russia.

The chapters follow a common analytical framework, each describing different aspects of an integrated whole. The introductory and concluding chapters, as well as the chapters on the macroeconomic dimensions of fiscal federalism in Russia and the description of the Russian system, were written by the editor. Jorge Martinez-Vazquez is the author of the chapter on expenditures and expenditure assignment. Roy Bahl wrote the chapter on revenues and revenue assignment. Charles McLure, Jr., is the author of the chapter on natural resource taxation and sharing of resource rents. Jennie I. Litvack prepared the chapter on regional demands in federal and nonfederal systems.

The analysis focuses on the 1992–93 period, and much of the analytical and empirical work draws on data from 1992. Although the speed of change in Russia is dizzying, this does not detract from the relevance of the analysis. Much of the change in the intergovernmental area has been more apparent than real; there is a very palpable sense of "plus ça change, plus c'est la même chose." As before, the "system" is not really a system at all; it basically retains its negotiated features. For example, in spite of new laws and ongoing adjustments to the fiscal system each quarter, our analysis suggests that the end results, in terms of expenditure and revenue distribution, were not much different than before 1991. The mechanisms might have changed, but the results have not. A detailed analysis of the years 1992–93 thus carries lessons that go beyond this period.

The book is aimed at those with an interest in Russia—general economists, practitioners of public finance, academics and advisers, and policymakers and their advisers in the Russian Federation and in other states of the former U.S.S.R. It may also be of interest to those working on other economies in transition. Those who are interested in social safety nets, macroeconomic stabilization, privatization, fiscal decentralization, and the critical role of intergovernmental fiscal relations in facilitating a successful transition to the market economy should also find this book relevant.

This book is based on work undertaken in the course of the World Bank's technical assistance program for Russia, which began in 1991. I am indebted to the World Bank for its support throughout the program and in the preparation of the book.

It was an especial pleasure to work with all the contributors to this book—on a personal and professional level. To Roy Bahl, Jorge Martinez-Vazquez, Charles McLure, and Jennie Litvack, each, heartfelt thanks.

Invaluable support and cooperation was provided by our Russian colleagues: Stanislas Korolev, vice minister of finance of the Russian Federation; Dr. Alexander Pochinok, chairman of the Commission on Budgets, Taxes, and Prices of the Supreme Soviet; Dr. Benjamin Sokolov, chairman of the Budget Subcommission of the Supreme Soviet; Dr. Sergei Shatalov, chairman of the Subcommission on Taxes and Prices; and Vladimir Ispravnikov, chairman of the Supreme Economic Commission. Insights, advice, and support were also received from Dr. Natasha Kalinina, Institute of Forecasting, Russian Academy of Sciences. Her knowledge of Russia, its economy, and its peoples added much to the richness of our understanding. Others who shared their knowledge and insights and to whom we owe a special debt include Sergei Vasiliev, Center for Economic Reforms; Alexander Lubianoi, Ministry of Finance; Viktor Vlasov, Moscow Oblast Administration; Evgeny Korolev, Nizhniy Novgorod Administration; Dr. George Polyak, College of Finance; Andre Sitnikov, Supreme Economic Council; Sergei Voblenka, Riazanskaia Oblast Administration; M. Churilov, Khanty-Mansiiskii Administration; Sergei Alexashenko, vice minister of finance; and Sergei Sibilev, consultant to the Budget Commission. This leaves out many other Russian experts—too numerous to name—who generously shared their expertise and insights, and whose help benefited the work greatly. We are also deeply grateful to the Ministry of Finance of the Russian Federation for permission to use hitherto unpublished data in this volume.

Closer to home, special appreciation goes also to Mario Blejer, Philippe Le Houerou, Helga Müller, Piroshka Nagy, and Horst Zimmermann, who were deeply involved especially at the early stages of the technical assistance process, and whose early insights contributed significantly to our understanding of Russia's federalism. Advice, comments, and valuable suggestions were received from many World Bank and International Monetary Fund staff and other experts. In particular, the study has benefited from the expertise and insights of Richard Bird, Nancy Birdsall, Milka Casanegra-Jantscher, Russell Cheetham, Martha de Melo, Shanta Devarajan, Gunnar Eskeland, Ved Gandhi, Elana Gold, John Holsen, Yukon Huang, Dani Kaufmann, Timothy King, Robert Liebenthal, Johannes Linn, Charles McPherson, Costas Michalopolous, Adrienne Nassau, Gur Ofer, Richard Podolske, Remy Prud'homme, Bertrand Renaud, Marcelo Selowsky, Carlos Silvani, Lawrence Summers, Emil Sunley, and Paulo Vieira da Cunha.

Outstanding, patient, and thorough secretarial support was cheerfully provided by Susheela Jonnakuty. Ritu Nayyar provided skillful, enthusiastic, and efficient research support. We are also deeply indebted to our outstanding editors, Bruce Ross-Larson and Vincent McCullough.

Finally, thanks to my husband, Leo Hakim, for his support, for the professional criticism he provided as a fellow economist, and for his patience with the long hours (and long trips) required for the completion of this manuscript.

Christine I. Wallich
Central Europe Department
The World Bank, December 1993

1

Russia's dilemma

Christine I. Wallich

Russia's moment of truth is fast approaching. It is in the midst of an economic and political transition never before attempted anywhere. Russia is trying not only to restructure its entire economic system but, at the same time, to protect the well-being of all citizens, stabilize prices and its external balance, and provide public services. It is also trying to establish a system of governance acceptable to far-flung regions whose cultural identity, natural resource endowments, and degree of economic development differ widely. It is a herculean task for the new Russian Federation.

The challenges of federalism

At the heart of all these challenges is an important issue: intergovernmental finance; more specifically, the division of expenditure responsibilities and the allocation of revenues to different levels of government. In a nutshell, it is about how Russia's national revenue pie should be divided between the federal government and its oblasts (Russia's basic unit of subnational government), and below them, its cities and rayons (Russia's third tier of government), and which of these levels of government should be responsible for which type of spending.

The challenge of fiscal federalism in economies in transition

Intergovernmental finance in Russia is not a "local matter." How services and goods are provided by various levels of government and who pays for them has consequences that extend throughout the economy. In most economies in transition, the design of fiscal federalism is crucial because it

affects almost all of the key goals of reform, including macroeconomic stabilization, the effectiveness of the social safety net, and private sector development. In the case of Russia it is also critical to nation building.

In Russia and other economies in transition, the first step in designing
a good system of intergovernmental finance is to delineate the role of the
public and private sectors and to define a budgetary role for the state that
is less economically pervasive than in the past. Next comes assigning expenditures. What are the respective roles of central and subnational governments? Traditional public finance theory suggests that an *efficient* expenditure assignment between levels of government is based on the geographic
dimension of benefits (chapter 4). Ideally, each jurisdiction should provide
and finance services whose benefits accrue within its boundaries.

Russia and other economies in transition provide a special challenge,
however, because the responsibilities and nature of enterprises and government are changing dramatically. Enterprises that played an important
role in providing social services and financing social assets (for example,
schools, hospitals, housing, urban infrastructure, and water and sewerage)
now must divest expenditures that are not directly related to production.
Some divested social assets could be privatized; but many other expenditure functions fall into domains that will be assigned to the subnational level.
The key challenge for Russia now is to determine the costs of these outlays
and to design a system of tax assignments, shared taxes, and intergovernmental transfers that provides oblasts with sufficient revenues to meet these
and other assigned expenditures, so that revenue-expenditure correspondence is ensured.

This chapter touches on these and other themes, each developed in
greater detail in later chapters of the book. Its purpose is to provide an
overview of Russia's dilemma and the major issues Russia will face in redesigning its system of fiscal federalism. The chapter follows the outlines of
the book. It begins with a discussion of the macroeconomic dimensions of
fiscal federalism in Russia, followed by a discussion of the role of government in the economy and of expenditure assignment and revenue-sharing
issues. It concludes with a discussion of the special challenges to federalism
posed by Russia's ethnic and natural resource–rich areas and how a well-
designed intergovernmental system can become a catalyst that binds together the Russian Federation.

The challenge for Russia

In Russia's present intergovernmental tax and expenditure system there is
no *correspondence* (or matching) of fiscal responsibilities and resources. Most
subnational governments do not have enough revenue to meet their spend-

ing responsibilities. So Russia must also design a system of transfers that will both meet the shortfall and support more efficient and equitable provision of services. These fiscal changes will determine the efficiency with which the economy performs, and its future direction.

The new intergovernmental fiscal system now evolving in Russia gives subnational governments new spending responsibilities (especially for investment and in the social sectors), as well as new budgetary rights and new fiscal resources. These are formalized in the Basic Principles of Taxation Law—the basic legislation defining the new fiscal system—and other new laws (see appendixes A and B for details). The major changes have not yet been fully implemented, however, and subnational governments are operating under transitional rules. Some oblast governments also want special treatment or *regimes* outside the laws.

The new intergovernmental laws, if implemented, would have some merit. They seek to move governance closer to the people, give subnational governments more budgetary discretion, make revenue sharing more transparent and less negotiable, and clarify and define the rights and responsibilities of subnational governments vis-à-vis the center. These are laudable goals, and supportive of the general economic reform under way. Much more, however, needs to be done.

The speed of change in Russia makes focusing on longer-term issues, such as the establishment of an intergovernmental financing system, difficult. However, there is now a critical window of opportunity for introducing refinements to the intergovernmental financing system because it is still in transition. Failure to seize the moment could weaken federal leadership and influence, especially when strong forces for oblast autonomy are pulling at the center. Indeed, the future of the Russian Federation depends importantly on a transparent, fair, consensus-based intergovernmental financing framework that matches resources and expenditures. An improved fiscal framework would provide an important mechanism for containing these centrifugal forces.

Ideally, any system of subnational government financing would:
- Ensure correspondence between subnational expenditure responsibilities and resources
- Incorporate some subnational revenue powers and provide incentives for subnational governments to mobilize revenues
- Support the macroeconomic policies of the central government
- Give appropriate spending discretion to subnational governments and improve the accountability of local officials
- Be transparent, based on objective, stable, non-negotiated criteria
- Be administratively simple
- Be consistent with national income-distribution goals.

In addition, in Russia any new system should also support the government's role, consistent with market-oriented reform.

The recent transition

The challenge for Russia's policymakers is to create an intergovernmental financing system that is compatible with short-term macroeconomic stabilization, combines rules with discretion, and is flexible enough to accommodate future structural shifts in the economy. At the same time, it must provide stability to subnational governments and essentially buy their cooperation, to build nationhood. How will this be achieved?

To begin, policymakers and legislators must change their approach to public finance reform. In Russia, certain fiscal issues and reforms have traditionally been viewed in isolation—expenditure assignment and spending mandates, tax-sharing policies and tax reform, and deficit-reduction and macropolicies. They must now be considered as a whole and the effects of each incorporated into the intergovernmental system. More generally, fiscal policy, tax administration, and intergovernmental fiscal relations are so interconnected in Russia that they must be addressed simultaneously (chapter 5).

Not surprisingly, because of the absence of an integrated framework, the benefits envisioned in the Basic Principles of Taxation Law, which lays the foundation for Russia's new revenue and revenue-sharing system and of other new legislation, could not be realized in 1992—or beyond. On the spending side, subnational governments still have less than full budgetary discretion. On the revenue side, Russia's old ad hoc tax-sharing system has not yet been phased out. Although huge strides have been taken to improve the intergovernmental system, Russia is still unable to move away from the prereform system of negotiated revenue sharing. And the Ministry of Finance still determines the volume of resources to be transferred to the oblasts, and which oblast gets what. The present system of intergovernmental finance thus remains ad hoc and contentious and could increasingly lead to more "ad hocery" and special regimes, bilaterally negotiated by separatist or disgruntled oblasts (chapter 7). As one Russian observer said: "This government has no regional (subnational) policy and it is killing itself."

This discretionary and bargained system gives the federal government great flexibility to determine the overall fiscal balance and, in principle, to pursue macroeconomic stabilization policies. It also gives the Ministry of Finance the flexibility to distribute resources among rich and poor oblasts to realize equalization or other objectives. For subnational governments, however, the system implies budgetary uncertainty and an inability to plan for service delivery. The lack of transparency is also perceived by oblasts as unfair. They must compete with each other for shares in a revenue pie that cannot sustain all equally. In practice, that means negotiating and bargaining with the Ministry of Finance to improve their lot.

Any new comprehensive and integrated intergovernmental financing system must not only respond to the problems of the current transitional period but also address fundamental longer-term issues. An important first step is to establish an institutional framework, including a special "blue-ribbon commission" to develop an intergovernmental strategy and plan its implementation. The commission would consist of informed leaders from the professions, academia, the Supreme Soviet and relevant ministries, oblasts, and cities, drawing on foreign advice where necessary.

What, precisely, would such a commission need to do? The commission should undertake a careful, empirical study of Russia's options, decide how to assign spending responsibilities to different levels of government, and quantify expenditure responsibilities by function to assess the spending requirements of subnational governments. It would then estimate likely expenditure and revenue growth trends—that is, their elasticities. It would need to analyze options for revenue assignment, tax sharing, tax surcharges, formula grants, and natural resource revenue sharing, to name just a few. Finally, it would need to simulate the effects of the newly designed system on central and subnational fiscal balances and on the distribution of the fiscal resources among subnational governments in the short and long term. Such applied policy analysis is critical to assess whether the system's effects on budgetary balance and on equalization across oblasts are acceptable. With consensus on the most appropriate strategy, the commission would report to the Supreme Soviet, which would legislate policy implementation.

The macroeconomic dimensions of intergovernmental finances

The government's stabilization program calls for reducing the state budget deficit substantially. How this reduction affects the different levels of government will depend on how governmental functions are reassigned among various levels. In the 1992 fiscal program there were major budgetary cuts in central government spending—enterprise investment, producer and consumer subsidies, and defense. An important part of social expenditures (early in 1992) and investment outlays (later) was delegated to subnational governments. The budget envisaged a major increase in taxes, primarily on petroleum products and foreign trade—revenues that are retained, in principle, fully by the federal government. Thus, most extra revenue would accrue to the *federal* government, while most additional spending would be by *subnational* governments.

There is now, it seems, a mismatch between expenditure assignments and revenue shares. This can undermine the national stabilization effort and put pressure on subnational budgets. Apparently, the center's basic strategy has been to push the deficit downward by shifting unfunded spending responsibilities down to the oblasts and hoping that the subnational governments will cut costs. Rather than cutting their outlays on the social safety net during transition, however, subnational governments might instead seek to negotiate greater central government subsidies. Or, caught without enough revenue to cover their newly assigned spending mandates, oblasts might simply fail to undertake important expenditures, might incur arrears, or might borrow from banks and from the enterprises they still own and control (and which have easier access to credit than do the oblast governments themselves). This adds to pressure for credit creation. Oblasts have also developed extrabudgetary revenue resources. Some oblasts have delayed federal tax remittances, leaving the federal budget singularly vulnerable because in the Russian system of tax administration all tax revenues are collected by tax offices at the county (or lower) levels and remitted *upward*. Ironically, focusing stabilization policy only on the federal deficit is leading to actions that can further destabilize the economy, reduce the transparency of budgetary accounts and, if oblasts are successful in their ability to obtain credit, subvert monetary objectives. (These and other dysfunctional coping mechanisms are described in chapter 3.) Since Russia's subnational governments account for almost half of total budgetary outlays, sound intergovernmental fiscal policies are crucial to a successful stabilization effort.

Efforts to reduce the budget deficit by squeezing the subnational sector are also harming privatization (see below). An important aspect of fiscal decentralization in Russia has been the transfer of enterprise ownership from central to subnational governments. Oblasts derive significant funds from enterprises they own, and they benefit significantly from the expenditures these enterprises finance. Hard-pressed oblasts may therefore oppose privatization and seek to reinforce their revenue base by holding on to the enterprises they own and control, in an effort to ensure the continued provision of services they find increasingly unaffordable under the current intergovernmental fiscal arrangements. At the same time, encouraging enterprises to continue to provide social services makes privatization even more difficult. Fiscal arrangements that address the needs of each level of government and match expenditures and revenues should thus be a high priority.

Government, enterprises, and privatization

Russia wants to move rapidly toward a market-oriented economy. However, at present, many activities of government go well beyond what is considered desirable in a market economy. Some government spending can no longer be justified—for example, oblasts and rayons producing and selling goods and services that are more appropriately the bailiwick of private enterprises (chapter 3). A major redefinition of the role of government vis-à-vis the private sector is in order.

Subnational governments in the role of entrepreneur

A major problem is that subnational governments still see themselves as entrepreneurs and producers. Indeed, their involvement in economic ventures (using their land, commercial assets, or industrial resources in partnership with other investors) appears to be increasing. Apart from being *fundamentally inconsistent with privatization,* this carries several dangers. The most significant is that such businesses will probably compete unfairly with emerging private competitors, thus undercutting the government's tax base. Moreover, pressures will be put on subnational governments to shore up their enterprises (and their employment) by subsidizing them. There are likely to be many poor investments. In market economies the small-business failure rate is high, with reportedly only one in five surviving the first three years. There is no reason to expect that Russia's oblast governments can beat the odds. There is a danger, too, that subnational governments will become involved in setting up banks, directing their credit or lending policies.

Enterprises and their social assets

A serious and looming problem concerns the traditional role of public enterprises in providing social services. Historically, Russia's state enterprises have financed many expenditures that would be shouldered by the public sector in a market economy (for example, schools, hospitals, roads, and sanitation). With marketization of Russia's economy, this kind of spending cannot continue to be an enterprise responsibility and some of it is likely to be transferred to subnational governments, since such outlays generally fall into so-called local areas of spending responsibility. The transfer is already taking place de facto because of the financial problems of many government enterprises. Public enterprises cannot continue to provide such services and successfully compete in an increasingly privatized and market-oriented economy. However, it is essential that they be transferred in a programmed and orderly way. Who will assume which responsibilities? Central government appears to have neither quantified this problem nor planned a solution. It needs to do both. In sum, any increase in subnational spending responsibilities must be accompanied by a corresponding increase in revenue flows to subnational government (chapter 4).

Expenditures and expenditure assignment

As in many other economies in transition, Russia has focused mostly on changing tax assignment and revenue sharing between federal and oblast governments. This puts the cart before the horse. Expenditures must be assigned to one level of government or another and the expenditure assignments quantified before resource requirements can be established. In Russia the availability of revenue is dictating the assignment of spending responsibilities among different levels of governments, rather than the other way around.

Consistency with principles

Three principles underlie the assignment of expenditure responsibilities in the mainstream academic literature. First, public services whose benefits do not accrue beyond local boundaries should be provided by local governments. Second, services that benefit several communities should be provided at the state level. And, third, services whose benefits accrue to the whole country should be provided by the federal government. (There may be exceptions when considerations of regional autonomy take on importance.) In most countries stabilization and income distribution policies are central responsibilities; allocative functions, largely subnational. These principles encourage the accountability of subnational governments and are the rationale for fiscal decentralization. They also seem to be well understood in the Russian Federation. Traditional spending assignments, largely continued through inertia under the Russian Federation, have seemed appropriate enough until recently. Recent assignment changes, however, made under cover of the current legal murkiness, violate general principles.

Shifting responsibility for the safety net

In early 1992 the central government—in an apparent effort to balance its budget—shifted responsibility for most subsidy and social welfare programs to oblast and rayon governments, where before they had been financed by transfers from the center. While price subsidies will cease when prices are freed, the need for social protection for those most hurt by Russia's economic change will not. Apparently the center has not estimated the cost of this social protection, or how this cost might be matched with available oblast revenues.

In addition, this safety net policy may contradict the traditional approach of assigning expenditure responsibilities. If the adequacy of the social safety net is a national priority for smoothing the difficult transition that lies ahead, should it be the responsibility of oblast and rayon governments alone?

Reassignment of capital spending

In mid-1992 most investment financing—even of nationally strategic areas such as highways, military housing, and airports—was shifted to subnational budgets, where before the federal government had approved, financed, and implemented all subnational capital investment. Shifting these to lower-level governments may ease short-run federal budget pressures, but it is inconsistent with expenditure assignment principles and efficient service delivery. It is also provocative at a time when subnational discontent is growing (chapter 7). Subnational governments should be responsible only for capital investments that correspond to their assigned recurrent expenditures—for example, for schools, local roads, and other subnational infrastructure.

The Russian government is also using spending mandates to require subnational governments to undertake expenditures without adequate funding. These include across-the-board wage increases and pension adjustments regardless of the budgetary position of each government. There should, ideally, be no mandates without funding.

The dangers of shifting expenditures down

There is a more general issue: there is little precision or consistency in assigning spending responsibilities. Both subnational governments and the central government reap advantages from this. Subnational governments use their broader responsibilities to bargain with the center for a bigger share of revenue. The federal government has an extra instrument—jettisoning spending—to help balance its budget. This cannot continue much longer if the intergovernmental relations in the Federation are to move toward greater certainty and predictability. If spending responsibilities are not assigned specifically, determining the revenue sufficiency of alternative tax allocations or assignments (including those in the Basic Principles of Taxation) will not be possible. And the desirability of alternative systems of sharing will be a moot point.

If this trend persists, moreover, what important spending functions will remain for the central government to justify its existence to skeptical regional governments and to give meaning to the union? Russia's federal government may inadvertently be contributing to its own worst nightmare—the disintegration of the Russian Federation.

Quantifying expenditure assignments

Quantifying expenditure responsibilities, function by function, is perhaps the most important first step in restructuring intergovernmental financing.

Estimates of subnational expenditure requirements would include those functions that continue to be local government's responsibility, those assumed by the government as enterprises give them up, and those that should no longer be the responsibility of any level of government (chapter 4).

Tax revenues and transfers

Russia's revenue-sharing system, inherited from the Union and still in place in 1993, had two distinct features. First, unlike most systems of intergovernmental finance, revenue is shared *upward* from the rayons and oblasts that collect it, to the federal budget. This upward sharing contributed to the breakup of the Union when the republics, beginning with Russia and Ukraine, stopped making their transfers to the union budget. Upward sharing makes the Russian Federation similarly vulnerable. Second, the intergovernmental system is not really a system. It is a series of ad hoc, bargained, nontransparent bilateral agreements, whose effects and incentives are not well understood.

A transition is now taking place toward a true system that seeks to allocate revenue sources to each level of government in a more transparent manner. The Basic Principles of Taxation Law, only partially implemented, assigns all taxes, in full, to one or another level of government and allows for no transfers. Value-added tax is assigned to the federal government, and personal and corporate income taxes are intended to flow to subnational governments. Twenty-one very minor taxes are assigned to rayon governments. Subnational governments, however, have been assigned only the *revenue* from these taxes. The distinction is important. Subnational governments have no rate-setting or base-setting authority—a major omission. All tax assessment and collection remains a federal responsibility, although executed in local tax offices.

These laws—if they are implemented—could improve intergovernmental financing and increase transparency by limiting ad hoc arrangements. They give subnational governments some prescribed revenues—and some incentives for increasing tax effort. But flaws remain in the Basic Principles, in subsequent laws, and in the present program, indicating the need for adjustments and, probably, a new law (chapter 5).

Mismatch of assigned revenues and expenditures

One flaw is that there is no correspondence (or matching) of current subnational tax assignments with expenditure responsibilities. There is no guarantee that the two major taxes assigned to the oblast level will be sufficient to finance "normal" subnational expenditure responsibilities—either for the subnational sector in aggregate, or for individual oblasts. If the personal and corporate taxes overfinance the subnational sector, there is no provision to "claw back" any surplus for the center; if oblasts are underfunded, there is no legal provision to provide grants or subventions (in Russian terminology) to make up the difference. A similar mismatch may emerge in the longer run, since there is no guarantee that the two subnational-assigned taxes and subnational expenditures will grow at the same rate. The revenue and expenditure elasticities may be very different.

Tax assignment and tax sharing

The Basic Principles represent a move toward a system of pure tax assignment very different from the present system, where most taxes are shared. Of course, some taxes can and should be assigned to subnational governments. But which ones? There are several arguments against changing in a radical fashion from tax sharing to tax assignment in the case of the major tax sources in Russia today. First, assignment of nationally uniform taxes leaves subnational governments no revenue discretion of their own and leaves budgets vulnerable to changes in central tax policy. A single tax rate change or tax policy change could reduce (or increase) subnational revenues significantly and have widely different impacts across oblasts. Thus, even though tax assignment appears to reduce the dependence of subnational governments on the center by giving each level of government its own taxes, this independence is illusory. Localities also remain vulnerable to any revenue volatility of their assigned taxes (corporate and personal taxes are particularly volatile), and they have no discretion over the setting of tax rates. Given the taxes proposed for assignment by the law—corporate and personal income taxes—this is probably a good thing. In Russia today it would be hard to argue for eighty-nine different corporate or personal tax rates. The confusion and tax competition that might arise would make Russia's revenue system a true "tax jungle" (chapter 5).

The assignment approach can also worsen resource allocation: oblasts' vested interests in enterprise tax revenues can, in an economy as regionalized and with as few antimonopoly policies as Russia, encourage domestic protectionism and interoblast trade barriers to protect local monopolies. This protectionism will ultimately reduce economic growth, just as impeding trade between the republics of the Commonwealth of Independent States (CIS) has done. The behavior of oblast governments plays a crucial role in determining the efficiency with which the Russian economy performs, and its future growth.

Equalization

Finally, the new legislation does not consider intergovernmental transfers or equalization. Assigning personal and corporate taxes (or any other taxes) to the subnational governments where they are collected (on a so-called derivation basis) necessarily means that Russia's higher-income territories—those with a bigger tax base—will receive more revenue. In most countries, grants are provided for those territories whose economic base is too weak to support adequate public services; in Russia, however, grants were not provided for in the law. Recognizing the problems this gave rise to, the Ministry of Finance has been providing ad hoc and negotiated grants (subventions) to oblasts since mid-1992, and a Law on Subventions was passed, but never implemented. It is unclear whether or not the current bargained process for subventions is equalizing.

Special fiscal treatment and regimes

The design of fiscal federalism in Russia is complicated further by the demands of some territories for political autonomy, greater devolution of responsibility for expenditures, and special fiscal regimes. There are three broad oblast groups making these demands. First, certain non-Russian *ethnic groups* (which form a near majority of the population only in Tatarstan) claim greater autonomy because of their different history and culture. Second, some *natural resource–rich* areas want special financial arrangements to derive greater benefits from natural resource revenues. They note that resource development has not benefited them but has instead resulted in sustained and severe economic and ecological damage. Third, *industrially well-endowed* areas that have greater growth potential than other areas want more fiscal autonomy and special fiscal arrangements that enable them to benefit from their stronger local economies.

Without a transparent revenue allocation system, there is a perception that the negotiated tax-sharing system works against better-off oblasts and that the rich oblasts subsidize the poor. Not surprisingly, some regions are reportedly insisting on taking matters into their own hands through a so-called single channel system, similar to the one that sealed the Union's fate, whereby all revenues flow initially to the oblast and a single payment—determined unilaterally by the oblast itself—is sent to the federal government. The Republic of Bashkortostan has reached such an agreement with the Ministry of Finance, though this has not been approved by the Supreme Soviet. In other reported cases (the Republic of Tatarstan and more than twenty other oblasts) this arrangement is being implemented de facto—and presumably illegally (chapter 7).

Options for a new structure

The Russian government can build on the direction suggested by its new laws but should consider some further restructuring of center-oblast financing, taking into account the need for macroeconomic stabilization, equalization, and greater subnational fiscal autonomy. Fixed and inflexible solutions should be avoided for the time being, given that Russia's economy will undergo continued change. Yet a structure is needed.

How can the arrangements be improved? A new framework might have four components. Expenditure assignments would be clarified and Russia's total revenue pool could be notionally divided between federal and subnational governments, based on the quantified and assigned expenditure responsibilities of each level of government. Part of the subnational revenues would accrue, via tax sharing, to the oblasts in which the revenue is collected (this is known as derivation-based sharing) and, if the sharing arrangements are made more transparent, would be similar to today's system. The remainder would be distributed to subnational budgets according to a fixed (and transparent) formula that has equalization as its objective—akin to a grant system. Finally, there should be some room for assignment of subnational taxes and surcharges that oblasts can levy at their own discretion.

This four-dimensional structure is flexible. It supports a combination of strategies and permits them to change over time. It is compatible with shifts in expenditure responsibilities between federal and subnational government: if extra expenditures are shifted "downstairs," the subnational revenue share can be increased. It is also compatible with a changing emphasis on equalization: the larger the fraction of subnational revenues shared with oblasts on a derivation basis, the more the better-off oblasts will benefit from their stronger fiscal base. The larger the fraction of the subnational revenue pool distributed by the equalizing formula, the more the poorer oblasts will benefit. However, equalization penalizes the better-off regions whose industrialization and growth potential is greatest. As in other countries, Russia must balance the tradeoff between growth and equalization. Finally, to the extent that greater scope is allowed for assigned taxes and surcharges, the more local revenue capability and accountability will be developed.

Choosing the degree of equalization is a political judgment, made differently in different countries and at different times. How much equalization does Russia need at present? It is true that there are vast disparities in income and wealth among oblasts. However, the need for political unity may be greater than the need for equity: if the system is overequalizing, Russia's better-off oblasts may become disgruntled and opt out, pulling resources from the equalization pool. Ironically, then, imposing too much equalization at this stage could impel wealthier areas to withdraw unilaterally from the system, thus reducing the scope for *any* equalization and leaving the remaining oblasts poorer. Emphasizing derivation-based sharing would give weight to the concerns of wealthier areas, making them more willing to participate (chapter 7).

Addressing special areas

This flexible framework can also help deal with those oblasts seeking special fiscal treatment within the Federation. In principle, demands for special treatment can be addressed in three ways—by "ad hocery" (individually negotiated payment arrangements), by granting special fiscal regimes, or by an intergovernmental fiscal system with a comprehensive formula.

In the past Russia's central government has dealt with disgruntled areas piecemeal, through bilateral negotiations. This might not work in the future. It is not transparent, and it creates a sense of injustice among oblasts, some of which perceive that others are striking better deals with the center. Transparency is crucial in Russia at this time, when sometimes-skeptical regions are testing out democracy.

If disgruntled oblasts continue to decide unilaterally what revenues they will provide to the center, it could threaten the fiscal viability of the Russian Federation—just as it contributed to the fiscal bankruptcy of the U.S.S.R. In fact, the experience of the Union raises the question whether special fiscal status should not be granted to some Federation territories to appease them. Some countries (for example, Spain and Canada) do provide special regimes within otherwise uniform systems (chapter 7).

A totally uniform fiscal treatment could threaten Russia's future if disgruntled groups opt out. That certain areas are demanding special treatment should not be taken lightly. Great care should be taken, however, when granting any special fiscal regimes. Demands for special treatment will spread rapidly as soon as one is granted. If there are to be such regimes, eligibility must be narrowly defined—according to objective criteria. For example, areas where most of the population is an ethnic minority might be granted a special regime, but only if there is potential for serious political conflict in those regions. Once granted, special treatment is nigh impossible to rescind.

The catalyst that binds: a formula-based intergovernmental system

Demands for special treatment can also be addressed within a formula-based fiscal framework that makes special regimes unnecessary (chapters 5 and

7). The framework would give Russian policymakers flexibility in deciding the emphasis to be placed on assigned taxes, equalization, derivation-based tax sharing, or other objective, formula-based characteristics. In India, for example, a revenue-sharing formula provides the politically sensitive state of Punjab with extra government funding because of the difficulties of being a border state. India's formula also assigns backward areas a special weight that gives them extra compensation. In Russia, too, areas with bigger ethnic minorities could be assigned a weight in the formula-based pool. The same could be done in resource-rich or other areas, whose development needs have been ignored and where environmental damage may be great.

Using formula-based sharing to meet diverse oblast needs is appealing for several reasons. While the formula would be uniform among all oblasts, its components would permit policymakers to direct special treatment to certain areas. It could appease disgruntled groups but at the same time maintain transparency and avoid engendering a sense of injustice; thus, it would encourage areas to stay with the system rather than opt out.

What should this formula-based system look like? It should be simple and easily understood, taking into account the oblasts' different expenditure needs and fiscal capacities. And as Russia seeks to define itself as a nation, the immediate need for political unity may be greater than the need for equity. So rather than allow oblasts to negotiate individually for special fiscal regimes or decide unilaterally to leave the federal system, the government should almost certainly seek to engender widespread participation by adopting a formula that does not overemphasize regional equalization and that is flexible enough to respond to special circumstances.

It is crucial to develop consensus for a transparent framework for intergovernmental finances that provides, based on fair criteria, revenue-expenditure correspondence. The future cohesion of the Russian Federation depends on it. It is, perhaps, one of the most important mechanisms available to contain the significant centrifugal forces pulling at the seams of the new Federation.

Sharing revenues from natural resources

As domestic energy prices rise to world levels, potential fiscal revenues from the energy sector could be enormous. Russia's policymakers need to examine three issues: how taxes on the natural resource sector should be structured; how natural resource revenues should be shared between the center and the oblasts and among oblasts; and how natural resource revenues should be used. For Russia the outcome is most important for oil and gas, where the money at stake is huge.

The design of natural resource taxes

Proceeds from the sale of natural resources often greatly exceed the costs of exploitation, creating economic rents, part of which should be captured for the budget. Taxation based solely on output volume or the value of output (as introduced in Russia's recent laws) can discourage economic production of marginal fields. Such production taxes also allow enterprises, instead of the government, to gain most of the rents from highly productive fields. Russia's natural resource taxes should be redesigned to specifically target economic rents, thereby avoiding both problems (chapter 6).

Dividing natural resource revenues between levels of government

Exploitation of natural resources often generates significant social costs— the budgetary costs of public infrastructure, such as specialized transport facilities, and of environmental degradation, including cleanup costs. Oblasts should be compensated for these and other expenditures. This could be done through environmental charges and levies channeled to the subnational governments of producing regions.

When oblasts have been compensated for their financial, social, and environmental costs, the remaining revenue from natural resource taxes can be divided in several ways (chapter 6). Precisely how is as much a political as an economic question and depends on the nature of the Russian Federation. If people see their primary allegiance as being to the Federation (if "we" are citizens of the Russian Federation) and if natural resources are seen as a common wealth that belongs to all, then resource taxes should flow to the *federal* budget. If, however, allegiance is to a smaller natural resource–producing jurisdiction (if, say, "we" are the citizens of the Khanty-Mansiiskii autonomous okrug, which produces the bulk of Russia's oil), revenue should flow to the oblast or okrug budget.

In many countries most natural resource revenue goes to the federal budget. In Russia, in principle, revenue from oil and gas could be allocated in almost any way: to tribal groups or native peoples residing on the producing lands, cities, and rayons; to the autonomous okrugs Khanty-Mansiiskii and Yamal-Nenets, Russia's largest oil- and gas-producing regions; to other okrugs and oblasts; or to the Federation. Given the parlous state of the federal budget in Russia, a large share should almost certainly go to the federal government. A more equitable, transparent, formula- and rules-based intergovernmental arrangement might make it easier to reach consensus on the politically divisive issue of natural resource revenue sharing. If oblasts perceive that they are being treated fairly under a uniform system, they may cede demands for asymmetrical federalism. Oil-rich regions would be less likely to adopt the attitude that "what is mine is mine, what is yours is negotiable."

Using natural resource revenues

Revenue from natural resource taxes can be used in three ways: to cover current budgetary spending; to establish a "heritage fund" for future generations; or to be used as grants to the local population (as in Alaska). Grants are tempting, especially if the oblast is poor. They are also inadvisable. Some financing of incremental expenditure (especially to redress deficiencies in the subnational infrastructure) might be appropriate. Many oil-rich countries place their substantial revenues in a trust fund, with earnings used to supplement general budgetary revenues or to help ease the region's transition to a post-oil economy.

Given Russia's budgetary difficulties, using the federal share of natural resource revenue to finance general public spending (the federal budget) might be appropriate. If the revenue flow to producing oblasts is significant, trust funds are essential. Most oblasts could not absorb massive funds in any productive way. Local and regional investments, under a policy of resource-based industrialization, inevitably have a low rate of return.

Scope of the intergovernmental system

This is the final, important unanswered question of the new legislation. It is unclear whether the central government should define only center-oblast tax and expenditure issues or whether it should also allocate fiscal resources to cities and rayons. Essentially, the issue is whether or not Russia sees itself as a federation. If Russia is truly a federation, the center should concentrate on establishing a proper relationship between itself and the oblasts and regions and leave intraoblast matters to the oblasts themselves. Local affairs can be handled more efficiently by each oblast than by Moscow, especially in a vast country with more than 2,000 rayon governments and many more districts and lower-level soviets. Some framework law might be useful, however, requiring oblasts to pass through some revenue to rayons or cities according to agreed guidelines (chapter 5).

Also, larger cities in Russia that have a greater taxable capacity and more complex and, perhaps, bigger spending needs could require special treatment. This may include assigning special taxing rights, providing special support in implementing property or vehicle taxes, or giving special rights to set prices for municipal services.

What, then, to do?

The intergovernmental system established now will be key to determining "whither Russia?" Russia could either transform itself into a market economy and shake off the shackles of state ownership, or remain dominated by the government's heavy hand. It could develop a nationally integrated market, where enterprises compete on the basis of price and quality, or remain regionalized and localized, with local fiefdoms circumscribing economic activity. Russia's oblasts could see the benefits of a close federation, or they could come to regard confederation and greater independence as more economically beneficial. The incentives of the intergovernmental financial framework adopted will influence all three and be crucial to what kind of country Russia becomes.

2

Intergovernmental fiscal relations: setting the stage

Christine I. Wallich

The Russian Federation has embarked on a bold process of economic re-structuring—privatizing industry, instituting agricultural reform and price liberalization, modernizing the financial sector, and reforming the tax system. These reforms will significantly change the role of the government in the economy, reducing its direct control over the allocation of resources and financing and strengthening the regulatory and other functions characteristic of government in market economies. The reforms also imply major changes in rural and industrial enterprises, which will divest social and other responsibilities as they strive to become profit-oriented in the emerging market economy.

Fiscal reform began in the U.S.S.R. in the late 1980s and accelerated after the U.S.S.R. was dissolved and the Russian Federation became independent in 1991. Fiscal reforms have changed responsibilities at all levels of government—from the federal parliament to the village soviet. In particular, reforms have changed the center's spending responsibilities, its need for revenue, and the ways in which revenue is collected. In intergovernmental relations and subnational finances, however, reforms have only just begun.

Fiscal reform and, in particular, its intergovernmental dimensions will continue to play an important role in the success of Russia's reform effort. First, sound fiscal policies are crucial to a successful stabilization effort, and since Russia's subnational governments account for almost half of total budgetary outlays, they have an important role to play. Second, with centrifugal tendencies now emerging throughout the Federation, *how* fiscal resources are divided among subnational units will, in the present environment of nation building, be crucial for establishing a cohesive federation. Third, the equity and incentive aspects of tax and decentralization policies are crucial to structural reforms—and to creating an environment in which the private sector can flourish. In this context the continued ownership role of subnational governments also makes them crucial as players in, or impediments to, privatization efforts. Finally, expenditure reform has given subnational governments important new responsibilities for the social safety net, which will take on a new shape, shifting away from subsidies toward targeted safety net programs.

The remainder of this chapter discusses the context and evolution of Russia's fiscal system, its current tax-sharing and transfer system, its expenditure and expenditure assignment policy, and questions related to the divisive issue of natural resource taxation and the demands by certain oblasts for special fiscal treatment.

Basic characteristics and the federal administrative and budgetary structure of the Russian Federation

The Russian Federation is the largest and one of the most diverse countries in the world, with regions whose cultures, politics, and resource endowments vary widely. This diversity represents a challenge to effective administrative organization, to budgetary management, and to nation building.

Russia's geography and its "nationalities"

With an area of 6,592,000 square miles the Russian Federation is geographically the largest country in the world. Russia spans eleven time zones and almost 10,000 miles. East to west it stretches from Kaliningradskaia oblast on the Baltic Sea to the Chukotskii autonomous okrug on the Bering Straits by Japan. North-south, it reaches from the Arctic Ocean to the Caspian Sea. Russia covers about one-eighth of the world's land surface. The Russian Federation retains many of the geographical features of the former U.S.S.R. (see map of the territories of the Russian Federation). The northernmost part of the country, and most of Siberia, is arctic desert and tundra. Indeed, two-fifths of the territory of the Russian Federation is permafrost. Russia's central regions contain the famous Russian pine forests (the Russian *taiga*) and its swamps; farther south lie Russia's flatlands (*steppes*). East-west, Russia is divided by the Ural Mountains, which represent its European-Asian divide. Industry is concentrated in the major centers of European Russia as well as near the Urals. Natural resources are located mostly in Siberia (see map of the resource endowments of the Russian Federation, chapter 6).[1]

With a population of about 165 million, the Russian Federation is the most populous country in Europe. It embraces many dozens of ethnic groups, although it was federated (in 1922) on the basis of areas where Russians were the majority. A little more than 80 percent of the population is ethnically Russian. Major "nationalities" and ethnic groups include Tatars (3.8 percent), Ukrainians (3 percent), Byelorussians (0.8 percent), Germans (0.6 percent), and Jews, Armenians, and Kazakhs (each 0.4 percent). Other nationalities include Bashkirs, Yakuts, Osetians, and Chechens, to name a few. Most of these latter nationalities are concentrated in certain geographic areas, although they are not typically the majority there, and some have their own homelands, for example, the Republic of Bashkortostan and the Republic of Sakha (Yakutia) in the Siberian far east. The nationality-based administrative units (namely, all republics and autonomous okrugs) cover about half of the territory of the Russian Federation.

Many of these regions have their origin in the period following the establishment of the Soviet state. The vast size of the U.S.S.R. lent itself to a territorial form of organization. As early as 1922 many territories in the U.S.S.R. had parliaments, presidiums, and presidents. The state—in statu nascenti—thus appeared early at the subnational level (Milanovic 1993). As communist power waned, the existence of proto-state structures provided the framework for real states—the union republics and, within Russia, the oblast-level structures—to emerge.[2] At the present time, with the authority of the center eroded, the existence of these structures within Russia itself makes the question "whither Russia?" a very real one.

The European part of the Russian Federation is relatively densely populated and includes the cities of Moscow (9 million inhabitants) and St. Petersburg (5 million). The Asian part is more sparsely populated, with major urban centers situated near the Urals and along the Trans-Siberian Railroad. There are about ten cities with populations of more than 1 million.

Resource endowments across regions

The Russian Federation has vast natural resources. Its large mineral deposits include coal, oil, natural gas, minerals, iron ore, gold, diamonds, copper, lead, tin, bauxite, manganese, silver, graphite, nickel, and uranium (see natural resource map in chapter 6). Indeed, Russia produces some 20 percent of the world's oil, and 15 percent of its coal. Most of Russia's most important mineral deposits are located in its republics and ethnic regions. For instance, a large part of the western Siberian oil fields is found on the territory of the Khanty-Mansiiskii autonomous okrug and in the Yamal-Nenets autonomous okrug bordering the Barents Sea. These together produce more than 80 percent of Russia's oil and gas. The remaining important oil fields are located in the Republic of Tatarstan on the Volga, north of the

Caucasus. The major diamond deposits are located in the Republic of Sakha (Yakutia), Siberia's largest territory, which reaches the Arctic circle and produces 99 percent of Russia's diamonds and 25 percent of the world diamond supply.[3] In contrast, the population of these ethnic territories counts for only about 20 percent of Russia's population. The territory and population of the resource-rich republics of Sakha (Yakutia), Tatarstan, and Baskortostan account for 20 percent and 6 percent of Russia's territory and population, respectively. Because natural resource endowments vary so much across regions, the right to resource revenues, which could become enormous as prices move to world levels, is a contentious issue in Russia. Although the Federation Treaty (see below) provides that the residents of an ethnic republic own the land and natural resources within the republic's boundaries, it also states that the ownership and the use of the natural resources should be regulated by the laws of both the Russian Federation and the ethnic republic. The proposed new constitution provides for the supremacy of federal legislation.

Income and expenditure differentials across regions

The varying natural resource endowments in Russia are reflected in per capita incomes, which vary widely across oblasts. Clearly, in a country where prices are as distorted as in Russia, per capita income is an imperfect measure of well-being. However, it serves to indicate the extent of dispersion. In 1989 the richest oblast (Tyumenskaia oblast, which until 1991 included the oil-producing Khanty-Mansiiskii okrug) had a per capita income of R 5,971 (or about US$9,000) (measured as per capita gross value agricultural and industrial output, GVAIO), approximately ten times the per capita income of the poorest, the Republic of Kalmykia.[4,5] In 1992 the dispersion remains about the same. With respect to the budget the regions are similarly differentiated: per capita expenditures ranged from a low of R 663 in the Chechen Republic, just north of Georgia, to R 4,488—seven times as much—in Chukotskii autonomous okrug on the Bering Straits. The standard deviation of per capita expenditure was R 729 (in 1991) around an average per capita expenditure of R 1,338 (appendix D).

The federal structure

The Russian Federation is a three-tiered federal state. It was proclaimed a sovereign country by the Supreme Soviet of the Russian Soviet Federal Socialist Republic on June 20, 1991, six months prior to the final dissolution of the Union. The Russian Federation claimed successor status to the

U.S.S.R. and took over many of its functions and responsibilities. With the resignation in December 1991 of Mikhail Gorbachev as president, the U.S.S.R. was effectively dissolved.

After the collapse of the U.S.S.R., the status of the federal-regional relations within the Federation were embodied in the Federation Treaty and its three associated agreements signed in March 1992. Administratively, the Russian Federation consists of eighty-nine states (second-tier governments, also known as "subjects of federation"), which are directly subordinate to the federal government but have varying legal and administrative status. In July 1992 the Federation Agreement, which binds these states together into the Federation, was formally signed. With varying degrees of administrative autonomy, the eighty-nine states comprise the oblasts, okrugs, and *krais* (native lands, see below); metropolitan cities with oblast status (Moscow and St. Petersburg); and republics (some were called "autonomous republics" before mid-1992). All of Russia's eighty-nine administrative units (except Moscow and St. Petersburg) are further subdivided into rayons (districts).

These administrative divisions have their roots in the administrative structure of the former U.S.S.R.—a four-tiered state that comprised the union government, union republics, oblasts, and cities or rayons (IMF and others 1991). The 1977 Constitution of the U.S.S.R. envisioned the Russian Federation as a confederation in which the ethnic republics were parallel in status with the former union republics and had the greatest autonomy from the federal government. (In the former U.S.S.R. the union republics had the right, in principle, to coin money, enter foreign trade agreements, and secede from the Union.)

The new Federation's republics include Adygeya, Altai, Bashkortostan, Buryatiia, Chechen, Chuvash, Dagestan, Ingush, Kabardino-Balkar, Kalmykia, Karachai-Cherkess, Karelia, Khakasia, Komi, Marii-El, Mordovia, North Osetia, Sakha (Yakutia), Tatarstan, Tuva, and Udmurt. These have their own governments ("supreme" soviets), with some autonomy—at least, in principle. Some have declared their independence, although this is not recognized by the Russian Federation's Supreme Soviet or by any other country. Tatarstan and the Chechen and Ingush republics have added special covenants to the Federation Agreement (signed by all other oblast-level governments in July 1992) and thus have special status within the Federation. The Federation's autonomous regions or okrugs consist of Nenetskii, Koriakii, Chukotskii, Komi-Permyatskaia, Khanty-Mansiiskii, Yamal-Nenets, Taimyrskii, Evenkiiskii, Ust'-Ordynskii Buryatskii, and Aginskii Buryatskii. In addition, there are six krais and two metropolitan cities (Moscow and St. Petersburg). With the establishment of these subnational governments, the stage was set for regional interests to emerge.

In Russia the central government deals directly only with second-level governments, the subjects of federation. These include not only oblasts, but also republics, krais (native lands that usually contain within their borders an autonomous oblast or autonomous okrug), and okrugs (an administrative unit that is nationality-based, although in fact populated mostly by native Russians). These have differing political status. The Federation Treaty began the necessary process of defining the relationships between the federal government and the eighty-nine subjects of the federation but did not accomplish it. Although the treaty confirmed the greater control of the ethnic republics over their foreign policy, foreign trade, relations with the federal government, and relations with other republics, krais, and oblasts, two republics refused to sign it. One, Chechenya, has in effect seceded. The other, Tatarstan, insists on signing a state-to-state treaty with Russia.

Traditionally, metropolitan cities, krais, autonomous okrugs, and autonomous oblasts have had somewhat more autonomy from the federal government than the oblasts—but less autonomy than the republics have enjoyed. However, the success of the republics in acquiring even more economic and political rights has encouraged many ordinary oblasts to move in the same direction. In the ongoing constitutional debate, the oblasts favor equal status among all the subjects of federation. (Subjects of federation are collectively referred to throughout this book as "oblast-level" or "subnational" governments or, in the Russian phrase, as "subnational administrations," reflecting their original role as deconcentrated organs of the central system.) Below them are municipalities and rayons, subordinate to the oblast government.

The administrative structure

Each oblast supervises urban and rural areas within its jurisdiction (figure 2.1). All local governments within an oblast report to the oblast government and carry out duties according to oblast regulations. For example, Moscow oblast at the end of 1993 contained 60 cities (with populations ranging from 60,000 to 200,000) and 650 independent (rayon, city, and rural) settlements. Each has a so-called independent (that is, separate and freestanding) budgetary and administrative status. This vertical relationship allows for some future fiscal decentralization to rayon governments.

The sovereignty of the oblast in directing the activities and administrative units within its jurisdiction reflects the *territorial principle* of administration (Gleason 1990). The territorial unit has full administrative jurisdiction, or "competence," for functions in its territory. Thus, under the territorial principle, the federal government is responsible for all governmental func-

Figure 2.1 Government structure in the Russian Federation, 1992

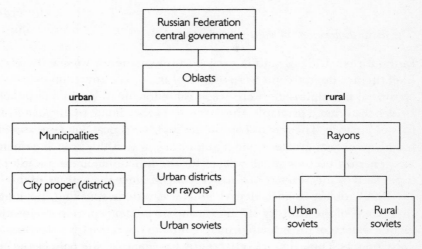

a. In some oblasts and in some other special cases, urban rayons may be directly subordinate to the oblast government.

tions within the federation (from diplomacy and defense to social spending and tax collection); the oblast government is responsible for governmental functions within the oblast; and the rayon government is responsible for activity within the rayon territory.

Because some subnational government functions (such as tax collection and some expenditures) are also federal domains, oblasts are subject to central subordination in these areas. Likewise, rayons are subordinated to oblasts. In these cases, it is the vertical *branch principle* of organization that gives the higher level its jurisdiction over the lower.[6]

Most ministries are organized along branch lines, in a vertical hierarchy, from the federal to the rayon level. The structure of administration is approximately duplicated for all levels. Federal ministries coordinate and supervise their corresponding oblast departments, which in turn coordinate the corresponding city and rayon activities. The Ministry of Finance, for example, is responsible for the budgetary function at all levels of government and is organized in a vertical (branch) fashion, an organizational structure that survives from the Soviet system (figure 2.2). The overlap of the branch and territorial jurisdictions means some activities and some administrative bodies (such as oblast departments of finance) were under so-called dual subordination—that is, they were simultaneously part of a branch organization (such as the Ministry of Finance) and a territorial administration (the oblast government). As long as there was good coordination of the territorial organs with the branch organs, this dual subordination worked smoothly (Gleason 1990).

The fiscal dimensions of dual subordination

In the former U.S.S.R. and in early postindependence Russia, the oblast-level finance departments were organs of the oblast governments (by the territorial principle) and were responsible for oblast-level fiscal policies. Under the branch principle, they were also subordinate to the *federal* Ministry of Finance. The recent Law on the Rights of Local Self-Governments has given oblasts greater budget autonomy, so that the branch principle has generally become much weaker for the functional areas traditionally supervised by the Ministry of Finance. Indeed, since the passage of this law (in 1992), oblast finance departments are, strictly speaking, no longer "branches" of the Ministry of Finance and no longer report to it. However, certain aspects of the branch principle remain operative for oblast finance departments. Their finance officers are, for example, still paid by the central government budget. So, although officially autonomous according to the Law on the Rights of Local Self-Governments, finance departments may still have one foot in Moscow and one in the oblast and may respond to competing realms of authority (figure 2.2).

Nonetheless, decentralization in Russia has generally strengthened the

Figure 2.2 Hierarchy of government administration and finance in the Russian Federation, 1992

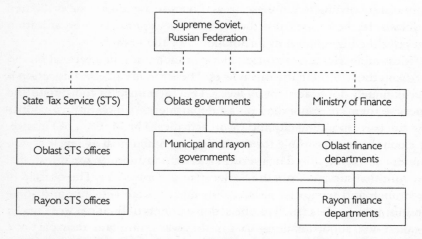

Note: Solid lines indicate hierarchy of subordination. Dotted lines indicate subordination in the Soviet regime and its absence in the present one. Dashed lines indicate legislative-executive branch lines. For the Ministry of Finance, since 1992, federal-oblast subordination no longer formally applies, given the present, more federal structure.

territorial side and weakened branch management, especially in the fiscal area. The State Tax Service—responsible for all tax collection—ceased being a territorial organ in l991, when it was formally completely centralized. Although it is now purely a "branch ministry" (oblasts have no formal jurisdiction for tax collection) and its local offices are therefore no longer formally under dual subordination, there appears still to be informal dual leadership, and substantial loyalty of local tax officers to the oblast administration (and potential conflict of interest) remains. This is because oblasts are still responsible for providing many amenities and services for State Tax Service local staff, from housing to all fringe benefits, including food allowances, education, and other subsidies. Only staff wages come from the federal budget, and some estimates put these at only 30 to 40 percent of the staff's total compensation package. These conflicting loyalties make the pursuit of regional fiscal interests by this central organ—but at the *expense* of the center—possible. The resolution of the dual leadership conflict will be crucial in determining how much control the central organs have over their administrations in the oblasts and rayons.

The structure of the state budget and the evolution of budgetary policies

For decades public finances in the U.S.S.R. were dominated by planning objectives, with little weight given to macroeconomic aspects.[7] In the traditional socialist system the state budget was used to massively reallocate resources in accordance with the national economic plan. Close adherence to the plan and strict controls over state enterprise finances ensured broad balance in public sector finances until the mid-1980s.

In the second half of the l980s there was a progressive deterioration in the budget. This was attributable to relaxation of planning and increased autonomy of state enterprises, combined with adverse external shocks and growing macroeconomic disequilibria. As a percentage of GDP, profit remittances to the budget by enterprises and receipts from turnover taxes (the major sources of revenue) declined. Social spending (mostly on price subsidies) rose rapidly, and defense costs remained high. Nonetheless, investment was not cut significantly. The result: fiscal imbalance worsened rapidly, rising in 1988 to an adjusted deficit equivalent to 11 percent of GDP. Late in the Soviet era efforts were made to reduce the budget deficit, and at the same time structural reforms were initiated to adapt public finances to a more market-oriented economy. On the revenue side, these reforms centered on taxation of enterprises and individual incomes and improvements in the transparency and neutrality of taxation (IMF and others 1991).

Russia's budget structure in the former U.S.S.R.

In the Soviet period Russia had a "unified budget," meaning it covered *all* budgetary accounts and the fiscal plans of both Russia's federal *and* subnational (oblast) levels. Until the late 1980s Gosplan, the state planning agency, controlled most major budgetary decisions. The Ministry of Finance implemented national financial policies and supervised the finances of oblast (and lower) governments. The Ministry of Finance was the planning "handmaiden" (that is, cashier to the government), as well as an accounting agency. As part of decentralized decisionmaking, Gosplan's role was progressively reduced (IMF 1992a).

Approval for the budget came from "bottom up and top down." Subnational finance departments prepared budgets based on information from *lower* levels; but oblast budgets were developed within the framework provided by the *upper* level—the federal ministry. Therefore, each level of government approved budgetary spending ceilings for those units immediately beneath it and also determined the amount of revenues that the lower level could retain. (In Russia all fiscal revenues are collected at the local, so-called grass-roots level and are retained locally or shared with higher-level governments. In other words they are shared upward; they are not collected, as in most market economies, by the central government and shared down with states and provinces.) Any ex post deficits had to be covered by budget transfers from the higher level of government that had approved the spending. Thus, a rayon could run a deficit only if its supervising oblast agreed to the deficit—and financed it. In principle there were no transfers between same-level budgets or from a lower level to a higher one. But in fact ex post surpluses could be "clawed back" by higher levels if this was approved by the central authority.

Subnational and rayon budgets in the Russian Federation

Under the new system of budgetary legislation (see below), each level of government now prepares its own budget. Although federal-oblast tax-sharing (retention) rates are in principle fixed by the Supreme Soviet, in practice the sharing rates are negotiated by oblasts with the Ministry of Finance. These tax shares are designed both to provide the oblast with sufficient revenues and to fund the federal budget. For oblasts in deficit the agreed level of authorized expenditures, based on standardized "expenditure norms" and grants (or subventions), is also negotiated. Oblasts in turn negotiate the tax revenues retained by rayon administrations (figure 2.3). Thus, Moscow oblast prepares its own budget governing oblast expenditures and negotiates the agreed tax retentions with the 710 cities and

Figure 2.3 Structure of the state budget in the Russian Federation, 1992

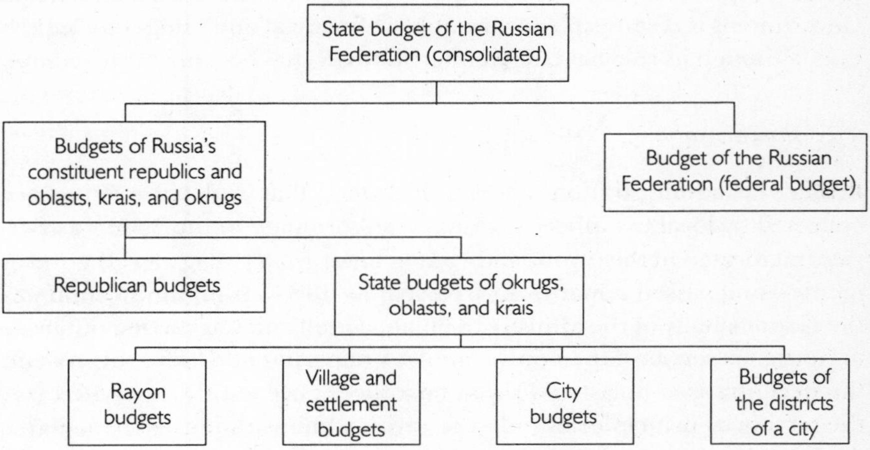

```
                    ┌─────────────────────────┐
                    │ State budget of the Russian │
                    │ Federation (consolidated)   │
                    └─────────────────────────┘
        ┌───────────────────┴──────────────────────┐
┌─────────────────────────┐              ┌─────────────────────────┐
│ Budgets of Russia's     │              │ Budget of the Russian   │
│ constituent republics and│             │ Federation (federal budget)│
│ oblasts, krais, and okrugs│            └─────────────────────────┘
└─────────────────────────┘
   ┌──────────┴──────────────────┐
┌──────────────────┐   ┌─────────────────────────┐
│ Republican budgets│   │ State budgets of okrugs,│
└──────────────────┘   │ oblasts, and krais      │
                       └─────────────────────────┘
   ┌──────────┬──────────────┬──────────────┬──────────────┐
┌────────┐ ┌────────────┐ ┌────────┐ ┌──────────────┐
│ Rayon  │ │ Village and│ │ City   │ │ Budgets of   │
│ budgets│ │ settlement │ │ budgets│ │ the districts│
│        │ │ budgets    │ │        │ │ of a city    │
└────────┘ └────────────┘ └────────┘ └──────────────┘
```

Source: Ministry of Finance of the Russian Federation.

rayons under its jurisdiction. Local governments that are *not* in deficit after retaining their agreed tax shares can theoretically determine their expenditures from their own resources. In practice expenditure autonomy for both oblasts and rayons is more limited, as discussed in chapters 4 and 5.

Fiscal policymaking

The current framework for formulating and implementing fiscal policy has two parts—the central government (that is, the executive) and institutions under the oversight (until its dissolution in late 1993) of the Parliament (the legislative). The legislative branch has recently been more populist, favors fiscal decentralization, emphasizes equalization and, in the early 1990s, has not been overly sensitive to macroeconomic stabilization concerns. On reforms in general, the legislative branch is more conservative than the executive and not supportive of changes that threaten the status quo. Executive proposals, in contrast, tend to be more centralized and to emphasize macroeconomic stabilization. These differences have led to ongoing tensions between the two and culminated in the dissolution of Parliament by the president in October 1993.

The Ministry of Finance is responsible for preparing and implementing the budget. Parliamentary committees, which handle fiscal policy legislation, including legislation on intergovernmental finance, are the Committee on Plans, Prices, Taxes, and Budgets, the Subcommission on Budgets, and the Subcommission on Taxes. There has been much parliamentary legislation recently on fiscal decentralization, often with limited Ministry of Finance input (and not always its approval). The Subcommission on Local Government is responsible for intraoblast financial and budgetary legislation, although its role has been limited as Russia has become more federal.

Tax administration

Russia's tax administration system is "inverted," that is, all tax revenues are collected by local tax offices—formally subordinate to the State Tax Service but located in the rayons and even in lower *gorat* (village-level) governments—and passed upward. Until November 1991, tax administration was the responsibility of the Ministry of Finance itself and was carried out by its in-house tax service—then only a ministry department. Under this system, the decentralized oblast and rayon tax offices were jointly supervised (on the territorial principle) by oblast or rayon administrations—but also (on the branch principle) by the federal Ministry of Finance. There was thus no single authority (such as a revenue commissioner) in charge of all tax administration. This "dual leadership" of the local tax officers was a major conflict of interest. Just how the conflict is resolved will have powerful implications for the future of Russia. Many taxes from locally owned enterprises flow to subnational governments, and oblasts and rayons benefit by keeping taxes low. Why? For those taxes that are shared with the central government, a light administrative touch (that is, low taxes) allows increased earnings to be retained by enterprises. These retained earnings are not shared with the center but remain in the local area and could be tapped for "donations" to local-government projects.

In 1991 the central government began implementing new fiscal policies for which better tax administration became crucial. The State Tax Service became an autonomous agency with ministerial ranking—no longer a department of the Ministry of Finance—and was charged with administering all taxes in the Russian Federation.

The State Tax Service is three-tiered—central, oblast, and rayon. Its central office or headquarters coordinates, but it has no collection responsibility. Oblast offices supervise rayon and local offices and provide the center with tax revenue and tax data. Oblast State Tax Service directors (eighty-nine of them) report directly (and only) to the ministerial head of the State Tax Service, thus formally eliminating the previous dual leadership structure. In theory the State Tax Service is managed fully on the branch principle of authority—that is, it fully controls all of its decentralized offices in the oblasts. It collects property taxes, the twenty-one local taxes, and all taxes accruing to federal, oblast, and rayon governments (except customs duties, which are collected by the customs department, and some extrabudgetary revenues, which are collected by off-budget entities). Tax policy design, however, remains the responsibility of the Ministry of Finance.

Evolution of the intergovernmental system

Prior to 1990, fiscal policy in the U.S.S.R. was strictly centralized.[8] In a traditional Western federal fiscal system, intergovernmental relations and revenue sharing between levels of government are relatively stable and well-defined. In the former U.S.S.R., however, policies changed yearly and were negotiated in an ad hoc manner between the Union and the fifteen republic governments. Revenue sharing was an administrative device to simplify resource allocation between the center and the republics: taxes and other revenues collected at the grass-roots level were either retained locally or passed up to higher-level governments to achieve budget balance.

In the late 1980s the U.S.S.R. state budget relied on four major revenue sources—the turnover tax (about 28 percent of budget revenues); transfers of state-owned enterprise profits (30 percent); foreign trade taxes (17 percent); and personal income taxes (10 percent) (IMF and others 1991). Unlike the practice in market-oriented economies, the turnover tax had no single fixed rate. Instead, there were thousands of commodity-specific rates that were used to transform administratively fixed retail prices into wholesale prices. This was, in effect, another means of controlling enterprise profitability since in a "fixed-price system," all taxes are shifted backward. Foreign trade taxes similarly taxed away the profits arising from differences in international and domestic prices.[9]

Expenditures were guided mainly by directives issued by Gosplan. Budgets of subnational governments (union republics) were always in (accounting) balance because the union budget automatically financed any shortfall, either by allowing higher revenue retentions by the republic governments or by direct but ad hoc and negotiated budgetary transfers (subventions).

The period prior to dissolution of the Union

After 1988 pressures for more autonomy from union republic governments intensified and caused a shift toward more regional fiscal decentralization. Revenue sharing came under scrutiny, with union republics reluctant to share revenues collected in their territory with the U.S.S.R.'s union budget. Some republics even proposed retaining all of the major taxes. Instead, it was agreed in 1991 that the union budget would be financed with mandatory transfers from republics, fixed in nominal terms.

Dissolution of the Union

In 1991 union republics began to demand still more independence, and some larger ones (notably Russia and Ukraine) assumed full responsibility for preparing their own budgets. Others f llowed suit. Other than expenditures for "common functions," most ur.ion spending responsibilities were moved out of the union budget into union "extrabudgetary funds."

During 1991 the union republics' efforts to achieve full independence intensified. Union tax laws were superseded by republican ones and some republics set their own tax rates, typically decreasing the tax load on their enterprises. Moreover, republics also introduced their own investment, subsidy, and social support policies without consulting the union government. Republics also began to retain higher-than-agreed shares of revenue, a practice that became widespread by midyear. Ultimately, the mandatory upward transfers from the republics to the union budget dried up. Russia, for example, had agreed to pay R 90 billion to the union budget in 1991 but remitted only R 30 billion.[10] As dissolution continued other republics' transfers did not materialize. Thus, 1991 saw a gradual diminution of the U.S.S.R. central government's power and activities, culminating in the dissolution of virtually all central government bodies by November 1991. That year also saw the takeover by Russia of most union revenue and expenditure responsibilities, including foreign debts and defense.

Early policies in the Russian Federation

The revenue-sharing system in place at the time of Russia's independence reflected an extension of the system that had governed intergovernmental relations in the preindependence period. Thus, many dimensions of the old system of negotiated tax-sharing rates between the central level and the subnational governments remained in place and were carried over. The bargaining inherent in this system made oblasts highly dependent on the center and created considerable uncertainty in subnational government finances.

Under the postindependence (1991) system in the Russian Federation, sharing of most major taxes was still achieved by negotiated arrangements between the federal Ministry of Finance and finance departments of oblasts, okrugs, republics, and krais. The sharing rates varied according to the tax and the oblast.[11] Each oblast negotiated an agreed level of expenditures with the federal ministry and was allowed to retain (just) enough tax revenue to finance those expenditures. Similar arrangements dictated tax sharing *within* the oblasts: taxes were collected at the local (city and rayon) level, and a negotiated share of each tax was retained by the city or rayon and a further share "sent upstairs."

Under these arrangements the Russian federal budget is as reliant on transfers from below as was the old Union. The vulnerability of the Federation to demands for "fiscal sovereignty" from its oblasts (especially those with ethnic populations) has now come to the fore. This materialized acutely in early 1992, when some subnational governments in Russia proposed to retain all taxes collected and to transfer a nominally fixed amount (determined at their discretion) to the federal budget. This vulnerability is central to recent Federation reforms in intergovernmental fiscal relations which, since independence, have included reforming the State Tax Service and strengthening control of banks (which process tax remittances).

Russia's special features

Thus, the Russian system of revenue sharing, which was inherited from the Union and was still in place at the end of 1991 as the Federation came into existence, has at least two unusual characteristics. First, unlike the practice in most systems of intergovernmental finance—where the central government collects most national revenues and shares them with lower levels of government—in the U.S.S.R. and in the Russian system revenues are "shared upward." The breakdown of this system, as the republics ceased to make their transfers, contributed to the dissolution of the Union. And the Russian Federation is similarly vulnerable. Second, the system is not truly a "system," but rather a series of ad hoc bargained agreements, nontransparent at best, whose effects and incentives are not well understood. Resolving these systemic intergovernmental problems will influence not only how the Federation develops and takes shape, but how Russia's tax system will perform in the future to underpin a market-oriented economy.

Expenditures and expenditure assignment

Expenditure policies have evolved since Russia emerged from the U.S.S.R. as an independent country, but the overall structure of government spending, budget policies and, most importantly, which level of government is responsible for which expenditures have their roots in the preindependence period.

National expenditure policies in the Soviet period

As in other socialist economies in transition, the role of the public sector in the Union was very large and the proportion of government spending in aggregate income or output correspondingly high.[12] The budgetary expenditure-to-GDP ratio in the U.S.S.R. was about 50 percent, broadly comparable to such other European countries as Germany, Sweden, and France. This, however, did not fully reflect the importance of the public sector in the Soviet economy. Outside the state budget there were the extrabudgetary funds of branch ministries, whose gross flor in 1989 were estimated to have reached almost 5.5 percent of GDP. Similarly, quasi-fiscal operations of government banks appeared to be substantial, as was public infrastructure paid for by enterprises. Interest subsidies meant that interest payments grossly understated the true cost of government borrowing. Thus, the 50 percent expenditure-to-GDP ratio should be viewed as a minimum. In other socialist economies in transition expenditure-to-output ratios of 60 to 65 percent were common at this time (IMF and others 1991).

National expenditures in the Russian Federation

Since the formation of the Russian Federation there has been a sharp decline in government spending relative to GNP.[13] This is in line with the economic stabilization and austerity program and has taken place despite Russia's assuming the expenditure functions of the former Union. The ratio has declined to about 33 percent in 1992 (appendix C).[14]

The allocation of expenditures also changed. In 1990, during the Soviet period, most expenditure had gone to subsidies and to transfer payments such as pensions and other allowances. In the 1992 budget, 33 percent was earmarked for "national economy" (a catchall category that includes price and other subsidies), 14 percent for defense, and 24 percent for social and cultural activities, education, and health. In the future more is likely to go to protecting the most vulnerable groups. Economic restructuring is expected to require more for unemployment benefits, retraining, and (possibly) public works employment. The cost is expected to be significant (appendix C).

For the future, as central planning is dismantled, budgetary wage costs should shrink and subsidies to enterprises should fall with the transition to a market economy. Defense spending may also decline. Government investment has already been cut sharply, especially now that since 1992 the centrally financed portion has been shifted totally to oblasts and rayons.

Introducing budgetary discipline has not been easy. The Parliament has stonewalled over politically contentious measures, and strong enterprise and regional lobbies have made it virtually impossible to do much about enterprise credit and subsidies. As a result the budget deficit for 1992 was some 20 percent of GDP.[16] In mid-1993 Parliament refused to approve the budget proposed by the executive branch, making instead a counterproposal for a budget with a deficit of 30 percent of GDP. And the inability of the federal government to provide a stable macroeconomic framework has contributed to regional skepticism about its role.

Expenditure issues in the longer term

For the longer term, economic restructuring calls for a substantial reduction in central and subnational government spending, although different levels of government will be affected differently. Government will withdraw from activities that can be undertaken more efficiently by privately owned (or, until privatization is completed, financially independent) "commercialized" or "corporatized" firms. At the same time government will assume responsibility for providing some of the services now delivered by enterprises. These include non-production-related services and "social assets" that enterprises have traditionally undertaken, such as road building, schools, hospitals, cultural centers, and kindergartens. Providing these services, however, would *increase* the size of government. In fact the *size* of government in this transition period and beyond will depend on how reform policy evolves in Russia. The government will eventually retire from direct intervention in enterprises. It will halt financing of enterprise investment and leave it to the financial sector; it will no longer provide budgetary investment funds or subsidies to unprofitable firms. In the same vein it would also end its accommodating credit policy to enterprises. These changes will have ramifications for *all* levels of government. However, many new functions are likely to increase the outlays of subnational governments (chapter 4).

Expenditure assignment in the former U.S.S.R.

Expenditure assignment in the former U.S.S.R. (and now in Russia) was generally consistent with the public finance principles of assigning expenditure responsibility according to "benefit areas." Under these principles public services whose benefits do not extend beyond the boundaries of a local community should be provided by local government, services whose benefits are enjoyed jointly by individuals in several communities should be provided by subnational governments, and services that benefit the entire country should be provided by the federal government (chapter 4). These principles seem to be well understood in Russia. Yet the lack of clarity in assignment to different levels of government has at times meant that responsibility has been ill-defined, leading frequently to overlapping responsibilities. Unlike in market economies, expenditure responsibility has included not only the public service functions assigned to each level of government but also ownership responsibility for some industrial sectors and enterprises.

Union expenditures. Expenditures solely financed from the budget of the former U.S.S.R. were defense, justice, internal security, subsidies to the external sector, and most budgetary investments in the economy. The union budget financed enterprises of the so-called group A industries (for example, transport and heavy industry), often thought of as the "commanding heights of the economy."

Union republics. Union republic budgets financed most price subsidies—including consumer price subsidies as well as all of social security pensions. Republics also financed enterprises in light industry (group B), the transport sector, and state farms and *kombinats* (collectives) in agriculture. On the revenue side each level of government received the fiscal revenues generated from "its" group of industries—including their profits and other budgetary remittances. As tax reforms were introduced in the early 1980s and profit remittances became profit (corporate income) taxes, these revenues also flowed to the level of government that owned the enterprise (IMF and others 1991).

Oblast, city, and rayon expenditures. Subnational governments were mainly responsible for health and education, financing 86 percent and 66 percent (respectively) of all national spending in these sectors in 1989. Oblasts were responsible for local transport, roads, and local environmental cleanup. Rayons financed housing, utilities, local services, trade, public food supply, health care, and primary and secondary education. Subnational governments were responsible only for local light industry (group C) and food enterprises, so their social role was more substantial. Most subnational government spending was on education (29 percent); public health, mostly primary care, clinics, and local hospitals (24 percent); and housing (17 percent). In fact most of this spending was by rayons—which undertook 80 percent of all subnational expenditures on housing, 86 percent of subnational expenditures on education, and 81 percent of subnational expenditures on public health (table 2.1).

Assignment of capital expenditure. While recurrent expenditures were assigned according to the principle of "benefit areas," until 1992 capital spending was fully centralized. All capital investments were financed and implemented by the Ministry of Economy (the former Gosplan), except for those funded directly by the Ministry of Finance or by public enterprises. Oblast and rayon governments in which these capital investments were made, however, were responsible for operation and maintenance costs. Unused investment funds had to be returned to the central government. They could not be used for other purposes (chapter 4).

Expenditure assignment in the Russian Federation: recent policies

Although their actual budgetary outlays are smaller than those at the federal level, the oblasts are responsible for most public services in Russia. The consolidated national budgetary expenditures amounted to 33.6 percent of GDP in 1992 (appendix C). Regional budgetary expenditures accounted for 43.6 percent of the consolidated national budget. However, the oblasts accounted for the bulk of the two major budget expenditure categories, that is, national economy (which includes subsidies) and social and cultural activities (which includes education and health) (appendix C).

In many ways the system inherited from the U.S.S.R. governs expenditure assignment in the Federation. In 1992 there were some major rear-

Table 2.1 Subnational budgetary expenditures of the Russian Federation, 1990

(in billions of rubles)

			Breakdown of subnational expenditures			
Expenditure item	Subnational expenditures	Percentage of total subnational expenditures	Krai and oblast expenditures	Percentage of subnational (sector) expenditures	City and rayon expenditures	Percentage of subnational (sector) expenditures
Agroindustrial complex	1,937	3.2	1,266	65.3	671	34.6
Social complex	718	1.2	301	41.9	417	58.0
Construction complex	462	0.7	248	53.6	214	46.3
Transportation complex	249	0.2	84	33.7	165	66.2
Items not included above:						
Communal services	376	0.6	183	48.6	193	51.3
Housing and utilities	10,163	17.2	2,063	20.3	8,100	79.7
Local industries	55	0.0	34	61.6	21	38.3
Fuel and peat industry	421	0.7	98	23.1	323	76.8
Environmental protection committees	79	0.1	74	93.8	4.8	6.1
Other expenditures	6,274	10.6	4,733	75.4	1,541	24.5
External economic activities	2	0.0	0.9	58.9	0.6	41.0
Social and cultural activities	32,696	55.5	6,037	18.4	26,659	81.2
Of which:						
Education	17,264	29.3	2,369	13.7	14,895	86.2
Public health	14,043	23.8	2,593	18.4	11,450	81.5
Physical education	51	0.0	24	46.5	27	53.4
Social welfare	1,338	2.2	1,051	78.5	287	21.4
Science	47	0.0	25	53.4	22	46.5
Public authorities and administration	1,625	2.7	333	20.3	1,292	79.5
Funds to be transferred through mutual accounts settlements	2,061	3.5	1,203	58.3	858	41.6
Other	1,675	2.9	1,635	97.8	40	2.2
Total expenditures	58,841	100.0	18,316	31.1	40,525	68.9

Source: Data provided by the Ministry of Finance of the Russian Federation, 1992; author's calculations.

rangements. These were, however, ad hoc, which conflicts with efforts to assign revenue responsibility clearly (see below). Even so, many responsibilities are distinct. Obviously, national defense, state apparatus, foreign affairs, and fundamental research are reserved for the federal government. Other expenditures can appear in the budgets of any level of government, according to the level at which benefits are received. For example, since most enterprises are still in state hands, outlays to support enterprises will be found in the budgets of all three levels of government.

Expenditure at the federal level. Almost all former union budgetary functions have been assumed by the Russian Federation. Russia's federal budget is now responsible for group A and group B enterprises and for pipelines, electric power, marine transport, and national (but not local) environmental problems, such as Chernobyl in Ukraine. Transfers to public enterprises, however, were severely restricted in 1992. The federal budget also finances foreign economic activity (such as export and trade subsidies) and fundamental science. In the social sector, the federal budget accounts for some (minor) financing of universities and other higher-learning institutions, specialized health care facilities, and culture and museums (table 2.2).

Expenditure at the oblast and rayon levels. Oblasts are responsible for their environment, river transport, oblast roads, forests, vocational schools, health care, and specialized clinics. Oblasts and republics are also responsible for group C enterprises—local light industry and consumer goods. Oblasts are increasingly transferring such enterprises down to rayons.

Expenditure responsibilities of rayons and townships are mainly in the social sectors. Rayon budgets account for almost 100 percent of all spending on basic education, some 85 percent of health expenditure, 60 percent of national outlays on kindergartens, 60 percent of housing expenditures, and 80 percent of public-utility spending.

Social expenditures and public enterprises

No discussion of expenditure assignment in Russia can be complete without a discussion of the "public expenditures" assigned to the enterprise sector. As in other former socialist economies, Russian enterprises provide many services for employees and families that elsewhere fall under the jurisdiction of the public sector budget. For example, enterprises build and support hospitals, construct and maintain housing, build and run kindergartens and preschools, and make "voluntary donations" toward financing public transport and to extrabudgetary funds of subnational governments.

This can have advantages for enterprises and oblasts. Nizhniy Novgorod oblast, for example, gives tax breaks (tax expenditures) to firms that finance their own kindergartens. Public enterprises also undertake capital investments in the social sectors by building, say, schools and hospital facilities and then transferring them to oblast or rayon governments. Even for oblasts that are not revenue constrained, shifting outlays onto enterprises makes sense. To finance their own spending oblasts must use tax retentions—"after-tax income." But the oblasts' share of many taxes is only 40 percent; the central government gets 60 percent. So if the enterprise finances the expenditures itself, profits and profit taxes fall, but 60 percent of the decline will be borne by the central government.

Capital spending of larger public enterprises extends to roads, sewerage, water lines, and environmental protection. Most enterprises provide housing for employees. Many also build and operate child care facilities, such as summer camps. Not only do they provide money for construction, they often contribute labor and materials and participate in upkeep of the facilities.

Subnational governments look to enterprises to finance many essential public services. Take, for example, the Volga car factory. The factory provides many social services and produces many outputs not related to its production activities. Located in Nizhniy Novgorod oblast (an industrialized oblast in the center of Russia), Volga produces cars and tractors and has some 120,000 employees. In early 1992 (when one dollar equaled about 20 rubles) it was financing:

- Meal subsidies of R 10-R 15 per person, per day.
- Operating and maintenance costs of a 1,000-bed hospital.
- Building and maintenance costs of housing, at a rate of about 200,000 square meters of housing per year, for about 22,000 people. In 1992 the outlay was R 650 million.
- 117 kindergartens and preschools, serving 20,000 students. Cost in early 1992: R 350 million.
- Mass transportation subsidies (bus, tramway, and subway).
- Collective farm purchases to help provide workers with food.
- Construction of roads, water, sewer lines, and other infrastructure, with operations then transferred to local governments in the oblast.

The recurrent cost of social expenditures was estimated at about 10 percent of profits (25 percent, including construction costs). The Volga car factory is perhaps exceptional. Even so, most Russian enterprises are unusually important providers of "public services." Structural change and privatization will require that enterprises off-load these responsibilities, to all levels of government. The question is: which level will assume what? The aggregate amount of these expenditures is large. Field visits in mid-1992

Table 2.2 Expenditure assignment in the Russian Federation, by level of government, 1992

Expenditure	Federal	Oblasts	Rayons	Village soviets
Defense	100 percent (except military housing)	Military housing	None	None
Justice and internal security	100 percent	None	None	None
Foreign economic relations	100 percent	None	None	None
Education[a]	All university and research institute expenditures / All technical and vocational schools	Several special vocational schools	Wages; operation, construction, and maintenance of all primary and secondary schools	None
Culture and parks[b]	National museums / National theater	Museums with oblast significance	Some museums / All recurrent expenditures of all sport and park facilities and all other cultural facilities	None
Health[c]	Medical research institutes	Tertiary hospitals, psychiatric hospitals, veteran hospitals, diagnostic centers, and special service hospitals	Secondary hospitals, primary health clinics, medicines	Paramedics
Roads[d]	Construction of all roads / Maintenance of federal roads	Maintenance of oblast roads	Maintenance of rayon and city roads	Maintenance of commercial roads
Public transportation	Previously, interjurisdictional highways, air, and rail transport	Most public transportation facilities (assigned earlier to federal government)	Some transportation facilities, including subway systems	None
Fire protection[e]	None	Most fire protection services	Voluntary, military, and enterprise services possible at this level	None
Libraries	Special libraries (for example, the Lenin library)	Special library services	Most local library services	None
Police services	National militia	Road (traffic) police	Local security police (since 1991)	None

Garbage collection[f]	None	None	Part of garbage collection	Part of garbage collection
Sewerage[g]	Infrastructure capital investment	Most of the operational expenditures	Some operational expenditures	None
Public utilities (gas, electricity, and water)	None	None	None	Subsidies to households (not enterprises)
Housing[h]	Building and development	None	Maintenance and small-scale building	None
Price subsidies	None	None	Fuels, mass transport, food (bread, milk), medicines	None
Welfare compensation	Part central government responsibility	Part oblast government responsibility	Managing programs funded by upper-level governments	None
Public enterprises (productive sectors)	None	Capacity to invest in joint ventures (keeping 50 percent of privatization proceeds if enterprise is rayon-subordinated	Capacity to invest in joint ventures (keeping 50 percent of privatization proceeds if enterprise is rayon-subordinated, 10 percent of any other subordination)	None
Public enterprises—new investment (productive sectors)	Group A enterprises (e.g., transport and heavy industry) Group B enterprises (e.g., light industry, transport, and agriculture)	Group C enterprises (e.g., local light industry, housing construction, and food industry)	If transferred to local level	None
Environment	National environmental issues	Local environmental problems (e.g., the preservation of forests)	None	None

a. Public enterprises also build schools but typically do not operate them. They frequently operate kindergarten services.
b. Some enterprises build sport facilities.
c. Some enterprises build hospitals and in some cases also operate them. Social insurance financed primarily by enterprises pays for the health services of those covered.
d. A Special Extrabudgetary Fund is financed by an excise tax on oil consumption.
e. Special fire-protection services are provided by enterprises, but such services are on the decline.
f. Separate user charges do not normally apply for garbage collection.
g. Separate user charges apply for sewerage.
h. Enterprises have been important builders of housing and own nearly half of the housing stock in Russia. The central government has transferred housing to local governments; maintenance is the responsibility of the level of government or enterprises owning housing. Capital expenditures are included unless otherwise noted.
Source: Based on fieldwork conducted in 1992.

suggest a figure as high as 40 percent of some oblasts' budgetary social spending, although nationally the estimate averages much less. A concrete estimate is hard to construct, however.

Postindependence expenditure shifts to the subnational level

Since Russia's emergence as an independent country, the broad pattern of intergovernmental assignment of spending responsibilities has been maintained. There are no Russian Federation laws addressing expenditure assignments, although there has been a *tradition* of intergovernmental division of responsibilities. However, in two key areas formerly federal outlays have been shifted to the subnational level.

Social expenditures. In early 1992 some traditionally federal spending was shifted to the subnational level—notably, consumer price subsidies (milk, meat, bread, baby food, and so forth) and cash subsidies for vulnerable groups, welfare programs for pensioners, family allowances and child compensation, and support for the homeless. Until 1992 the *central* government financed these price subsidies by transferring funds to oblasts, which in turn disbursed them to the rayons. But in the first quarter of 1992, responsibility was shifted to the rayon level. In mid-1992 expenditures on these subsidies (and those for coal, food, housing, heat, and transport) amounted to about 4 percent of GNP.[15]

Shifts in spending responsibilities to local government can increase the efficiency with which social welfare and other services are provided. They can also imply differences in levels of service provision between rich and poor localities, which may (or may not) be acceptable in Russia. If there is consensus that there should be few differences, the center should continue to play a role in financing these important areas. Consumer subsidies and the targeted cash benefits that will replace them are typically justified on grounds of income distribution, which in many countries is a function assigned to central government. (Efforts by lower levels of government to redistribute income may prove self-defeating.) For administrative efficiency it may make sense to delegate the administration of social programs to the subnational level, with financing retained at the center.

Capital investments. In mid-1992 responsibility for all capital investments was shifted to subnational governments, including large and nationally significant projects, such as airports, highways, utilities, and military housing. This was announced by the federal government as a permanent policy although in some spending areas it has since been reversed (chapter 4). But the issue, particularly military housing, is complex. Russia is committed to bringing back union (now Russian) army personnel from the former republics (especially the Baltics); but finding and building homes for them has been a major barrier to repatriation. Scant attention has been paid to the inappropriateness of this policy, and no thought has been given to assisting local governments. Shifting investment "downstairs" seems to have been designed to draw down the apparent budget surpluses generated in many oblasts by the 1992 transitional revenue-sharing arrangements. This was seen as the only way to "claw back" revenues, given that recent legislation disallowed extracting surpluses (see below).

Shifting investment responsibilities for capital goods with a *local* benefit zone can increase efficiency significantly, provided subnational governments have adequate funds. Oblasts and rayons have a better understanding of the investment required. For capital investments whose scope is more national, however, the provision of services could be greatly weakened. It has already met with much resistance from oblasts and rayons, who are wondering what functions are now served by the center.

More generally, because a large chunk of social and capital expenditures has been pushed down to the subnational level, overall subnational spending may not have been reduced much—if at all. It will probably have increased. Revenue adequacy is, therefore, a major issue. Quantifying the spending implied by these new subnational responsibilities is an important—but often forgotten—first step in defining resource requirements. By focusing only on revenue assignment Russia's policymakers put the cart before the horse.

Expenditure autonomy

For economic efficiency, subnational governments require flexibility and discretion in budget decisions. In principle these are accorded to oblasts and rayons by the Law on the Rights of Local Self-Governments (appendix A). The same law also prohibits passing on expenditure mandates to lower-level governments without adequate funding and forbids higher-level government from extracting surplus funds from oblasts. Budget independence is in principle also protected by the jurisdictions' autonomous sources of revenues and by the oblasts' power to determine how all funds should be spent.

Budgets are regulated by the Law on the Basic Principles of the Budget System and Budgetary Process (appendix A). This distinguishes between recurrent and capital budgets, which are to be voted on and approved separately. As with the Law on the Rights of Local Self-Governments, this law espouses the principle of balanced budgets for oblasts and rayons. Balanced budgets are required ex ante, although transfers from higher-level governments can be incorporated. In this case the oblast soviet may establish a deficit ceiling for the lower-level subnational governments in its jurisdiction.

Even though there is full legal autonomy, subnational budgetary activities are constrained in several ways. First is the constraint on the overall level of budgetary outlays, which comes from the negotiated tax-sharing rates. These can be set by the Ministry of Finance so as to finance local budgets at just the level deemed appropriate by the Ministry of Finance—no less, no more. Then, there are the unfunded "central mandates" that govern much subnational spending. For example, the federal government determines wages for all public employees, and federally mandated wage increases affect subnational budgets directly. The central government also still sets ceilings on some public sector prices—notably, tariffs on public transport and utilities, which affect cost recovery of oblast- and rayon-owned enterprises. Rents on housing owned by enterprises and local governments were also controlled by the center until mid-1992. The central government also sets ceilings on the tax rates that can be levied by oblasts and rayons. This alone implies that subnational governments do not determine the aggregate level of their budgets autonomously. Finally, rayon budgets are subject to scrutiny and approval by oblasts. Until the second quarter of 1992, and the passage of the above-mentioned law, oblast budgets were, in turn, approved by the Ministry of Finance.

Another constraint has been the use of so-called expenditure norms. Budget norms have traditionally been used to determine financial requirements for each subnational expenditure item (for example, hospitals) in the oblasts. These norms translated minimum physical quantities into a ruble cost figure (box 2.1). Norms were used to determine the costs, for example, of maintaining a hospital bed. They were not used, however, to determine the funds required for an adequate number of hospital beds per capita; the sufficiency of these was left to capital budget determination. Until 1988 all subnational spending was based on these norms, determined annually by the Ministry of Finance and the various sector ministries. Funds allocated to one budget item could not be transferred to another. In the past these norms (and there were thousands) may have been population-based, yet, given migration and growth, current norms are almost certainly not. Many areas may be vastly underserved.

A workable system of defining subnational expenditure needs has yet to be established. In 1988–89 the Ministry of Finance simplified and standardized the norms. Their primary disadvantages remained, however. They do not incorporate regional cost differentials, their costs may be obsolete, and they reduce budget flexibility. For 1992 the Ministry of Finance adjusted 1991 expenditures upward by an inflation norm (coefficient), thus prolonging the biases and problems of the past. In the June 1992 round of quar-

Box 2.1 Expenditure norms in the health sector in the U.S.S.R. and the Russian Federation

Expenditure norms existed at each level of government for most expenditure items in the social sphere of the budget. The norms for the health sector were released by the Ministry of Finance and the Ministry of Health. They included extremely detailed standards for the cost of each part of the health care sector's operations and outlays—that is, cost standards for the acquisition of beds and uniforms, for doctors' visits, for the acquisition of medicine, and so forth. The standards differed according to the specialization of the hospitals or hospital departments. The following is an example of the cost standards for *one* patient's food ration *per day* at each of the seventeen different types of health institution. (Similar norms applied to each patient's medicine, heat, supplies, and the like.)

Type of patient or type of hospital	Budgetary norm (per capita per day, in rubles)
Children	7.00
Maternity	7.00
Infants	1.00
Gynecology	5.60
Gastroenterology/hematology	5.60
Necrology	5.40
Leprosy	4.71
Pneumoconios	4.71
Oncology	3.89
Endocrinology	5.18
Burn unit	4.56
Tuberculosis ward	4.71
Children's tuberculosis	5.18
War invalids	6.48
Daytime in-patient	3.89
Unpaid blood donors	3.91
Paid blood donors	1.71

This ruble amount would be multiplied by the estimated patient-days for each year in each type of hospital to yield a budgeted amount for "food." A similar exercise would be undertaken for medicine and every other type of hospital expenditure, as well as for expenditures in every other sector.

In 1992 price liberalization precluded establishing norms. Rather, the physical norms were costed out by each individual locality (which asked the hospitals, schools, and so on to estimate the cost of providing each service item). Costing was done each quarter. Some expenditure items (drugs, food) must be indexed according to figures still provided by the central government; for others (heat), local costing is acceptable. With price liberalization different regions have experienced different inflation rates: in one region visited, the index provided by the center allowed for a sixfold increase in prices, while the actual price rise in that region (a northern Siberian territory) was fifteenfold.

Note: The then-prevailing exchange rate was approximately R 20 = US$1.
Source: U.S.S.R. Ministry of Finance and Ministry of Health; Resolution #105 of March 19, 1991, "On Retail Price Reform and the Social Protection of the Population."

terly oblast budget determinations, eighty-five of Russia's eighty-nine oblasts protested the budgets arrived at by the Ministry of Finance and sent delegates to Moscow for negotiations.

The current state of affairs has a number of implications for intergovernmental relations. Oblasts with growing populations are underserved because of the absence of population-based norms. Some face higher costs than the national average, but are limited by a centrally determined index for certain cost components. And there are disincentives to reallocate existing resources into other expenditure categories because the budget is based on norms that differ for each spending category. In principle, subnational governments have autonomy for reallocating spending across categories. In practice, however, they must reallocate funds judiciously or risk a reduced budget the next year. All oblasts feel shortchanged in their treatment by the center. Lack of transparency allows each oblast to feel that all others are better off. Frustrations are manifest in poor interoblast relations, which in turn exacerbate regional tensions.

The intergovernmental tax-sharing and transfer system: one year after independence

The revenue and tax-sharing system in place when Russia gained independence in 1991 was an extension of the system that had governed intergovernmental relations in the preindependence period.[17] In November 1991 the Russian Federation took over the union budget's revenue and expenditure responsibilities and began to introduce "sovereign" tax policies. Thus, much of the old system of negotiated tax sharing between central and subnational governments remained in place, and there is also a lack of transparency in the revenue system itself. The bargaining inherent in this system made subnational governments dependent on the center and has aggravated center-oblast relations. It has also pitted oblasts against each other, as they fight for a larger share of the pie, and has intensified tensions.

Revenue structure and tax sharing

The major tax source for subnational governments has traditionally been the local share in a limited number of taxes of the federal level: personal income taxes, company income taxes, and sales tax. As shown in appendix C, total revenue of the consolidated national budget (that is, the consolidated federal and regional budgets) amounted to 30 percent of GDP in 1992. The regions accounted for a little more than 43 percent of this total. During the first quarter of 1993 the implicit share of the regions in total budget revenues increased to just less than 50 percent. Although regional and local governments were assigned a large number of various taxes and fees, most of the aggregated regional revenues came from four taxes in 1992 —the profit tax, the value-added tax, the personal income tax, and excises. Except for personal income tax, all of which flows to the oblast budgets, the revenues from the other three taxes are shared between federal and subnational levels of government.

In 1992 and 1993 major changes in the tax system and unfinished plans for reform of the system of intergovernmental finances have led to ongoing difficulties in putting together a Russian Federation budget. (See figure 2.4 for the percentage distribution of subnational revenue in 1992.) Only a first-quarter budget was presented to the Supreme Soviet in mid-January 1992. Quarterly budgets combining reform and stabilization objectives were also presented for the rest of l992 and 1993.

Reforms of tax policy and tax assignment

Recent tax reforms in the Russian Federation are a continuation of fiscal reforms initiated by the U.S.S.R. in 1990 and 1991. These aimed at replacing the former system of budget financing from turnover taxes and enterprises' profit remittances with a system based on taxes on income, profits, consumption, and trade, similar to systems in market economies. The primary feature for intergovernmental relations was a planned, radical shift from the earlier negotiated, bargained tax sharing to a system of pure "tax assignment" that eschewed the use of transfers. By mid-1992 there were many new tax laws and new taxes—value-added tax, excise taxes, and personal

Figure 2.4 Distribution of tax revenues in the Russian Federation budget, central and subnational levels, 1992

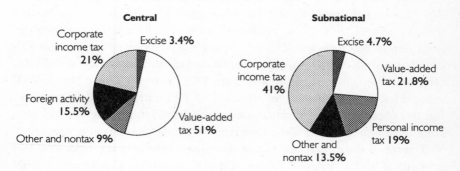

Source: Ministry of Finance of the Russian Federation; appendix C.

income tax. These changes were laid out in the Law on the Basic Principles of Taxation and other laws and are described below.

Personal income tax. In Russia the personal income tax is a federal tax withheld by employers that applies to most wage earners. In the law, rates range from 12 to 60 percent; in fact, because of wage compression this is essentially still a flat rate tax. The 12 percent bracket is wide, applying to annual income up to R 250,000 (July 1992)—more than ten times the (then) minimum wage. Most wage earners pay this rate. The 60 percent rate applies to earned income that was 100 times the minimum wage. All personal income tax revenue is shared 100 percent with oblasts, which may pass it on to rayons. A peculiar feature is that the revenue is assigned to the locality of the taxpayer's place of *employment,* not his rayon of residence. This means that in commuter areas revenues go to the city providing employment, even though residence services are provided by another jurisdiction (chapter 5).

Corporate profits tax. Modeled on industrial countries, this tax is levied at 32 percent (1993). Although according to the Basic Principles of Taxation 100 percent of corporate income tax accrues to oblasts, it has been shared, in the transitional revenue-sharing system, between levels of government. In early 1993 the center reduced its share to 30 percent, oblasts took 70 percent (22 of 32 percentage points). The corporate income tax has shortcomings. No adjustments are made for inflation, and Russian depreciation does not conform to any notion of economic depreciation. There is a move to reform the tax and replace it with one on enterprise "income" (defined as profits plus wages), to discourage excessive enterprise pay increases. Any such change would, of course, reduce subnational revenues.

Value-added tax (VAT). Introduced on January 1, 1992, the federal VAT replaced both turnover tax and the 5 percent union sales tax that had gone into effect in February 1991. Under this origin VAT, exports are zero rated—that is, the VAT on them is rebated. However, under a holdover from the preindependence period, VAT rebates are not paid on exports to other CIS member countries—they are treated as if they are still domestic transactions. (Imports from the rest of the world are VAT exempt.) There are no VAT rebates for capital goods. The standard VAT rate in 1992 was 28 percent, but in February 1992 the rate on some foodstuffs was changed to 15 percent. Some oblasts have also made unilateral (downward) adjustments to VAT rates in their territory. Under the Basic Principles of Taxation, 100 percent of VAT is assigned to the federal government. Under transitional arrangements, however, it has been split between the center and oblasts, the sharing rates varying both over time and across oblasts. Oblasts received a variable, negotiated share in early 1992 (some oblasts kept as little as 1 percent, some as much as 100 percent). Oblasts retained a uniform 20 percent of VAT in the second and third quarters and hoped for more by year-end. In early 1993 some oblasts got as much as 55 percent of the VAT; others as little as 20 percent. In late 1992 the Supreme Soviet voted to permanently lower the VAT rate to 20 percent beginning in 1993; this would significantly lower subnational government revenues.

Excise taxes. Federal taxes are levied on alcoholic beverages, tobacco, automobiles, and some luxury goods, at rates ranging from 14 to 90 percent (of the tax-inclusive price) and corresponding to an implicit rate on the tax-exclusive price that is far higher. Excises are not levied on exports outside the CIS area, nor on imports. Excises are shared between federal and subnational governments at rates identical for all oblasts. Shares, however, depend on the commodity. They are levied and collected at the point of production, not consumption. All excise taxes on beer, leather, fur, and some other luxury items flow to the oblast government. The excise on vodka is shared 50/50, and all motor vehicle excises go to the federal government. About 60 percent of all excise taxes are allocated to subnational governments; most come from vodka. In September 1992 an 18 percent excise tax on petroleum was introduced, destined for the federal budget, although it has since come to be shared (chapter 6).

Taxation of international transactions. Taxation in this area remains in a state of flux. In addition to customs tariffs the most important new tax is the export tax on oil, introduced on January 1, 1992. Designed to capture 30 to 40 percent of the value of taxed exports, the tax is denominated in ECU per ton of exported oil. Although there has been pressure from producing oblasts for a share, this was introduced as a federal revenue, earmarked to service external debt and to support government imports. Since mid-1993 it has become shared. All customs revenue accrues to the federal level.

Other taxes. Other legislation imposes taxes on inheritance and gifts, individual property (automobiles and real estate), and transfers of bonds, stocks, and other securities. Many are federal taxes. A petroleum/natural resource production tax was introduced in 1992. All of it was to go to the federal budget. Indeed, it was seen as a way to balance the budget. Following negotiations with increasingly powerful and disgruntled producing regions, however, the tax was split—80 percent to producing oblasts and 20 percent for the federal budget. Natural resource ownership and the sharing of resource revenues is one of the most contentious issues in Russia today (chapter 6).

Revenue sharing between center and oblasts

Enacted in January 1992, the Law on the Basic Principles of Taxation is part of the fundamental framework for taxation in the Russian Federation at all levels of government. It is in two parts. The first part establishes the "unified" (meaning national) tax structure, rules, penalties, and administrative powers. The second specifies which taxes may be levied by federal, oblast, and rayon governments and assigns the revenue from each tax to the budgets of one of those governments—in theory. In fact, which taxes are assigned in full to subnational governments is ambiguous—deliberately so, according to one adviser to the drafting committee.

According to the Basic Principles, personal income tax and corporate income tax are "regulating revenues" of the oblasts—that is, a revenue collected at the grass roots, but shared between higher and lower levels so as to regulate the revenue retained by the lower level and ensure that it can balance its budget. (See box 2.2 for sharing rates of each tax.) Thus, the term "regulating income" can refer to revenues *of the oblast,* which the oblast can use to regulate rayon budgets, or revenues for the center *to regulate oblast* budgets. The latter, according to some, is an ex post interpretation, invoked when it became clear that the revenues assigned to the federal budget were inadequate. Value-added tax, export taxes, and certain excise taxes (vehicles) accrue 100 percent to the federal level. Excises on vodka are shared, while excises on most other products go to the oblasts. Revenues from taxes on natural resources, petroleum, and natural gas products, although federal by law, are shared, largely in favor of oblasts. Subnational governments are assigned twenty-one different minor taxes and fees, although the federal level defines the tax bases and sets maximum rates for almost all of them. For the most part oblasts have the final word on how revenues will be shared with rayons, but the law makes some provisions for tax sharing with the rayon level and below.

The Basic Principles Law represents a major change in intergovernmental fiscal relations in the Russian Federation. If fully implemented, it would be a complete switch from the former bargained tax sharing to a system of pure tax assignment. (Strictly speaking, since subnational governments cannot set the rate or base of the federal taxes assigned to them, the law envisages only *revenue assignment.*) The Basic Principles envisages the "independence" of subnational budgets and would guarantee them the revenues from their assigned tax sources. The locally assigned revenues would accrue fully on a pure "derivation" basis—that is, to those subnational governments where they were originally collected. Thus, oblasts with a larger tax base and larger collection volume would receive proportionately more. This has important implications for the future shape of—and the emerging interoblast differences within—the Russian Federation.

**Box 2.2 Proposed tax assignments:
the Basic Principles of Taxation Law**

Federal taxes. These taxes accrue fully to the federal level. The federal government has full control over the rate and the base. These include:

- value-added taxes
- export taxes
- excises on motor vehicles and alcohol (which is 50 percent local)
- tax on bank profits
- tax on insurance profits
- tax "exchange activities"
- tax on securities operations
- customs duties
- natural resource "payments."

Subnational taxes (assigned federal taxes and local "own" taxes). The regulating revenues of subnational governments include three federal taxes. Oblast governments have no control over the rate or base of these taxes:

- personal income tax
- corporate income tax
- 50 percent of vodka excises and 100 percent of all other excises except motor vehicles.

In addition, subnational governments receive all of the revenue from the collection of:

- road fund taxes
- stamp duty
- estate duty
- gift tax and inheritance tax.

Some taxes are designated as oblast-level taxes. The center defines the base of these taxes; the subnational level has control over the rate and receives all of the revenues. (Not all these taxes have yet been introduced in all regions.) These include:

- property tax/tax on enterprise assets
- forestry tax
- payment for water use.

Rayon and local taxes. Rayon and local-level taxes include twenty-one taxes and fees, some of which are best thought of as "nuisance taxes," noted below. Their rate and base can be set locally, but the law sets maximum rates for most:

- property tax on natural (not juridical) persons
- land tax
- business registration fees
- construction in resort areas
- resort fee
- tax on the right to trade
- special-purpose taxes for the maintenance of militia
- tax on advertising
- tax on the resale of cars, computers
- tax on owners of dogs
- license fee for the sale of wine and liquor
- license fee for the right to hold auctions
- fees to move into apartments
- fees for car parking
- trademark fee (use of logos)
- fee to participate in horse races
- fee on winnings at horse races
- fees on participating in the "totalizer game at races"
- fees for commodity exchange transactions
- fees on cinema and TV filming
- fees for cleaning of cities, towns, settlements, and so on.

Note: Taxes above are given in the order of their listing in the Basic Principles Law (appendix B).
Source: Law on the Basic Principles of Taxation, Russian Federation, December 1991, unofficial translation.

The Basic Principles did not make specific allowances for intergovernmental transfers. The absence of grants from higher levels to lower levels preserves the appearance of local independence—an important political consideration for some in present-day Russia. No oblast is "transfer dependent" on the center, and each tub appears to "sit on its own bottom." But under any assignment system, revenue shortfalls will occur, and a supplementary grant ("subvention") system seems to be necessary. The apparent independence, therefore, comes with a heavy price for those poorer oblasts whose collection receipts are low, for oblasts for which the system would mean wrenching changes, or for oblasts which under the new system do not achieve revenue-expenditure correspondence (chapter 5).

Implementation of the intergovernmental system in 1992

Given the difficulty of moving quickly from tax sharing to pure tax assignment, the Basic Principles Law passed in December 1991 was superseded almost immediately by quarterly budget laws, beginning with the first-quarter 1992 budget. The system of tax assignment has not yet been truly implemented. Revenue volatility created difficulties in formulating a budget for the whole year. Thus, the old sharing system, amended in various ways, continued to prevail in the four quarterly budgets of 1992 and in 1993. Revenue from all major federal taxes (personal income tax, corporate income tax, VAT, and excise taxes) was shared between federal and subnational governments in varying degrees.

In the first quarter of 1992, for example, 47 percent of corporate income tax went to the federal budget and 53 percent to the subnational level (15 and 17 percentage points of the 32 percent rate, respectively). In the second quarter, subnational governments kept 60 percent (19 percentage points of the 32 percent rate, with the center receiving only 13 percentage points). Personal income tax, legally assigned to oblasts, was indeed channeled in full to them and, in turn, most oblasts gave some 5 to 10 percentage points of it to rayons. VAT, which had been assigned (in the Basic Principles Law) 100 percent to the federal level, was shared with oblasts on an ad hoc basis that differed across the eighty-nine oblasts. These variable, negotiated rates were set so that, in the estimation of the Ministry of Finance, the revenues accruing to each oblast would be exactly sufficient to enable it to meet its normed expenditures. The average subnational share of the VAT (in the first quarter) was budgeted to be 17 percent, but it varied widely (from 1 to 100 percent) across oblasts. In the second quarter, with oblasts protesting that nothing had changed from the previous system, it was decided that the VAT sharing rate should be fixed and uniform across all oblasts. So each oblast was given 20 percent, allocated on a derivation basis. According to the Ministry of Finance this share of the VAT—together with the oblast shares in other taxes—was to provide in full for the budgetary expenditures of oblasts. No provision was made for transfers or grants to oblasts or rayons in the first half of the year.

In the first quarter there was, it could be argued, less need for grants, since much discretionary gap-filling could be done by allowing oblasts to retain more VAT. Indeed, the purpose of ad hoc negotiated VAT shares was to eliminate any ex ante budgetary oblast deficits. When VAT rates became fixed, however, there was a need for transfers, and the Ministry of Finance introduced, at the end of the second quarter, a series of negotiated, ad hoc subventions in response to oblasts' demands. In the third-quarter budget, VAT shares continued to be fixed and uniform, and Ministry of Finance–determined subventions were granted ex ante to oblasts with outstanding fiscal gaps. In addition, further subventions were granted, on a negotiated basis, for oblasts deemed by the Ministry of Finance to need them. Thus, although there was de jure a more fixed structure, in practice the Ministry of Finance still controlled oblast budgetary flows (table 2.3).

Further adjustments to the systems of sharing and subventions are ongoing. In early 1993, for example, the first-quarter budget reintroduced variable tax-sharing arrangements, both for the VAT and the natural resource tax. Under this new arrangement the oblasts' share of the VAT ranges from 20 to 55 percent, depending on the oblast (the federal share is 45 to 80 percent). These changes are a step away from the uniform tax-sharing arrangements maintained in mid-1992 because determination of each oblast's sharing rate is again negotiable. However, the higher VAT retention rates are expected to be at the expense of lower and fewer subventions, so the net budget cost to the federal level and the net implication for oblasts' revenues may be quite small. The other major change relates to the tax on

Table 2.3 Intergovernmental sharing rates of major taxes in the Russian Federation, 1992 and 1993

(percentage of total collection)

Revenue source	As set in the Basic Principles		First quarter 1992		Second through fourth quarter 1992		1993	
	Federal	Oblasts	Federal	Oblasts	Federal	Oblasts	Federal	Oblasts
Value-added tax	100	0	ad hoc negotiations		80	20	80-50	20-50
Profit tax	0	100	46	53.1	40.7	59.3	31.2	68.7
Personal income tax	0	100	0	100	0	100	0	100
Excise on alcohol	50	50	50	50	50	50	50	50
Subventions	none	none	ex post, negotiated		ex ante, negotiated		ex ante, negotiated	

Source: Ministry of Finance of the Russian Federation.

petroleum exports, which will now be shared 25-65 percent (depending on the oblast) with the producing oblast, with 35-75 percent going to the center. As this was previously (by law) a 100 percent federal tax, this represents a major concession to territories.

More transitional arrangements:
the Law on the Budgetary Rights of Local Self-Governments

The Law on the Budgetary Rights of Local Self-Governments, adopted by the Supreme Soviet in April 1993 and implemented in June 1993, is the most significant piece of recent legislation likely to affect the intergovernmental relations in Russia in the near future. In substance this law does not fundamentally change intergovernmental relations as they have evolved in Russia over the past few years; rather, it essentially codifies the transitional tax-sharing system.[18] Budgets at different government levels are still interconnected through revenue sharing of several "regulating" taxes, and the process of expenditure determination still leaves ample room for the continuation of "negotiated" budgets. The transitional system thus continues.

The objective of the law was to define the budgetary rights and obligations for each of the three tiers of government in Russia. The law goes beyond the traditional federal structure because it regulates not only budget relations between the central and oblast governments, but also the fiscal relations between the oblast government and the rayons.

The Law on the Budgetary Rights of Local Self-Governments preserves the principle of budget independence at all levels of government: each level of government retains the right to formulate and execute its budget, independent of higher levels of government. However, it does *not* guarantee that resources will be provided for the achievement of full financial autonomy by each level of government. The law also gives the central government the right to gather statistical data on the consolidated budgets of the subjects of federation (oblast governments).

Different aspects of the budget process are regulated by the Law on the Budgetary Rights of Local Self-Governments. In particular it is stipulated that the preparation of the budget, including the "minimum required budget," should be made according to approved norms. (The norms will be uniform for the entire national territory but some regional variations will be allowed.) A minimum required budget is guaranteed by the higher-level government; thus, the minimum budget for the oblast includes the minimum expenditures that the oblast must guarantee to its rayons. The "minimum necessary expenditures" are *not* defined in the law. The norms to be used in the definition of minimum expenditures are being developed in the Ministry of Economy, the Ministry of Finance, and the line ministries (see below). The law does not provide a concrete assignment of expenditure responsibilities among the different levels of government. Instead it provides that the annual budgets will list those expenditures that will be reassigned "up" or "down" in that particular year.

The Law on the Budgetary Rights of Local Self-Governments distinguishes between "fixed" and "regulating" revenues. Fixed revenues are stipulated as constant amounts or fixed shares of certain taxes (neither the amounts nor the shares are specified), and regulating revenues are those whose amount is determined annually (by negotiation) in the budget. The relative size of the fixed revenues cannot be less than 70 percent of the required minimum budget (60 percent in 1993 only). In order to achieve this minimum level of funding, the higher-level government must also assign to the lower-level government (central government to oblast government and oblast government to rayon government) for a period of not less than five years either a fixed percentage or the entirety of the regulating taxes.

The fixed taxes, to be assigned or shared either in full or at a fixed sharing rate (determined by the Ministry of Finance) with oblast governments, include the following: tax on enterprise income, tax on personal income, taxes on natural resources, 50 percent of the tax on corporate assets, and other minor taxes newly assigned by the Supreme Soviet to the oblast governments. This is not dissimilar to the list of subnational taxes in the Basic Principles. The distinction is that they are to be posted to the oblast budget in part or in full, with no sharing rates specified. (The list of fixed taxes to be assigned to rayon and city governments by their oblast is exactly the same.) The remaining regulating taxes will be shared among the different levels of government at rates determined in each year's budget to reach the 70 percent minimum budget. The remaining 30 percent of normal expenditures are presumably to be financed out of own sources or, possibly, subventions, although this is not specified.

The Law on the Budgetary Rights of Local Self-Governments requires that the budget formation cycle begin seven months before the start of the fiscal year. It also reaffirms the existence of extrabudgetary funds at all levels of government, including the right to keep hard currency funds.

In summary, the Law on the Budgetary Rights of Local Self-Governments does not introduce significant changes in the *existing* structure and practice of Russia's fiscal federalism (although it differs from past laws, some of which were only partly implemented). An important exception is that it mandates a specific structure for the relationship between oblast governments and their constituent rayons. Otherwise the law maintains the status quo, preserving the rights of the central government to determine the funding level of oblast governments and the right to "negotiate" tax shares with them according to unspecified criteria.

Intergovernmental transfers

An important element of most federal systems, intergovernmental transfers address the *vertical imbalances* that exist when assigned revenues are not perfectly matched with spending responsibilities. Transfers also address *horizontal imbalances* among subnational governments, narrowing inequities from disparate resource endowments. Transfers can also be used to influence the spending behavior of subnational governments.

The role of transfers in most countries—to achieve fiscal balance and parity—was supplanted in the former U.S.S.R. (and now in the Russian Federation) with variable, negotiated tax sharing. The disadvantage was that a single instrument (the sharing rate) was attempting to address simultaneously two problems—vertical and horizontal balance, that is, how much the oblasts got in total and which oblasts got what. The tax-sharing rates were chosen to balance the division of revenue between the subnational and central levels in aggregate *and* to achieve fiscal parity among oblasts.

Neither the Basic Principles of Taxation, nor the Law on the Budgetary Rights of Local Self-Governments, nor other laws governing subnational fiscal policies included any explicit arrangements for intergovernmental transfers. Without transfers, tax assignment implies that each tub will sit on its own bottom—that is, that an oblast's assigned revenue will determine its expenditure. True revenue-expenditure correspondence is unlikely, however, either for subnational governments in aggregate or for each oblast. Thus, differentials in expenditures and service provision will grow, since lower-income territories will collect less revenue.

Even if Russia's equalization and redistribution objectives are limited, some transfers will be required to secure fiscal balance in all territories. Indeed, for each quarter of 1992 most oblasts negotiated such gap-filling transfers. The 1992 Law on Subventions (appendix A) (never implemented) provided for targeted, specific grants to oblasts, not to meet general deficits but to help finance specific expenditure deficiencies in the social sectors. (Most grants appear to be for deficiencies in social and physical infrastructure.) Neither the overall volume of such subventions nor the criteria for distribution are specified.

The challenges posed by the Basic Principles of Taxation and the transitional system are acute. It is not surprising that the intergovernmental system remains in flux and that significant tensions remain. Indeed, these tensions are such that throughout 1992 and 1993 Russia has had difficulty in securing compliance from several oblasts to the agreed system.

Special fiscal regimes

In l992 several oblasts hammered out special fiscal relations with the federal government. These include some ethnic regions and better-off industrial oblasts, which argued that the fiscal regime is excessively equalizing and that they no longer wished to support cross-subsidies. Some areas rich in natural resources also felt entitled to special arrangements. They said that they had not benefited from natural resources or their development and that their area had, in fact, sustained severe economic damage from resource exploitation. In the Republic of Bashkortostan the subnational government has a "single channel" agreement with the federal government, retaining *all* revenue from *all* taxes collected in its territory and transferring a fixed nominal amount each month to the federal budget. This agreement has not been sanctioned by the Russian Supreme Soviet. In Tatarstan—an oil-rich republic with potentially huge natural resource revenues that could accrue to the center—the administration has yet to reach agreement with the Ministry of Finance. Since March l992 Tatarstan has withheld transfers to the Ministry of Finance, and negotiations are continuing. In the Udmurt Republic, which had also not reached agreement with the center in 1992, the government seeks a single channel agreement similar to the one exercised by Bashkortostan.

A further twenty oblasts reportedly decided in 1992 (this number has risen to a reported thirty oblasts in 1993) to determine unilaterally the proportion of taxes to be shared with the center. Discussions with all are continuing, and the Supreme Soviet has taken a hard line with them. It has threatened to apply sanctions that would call for a halt to all central expenditure in the territory, withholding export and import licenses, denying central bank credit, halting material supply from the central supply system, and withholding cash and currency. The Republic of Sakha (Yakutia) reached an agreement in late 1993 whereby it would retain all revenues collected from natural resources (gold) on its territory but would self-finance all expenditures, including traditionally federal outlays, on its territory.

The proliferation of such regimes could spell the dissolution of the Russian Federation—just as the failure of union republics to contribute to the union budget helped foster the dissolution of the U.S.S.R. in l991. Certainly, demands for special treatment and greater "fiscal sovereignty" complicate the design of a future intergovernmental system. The political structures giving oblasts the ability to conduct themselves in this manner have early roots. Ironically, in its early days the former U.S.S.R. took many steps to reinforce proto-state structures that would later lead to its demise and that are now causing Russia such problems. As noted by Milanovic (1993, p. 2),

Communists traditionally paid great attention to "nationalities" issues—indeed Marx boasted that communism would solve the "nationalities" problems. The Soviet state took great care to "discover" and catalogue new nationalities, which often lacked written literature and had no consciousness of their own distinctiveness. Most Siberian peoples could well have been absorbed into Russia, but instead were given special status, rights and proto-state structures. For nationalities that already *had* strong national feeling, the Soviet State assumed that nationalist aspirations would be satisfied by this step. No problems existed as long as communists were at the helm in these states. However, when the system began to crumble, these ethnically distinct political states and elites had all the accoutrements of state power and the proto-state could become a state. The seeds of destruction were thus sown early.

How Russia resolves these demands will determine the future shape of the Federation and "whither Russia" (chapter 8).

Sharing revenues from natural resources

Because it is potentially so divisive, taxation of natural resources deserves special attention. Natural resources in Russia are legally the property of the state, and thus part of the "common wealth" of Russia. As Russia's domestic natural resource prices rise to world levels, however, fiscal revenues from natural resources could become enormous. Formally, natural resources are governed by Russia's unified national tax system, subject to direct and indirect taxes (VAT, corporate income tax, and personal income tax) as is any other productive sector. In addition there is the (38 ECU per ton) export tax on petroleum. To capture additional revenues from natural resources for the budget, a royalty or severance tax was introduced in 1992, levied at 8 percent of the value of oil and gas production. This tax is now shared, with the proportions favoring producing oblasts.[19] While there are no *retail* excise taxes on oil and gas or other natural resources, an excise tax of 18 percent was introduced in 1992 and levied at the wellhead. It was assigned to the federal budget, but already in 1993 there is sharing with the producing oblasts. Domestic price controls are an additional "tax." With the domestic wholesale price of crude oil at about 17 percent of world prices (in 1992), price controls are equivalent to a tax of 83 percent.

The natural resource sector is one of the most heavily taxed sectors in Russia. Taxes and quasi-taxes based on production, rather than on profits, take more than half of the market value of exported oil. This means only the most productive fields could cover expenses and show a profit, even before profits tax. The heavy reliance on production taxes discourages production that would otherwise be economic. Indeed, the Russian tax system is ill-suited to capture economic rents from resource exploitation and Russian policymakers need to reexamine the taxation of natural resources. They should focus on an appropriate structure of taxes, the sharing of revenues among jurisdictions, and an equitable use of the proceeds (chapter 6).

Asset transfers to subnational governments

One of the features of fiscal decentralization in Russia and other economies in transition has been the transfer of enterprises (as well as land and housing) from central ownership to ownership by subnational governments. An inadequate revenue base and lack of intergovernmental transfers means that oblast and rayon governments have become increasingly financially dependent on the ownership of these public assets. Oblast and rayon enterprises provide vital social services ranging from housing, education, and health to water supply and sewerage. As oblasts become financially pressed, they may rely even more on enterprises they now own to meet these needs. This means that oblast and rayon governments could play an important role as either supporters of, or impediments to, privatization.

Until 1990 the ownership of enterprises in Russia was centralized. After the dissolution of the Union, there was broad agreement that ownership of real property should be reassigned to the different levels of government.

Federal property

National resources, such as national parks, health resorts, wildlife sanctuaries, art, and historical and cultural items, all became federal property. All state property with a national function is also assigned to the federal balance sheet, including the Pension Fund, the Social Insurance Fund, and other extrabudgetary funds, the central bank, the stock of gold, hard currency, military property, railroads, and other property that was formerly financed by the state budget of the U.S.S.R.[20] Also included are institutions of higher learning, research institutions, institutions jointly serving several ministries, geological and agricultural institutions, the defense industry, natural resources enterprises, and the transportation and communications sectors.

Oblast and rayon property

Subnational governments also own state property. Rayons and cities own buildings, housing, urban infrastructure facilities (including subways), retail sales outlets, consumer service enterprises, wholesale depots, public health institutions, and schools. Many provide local public goods and services—and are loss-making. Privatization of the housing stock, which was transferred to rayon and city governments in 1992, is considered a priority but will take time. Housing rents were frozen until mid-l992 (at their nominal January 1928 levels), and the failure to cover maintenance from rental incomes led to significant deterioration of the housing stock. Moreover, until the large subsidy to renters is reduced, privatization will be an unattractive option because home ownership will be much more expensive than renting (Renaud 1991).

Privatization and the provision of public services

The realization that markets can do a better job in the production of most commodities has led all levels of government in Russia to begin privatization. Privatization should mean a higher level of budgetary revenues because better allocation of resources results in higher output. Privatization may also bring potential savings to all levels of government, because of reduced subsidies to unprofitable enterprises. With competitive markets all governments stand to realize significant savings by contracting out the production and delivery of different public services without relinquishing the final responsibility for their delivery.

In the former U.S.S.R., not only did government have commercial functions, but state enterprises played a major role in the provision and direct financing of many social services that in market economies are the responsibility of government institutions. The most substantial were in health, education, and culture. The significance of contributions by public enterprises to oblast and rayon budgets has varied considerably, depending on the size of the enterprise vis-à-vis the local jurisdiction. Unofficial estimates put their magnitudes as high as 40 percent of some oblast and rayon social expenditures in 1991. In some single-enterprise "company towns," virtually all social outlays may be provided by the enterprise rather than by the budget.

There are strong incentives for state enterprises to discontinue support of public services. Of all their contributions only housing maintenance is formally tax deductible (although local governments may give special tax allowances). Construction of schools, health facilities, and housing are funded out of after-tax surpluses, which are now more urgently needed for investment in plant and equipment. Before 1991 most financing of state enterprise capital investment was centralized. In 1991 and 1992, however, about 80 percent of investment in plant and equipment came from enterprises' own funds.

However, divestiture of public service responsibilities has been less than complete—and uneven. Subnational governments have resisted change and, in some cases, are still able to extract sizable contributions from state enterprises. Not surprisingly, enterprise directors consider enterprise expenditures for local services as concealed taxation.

As privatization of state enterprises proceeds, divestiture will have to proceed. Provision of public services cannot be voluntary or ad hoc via the private sector. State enterprises cannot compete in a market-oriented economy if they continue to be burdened by these responsibilities. At some point local governments must stop attempting to coerce state enterprises to remain in their traditional role. State enterprises should contribute to the provision of local services in the same way private enterprises do—through taxes and user fees. More generally the Russian government needs to fully internalize the divestiture of public responsibilities by state enterprises into the design of the new system of intergovernmental relations.

Divestiture of enterprise social responsibilities should be to those levels of government presently responsible for the respective services (in most cases, oblasts and rayons) rather than to the government owning the public enterprise (most often, the central or oblast government). Ironically, to the extent that the new system of intergovernmental relations fails to internalize the divested social expenditures, it will tend to penalize most those local governments which in the former U.S.S.R. benefited most because they were chosen as the sites of large state enterprises.

Whither Russia?

Subnational finance and local government policies are emerging as crucial elements of ongoing reforms in Central and Eastern Europe's economies in transition. Subnational governments play a large role in economic activity, account for a major share of public sector outlays, and own many public enterprises and much of the housing stock. Recent attempts to streamline government budgets have led to increased subnational and local government responsibility for such crucial matters as capital investment, health, education, and safety net expenditure. Russia is no exception.

In Russia the changes are both economic (for example, intergovernmental relations) and political—and they are by no means over. Discussions have been held to reform the Constitution of the Russian Federation and to rethink the governmental structure. This reflects dissatisfaction with the rights of the oblasts vis-à-vis the federal level—is Russia a federation or not? Are the current oblast boundaries appropriate? Either constitutional reform, or the reform of governmental structures, would easily have major impacts on the Federation. At the constitutional level, although the precise proposals are murky, it appears that one proposal would consolidate the eighty-nine oblasts and autonomous regions into forty states (*zemlya*), along the lines of the German Federation's Länder, which have equal standing. The restructuring may not recognize present boundaries. Hence, the zemlya could be closer to their historical Russian origins, unlike the present-day oblasts, which were, allegedly, formed as part of the Leninist/Soviet "nationalities" policies. Another is to introduce a two-chamber parliament, with a lower house or "chamber of nationalities" comprising regional representatives. Such a system would almost certainly heighten the influence of regional and ethnic interests. The constitution proposed by the president in late 1993 may not be the final word in this complex area.

What is clear from all this is that the nature and structure of Russian federalism is in flux. The U.S.S.R. was dissolved only recently. Since Russia is in a period of nation building, it would be surprising if relations between the federal government and the republics and oblasts were not changing, as are those among the subnational governments. The okrugs are assuming a status akin to that of republics and oblasts. Expenditure functions that formerly were the responsibility of the central (U.S.S.R.) government have been devolved to subnational governments, and tax revenues of the federal government are now being shared with subnational governments under procedures that are changing frequently and unpredictably.

In Russia the question of resource rents is intertwined with ethnic independence (and special fiscal regimes for ethnically different groups) perhaps more strongly than in most other countries. If any resource-rich republics are allowed separate fiscal regimes that increase their share of resource rents at the expense of the central government, others are likely to demand the same treatment, including resource-rich oblasts and okrugs. Given the importance of natural resources in the Russian economy (for the foreseeable future), such a chain of events could lead to severe fiscal (and political) strains on the Russian Federation.

One huge problem is that the executive branch in Moscow lacks the political strength of the federal governments of Australia, Canada, or the United States. It has no obvious political recourse when subnational governments refuse to allow tax revenues to be remitted to the federal government. One daunting alternative, mentioned by the Russians themselves, would be the use of military force by the central government to prevent fiscal disintegration. But that may bring about the destruction of the Federation more swiftly and surely than could any fiscal disintegration. Rather, the challenge is to find the catalyst that binds, in the form of a consensus-based intergovernmental system that is perceived as fair and transparent.

Notes

1. This section draws on *Encyclopedia Britannica*, 1967, volume 19, s.v. Russian Soviet Federated Socialist Republic, and IMF (1992a, 1992b).

2. This section draws on Milanovic (1993). Milanovic argues that since indepen-

dent political activity was banned under communism and groupings based on shared economic interests could not emerge, the only accepted form of government was territorial.

3. See note 1.

4. Data are taken from the 1989 Statistical Yearbook of the U.S.S.R. and are the most recent available for these subnational aggregates.

5. Converted at the then-prevailing exchange rate of R 1.6 = US$1, which was generally agreed to be overvalued.

6. This section draws on Gleason (1990, pp. 61–90).

7. This section draws on IMF and others (1991); IMF (1992a, 1992b); and discussions with the Russian Ministry of Finance.

8. See note 7.

9. See IMF (1992a) and Tanzi (1992, 1993b) for a description of prereform taxation in economies in transition.

10. This is taken from discussions in April 1992 with Alexander Lubianoi, who was director of the Territories Department, Ministry of Finance of the Russian Federation.

11. This parallels fully the arrangements in the U.S.S.R., in which the individual republics in the Union negotiated tax shares for each tax with the Union's Ministry of Finance.

12. This discussion draws on IMF and others (1991).

13. See note 7.

14. Data referred to in the text or presented in tables have been made available to the authors by the Ministry of Finance of the Russian Federation (unless another source is noted) and have not hitherto been published. Data may not correspond fully to other sources or to data from the same source obtained at a different time as revisions and definitions are ongoing (dates have been specified whenever possible). This is especially so for oblast-level data.

15. Data were provided by the Russian Ministry of Finance.

16. Data were provided by the International Monetary Fund, April 1992.

17. The discussion of tax policy in 1989 draws on IMF and others (1991); the discussion of tax policy in 1990–91 draws on IMF (1992a, 1992b) and discussions with the Russian Ministry of Finance.

18. This section draws on material provided by Jorge Martinez-Vazquez based on meetings with deputies in the Supreme Soviet and representatives of the executive branch. These left the clear impression that the Law on the Budgetary Rights of Local Self-Governments is the best compromise that could be reached at the present time. There is desire and intention to further reform the system to make budgets at the different levels of government much more independent than allowed by the present versions of this law.

19. The Law on the Subsoil was passed in May 1992. Other taxes currently being considered include an exploration fee of 1 to 3 percent of the value of exploration expenditures and a fee for exploitation of the continental shelf.

20. This draws on IMF and others (1991), IMF (1992a), and discussions with the Russian Ministry of Finance.

3

Intergovernmental finances: stabilization, privatization, and growth

Christine I. Wallich

Russia's reform program has the dual aims of stabilizing the economy to reduce inflation and privatizing the economy to transform it into a market-oriented system. Russia's oblasts and local governments are crucial to its success in both endeavors. Oblasts own many of Russia's enterprises. Thus, the future of privatization rests in their hands. Oblasts are also key, if indirect, players in the budgetary and monetary processes. This chapter focuses on stabilization and privatization—areas in which the behavior and incentives facing oblast and rayon governments are especially important. The first section discusses the role of subnational governments in promoting or impeding stabilization, with particular focus on national fiscal policies and the intergovernmental dimensions of macroeconomic policymaking. The second section addresses Russia's privatization policy and the role of the subnational sector in promoting—or impeding—privatization and the transformation of Russia into a market economy.

Neither topic would typically be the focus of analysis of fiscal federalism in most countries. Traditional analysis of subnational public finances in market economies focuses on the responsibilities of state and local governments as "service providers" (Rosen 1988). This stems from the twin assumptions that stabilization and macroeconomic management are the responsibilities of the central government and that subnational governments are unlikely to have a major effect on the macroeconomy. This is likely to be true in countries where local governments are small and have limited powers. In Russia and many other economies in transition, however, the subnational sector is large. And as the subnational sector in Russia becomes increasingly powerful, the repercussions of oblast and rayon behavior gain significance, and the macroeconomic dimensions of subnational finances become crucial to stabilization.

Traditional analysis of subnational finance also focuses mostly on the allocative and equity dimensions of the subnational fiscal regime. This ignores the pervasive role of government (especially subnational government) as owner and producer in economies in transition, including Russia. With subnational governments owning most of Russia's enterprises, the effect of intergovernmental fiscal relations on Russia's privatization effort is also critical. Thus, in Russia, where subnational governments account for almost half of total spending, and where a significant number of these governments' responsibilities and outlays are linked to their ownership of enterprises, both stabilization and ownership are key dimensions of subnational finance.

The problem in a nutshell

Russia's central government has twin aims—stabilization and privatization, both of which require initiative and leadership. Stabilization, however, requires the center to *increase* its role and control over parts of the economy (such as the budget and monetary policy), while privatization means a *reduced* role for government. These signals are potentially conflicting and, given the current weak central government, they are not being transmitted well. The result is that neither objective—privatization or stabilization—is being successfully implemented (Litvack and Wallich 1993).

Intergovernmental relations are at the heart of this dual challenge and are key to the economic and political tasks ahead. Critical in the design of a revenue and transfer system is ensuring that each level of government has enough resources to deliver assigned services. When expenditure needs and revenue assignments are ill-matched, one level of government (usually the subnational) is left with inadequate resources to provide needed services to the population. In most countries this leads to a fiscal squeeze on local economies and, generally, to the required reduction in the government's overall fiscal program. In economies in transition the peculiar nature of the soft budget constraint (Kornai 1992) can lead to a somewhat different outcome.

Searching for ways to finance service delivery, subnational governments in economies in transition may revert to coping mechanisms that may allow services to be delivered, but at the cost of many important national objectives. The center's pursuit of tight monetary policy has, for example, met with strong opposition from oblast and enterprise groups that want expanded credit to the state-owned sector in order to keep ailing enterprises alive. This is hardly surprising since oblasts and lower-level governments now own many enterprises following their transfer from the central state ownership after Russia's independence. Subnational governments may also try to develop extrabudgetary sources of funds, which reduce budgetary transparency. All these coping mechanisms can be especially harmful in economies in transition such as Russia, where the national government has so many crucial objectives, and where central institutions are inexperienced and do not have the strength to resist.

The absence of revenue-expenditure correspondence is a striking feature of Russia's new Basic Principles of Taxation Law and of the transitional arrangements for the intergovernmental fiscal system (chapter 5). The fiscally squeezed national government has sought to strengthen budgetary control and reduce its deficit by shifting expenditures downward and taking more revenues for itself. The result: direct and indirect opposition from oblast governments. Directly, oblasts have successfully lobbied for greater, though one can argue still inadequate, revenue shares. Some have taken the correspondence issue into their own hands by withholding revenues from the center, thus leaving the federal budget exposed and vulnerable. Each of these coping mechanisms indirectly undermines the center's budgetary controls.

Reducing the federal budget deficit by squeezing the subnational sector may also harm privatization. Oblasts have few independent revenue sources under the present regime, other than the very minor taxes that have been assigned to them (chapter 5). In contrast to governments in market economies, subnational governments in economies in transition such as Russia still see themselves as owners—who can make direct economic interventions—rather than as service providers. They have a major stake in the assets and enterprises transferred to them during decentralization, and they derive significant funds from them. Hard-pressed oblasts may, therefore, want to hold onto *their* enterprises to ensure the continued provision of services that are becoming increasingly unaffordable under the present intergovernmental fiscal arrangements. Alternatively the oblasts may encourage enterprises to provide such services, making it even harder to privatize them with their ancillary activities.

A fiscal squeeze on subnational governments can also affect resource allocation. In an economy as regionalized and with as few antimonopoly policies as Russia, subnational governments' vested interests in enterprise ownership and revenues may encourage protectionism and interoblast trade barriers to prop up local monopolies. Fieldwork in a number of oblasts suggests that there is frequent use of "local-content" purchasing requirements, and "export" barriers have been introduced to ensure that tax revenues do not flow into the coffers of neighboring oblasts. Just as international trade barriers reduce countries' growth, Russia's oblast economies will be hampered by the failure to exploit economies of scale and the national marketplace.

Ironically, then, attempts to squeeze the local sector can create incentives to pursue the very mechanisms that threaten the center's objectives. The techniques used to regain control allow subnational governments to react in ways that can lead to further destabilization or are inimical to privatization. What is more, the approach of shifting the deficit down pits the center against the oblasts and is inconsistent with gaining the trust of the oblasts, so crucial at this time of nation building (a theme discussed in chapter 7). In sum, subnational governments and their behavior will help determine the efficiency with which the Russian economy performs in the future.

Why subnational finances are crucial for stabilization policy

There has always been controversy over the proper macroeconomic policies to stabilize the economy at high levels of output and employment, with reasonable price stability. Indeed, some analysts doubt that the economy can be fine-tuned at all (Dornbusch and Fischer 1987). However, there is general agreement that macroeconomic stabilization is a responsibility of central government.

Theory and central stabilization policies

In traditional public finance theory, the purpose of the government budget is to stabilize the economy, redistribute income, and allocate fiscal resources. The first two tasks are typically assigned to the central government (Musgrave and Musgrave 1989); mobility of capital and labor will likely prevent subnational or local governments from being successful in either stabilization or income redistribution. Because stabilization is so important, theory also assigns those taxes with greater stabilization properties (such as personal income tax and corporate income tax) to the center (Musgrave 1959). This leaves allocation—that is, deciding how much is spent on each service and how this is financed—as the main role of subnational governments.

The claim that the primary responsibility for the exercise of counter-cyclical policy must rest with the central government has been developed along two other lines (Oates 1990). First, stabilization policy must be a central responsibility because in most countries only central governments control money supply and credit. Subnational governments do not have this stabilization tool, for good reasons: if each level of government were able to create money, there would be a powerful incentive for them to finance purchases of goods and services with newly created money rather than local taxation. This would result in rapid national monetary expansion and inflation. Indeed, the lack of control over the money supply of central banks in the republics of the former U.S.S.R., which found it easier to create money than to tax, led to the abandonment of the ruble as a common currency—and to the breakup of the ruble zone—in early 1992. This was followed by the introduction of individual national currencies across most of the now-independent states. Similarly, the Czech and Slovak monetary union continued only until early 1993, when the Czech Republic became concerned that economically weaker Slovakia would not keep to the agreed monetary emission guidelines and both countries agreed to establish separate currencies.

The second rationale for pursuing stabilization policies at the center is that subnational economies tend to be highly open—that is, they import and export relatively large shares of the goods they consume and produce in trade with other provinces or regions. Such openness implies serious constraints on subnational governments' ability to employ countercyclical fiscal measures. For example, if the subnational government wanted to stimulate the local economy with a tax cut, most of the newly generated spending would flow out in payment for goods and services produced elsewhere and would have little ultimate effect on local employment. Thus, the absence of monetary prerogatives and the openness of regional or local economies suggest that the potential for effective macroeconomic stabilization is limited at subnational levels.

Subnational finances and stabilization policy

Whether the converse is true (that subnational government has a de minimis effect on national stabilization) is less clear. Even though many theorists believe that subnational governments lack the scope and ability to have much impact on macroeconomic stabilization, some empirical evidence shows otherwise (Oates 1972). Some argue that although central government, with its broad monetary and fiscal powers, must assume the primary role for an active countercyclical policy, local governments can make a contribution to that policy. Gramlich (1984) alludes to the role of "rainy day" stabilization funds that can be used countercyclically by local governments during recession as a means of stabilizing spending and tax revenues over the business cycle.

Studies in Germany suggest, moreover, that local governments' behavior can be destabilizing. In the 1960s, when Länder governments (the German equivalent of a state) accounted for roughly two-thirds of all investment, their investment pattern was apparently procyclical and destabilizing in the 1967 recession and subsequent boom (Wilson 1984).

In China, too, decentralization of public finances in the mid-1980s, and even now, may have compromised the central government's ability to pursue stabilization policy. As in Russia, subnational governments collect all tax revenues. Fiscal arrangements (known as *tax contracting*) allowed provincial governments to retain everything they collected in excess of an agreed amount (or *quota*) that was to be remitted to the federal budget. Since these quotas were fixed over time and set in nominal terms, provincially retained revenues grew in a boom and shrank in a slump. Because provincial governments typically spent all their resources and more than 50 percent of all spending was at the subnational level, provincial budgetary behavior could dominate the economy, fueling a boom and further starving a recession. The center, which received a fixed nominal revenue flow regardless of economic conditions (and whose real revenue was shrinking over time, due to inflation), was not able to offset the procyclical budgetary behavior of the provincial governments. To do so, it would have had to generate budgetary surpluses, but it did not have the revenue flexibility to do so (Bahl and Wallich 1992; World Bank 1990b; Szapary and Blejer 1989). An expansion of the *single channel approach* of remittances in Russia, which resembles China's quota system, would imply similar risks to macroeconomic policymaking.

In like fashion, macroeconomic stability can be jeopardized by intergovernmental arrangements that give subnational governments unfettered borrowing rights. Stabilization by the federal government hinges on its ability to control key policy instruments—that is, fiscal and monetary policy. The success of fiscal policy depends not only on how the federal government administers taxes and public spending but also on the size of the subnational deficit, and how it is managed and financed. Fiscal discipline at the national level can be offset by provincial indiscipline and uncontrolled borrowing. Both Brazil and Argentina have shown how subnational financing of deficits through borrowing from banks owned by provinces can jeopardize macroeconomic stability and the integrity of government finances. Extensive borrowing and deficit financing by subnational governments can offset attempts by the central government to balance its budget (Bomfin and Shah 1991; Shah 1990; World Bank 1990a). Indeed, in Argentina macroeconomic stabilization has been at the forefront of debates about fiscal federalism. Provinces have tried to obtain federal resources by running up high fiscal deficits and asking the federal government to step in. Provinces have also borrowed from the central bank through provincial banks, usually via rediscounts or overdrafts. (In 1986 provincial deficits in Argentina before transfers from the central government were 6.2 percent of gross domestic product, GDP.) There are no winners in this struggle and a coordinated effort is required from both levels of government to achieve price stability.

More generally, giving subnational governments access to major tax bases may reduce the revenue flexibility of the central government, diluting its freedom to manage the economy (Bahl and Linn 1992). Such freedom is important in developing countries and in countries in transition, where economies are more susceptible to economic fluctuations, shifts in terms of trade, or worldwide recession. Therefore, for stabilization and growth, there is a case for central government to retain control of the main taxes and borrowing instruments.

Oblast finances and national stabilization efforts

Across Eastern Europe stabilization has been complicated by the intergovernmental dimension (Bird and Wallich 1993). Fiscally burdened national governments have strained to pare down their expenditure responsibilities and generate revenues for fiscal balance. Local outlays have been viewed as a compressible type of expenditure, and intergovernmental transfers have been a tempting target for reducing central budgetary outlays. Expenditure responsibilities have also been transferred to local governments, especially those where central spending was never really justified, and the center has taken the better revenue sources for itself. In Russia, too, intergovernmental fiscal relations both affect and are affected by macroeconomic policy. Under pressure to meet stabilization objectives, central policies have affected subnational well-being, as the central government has pushed the budget deficit down by shifting unfunded expenditure responsibilities to oblast governments, hoping the resource-constrained oblasts would do the cost-cutting.

Experience beginning in early 1992 suggests that the reverse is also true—that the intergovernmental fiscal system and oblast behavior can also strongly affect the federal government's ability to conduct macroeconomic policy. It can be argued that the present transitional approach to intergovernmental fiscal relations is a potential threat to the success of Russia's macroeconomic stabilization. There are three dimensions to this. First, the system's design is flawed because it fails to provide the needed correspondence between subnational revenues and expenditures—both for the subnational level in aggregate and at the level of the individual oblast (chapter 5). This places significant pressure on subnational budgets, which must still cover the local budgetary cost of ongoing expenditures for the social safety net and for social subsidies and housing outlays, as well as expenditures resulting from wage and other spending mandates imposed by the center. On the revenue side, there are pressures (and frustrations) from oblasts' inadequate, though increased, share in total revenues and the erratic way in which the Ministry of Finance negotiates oblasts' revenue retention shares.

Second, as some oblasts have sought greater autonomy, their hostility toward central tax and tax-sharing policies has increased. In a system characterized by an inverted, bottom-up tax administration, Russia's federal budget is vulnerable, particularly now when its executive is weak, its tax administration system is inadequate, and there is an absence of adequate federal budget controls and treasury function (Szapary and Blejer 1989). The vulnerability of the federal budget to revenue withholding is potentially highly destabilizing. Indeed, it has been argued that factionalism in the economy could ultimately destabilize the economy (Bookman 1991). Should greater conflicts between regions and the center emerge, the present weakness of the central organs (plus de facto power of the purse, which lies in the oblasts' responsibility for tax administration) could threaten the federal budget. Any design for an intergovernmental fiscal system must carefully consider its potential for alleviating or exacerbating these tensions (chapter 7).

Third, the fragmentation of expenditure and revenue accounts in the form of extrabudgetary funds complicates macroeconomic management by reducing budgetary transparency and control. The emergence of such funds subnationally (they have also mushroomed nationally) reflects the difficulties of designing and implementing an integrated and coherent fiscal policy and will further complicate stabilization. Finally, legislation that endorses subnational borrowing is cause for worry. In Russia the combination of underfunded subnational governments and own-credit creation (as in Brazil or Argentina) could result in major macroeconomic distortions (see below).

Without a coherent and effective macroeconomic policy, there are risks that go well beyond the failure of stabilization policy. In the present center-oblast tension, skeptical regional governments may ask what function the central government plays if it cannot meet its fundamental responsibility of providing a stable price level and functional economic environment.

Russia's stabilization policies

The main aim of Russia's present macroeconomic stabilization policy is to stem the enormous inflationary pressures of recent years. Inflation was hidden during the command economy period but was reflected in scarcity and queuing. It became overt in the postcommand period. While inflation has almost certainly receded since its peak in 1992 of almost 2300 percent a year, fighting inflation is still the focal point of Russia's macroeconomic and stabilization policy.[1] It is generally agreed that rates of inflation greater than 30 to 40 percent a month risk the plunge into hyperinflation, which is thought to occur when inflation rates reach 50 percent a month (Cagan

1956). Russia, only a year after dissolution of the Union, has come perilously close.

The stabilization policies invoked by Russia's reformers are orthodox. On the monetary side, policymakers are committed to tightening credit and raising interest rates, as well as eliminating interenterprise arrears, which are an important source of credit creation in virtually all economies in transition including Russia.[2] (Interenterprise arrears can dwarf the budget in their potential impact on credit and other macroeconomic variables, paralyzing the payments system and tying up liquidity in the economy, so that further credit is needed to unfreeze the system.[3])

To support stabilization, Russia's central bank was also strengthened. The call for an independent central bank was an important initial step proposed under the 1992 reform program of then-acting Prime Minister Yegor Gaidar. However, this was subsequently opposed by Parliament and by enterprises that would suffer under such a policy. The central bank now reports to Parliament, which some see as a recipe for loose money.

In the external sphere, the reform program envisions a freer exchange rate and more trade liberalization, although plans for the CIS common currency zone and free trade area began to fail as early as 1991. As a result, in all ex-republics (not just Russia) trade and output have dived, taking these countries into deep recession. Economic growth in the Russian Federation averaged 3.2 percent in the first half of the 1980s (IMF and others 1991). In 1992 output fell 20 percent, and in 1993 growth is also expected to be negative (World Bank 1992b). These recessions have had deep effects on fiscal revenues, with virtually all republics of the former U.S.S.R., and Russia in particular, facing severe budgetary crises.

Finally, Russia is trying to improve its international creditworthiness by working closely with international banking groups to tackle the U.S.S.R.'s outstanding debts, which Russia has assumed. The macroeconomic program, together with other reforms toward a market economy, seeks to clear the way for foreign financial support and private investment to restore and further Russian growth.

National fiscal policies

Fiscal policy plays a crucial role in stabilization in Russia. As a result of the severe decline in output since the breakup of the Union, the failing state-owned enterprise sector no longer provides the revenue base or the tax handle of earlier days. Private entrepreneurship has the potential to contribute to a more vital economy in the future. In the near term, however, private sector development has accentuated the problem of a shrinking national revenue base, as many new smaller private enterprises elude the tax net and present major challenges to compliance and tax administration. The new tax reforms, which began in 1991–92 are undoubtedly desirable for market efficiency, but until experience with the new system is gained, revenue shortfalls seem likely.

The expenditure side of the budget continues to be burdened with heavy outlays for both consumer and producer subsidies. Both have been difficult to phase out, and consumer subsidies remain an important, although inefficient, means of social protection. Russia, like other economies in transition, has a generous cash benefit program of pensions, child benefits, allowances, and other transfers (Holzmann 1989; Barr 1992). Although these programs are financed in principle by payroll taxes with high contribution rates (37 percent of wages, levied mostly on employers), they nonetheless burden the budget because some extrabudgetary social insurance funds are in deficit (and they consume tax "headroom" that could be exploited for other spending programs). Finally, new and sometimes large outlays (to support failing enterprises, to restructure state-owned enterprises prior to privatization, and to convert military enterprises to civilian production) have created budgetary demands. Future demands may well come from the recapitalization of banks and from environmental protection and cleanup.

These problems are not unique to Russia. Recent economic reform programs in the economies in transition of Eastern Europe (including Poland, Hungary, Romania, the Czech Republic, Slovakia, and Bulgaria) have also had to deal with a weak overall macroeconomic position and fiscal deficits. There is an almost universal experience of sharp declines in growth in the early years of transition, with a corresponding decline in government revenues at a time when demands for additional outlays from the public purse are also present, especially for the unemployed, for pensioners, and for those seriously affected by the price increases (Milanovic 1992a; Calvo and Coricelli 1992).

To address the revenue-expenditure gap in Russia, broad measures to reduce the budget deficit call for prioritizing and further cutting expenditures, as well as implementing additional tax reforms to raise revenue. The Union fiscal deficit (on a commitments basis) reached 26 percent of GDP in 1991, as revenue sources dried up after republican transfers were cut in mid-year. Russia's budgetary stance (as a republic) just before independence was expansionary. After the dissolution of the Union, when Russia took on virtually all the former Union's budgetary functions, the estimated Russian budget deficit for the year as a whole was 31 percent of GDP (IMF 1992b). Since then, the federal government has aimed to reduce the fiscal deficit from this high level to about 10 percent for 1992. Although these efforts initially seemed feasible, 1992 ended with a deficit closer to 20 percent.

Russia's revenue plans

On the revenue side, Russia's fiscal program calls for a marked increase in taxes, primarily on petroleum products and foreign trade. If successful, these taxes will contribute significantly to balancing the federal budget. Reliance on these revenues is potentially problematical, however. Ownership of natural resources (such as oil and gas and gold) and rights to natural resource rents and taxes is being contested between the central government and some oblasts, notably Khanty-Mansiiskii and Yamal-Nenets in western Siberia, Sakha (Yakutia), and Tatarstan. These oblasts, some with large ethnic populations, are increasingly concerned about the continued exploitation by Russia of what they consider *their* heritage (chapter 6). The ability of the federal government to access these natural resource revenues—huge if oil prices rise to world levels—cannot be taken for granted. Indeed, preliminary parliamentary discussion of both the petroleum excise tax and the export tax proposed sharing both taxes with producing oblasts at rates ranging from 25 to 65 percent—and this at a time when oil prices remain low, when revenues are limited, and when dividing the spoils is still an academic point.

Fiscal revenues in 1992 were budgeted at 28 percent of GDP (the actual revenue at end-year came closer to 30 percent—see appendix C). This is far less than in the days of the command economy, when the government appropriated most enterprise and household surpluses for the budget, and revenues ranged from about 45 to 50 percent of GDP. The high revenue-GDP ratio was consistent with the dominant role of government in the command economy (Gray 1990). The ratio declines pari passu, however, as the government withdraws from the productive spheres. This has occurred in countries as diverse as China and Hungary. In Russia, as the government's role in the economy changes, the overall expenditure- and revenue-to-GDP ratios are also targeted to decline. However, as has been true elsewhere in Eastern Europe, the decline in revenue during Russia's early independence has been greater than generally expected, reflecting both the economic slump and difficulties in collecting taxes from the private sector (Tanzi 1992, 1993a, and l993b).

The 1992 and 1993 performance of individual taxes in Russia showed contrasting trends (chapter 5). Indirect taxes at times performed sluggishly, because of the impact of interenterprise arrears on value-added tax, which is collected only when sales revenue is realized. And there have been problems with collecting the new export taxes, which required payment at the time of export but which, in the absence of credit facilities, exporters could not pay.[4] Income taxes, however—and particularly corporate tax—were buoyant and grew rapidly because of the positive impact of inflation on reported corporate accounting profits, since depreciation is not indexed. Arrears did not affect corporate tax because sales revenues (even if unrealized) are taken into income as soon as the transaction is booked. Wages, which were adjusted frequently during the year, contributed to rapid growth in personal income tax. Revenue growth in 1993 was similarly uneven across the different taxes. For the future, improved tax administration, improved tax design, and economic recovery should help stabilize the revenue base and tax collections along the new, lower, revenue trend line.

Streamlining Russia's expenditures

On the expenditure side, and consistent with the changing role of government, Russia planned to reduce expenditures from about 48 percent of GDP in 1991 to slightly less than 37 percent in 1992. (In fact, end-of-year figures were closer to 33 percent of GDP—see appendix C.) Major cuts were planned in investment and subsidies to enterprises, as well as consumer price subsidies. Operation and maintenance outlays and defense expenditures were also to be reduced. More generally, the budget was to be restructured toward priority areas such as social protection, where spending was projected to increase significantly in the transitional period. It was expected that these priority areas would be financed from subnational budgets. For the future, continued budgetary streamlining is planned, as the government moves away from its role as owner, entrepreneur, and social provider—a development seen in other economies in transition where reforms began sooner.

Balancing the budget: the regional fiscal squeeze

The stabilization program implies austerity at both the central and subnational levels. It has had (and will have) a major influence on intergovernmental relations and subnational finances. Restrictive budgetary measures will affect each level of government differently, depending on how government expenditure functions and revenue flows are adjusted and reshuffled between the center and oblasts. The design of intergovernmental finance, as implemented in Russia's 1992 and 1993 budgetary legislation and its subsequent implementation, suggests a worsening picture for subnational governments.

Expenditure pressures at the subnational level

In the 1992 stabilization program most cuts in expenditures—except for consumer subsidies, which are now a subnational responsibility—have benefited primarily the *central* government budget. Shifting responsibility for

large components of social expenditures and capital investment to the regions suggests an *increase* in subnational expenditures.

How will demands on the regions for expenditures in these new areas
emerge? With the severity and duration of unemployment likely to accompany structural adjustment, and the impact of inflation on fixed incomes,
pressure to help the most vulnerable groups of society will increase. Although
expenditures on social welfare are to be funded by a central extrabudgetary
fund, the "social support fund," this fund could be in deficit by the end of
1992, and subnational governments will almost certainly have to use their
own funds to address these needs. Plans to make all consumer subsidies
means-tested and to streamline family allowances should yield some savings—but with a lag, because these programs will take time to implement.
In the meantime, subnational governments will still be under pressure to
use local funds to continue social subsidies. The number of families below
the poverty line is also likely to swell with economic readjustment.

Subnational expenditures triggered by economic reform also include
those associated with enterprise subsidies: many public sector prices (some
of which represent potential fee income to subnational governments) have
not been deregulated. These include the prices of most public utilities and
public transportation, whose services are provided by subnational governments but whose prices are determined by the central government. (At
present only gas and electric utilities are operated by the central government, and their prices are scheduled to rise to world market levels within
two years.) Housing rents may now be set by subnational governments, but
they are hostage to national wage policies and low wage levels. Subsidies to
these enterprises and to housing maintenance companies will be heavy
burdens until price and wage liberalization is complete. Expenditure pressures will continue to come from these pricing policies, the cost of the social safety net, and the need for neglected and long-postponed capital investment; and there will be pressures from wage and other mandates.

Finally, subnational governments may have to assume some of the social expenditures of their state-owned enterprises once these are privatized.
The budgetary implications of privatization may well be negative, as social
expenditures on the budget rise and as enterprises in the private sector become harder to tax. Jettisoning of social expenditures by enterprises is already disrupting local budgets (see the discussion of Yaroslav oblast later in
this chapter). The practice will reduce the need for government subsidies
to enterprises (or increase enterprises' disposable after-tax profits) but it is
not certain that these revenue benefits will accrue to the same level of government that must then pick up the expenditure tab. Analysis of the budgetary implications of this divestiture is needed to determine whether the
reassignment of these expenditures corresponds with the oblast govern-

ment's ability to finance them. Although in aggregate these enterprise social expenditures are estimated to range from 2 to 5 percent of GDP for the
nation as a whole, they are unequally distributed across oblasts —and allegedly account for as much as 40 percent of some oblasts' social expenditures.
Paradoxically, the regions of Russia that benefited most in the past from
the presence of enterprises are now most at risk from enterprises' divestiture of social assets. These regional differences should also be incorporated
in the (re)assignment or sharing of tax revenues and the design of transfers. If not, many regions may lag in privatization or may pursue coping
mechanisms to make their continued functioning possible.

The oblast revenue squeeze

Although most additional (social) expenditures will be borne subnationally,
most additional revenue (from trade and energy taxes) will likely accrue to
the *federal* government. To the extent these revenues do accrue to subnational governments, they will not benefit *all* subnational governments.
In the case of resource taxes, revenues will flow only to the three or four
resource-producing oblasts, whose combined population barely exceeds 5
million to 6 million of Russia's 165 million people. Indeed, this could be
considered a "worst case," because both federal and subnational budgets
are worsened while a few oblasts benefit inordinately.

   Moreover, tax revenues in the transition period will continue to be
volatile. Enterprises are being restructured and wages and prices are being
adjusted. These measures could mean erratic behavior of major tax bases—
and major revenue shortfalls. This highlights the risks of assigning any one
revenue (base) to a particular level of government. For example, in the long
run, as both direct and indirect enterprise subsidies are reduced (including interest and exchange rate subsidies, as well as subsidies in the form of
controlled energy and other prices), economic reform will reduce the
(largely fictitious) taxable profitability of state enterprises in the medium
term. This will severely erode the base of the corporate income tax, an
important source of revenue for subnational governments. Each of these
changes can throw subnational budgets into deficit—and subnational governments have little control over them.

   The fiscal squeeze is thus also felt on the revenue side. The result has
been a severe mismatching of revenues and expenditures in some oblasts
(chapter 5). The federal government is aware of this squeeze. Indeed, it
has been suggested that the 1992 transitional system was *designed* to generate inadequate subnational revenues, to force subnational governments to
draw down large accumulated cash balances to finance their newly assigned
expenditures. Based on the Ministry of Finance's expenditure figures, there

was a "surplus" (a positive cash balance) at the subnational level. Monetary statistics also showed an increase in bank deposits of oblast governments, which suggested that they were building up, in aggregate, a cash surplus equivalent to 1.7 percent of GDP in 1992 and about the same in 1993.[5] Across oblasts there was, of course, significant variance in estimated fiscal positions and cash balances.

Given the fiscal squeeze, this subnational surplus is surprising but is not difficult to explain. In many respects, it is illusory. First, this is a *cash* budget surplus, and it does not reflect oblasts' accrued commitments, which may be large if arrears in the government sector parallel arrears in the enterprise sector. Fiscal balance in one locality visited had been achieved by cutting monthly pensions from the then-official minimum pension of R 900 to R 300. Second, subnational governments must run balanced budgets, so they keep cash on hand to meet continuing obligations. Third, subnational governments must make many outlays on social benefits and wage increases for which they receive compensation (sometimes delayed by months and unindexed) from the federal government. Since subnational governments cannot have a deficit, these transfers immediately generate a surplus when they are credited (indeed, the magnitude of these transfers, which is almost equal to the overall subnational surplus, suggests the two are related). Fourth, uncertainty about the overall economic situation and revenue flows has led to cautious spending, and localities have delayed expenditures on operations and maintenance and other outlays. Finally, interenterprise arrears may have mitigated the budgetary burden of oblasts' social spending, since enterprises' arrears allowed them to continue these expenditures. The explosion of arrears also saved localities the costs of unemployment and the safety net associated with enterprise bankruptcy.

Given the balanced budget rule and the need for operating cash, subnational budgets will virtually always show a cash surplus. Perversely, neither extra spending responsibilities nor revenue cuts will ever eliminate the surplus. Localities will cut or shift expenditures (or accumulate arrears) to stay within available resources.

In sum, the budget position of subnational governments is fragile and, with the correspondence of expenditure and revenue assignments far from guaranteed, subnational governments may be caught in a vise of declining tax revenues and increased expenditures. This is also seen in other economies in transition in Eastern Europe, where the subnational expenditure envelope has expanded as a result of both decentralization and downward expenditure shifts related to short-run macroeconomic expediency, while revenues for the budget as a whole, and for the subnational level in particular, have fallen (Bird and Wallich 1993).[6]

Trends in center-local finances and consequences of ad hoc approaches

The dynamics of center-oblast sharing in each budgetary quarter of 1992 and 1993 appear, at first, consistent with strengthening the relative position of subnational governments, although both central and local budgets seem to be weakening. The oblasts' average retentions of value-added tax increased from 14 percent to 20 percent between the first and third quarters of 1992, reached 25 percent in the fourth, and ranged between 20 and 55 percent in early 1993. Of the 32 percent tax on corporate income, the subnational share rose from 17 to 19 percentage points in 1992 and to 22 percentage points in 1993. Both the export tax and the excise tax on petroleum have become candidates for sharing—at rates of 25 to 65 percent, depending on the oblast. This shift was introduced following pressure from better-endowed and politically strong oblasts (which might otherwise decide on sharing rates unilaterally) and from a legislative branch with populist interests.

However, in response to—or perhaps in anticipation of—these trends, the federal government reduced subventions and shifted expenditures downstairs. Each of these actions has limits: subventions cannot be reduced beyond zero, and further downward shifts of expenditures will become politically provocative. Moreover, these measures are risky and unsustainable macroeconomically and reflect the failure of the intergovernmental system to capture either consensus or revenue-expenditure correspondence.

If institutionalized, the ad hoc approach will at best perpetuate negotiations between central and subnational governments. And, as was true of the Union budget, the Russian Federation budget is exposed to the exercise of fiscal sovereignty by better-endowed, powerful oblasts, and the central government is constrained from strengthening its position by the absence of both a strong tax administration system and an intergovernmental system whose rules are agreed upon and followed.

Thus, at worst, extensions of the single channel approach (or of unilaterally determined sharing rates) could seriously destabilize the federal budget. If, as has happened in Bashkortostan and Tatarstan, subnational governments negotiate a fixed nominal share for remittance to the central government, the single channel approach will not only mean a lower federal yield: it will also mean a procyclical revenue yield, with the center's share prone to inflation erosion, thus leading to more stabilization problems. The experience of China, where such fiscal contracts became the norm, shows how big a problem they can be (Bahl and Wallich 1992; World Bank 1990b; Blejer and Szapary 1989). While strengthening and centralizing the State Tax Service would address the loose central control over revenue collections, the political-economy dimensions of the single channel approach to tax remittance—and the centrifugal forces that might sweep over Russia— must also be addressed (chapter 7).

These factors highlight the need for a flexible, transparent, and equitable, perhaps formula-based, revenue-sharing framework and the contribution (for good or bad) the intergovernmental system can make in determining Russia's future.

How oblast coping mechanisms may undermine stabilization

The basic strategy of the central government has been to push the deficit down by shifting unfunded spending responsibilities to the subnational sector in the hope that it will do the cost-cutting. This pressure on subnational budgets may undermine the national stabilization effort, and fiscal arrangements are necessary to address the needs of each level of government and provide correspondence between expenditures and revenues. Without adequate revenue and transfers, and with increased expenditure responsibilities, subnational governments are likely to resort to solutions that could threaten reform.

Subnational governments react to revenue insufficiency in several ways—none of them easy to quantify or amenable to statistical descriptions. First, they may simply spend and accumulate arrears. Second, they may negotiate unilaterally for lower tax sharing with the center. Third, they may borrow from locally owned banks or from "their" enterprises, potentially monetizing the subnational deficit and subverting national monetary objectives. Finally, subnational governments may rely heavily on their enterprises to finance current outlays and infrastructure investments in the locality. This is made possible by (and helps to explain strong pressures for) continued credit expansion to the enterprise sector. Some of this credit reaches the oblast government indirectly. All of these tactics are inconsistent with stabilization.

Revenue-short subnational governments also have the option of shielding their tax base by protecting local enterprises that are important providers of social services. They can also pressure banks to increase credit to enterprises in their area.

How has all this worked in the concrete case of one oblast? As described by the head of the finance department of the regional administration in Yaroslav oblast, a middle-income oblast on the Volga River just northeast of Moscow, the "level of uncertainty and resulting chaos in budget management in 1992 was unprecedented in Yaroslav since World War II" (Le Houerou 1993).[7] This official noted that the unsettled economic environment prevailing since 1992 was compounded by the new expenditure responsibilities shifted to the oblast and the uncertainty concerning the level of tax collection and federal transfers. Tax-sharing rates were adjusted erratically—sometimes two or three times in a quarter. And often the oblast would receive notification from the Ministry of Finance, *after* the fact, of the shares to be retained in the *previous* period. Furthermore, disbursements of committed federal transfers were generally delayed by a few months and, with a 20 to 25 percent *monthly* inflation rate, this significantly complicated financial management. As a result, proper budgeting was nearly impossible in 1992 and boiled down to short-term cash management: as soon as they were collected, revenues were allocated to the highest priority of the day.

In this context, the oblast authorities described multiple ad hoc solutions to emerging problems—most of them inconsistent with transparent and efficient fiscal management—including temporary borrowing of the road fund revenues; extensive unrecorded tax expenditures or tax remissions to enterprises undertaking social outlays; "asking" enterprises to supplement the city's investment budget to enable it to increase local heat generation capacity; instructing banks to grant interest-free credit to enterprises; and diverting resources into extrabudgetary funds such as the engineering, environment, and social protection funds.

Although faced with increasing social problems and a hardening budget constraint, the authorities in this oblast (at both the oblast and rayon levels) appeared to be making commendable efforts to rationalize the existing social programs by consolidating programs and targeting benefits. Enterprises engaged in restructuring were permitted to charge fees for the use of their social facilities. On the economic front, the overriding economic objective of the oblast administration was to support production and maintain employment. This translated into important subsidies and capital transfers to enterprises. It also involved lobbying the central government for directed credit and actively seeking foreign financing and partners for local enterprises.

The activities undertaken by Yaroslav are hardly consistent with supporting macroeconomic stabilization. Moreover, they demonstrate how important it is to the oblasts to retain local enterprises, which have been an important provider of social services.

Subnational borrowing and stabilization

Oblast and rayon governments can in principle finance their spending by borrowing. Laws in the U.S.S.R. permitted borrowing by subnational governments through liquidity loans from the central bank and from commercial banks under the official credit plan. The borrowing that took place was little different from budgetary finance, since state-owned banks were simply the executing agency (or financial arm) of the planning-cum-finance mechanism.

Long-term subnational borrowing in the traditional sense does not have much of a history in Russia. New budget laws passed by the Russian Federation give subnational governments virtually unfettered rights to borrow and to set up and own banks. Facilities for borrowing by subnational governments, as provided for in postindependence legislation, have their roots in the planning period when the credit plan determined investment and its financing across all oblast and rayons. This translated into debts to the (then) state bank (Gosbank) in virtually all oblast administrations. Because they were part of the credit plan, these loans were guaranteed by the government. The Law on the Basic Principles of the Budget System and Budgetary Process includes the subnational governments' right to take on loans from higher-level governments or commercial loans and states that the capital budget (deficit) may be financed through government bond issues or "credit resources." The Law on the Rights of Local Self-Governments allows local soviets to use credit for production and social purposes, to establish and operate financial and credit institutions on a shareholder basis, to grant interest and interest-free loans to government organizations and enterprises, and to issue local debt for developing social and production infrastructure. The Law on the Budgetary Rights of Local Self-Governments permits deficits or "temporary financial difficulties" to be financed by loans and does not appear to tie borrowing to capital financing; the only limit appears to be a nebulous "financing-capacity" rule. In fact, in the end, subnational credit is limited by the lack of bank facilities and financial markets.

These laws are hard to reconcile with the ban on subnational governments' running deficits also prescribed in the Law on the Basic Principles of the Budget System and Budgetary Process. Fieldwork suggests that localities do make strong efforts to balance budgets and that the balanced-budget rule applies ex post, taking into account transfers from higher levels and other coping mechanisms. However, field visits also suggested that some subnational governments still borrow for liquidity reasons. For example, in Mytishchi rayon, a loan from the local bank covered 16 percent of the rayon's budget in 1992. Subnational governments, as noted earlier, can also borrow indirectly through their enterprises. It is not uncommon for enterprises to make so-called donations to the oblast administrative budget—or for oblasts to request contributions to local projects. Since enterprises may finance these by borrowing, oblast and rayon governments have an indirect window into the banking system.

In early 1992 subnational governments' rights to borrow were suspended by the Central Bank of Russia, which issued instructions to its branches and to Russia's roughly 2,000 commercial banks. This was a wise decision. In today's circumstances the oblast governments' unlimited right to borrow seems misplaced. Subnational borrowing is a critical issue in intergovernmental finance, and in many countries it is restricted, controlled, or sometimes prohibited. Central government often establishes the total credit available to local governments, sets the terms of loans, defines the acceptable uses of debt financing, and controls the flow of loan funds (Davey 1988).

The reason for imposing such discipline is that, first, central government uses debt finance as a stabilization tool, and it does not want local governments to counter its policies. Second, subnational borrowing may crowd out private sector borrowing, which may be more economically beneficial. Third, central governments implicitly guarantee local government debt, so that subnational government borrowing may become an open (and destabilizing) door to the national treasury. (A strict rule would prohibit bailout by the upper government, thus permitting subnational bankruptcy to take place; but while this works in the private sector, it might not in the public sector [Zimmermann 1992].) Fourth, extensive subnational borrowing can make it difficult for the center to achieve its macroeconomic objectives, especially in the absence of reliable information on all public sector borrowing. Finally, uncontrolled facilities for deficit financing by lower government could also hamper central government control of budgetary imbalances. The risks to macroeconomic stability are even worse if these deficits can be monetized by giving subnational governments direct or indirect access to central bank financing, as in Brazil and Argentina.

All this does not argue for a total ban on subnational government deficit financing but rather for the right of the central government to control and monitor subnational borrowings both from banks and from the bond markets, to avoid excessive total public sector borrowing. Suspension of the borrowing rights of subnational governments by the Central Bank of Russia since 1992 makes sense for the medium term to underpin Russia's stabilization program. The fear is that some oblast governments would incur heavy debts, given their currently highly volatile revenues and expenditures.

The *indirect* access of subnational governments to borrowing through their ownership of banks and enterprises poses a severe problem and is a potential source of credit expansion. This requires both control of national credit expansion as well as the end of government ownership of banks. Not only does ownership inevitably lead to pressures for excessive overall credit, it also leads to misallocation of credit in favor of government-chosen enterprises at the expense of those in the private sector that may have higher potential (Long and Sagari 1991; Hinds and Pohl 1991). As Russia tries to reap the benefits from a diversified private sector, such government intervention in the banking system will have a palpable cost—and not only from a macroeconomic perspective. It will affect long-run growth, as savings are poorly allocated and interregional capital flows impeded.

How to develop more appropriate subnational borrowing mechanisms

For the longer run, subnational debt financing is almost certainly something Russia must develop, given the huge need for infrastructure development, rehabilitation, and reconstruction that faces Russia's oblasts and rayon governments. Theoretically, there is no reason subnational governments should not borrow; in practice, they often do. Arguments in favor of debt financing are microeconomic: if an infrastructure investment delivers services over many years, it is appropriate to finance the lumpy costs through borrowing and to repay them over time (Bahl and Linn 1992). Short-term liquidity borrowing is also necessary to cover revenue and expenditure fluctuations in the execution of the annual budget—and it is not controversial.

Mechanisms for state and local borrowing are in place in most developing and industrial countries. Relative to industrial countries, however, borrowing is a minor source of finances for subnational governments in developing market economies, reflecting the generally conservative position of most such governments and their limited sources of finance.

In Russia the oblasts or large cities might be granted some discretion to use debt. Appropriate borrowing sources for Russia's oblasts could differ for the short and longer terms. Borrowing from central bank branches should probably always be banned. Commercial banks, as soon as they develop, might be the first source for borrowing and might remain the major source, as in Germany (Zimmermann 1992). Bond issues would have to come later, since markets for bonds and other such financial instruments must be developed, and subnational governments must establish their creditworthiness. In fact, local government bond markets are unusual in countries whose capital markets are thin and where long-term financing is generally scarce.

State and municipal development banks might also be a source, although the international experience has not been positive. Few have developed the capacity to assist on the scale needed; instead, they have limited their focus to technical assistance in infrastructure finance or to purely financial assistance. Most have been undercapitalized and have tolerated significant arrears. Loans have often not been repaid. New loans were even made to borrowers who had defaulted on existing loans (Davey 1988).

Perhaps a better solution would be a development bank that is not established by the central government but that is a cooperative of, say, groups of oblasts or cities. Alternatively, one could envisage a subnational infrastructure financing facility that would have sunset provisions and would phase out once capital market finance was available. Restricting long-term borrowing to capital investment might also be right for Russia. And foreign borrowing should be restricted to the federal government.

Diverting oblast revenues into extrabudgetary funds

Central and subnational government have access to revenue outside (as well as in) the budget. Until recently extrabudgetary funds in Russia were insignificant and were dispersed over many budgetary organizations. Major federal extrabudgetary funds include the Road Fund, the Pension Fund (created in 1981), the Social Support Fund of the Population, the Fund for Medical Insurance, the State Social Insurance Fund, the Employment Fund, the Environment Fund, and some industrial funds, such as the Conversion Fund (for military industries), the Fund for Energy and Fuel Industry, and the Scientific Research Fund (IMF 1992b). Most others are recent creations and are smaller kitties managed independently by different agencies, including the Ministry of Finance and the Supreme Soviet.

Use of subnational extrabudgetary funds is formalized in the Law on the Rights of Local Self-Governments and, since 1991, these funds have been growing rapidly. Under the law, extrabudgetary funds can include unspent funds earmarked for local social and economic programs; voluntary contributions and donations; revenues from local loans; local commodity and monetary lotteries and auctions; and certain fines and penalties on enterprises, including all penalties for nonpayment of tax (a feature that allegedly encourages local authorities to collude with enterprises in tax evasion). Certain nontax revenues have been designated local extrabudgetary funds. Penalties for environmental pollution or damage of historical or cultural items are also included but are earmarked for environmental spending or restoration. Other sources may include profits from joint ventures and sales of unclaimed and confiscated property.

In general, all these funds can be spent fully at the discretion of the subnational government. This independence is a great attraction and lies behind their rapid proliferation. Another attraction is that they need not be shared at all with the central government. Local governments therefore try to shift as much of their revenues as possible into the extrabudgetary category. The size of the funds cannot be quantified, but indications are that they have grown to the equivalent of 10 percent of total subnational budgetary funds in 1992. There are also many rayon extrabudgetary funds, in particular municipal extrabudgetary entities, with special earmarked extrabudgetary revenue sources.

The proliferation of subnational extrabudgetary funds since mid-1991 presents serious problems for effective budgetary management at the macroeconomic level. These funds reduce the transparency of budgetary operations and weaken fiscal policy. They are parallel budgets outside the strictures of conventional budgetary procedures. Multiple budgets imply a loss of control and information and provide loopholes for public sector operations not approved through proper budgetary channels. By contrast, consolidated public sector accounts provide an institutional setting that promotes better public decisionmaking by compelling a more explicit recognition of the costs of public programs.

In addition, such funds are inefficient because they involve earmarking revenues and expenditures, which could lead to a misallocation of resources. Earmarking could also hamper effective budgetary control; furthermore, it impinges on the powers and discretion of the legislative and executive branches of government to allocate expenditures. Using earmarked extrabudgetary funds also imparts inflexibility into budgets when such systems outlive their usefulness.

Classifying some nontax revenues from enterprises (such as profits and dividends from local joint ventures), voluntary contributions by enterprises, and revenues from privatization as extrabudgetary revenues has other implications that go beyond the macroeconomic. It creates incentives to tap into enterprises in an extralegal way. It also contributes to the pervasive culture of misgovernance that has emerged in the postsocialist transition, in which corporate governance frameworks are unclear and ownership is unclarified.

Discouraging extrabudgetary flows

Including extrabudgetary funds in the budget would contribute greatly to budgetary transparency. Such funds might have been justified in the past when oblast governments were not protected against the extraction of surpluses or unspent balances by higher levels of government. At present their main attraction is that they shelter oblast revenues from sharing arrangements with higher levels of government when budgetary resources are negotiated. This gain is minor compared with the damage to the efficient allocation of resources and the potential loss in accountability and control of budgets.

Consistent with standard government accounting practices (IMF 1986), legitimate extrabudgetary revenue should be included in the regular budget for full accountability of fiscal operations. The problem is that the present intergovernmental fiscal sharing is not perceived as fair (or based on fair criteria) by some of Russia's diverse subnational governments seeking increased budgetary autonomy and greater transparency of federal-oblast sharing systems. Thus, one can expect extrabudgetary funds to grow and to remain an impediment to macroeconomic management.

And, in spite of the macroeconomic disadvantages and informational complications of loose budgetary control, extrabudgetary funds may be difficult to abolish because they are now entrenched. A realistic transitional approach for the central fiscal authorities would be to require that subnational governments disclose full information about, and sources and application of, all extrabudgetary funds.

Intergovernmental finances and privatization

A major feature of fiscal decentralization in Russia and in many economies in transition has been the transfer of assets such as enterprises, land, and housing from *central* state ownership to subnational governments. Until 1990, enterprise ownership in Russia was fairly centralized. After the dissolution of the Union there was broad agreement that ownership of real property should go to different levels of government (chapter 2). For a variety of reasons, oblast and rayon governments could be either strong supporters of privatization or impediments to it.

Why Russia wants to privatize

Russia, together with many other socialist economies in transition, is committed to the transformation of its economy into a market-oriented system. The shortcomings of central planning—inefficiencies, internationally uncompetitive and domestically undesirable products, outdated production methods and technologies, environmental disregard, and underlying distributional problems—have become apparent. Even the benefits of a mixed economy are now dubious (Kikeri, Nellis, and Shirley 1992). Government intervention in national economies was first witnessed in the post-World War II period, particularly in the 1960s and early 1970s, when the public sector was seen as a major contributor to economic growth and social-political stability. Other economic arguments in favor of public ownership related to the failure of markets to secure economic and social objectives, such as social equity and employment.

In the past decade, however, it has become increasingly clear that dissatisfaction with public enterprises is broadly based, and that the source of this dissatisfaction is not solely ideological. There is now widespread doubt as to whether the benefits of public ownership are worth the cost. Of particular concern to many governments is the burden of loss-making state-owned enterprises on hard-pressed public budgets. In Argentina state-owned enterprise losses as a percentage of GDP reached 9 percent in 1989; through the 1980s, about half of Tanzania's 350 state-owned enterprises persistently ran losses that had to be covered from public funds. A study by Floyd, Gray, and Short (1984) concluded that the overall subsidy requirements of state-owned enterprises (excluding government current transfers) was 3.5 percent of GDP in industrial countries and 5.5 percent in market developing countries. (Of course, there are a number of reasons state enterprises lose money, and not all losses can be laid at the door of state ownership per se. For example, there may be decreasing-cost industries, or prices may be held below marginal costs, for social reasons.)

Among socialist economies in transition, the experience has not been much different, although the magnitude is, if anything, more extreme. In China about 30 percent of state-owned enterprises have traditionally been loss-making, and enterprise subsidies account for about 6 percent of GDP. In Poland enterprise subsidies reached 9 percent of GDP in 1989. In Russia budget subsidies to state-owned enterprises account for 7 percent of GDP. The sheer size of state-owned enterprises' deficits and their increase over time has led some to conclude that public enterprises have been a major cause of stabilization problems (Bird and Brean 1984).

This realization has led all levels of government in Russia to begin privatizing many economic enterprises. The process, however, has been slow. A major roadblock has been the delay in assigning private property rights to land. (All land remains the property of the different levels of government, with the exception of individual ownership now permitted for land used as a housing site—an exception made by a constitutional amendment in December 1992 and one that the new draft constitution will further liberalize.) Other impediments include a weak legal framework; insufficient local (or expensive foreign) auditing, consulting, and financing capacity; and thin local capital markets, lack of liquidity, and suspicion of foreign investors.

Nonetheless, there is widespread awareness in policy circles that privatization should not be delayed because it will mean better allocation of resources, increased output, and expanded revenues for the public sector. Privatization brings savings to all levels of government by reducing subsidies now paid to unprofitable enterprises. Privatization revenues, which can be treated as "above-the-line" capital revenues or as "below-the-line" reductions in financing in fiscal accounts, immediately reduce the deficit, if only on a one-time basis. Efficient and profitable private enterprises will benefit the budget on a permanent basis—through enhanced tax and revenue flows.

Russia's privatization program in context

In mixed economies, privatization is a tool for increasing efficiency. In economies in transition it is an end in itself, essential to the transformation from a command to a market system. Approaches to privatization in Eastern

Europe vary. In economies that have taken the initiative to divest (the Czech Republic, Slovakia, Hungary, Poland, and the former East German territories), innovative privatizations are being devised. There is no blueprint; rather, each program is shaped by the institutional resources that have survived state socialism. It is generally agreed that there is a tradeoff between the speed of privatization and the revenues from sales proceeds (Milanovic 1992b). Rapid sales may mean distress prices—and no time to do the enterprise restructuring that might bring a better price. This tradeoff also relates to the still-nascent markets for assets (which take time to develop), pricing techniques (which are still in their infancy), and privatization procedures (which are often poorly understood by potential local buyers). Moreover, the "wealth constraint" in most economies in transition is a major impediment. Incomes are too low, especially in the early postreform period, when the output decline is severe and inflation has wiped out savings. Thus, the mismatch between the stock of assets to be sold and the income (or stock of savings) available to buy them is so great that prices will be very low if enterprises are sold quickly (van Wijnbergen 1992). This does not mean that privatization should be delayed; rather that rapid privatization is desirable in its own right, in spite of the opportunity cost of revenue forgone.

In Germany the state agency, Treuhandanstalt, has been given the job of imposing rapid, radical, and sweeping change in ownership; the goal is speed, explicitly forgoing the revenues that might be gained in a more drawn out process. Offers are assessed according to four criteria: price, long-term business plan, investments, and promises to maintain or create jobs. Firms that cannot be sold remain under the authority of the Treuhand, which can intervene directly in the firms' reorganization, while keeping them afloat through subsidies. The cost, however, has been high in budgetary terms and is generally not feasible in the rest of Eastern Europe. The Czech and Slovak coupon schemes gave citizens vouchers permitting them to bid in a series of auctions designed to reveal appropriate prices. Individuals had the option of giving their coupons to private investment funds in exchange for shares in the fund; fund managers then bid in the auction and managed the resulting portfolio. In Poland voucher privatization is also one component of a wide-ranging privatization program. Poles, however, do not hold shares in privatized enterprises, only shares in investment funds, which manage privatized enterprises. This scheme targets citizens as owners but uses the funds to concentrate corporate control. In contrast, Hungary's State Privatization Agency has used conventional methods to target foreign investors and is working closely with international investment banks and consulting firms.

Russia's approach to privatization has been multitrack. The State Committee for the Management of State Property, Goskomimushchestvo (GKI), uses different approaches for medium- and larger-size enterprises, small enterprises, and strategic enterprises.[8] Beginning in December 1992 medium- and larger-size enterprises have been converted into joint stock companies, with citizens using privatization checks (vouchers) to buy shares at auction. Vouchers can also be deposited in investment funds, or they can be sold freely.

Smaller enterprises are to be privatized through competitive auctions and tenders, by oblast or rayon committees of the GKI and the corresponding local Property Funds, both of which are subordinated to the oblast or rayon government. Most small firms are owned by oblast or rayon governments and are active in businesses such as trade, construction, engineering, agriculture, food processing, and road transport. Foreign investors are excluded from strategic and large enterprises. The state will retain controlling shareholdings for up to three years in key branches of the economy, including energy, communications, military hardware, and (because of the revenues from state-owned factories) alcoholic beverages.

Revenues from privatization (as is true of revenues under the fiscal system generally) are to be shared between all levels of government. For nationally owned enterprises, 70 percent of the proceeds of sales is expected to go into the federal budget. Oblast councils are expected to receive 20 percent from the sale of nationally owned enterprises on their territory, and rayon governments 10 percent. From the sale of oblast-owned enterprises, oblasts get 55 percent, with the rest shared between the center and the rayons. Whether this is a sufficient inducement to privatize, given the possible budgetary costs of losing enterprise services, is an open question. Currently, only a small fraction of all industrial enterprises' assets are privately owned.[9]

Why subnational governments may hesitate to privatize

Russia is trying to move rapidly toward a market economy, but interventions by the central, oblast, and rayon governments in the economy remain well beyond what is considered desirable in a market-oriented system. For example, the city of Nizhniy-Novgorod owns and subsidizes many enterprises, which it carries on budget, including heat and electrical supply, transport, water supply, hotels and laundry, local construction, repair and maintenance enterprises for local services, public housing, garbage collection, horticulture, and subways. The hotel and laundry sectors have operated without subsidies from the budget since early 1992 (although it is unclear whether they are up to date on obligations to banks or have cleared arrears to other enterprises). All of these enterprises also supply public services, such as schools and hospitals, that cannot be carried in a market system.

The city appears to be trying to transfer these enterprises, as well as enterprises with high losses (such as those enterprises responsible for road repairs) to the rayons.

Subnational governments can either play an important role as supporters of the privatization drive or they can impede it. Their choice will depend on the incentive framework.

Privatization incentives

The squeeze on subnational budgets that emanates from the design of the intergovernmental fiscal system in Russia seems to create disincentives for subnational governments to privatize their enterprises. For one thing, oblast-owned enterprises can earn profits that accrue to the extrabudgetary accounts of subnational governments. And for another, the tradeoff between speed and revenue in the privatization process suggests that enterprise sales may not generate much income—certainly not an amount equivalent to the present discounted value of the profitable enterprises' net profits.

When enterprises make losses, however, one would expect that a quick sale would be the preferred choice. In cases where the central government has transferred assets to local governments—assets that are better thought of as liabilities in many cases—it has in effect shifted the subsidy responsibility downward, protecting its own budget. Subnational governments will thus face major maintenance and subsidy burdens unless costs can be recovered quickly or the assets privatized quickly.

However, if the soft budget constraint prevails and credit is available from the socialized banking system, loss-making enterprises can remain suppliers of public services and employers of local residents, at a time when oblast government budgets may no longer be able to do so. Thus, the fiscal squeeze on subnational governments may make it advantageous to keep unprofitable enterprises alive if they can successfully lobby for extra credit or subsidies from the center.

The same fiscal squeeze may encourage subnational governments to push more social assets and spending onto the enterprises they do own. Loading enterprises up with social assets and additional nonproductive spending will make them harder to privatize. They will be less profitable and thus less attractive to buyers. However, divestiture of social assets will be difficult unless there are mechanisms for the public sector to assume the social assets that cannot be privatized. (Some ventures can be spun off as income-earners, for example, a sports club.) Indeed, as revenues diminish and expenditure mandates increase, subnational governments may rely increasingly on enterprises to provide basic services. And, because enterprises

have greater access to credit than subnational governments, often responsibilities have been transferred toward—not away from—enterprises.

The behavior and incentives facing subnational governments are key
to the successful privatization of Russia's economy. Oblast and rayon administrations currently own the vast majority of Russia's state-owned enterprises. The future of the privatization program is in their hands. Establishing the correct incentive framework for them—one that makes privatization
attractive—is crucial. Unfortunately, the present intergovernmental framework does not provide this.

Reverse privatization: Russia's "entrepreneurial oblasts"

The subnational revenue squeeze has had another perverse side effect in
Russia. Increasingly, some subnational governments view themselves not
only as service providers (as in a market economy) but as entrepreneurs
and producers. Fieldwork shows that they are involved in a wide range of
economic ventures, a pattern that is worrisome and antithetical to privatization. For example, they have entered joint ventures with domestic or foreign partners, or with other state enterprises, using (or sometimes infor-
mally mortgaging) local assets as their equity share (the McDonald's joint
venture partner is the Moscow city government). Land-rich localities use
land as the preferred equity contribution; some appear to see potential in
developing and servicing vacant land to enhance its value as equity, even
though real estate is one of the riskiest businesses in market economies. In
Russia ventures typically involve private market-oriented activities, such as
industrial products or hotels. Where localities have inherited important real
properties, joint ventures-in-process have been concluded with domestic
commercial and industrial companies such as bakeries, food processing
companies, and construction firms. Some oblasts and rayons have bought
up shares in state enterprises formerly owned by the central government,
and some oblast governments are also planning to buy or set up commercial banks.

In the oil- and gas-producing oblasts and okrugs of Siberia (Khanty-
Mansiiskii and Yamal-Nenets), there are plans for the joint exploitation of
the still federally owned resources through oblast-foreign joint ventures. In
the mineral-rich oblasts farther east, diamond and gold extraction joint ventures are being discussed. These ventures in particular are not only counter
to privatization but could threaten the fabric of Russian unity (chapter 6).

On the surface, there may be good reasons for government involvement in new joint ventures. With land or enterprise assets frequently idle
and difficult to privatize, the perceived cost to the government of contributing such resources to a joint venture may be low. Public officials may also

want to create immediate employment opportunities in economically depressed areas. It is also understandable that local governments feel responsible for promoting economic activity, especially with a shortage of private entrepreneurs. They also see the possibility of obtaining extrabudgetary revenues (enterprise profits or dividends) to supplement rapidly dwindling budgetary sources. However, such joint ventures will slow, if not reverse, privatization.

Risks of "government entrepreneurship"

Government entrepreneurship carries significant risks. It should not be necessary: if the venture is profitable, it can be performed well in the private sector; if not, it should hardly be undertaken by any entity. Government entrepreneurship is also economically risky because governments will likely compete unfairly with private concerns and, in doing so, undercut their own tax base. In market economies, economic pressures often require that these enterprises be subsidized, and the rate of small business failures is high. Most important, these local entrepreneurial activities are inconsistent with the "proper" role of governments in market economies.

Public officials (in Russia and worldwide) tend to be poor business managers. Bureaucrats and politicians mix such objectives as maintaining income or keeping jobs and maximizing profits. Experience in other countries, and now in Russia and the republics of the former U.S.S.R., has demonstrated the difficulty of shutting down enterprises, even when their value added is negative. If subnational governments in Russia retain unprofitable enterprises, local fiscal burdens increase and the revenue base declines. This only exacerbates the subnational fiscal squeeze.

Most important, such entrepreneurial activity is *fundamentally inconsistent with the privatization drive* and a barrier to true decentralization—that is, decentralization from the state to the private sector. Subnational entrepreneurial activity is neither privatization nor decentralization. The more rapidly the risks are understood by subnational governments in Russia, the better they will be able to protect themselves and concentrate on the true business of government—to provide services. Improving the design of subnational government finances may help eliminate such activity by removing pressures on localities that must rely on revenue sources, transfers, or tax shares which they perceive as inadequate or unreliable.

How should the proceeds from privatization be used?

When enterprises are sold or privatized in Russia, most proceeds accrue to the budget (or extrabudgetary funds) of the selling government. Each level of government also receives the profits and dividends from the enterprises it owns; similarly, rents and lease income accrue to the oblast budget or extrabudgetary accounts. Local governments lack guidelines or rules on using revenue from privatization. The most common practice is to use proceeds as current budgetary revenues. When privatization is feasible and profitable, what should be done with the proceeds? Should they be capitalized in special funds, invested in capital projects, or used to finance current expenditures?

In practice, no special strings have been attached to using revenues from privatization. But using privatization revenues to finance the *operating* budgets of subnational governments is unsustainable because they will eventually be depleted. Alternative sources of revenue will need to be found, and the decline in privatization income will have to be factored into the redesign of the revenue-sharing system. A more conservative public finance principle would call for using the center's proceeds to retire the national debt. (The same would hold for local governments if they had significant debt.) Subnational proceeds could also be invested in long-term assets (infrastructure), thus allowing subnational governments to draw income from those assets over a long period. The revenue from privatization should also be viewed as budgetary, not extrabudgetary resources.[10]

Conclusion

Macroeconomic stability and successful privatization are key to Russia's economic future. The incentive framework of the intergovernmental system is crucial to macroeconomic stabilization and to privatization by oblasts and rayons of the enterprises they own. Revenue-expenditure correspondence is an important fiscal goal. Without it, subnational governments will continue to exploit enterprises in order to provide services, thus impeding privatization. They will also look to coping mechanisms that subvert stabilization. Successful stabilization is necessary for the future cohesion of the Federation: regional entities may have little use for a national government that cannot provide the most basic commodity—a stable price level.

A more transparent system of intergovernmental relations holds great hope for Russia and will be crucial in determining "whither Russia."

Notes

1. The average yearly percentage change in inflation for 1992 was 2318 percent, based on the retail prices for goods.
2. Ministry of Finance estimates of net arrears put them at about one-third of the gross amount of interenterprise arrears (R 1 trillion on July 1, 1992).

3. Some countries have sought to eliminate such arrears through a netting exercise in which all interenterprise arrears are matched with the outstanding claims of enterprises on each other. The remainder (credit positions for some enterprises, debtor positions for others) can be written off, although this is unfair to net creditors and may cause them to fail. (Nonetheless, this is being tried in Albania.) Or they can be made good, leading to an expansion of credit, as happened in China in the late 1980s and many other economies in transition in the 1990s.

4. As initially introduced, this tax called for payment of the export tax (most of it from oil and gas) in advance at the time of export, before any revenues had been received. The system needed a credit mechanism to serve as a bridge until export receipts were received. Without credit facilities, enterprises lacked the resources to meet their tax liability.

5. The sources for these figures are the Ministry of Finance of the Russian Federation and the International Monetary Fund.

6. In Hungary, for example, the responsibility for welfare expenditures was transferred to localities. In Poland deconcentrated units of the central government (voivodships) that were responsible for the provision of may local public services are now in the process of handing over these enterprises to the local government.

7. The author is indebted to Philippe Le Houerou for this description and series of anecdotes on Yaroslav and has drawn on his unpublished report, "Fiscal Management in Yaroslav"(November 1993), for this chapter.

8. Large-scale enterprises were defined as having a book value (of capital) from R 50 million to R 150 million, as of January 1, 1992, and small-scale enterprises as having a book value of less than R 10 million. Inflation has made these figures virtually meaningless, and it is not clear how they will be applied in the privatization program. (See World Bank 1992b.)

9. For a good discussion of privatization, see World Bank (1992a) and Vickers and Yarrow (1988).

10. See Newbery (1991). His argument is that many of the assets may have been financed with debt (localities have substantial liabilities), in which case the proceeds should be used to pay off this debt, rather than burdening present and future local taxpayers with debt service.

4

Expenditures and expenditure assignment

Jorge Martinez-Vazquez

The Russian Federation is going through a radical transformation. Nowhere is this more true than in reform of the government expenditure budget. Success, however, is in jeopardy, and surprisingly, the biggest threat comes from central government policies.

The decentralization of government spending responsibilities is one major plank of Russia's public finance and budget reforms. It should increase the efficiency with which resources are allocated in the public sector. But the federal government must grant more expenditure discretion to oblasts and rayons and stop pushing its own spending responsibilities onto subnational governments. Otherwise, the efficiency of public spending will be impaired and, more importantly, the political integrity of the Russian Federation could be at risk. Given the enormous diversity and ethnic tensions in Russia, a truly decentralized government may be the only kind that can hold a democratic and market-oriented federation together. The transformation and marketization of any socialist economy mean less government spending. In Russia, total government expenditures (federal and subnational) have fallen from 50.6 percent of GDP in 1990 to an estimated 33.6 percent for 1992. The steepest declines have been in the traditionally federal expenditure areas of "national economy," especially in subsidies and in capital outlays for the so-called productive sectors. Defense spending has also fallen sharply, but in other traditionally subnational areas of responsibility, including health and education, the declines have not been as marked.

As the central government has cut back its own spending, it has also shifted (or assigned) more expenditure responsibilities, especially for social services and the safety net, onto lower levels of government. Both processes have increased the relative importance of subnational governments in overall government spending. For 1992, subnational spending was some 40 percent of total budgetary spending.

Recent policy changes suggest that the trend toward more subnational spending is likely to continue. Most conspicuously, privatization will sooner or later force the transfer of state enterprise spending—especially on social services and infrastructure—back to the government. Given that much of this enterprise spending falls into areas traditionally the responsibility of the subnational level—outlays are largely of a local public service nature—subnational governments will most likely bear these responsibilities. In addition, some spending responsibilities that were recently shifted to subnational governments should be reassigned to the federal government in line with the basic principles of efficient public finance. Examples of these include capital investments of national significance (for example, in transport, aviation, and other infrastructure) and social safety net and income redistribution programs.

The importance of expenditure assignments

Recent changes in the spending responsibilities of different levels of government have been either the unplanned by-products of other policy decisions (for example, enterprise privatization) or ad hoc measures by the federal government under budgetary pressure. Instead of studying policy options and developing legislation—as took place in the case of tax policy and revenue assignment—Russia's central government has not given serious consideration to the proper assignment of expenditure or functional responsibilities between the federal, oblast (state), and rayon (local) governments. All this has led the Federation along a politically dangerous path.

Lack of awareness, inexperience, and the inherent complexity and time-consuming nature of many issues partly account for the failure to assign responsibilities. However, the lack of clearly defined spending responsibilities was also politically attractive to both federal and subnational governments in this transitional period. The lack of clearly defined spending responsibilities gave the federal government more freedom to deal with budget deficits: it could, for example, shift expenditure responsibility for some items to oblast and rayon governments. The subnational governments were eager to accept new responsibilities, as long as they could be used to increase their bargaining power with the central government to get larger tax revenue shares. Thus, the shift of an important part of social spending to local governments early in 1992 may have seemed mutually convenient; in the larger context, it was unwise, as bargaining over tax shares was removed from the system soon thereafter.

Many oblasts withdrew tacit support for the murky spending assignments after June 1992, when the Supreme Soviet fixed uniform tax-sharing rates for the major shared taxes. These fixed sharing rates, and the fact that the federal government could no longer extract budget surpluses from subnational governments, meant that neither level of government could bargain for extra resources based on shifts in the ill-defined spending assignments.

While bargaining over tax shares has been reinstituted, the lack of explicit expenditure assignments still allows the federal government flexibility to shift other expenditure responsibilities to subnational governments—and thus, indirectly, to extract budget surpluses from oblasts. The problem here is that all oblast governments, including those in deficit, are forced to take on the additional spending responsibilities. This became especially severe in mid-1992, when the jettisoned responsibilities included many capital investments of national significance (such as national highways and housing for military personnel) that should have stayed with the federal government. These actions have set a dangerous precedent and put Russian intergovernmental relations on a perilous path with significant political risks.

If this trend of shifting responsibilities were to persist, what would be left to justify the existence of the central government to skeptical subnational governments? Put another way, what will be left to give meaning to the union of the Russian Federation? The short answer to both is less and less. If budgetary pressures tempt the federal government to shift further responsibilities, the federal government could be contributing to the fulfillment of its worst nightmare: the disintegration of the Russian Federation.

Principles of expenditure assignment

What level of government should be responsible for which spending functions? Expenditure assignment is the important (and often overlooked) first step in rationalizing an intergovernmental fiscal system. Only after this is done (and the overall volume of spending is known for each level of government) can taxes or revenue flows be assigned and intergovernmental transfers initiated. Economic theory does not, however, provide a neat and tidy set of rules defining the best assignment of expenditure responsibilities. Instead, economic theory provides only general principles about the performance of a system of intergovernmental relations and the tradeoffs among equally attractive systems.

So what should be the responsibilities of each level of government? The proper division of responsibilities should be guided by the three fiscal policy functions of government—efficiency in resource allocation, equity in income distribution, and stability in the macroeconomic environment. Not all levels of government are equally well positioned to fulfill these objectives. And in heterogeneous federations, considerations of autonomy may be important to address the concerns of culturally distinct groups.

An efficient assignment of expenditures ensures that the level and type of services provided by government maximize the welfare of citizens. Generally, expenditure assignment is efficient if welfare cannot unambiguously be increased by redirecting existing funds within (or across) different levels of government. One rule of thumb is to assign expenditure and service responsibilities according to the benefit area of each service. Thus, services whose benefits do not go beyond the local community (say, neighborhood parks) should be provided by the rayon governments; services that benefit multiple communities (such as intercity highways) should be provided by the oblasts; and services that benefit the whole country (national defense, courts) should be provided by the federal government (Musgrave 1959).

In most cases the greatest efficiency will come from an expenditure assignment that places the responsibility for each function with the lowest level of government capable of delivering it efficiently (the so-called principle of subsidiarity). Because subnational governments are closer to the preferences and needs of taxpayers, they are more likely than the central government to deliver services that local residents want. And, to the extent that preferences for public services differ, efficiency will lead to (indeed, will require) diversity among subnational jurisdictions. Reliance (to the extent possible) on locally imposed taxes to finance subnational expenditures internalizes the costs of providing these services and leads residents in turn to demand more accountability from public officials. When the beneficiary pays, there is greater efficiency and responsibility in government decisionmaking.

What are the exceptions to the subsidiarity rule? First, if there are major economies of scale to be captured, it might make sense for the central government to provide the service. Some efficiency will be lost as the decisionmaking is distanced from the residents and beneficiaries, but the loss might be more than offset by more economical production costs. This might apply, for example, to the centralized procurement of textbooks or pharmaceuticals, where there are many purchasers and few suppliers. It might also apply to some services where the costs of duplicating subnational administrations are high. In some cases, such as public utilities, regional governments are large enough to capture economies of scale.

Second, central provision might be desirable where a service (environmental policy, for instance) significantly affects citizens outside local jurisdictions, indicating that externalities or spillover effects are present. Leaving provision to lower levels of government might result in underprovision (or overprovision) because of the lower-level governments' failure to incorporate external effects into decisions. Third, central government provision of some services, such as education, might be justified because it is important for other national objectives, such as economic growth and development or better income distribution.

Finally, the considerations that go into fashioning intergovernmental fiscal relations in a country with a highly heterogeneous population or with peoples in different regions displaying cultural diversity might have to be somewhat different than those just described. For example, where cultural or ethnic diversity is present, assignment of functions to subnational governments might be affected by those governments' particular wish to take charge of certain areas in order to assert their identity or autonomy. Thus, the design of intergovernmental fiscal relations, in addition to meeting efficiency, equity, and stability goals, might need to respond to the need for autonomy in federations with heterogeneous populations.

Equity, or a more equal income distribution, is generally accepted as a proper government objective. And where there is a consensus on the importance of the government's role in income distribution, it is often argued that any serious attempts to affect it should be undertaken by the *central* government. Subnational governments' efforts to improve the well-being of their lower-income households can be self-defeating, since redistributive programs can attract the needy from other parts of the country. Such efforts may also encourage migration of the better-off, who see their taxes being used for services from which they do not directly benefit. That will simply undermine the local tax base. Thus, unless there is little mobility among taxpayers (or strict eligibility rules, such as ration books or residence permits that entitle only local families to benefits), a subnational government may not succeed with aggressive redistribution policies.

From an equalization perspective the design of a system of intergovernmental fiscal relations depends partly on the presence (or absence) of labor mobility within the country. With little geographic mobility, residents of poor regions will stay poor, and the fiscal system may need to address this, via equalizing transfers or other means, if the poorer regions are to even out service provision. Russia's size and its regional diversity suggest that even in the medium term, mobility may be low. In the near term, Russia's system of household registration (the so-called *propusk*) ensures that mobility is virtually nil. It could be argued that in such a case attention to equalization is essential. However, Russia faces a difficult tradeoff here (as argued in chapters 5 and 7). With powerful industrial oblasts, natural resource–rich jurisdictions, and ethnic areas taking an increasingly proprietary approach to their economic resources, a fiscal system that cross-subsidizes too much might not be acceptable. It might also be that to promote more rapid growth a choice has to be made in favor of allowing the better-off oblasts to reap the benefits of their larger and more prosperous economic bases.

Stabilization, too, is often thought to be better pursued by central government because it is better equipped to implement those expenditure and tax policies that are sensitive to the overall level of activity and must be coordinated with monetary and exchange rate policies. It is sometimes argued that, to manage a stable economy, central government needs to have tight control over subnational government budgets, with limits on subnational expenditure, tax rates, or borrowing capacity. However, international experience shows that despite more complicated macroeconomic management, decentralized systems do not necessarily mean more economic instability (chapter 3). There is less than perfect consensus on whether limits or controls should be placed on the fiscal activities of subnational governments.

The fundamental justification for a decentralized system of intergovernmental relations is to make the government more responsive to the needs and preferences of local residents. Although centralized (or unitary) systems can be as effective—and sometimes more effective—in achieving stabilization and equity, they fail to deliver the efficiency gains of decentralized systems. But efficiency in local service provision (maximizing the welfare of local taxpayers) is hard to achieve even in decentralized systems. Several specific characteristics are essential if a decentralized government system is to achieve marked efficiency gains over a centralized system.

What are these critical requirements for efficient subnational government? First, local officials must have discretion in budget matters—the level and composition of expenditures and the setting of expenditure priorities. They also need flexibility in setting wages and employment, and they must have some independent authority to raise revenue. Limits on the autonomy of local authorities make it hard (or impossible) for them to take into account local preferences. This lack of discretion forces inefficient expenditure choices, and it eventually forces local residents to look to the central government for solutions (and revenues).

Second, efficiency requires some way for taxpayers to convey to local authorities their preferences and desires, together with a mechanism to make local officials accountable. In this context, voters' ability to remove or reappoint elected local authorities is a critical element—a simple enough democratic principle but one of the hardest to put into workable reality. For example, the Moscow City Council, with its 800 elected representatives, is too big and unwieldy to be effective as a governance unit responsive to local citizens' needs.

Third, taxpayers must be made aware of the link between the costs of providing a service and the quality and quantity of the service they demand.

The best way is to partly finance a service with taxes that fall on the local population. The higher the share of spending that is financed this way, the more likely it is that taxpayers will hold local officials accountable. Using local taxes also allows local authorities to determine the overall level of public services. To promote accountability and efficiency, a system of shared taxes (or better yet, a shared tax base) is thought by many to be better than using central government grants. Exclusive reliance on own-taxes may lead to unequal service levels because of unequal tax bases and levels of development. In this case, such gaps can be closed with appropriate intergovernmental transfers.

In many countries with decentralized government, expenditures relating to economic stabilization (such as unemployment benefits) and those affecting income distribution (such as social safety net expenditures) are financed by the central government. Expenditures for which an efficient allocation of resources is imperative are assigned to different levels of government according to their economies of scale or spillover effects. Specifically, those typically assigned to the center include defense, post and telecommunications, national roads and highways, civil aviation, the judiciary, law enforcement, foreign affairs and diplomacy, scientific research, and the environment. Regulation of private industries and interstate commerce are also the responsibility of central government.

Expenditure responsibilities of subnational government traditionally include public services with well-defined benefits in local areas: police, hospitals, public utilities (such as electricity, water, and gas), sanitation, sewerage, local transport, roads and road maintenance, street lighting and cleaning, public markets, and building permits.

The design of expenditure assignment needs to draw a clear distinction between the provision, production (if any), and financing of services. Many functions may be provided subnationally but financed centrally—for example, social welfare. Here, the central (or federal) government may have a legitimate interest in equalization and in ensuring that the service is provided according to a certain standard. A further distinction must be drawn between the financing and production of goods and services, which may be contracted (wholly or partly) to the private sector by any level (or across different levels) of government.

In some areas—health education and social welfare—the principles of expenditure assignment are ambiguous. On the one hand, local clinics and schools clearly benefit residents in their area; on the other, a healthy and well-educated population benefits the nation. Equity also calls for minimum quality and service standards to be maintained throughout the country. Because of these equity concerns and spillover benefits, health and education are often provided by central government or shared between subnational and central governments. In many countries the central government extends grants to subnational governments to provide services up to a common standard.

Although general guidelines are useful, there is no best-practice expenditure assignment or service decentralization across countries and over time. There are as many good systems as there are packages of policy goals. Changes in preferences, household mobility, and production technologies can also mean changes in the most desirable expenditure assignment. Ideally, a system of intergovernmental relations would be adaptable to these changes and to changes in the relative weights given by government to efficiency, equity, and economic stability. As is true of any country, Russia needs to find its own compromise and approach to the assignment of expenditure responsibilities.

Once government policy objectives are stated, there will be assignments of responsibilities that more or less conform to those objectives. Also, there may be structures and assignments that can be improved unambiguously. For example, the system's efficiency may be improved through reassigning expenditure responsibilities, without losing ground in the other two policy goals of equity and economic stability. Among the desirable features of assignment are transparency and objective rules. International experience, not surprisingly, shows that these two features are associated with more stable intergovernmental relations.

The efficiency of Russia's expenditure assignments

On the surface the regime in the former U.S.S.R. had an efficient assignment of expenditure responsibilities among the different levels of government. In substance that assignment, which did not change much in seventy years, is similar to the assignment of expenditure responsibilities in the new Russian Federation.

Despite centralization the massive involvement of the government throughout the economy of the U.S.S.R. meant that many public services were provided by oblast and rayon governments, while the federal and republican governments in the U.S.S.R. concentrated on economic activities (such as industrial production) that, in Western market economies, traditionally have been part of the private sector.

Fundamentally, the division of expenditure responsibilities in the former U.S.S.R. was predetermined by the ownership of property (state assets) by different levels of government. The central budget included activities and enterprises of national importance (for instance, transport, heavy industry, and defense). The republics were responsible for light industry (such as tools and machinery), and oblasts for small businesses, local consumer goods, and public services and regional roads. Rayons and cities had responsibility for housing, utilities, trade, and public services such as health care and pre-university education. After the dissolution of the U.S.S.R. in 1991, the federal share of the Union budget's responsibilities was taken over by the federal budget of the Russian Federation. With the exception of a few important items, the detailed assignment of expenditure responsibilities in Russia in 1992 did not look much different from expenditure assignments in 1991 under the U.S.S.R.

Despite appearances, however, the assignment of expenditure responsibilities in the former U.S.S.R. was not fully efficient. Although republic, oblast, and rayon governments had the responsibility for public services with regional and local significance, they never had the autonomy to determine either the composition or level of those services. Subnational (republic) governments played a passive role. All substantive budget decisions were made at the highest level of government. Practically no consideration was given to the preferences (or desires) of local residents. Although some gains in efficiency could have come through lower costs of service provision in the old regime, it is doubtful that there were any such gains—subnational governments, with no discretion to use any budgetary savings they might have made, had no incentives to operate efficiently. Such savings, as was the case with any other surplus funds, were automatically extracted by the higher level of government at the end of the fiscal year. Production inefficiencies were also present because of an institutional dichotomy in the central planning system between capital expenditures—the responsibility of Gosplan (the state planning commission)—and operations and maintenance spending, funded by the Ministry of Finance. Subnational governments had little incentive to maintain that capital.

Many of the issues the Russian Federation needs to address in the area of expenditure assignment have been inherited from the past regime. Some, however, are the creation of the new government.

Two changes have taken place that affect the efficiency of expenditure assignment in Russia, compared to the previous regime in the U.S.S.R. First, new legislation approved by the Supreme Soviet in 1993—that is, the 1992 Law on the Rights of Local Self-Governments and the Law on the Budgetary Rights of Local Self-Governments (appendix A)—has given local governments the power to formulate budgets and raise revenues without fear of surpluses being extracted by the central government. Before these laws were passed, subnational governments could raise revenues according to the powers given them under the law, but if their overall revenues (own and shared) exceeded the Ministry's estimates of their budgetary needs, the surplus could be "clawed back" (via a transfer of their cash balances with the banking system). Under the present system this is no longer permissible. However, it remains possible for the Ministry of Finance to adjust the negotiated tax-sharing rates and the subventions in such a way as to ensure that no surplus emerges. It is also possible for the federal government to adjust the tax-sharing rates or the intergovernmental subvention in a *future* period to offset a surplus obtained in the previous period. Nonetheless, the new legislation is a clear break with the past and the beginning of a more responsive, accountable, and efficient system of government.

The second change was the reassignment of some important central spending responsibilities to oblast and rayon governments, changes that clearly violated the principle of efficiency. This was the result of the pressures and, at times, constraints and perverse incentives of the current system of intergovernmental legislation, which has been only partially reformed. The present intergovernmental expenditure assignments are basically those inherited from the previous regime, but there is no law that concretely spells out the responsibility of different levels of government. This is, perhaps, the most serious obstacle to distancing Russian intergovernmental relations from the old ways. This lack of expenditure assignment is in stark contrast to the very explicit tax assignments in the Basic Principles of Taxation. By focusing policy efforts exclusively on tax assignment and revenue sharing between the federal and oblast governments, the Russian government is putting the cart before the horse. Revenue availability has been dictating the distribution of responsibilities between the different levels of government, rather than the other way around.

Why is there no clear definition of service and expenditure responsibilities? Both subnational and central governments see advantages in the lack of specifics. Lower-level governments have used increased responsibilities as a lever to argue for more revenues from upper levels. The federal government has used the lack of legal definition to offload its own budget deficit onto the subnational level. In the first quarter of 1992 changing expenditure assignments were paralleled on the revenue side by a system of bargained nonuniform tax-sharing rates, negotiated between the Ministry of Finance and the oblast governments. Not surprisingly, when these rates were fixed in mid-1992, oblasts were less willing to accept additional expenditure responsibilities.

Another aim seems to have been to force oblast governments to discontinue some public sector expenditures (for example, price subsidies). In fact, the shift in expenditure responsibilities has created serious budget pressures for subnational governments, risking the crowding out of other expenditures, including health care and education. Though too early to quantify, the impact is visible on expenditures in the traditional subnational expenditure spheres. Such ad hoc spending reassignments, in which the federal government jettisons responsibilities, enterprises, or assets onto lower levels without corresponding adjustments in revenues, is likely to be unsustainable. If the practice continues, what expenditure functions will the central government have left to justify its existence to skeptical subnational governments and to give meaning to federation? In pursuing this provocative policy, the federal government may be inadvertently contributing to its worst fear and the new Russian Federation, like the old U.S.S.R., may simply disintegrate.

The equity of expenditure patterns

We have seen that the efficiency of public expenditures, as measured by the responsiveness of those expenditures to the specific needs of local communities, was sacrificed in the centralized system of the former U.S.S.R. and now, to a lesser degree, in the Russian Federation. But were public expenditures under the old regime at least equally and fairly distributed across communities in a way that might justify the lack of efficiency? Or did some communities benefit more than others under this budgetary system?

Subnational public officials frequently say that, under the past regime, their local community was treated unfairly because it retained only a small portion of locally collected taxes and yet received few discernable benefits from central budgetary spending. This perception may be quite justified: a large slice of GDP was used for military purposes or was dissipated in prestige projects—expenditures that likely benefited few local communities. Even more interestingly, public officials also claimed that under the old regime their community had been treated unfairly compared with others.

How equally distributed public expenditures were in the former U.S.S.R. is more difficult to assess than for most countries. The reasons for this are relevant to the equity issue in the Russian Federation. In examining regional distribution of public expenditures in most other countries, it would be enough to look at just the distribution of budgetary outlays across jurisdictions. In the former U.S.S.R. and the Russian Federation, it is necessary to go well beyond this.

Comparisons of local services and levels of provision, based only on budgetary data for subnational governments, would be highly misleading. State-owned enterprises in Russia, as noted in chapter 3, provide many of these social services, as well as infrastructure, in many Russian communities. Schools, kindergartens, housing, and clinics and hospitals, as well as urban maintenance, are provided in some measure by enterprises. The problem is that data on such enterprise outlays are not available. Nonetheless, one might presume that the better off the enterprise, the better the services it could provide out of its higher retained earnings. And, probably, the more heavily and profitably industrialized the oblast is, the better served is its population.

More generally, in the unified budget policy of the U.S.S.R. the only way to obtain more resources was to increase lobbying and bargaining power with central agencies and organizations in Moscow. This, of course, opened the door for inequalities in the distribution of expenditures in favor of regions that were more vocal or better organized. The importance of bargaining power has been more significant for capital investment funds allocated by the Planning Ministry (now the Ministry of Economy) than for recurrent budget allocations made by the Ministry of Finance, which had somewhat greater transparency. Allocations for recurrent expenditures in all areas were based on detailed budgetary "norms," which were designed to provide the operating and maintenance costs of the existing infrastructure capacity. However, the very fact that they were designed to finance operation of existing facilities rather than to meet the needs of the population meant that such recurrent allocations may have reinforced, rather than offset, the unequal distribution of capital investment resources achieved by differential bargaining powers.

Almost all empirical evidence on the issue of the regional distribution of public expenditures in the former U.S.S.R. has been at the level of the fifteen union republics (Bahry 1987). Official policies in the Stalin and Khrushchev eras called for standardized per capita spending in both investment and social expenditures, part of a long-term strategy to close the ethnic gap by reducing economic inequalities between territories in the Union. Bahry (1987) found no evidence that the political status of any republic leaders had an impact on the distribution of fiscal resources—that is, bargaining did not produce winners at the republic level. However, Bahry also found that both investment and expenditures on education and health were unequally distributed and increased significantly with the level of economic development of the republic.

Whether some regions or communities benefited more than others under the old regime is interesting from both a historical and a contemporary perspective: it gives us a better idea of the starting conditions of oblast governments under the new regime. Perceptions about past inequities in treatment appear to play an important role in oblast governments' views on the design of Russia's system of intergovernmental fiscal relations. Are we departing from an egalitarian system or a system with pronounced inequalities?

Any study of oblast and rayon governments is difficult because of the lack of data and their disparate sources.[1] To reach an approximation of public service disparities within the Russian Federation in more recent times, we analyzed 1989–91 data for public service infrastructure of the eighty-nine oblasts. For example, regressing an indicator of capital outlays in the social sectors on per capita incomes, population density, and urbanization suggested that capital expenditures were positively and significantly related to per capita incomes (as proxied by the average monthly wage) (appendix 4.1). Our results supported Bahry's conclusion that, in the old regime, expenditures were not always equalized among different regions, but rather varied positively with the average regional per capita income.

It is too early to say what impact the recent policy changes may have had on the distribution of expenditures per capita across oblasts. The available evidence, however, points to wide expenditure disparities. For 1992 (for which data were made available by the Ministry of Finance), expenditures per capita ranged from R 5,077 to R 83,665, with a mean value of about R 18,410 and a coefficient of variation of 0.80 (defined as the standard deviation divided by the mean). This suggests significant disparities among oblasts, and, if taken at face value, a noticeable increase in the degree of variation in per capita total expenditures among oblasts. (In 1991 per capita expenditures among oblasts ranged from R 663 to R 4,488, with a mean value of R 1,338 and a coefficient of variation of 0.54.) Several other ways of testing the relationship between expenditure levels and per capita oblast income were explored (appendix 4.2), and the results parallel those for fixed social capital. Regressing per capita expenditures on average monthly wages and other independent variables showed that these were positively and significantly related to average incomes and negatively related to the degree of urbanization and the number of rayons within the oblast. Better-off regions receive higher budgetary expenditure allocations, while the urban areas are relatively underserved in expenditures.

Again, it is too early to draw conclusions about equity in the new regime. The regressions, however, show that per capita expenditures were not equalized in early 1992. This was at a time when the Ministry of Finance of the Russian Federation agreed to keep a bargained tax-sharing system with oblasts, precisely to avoid major inequalities in the distribution of resources. When the system moved toward derivation-based, fixed sharing rates for all major taxes in mid-1992, there was an increase in potential inequality of per capita expenditures across oblasts. These trends show the importance of a system of intergovernmental transfers (chapter 5).

Budgetary autonomy in the new regime

A series of new laws passed beginning in early 1992 constitutes a firm foundation on which to build the decentralized budget-making that is crucial for efficient public spending. Practices inherited from the old regime, however, still undermine local autonomy. The key pieces of legislation are the Law on the Rights of Local Self-Governments, the Law on the Budgetary

Rights of Local Self-Governments, and the Law on the Basic Principles of the Budget System and Budgetary Process.

The first of these grants local (oblast and rayon) soviets complete independence in forming and executing budgets. Specifically, the law states that interference by other governments will not be allowed, except by express legislation from the Supreme Soviet. This principle of budget independence is perhaps as strong as possible without being written into a constitution. The law also forbids imposing spending mandates on subnational governments without adequate funding and prohibits any extraction of local surplus funds by any higher level of government. The Law on the Basic Principles of the Budget System and Budgetary Process gives local budgets independence by protecting autonomous sources of revenues and by ensuring local discretion over how funds should be spent. But the law also requires a balanced budget and indicates how this is to be achieved (see below). The Law on the Budgetary Rights of Local Self-Governments defines the rights and obligations of all three levels of government, all the way to the rayon level. It guarantees expenditure freedom (but not funding) and defines taxes that are to be shared with the oblast governments, as well as other taxes that are to be assigned.

This is all very good but, de facto, discretion is limited in a number of ways. One is the use of central mandates that compromise subnational governments' ability to control expenditures. Other limitations are the unpredictability in local budgetary resources; a balanced-budget act that includes central directives for expenditure reductions to be taken by oblast and rayon governments; central wage policies; and the continued influence of higher-level governments in the appointment of local finance officials.

Central expenditure mandates

Central mandates—or orders from upper to lower levels of government to undertake certain expenditures without adequate funding—have been a source of growing friction between the different levels of government. The incentive for the federal government to mandate expenditures by oblasts has increased since mid-1992. Fixed sharing rates (for 1992) on some major taxes have resulted in budget surpluses for some oblast governments, and expenditure mandates have been seen as the only tool left to the Ministry of Finance to extract subnational surpluses. Mandates are not restricted to the central government: oblasts also impose them on rayons. For example, price ceilings are fixed by oblasts for heating, bread, milk, and meat, but the rayon pays for the subsidies. The incentive to impose mandates on rayons is less, however, because they are more financially dependent on the oblast budget.

Budget review and expenditure control

Budget practices today are still anchored to a large extent in the old regime. Under the pre-1992 regime and before the new laws were introduced, budget formulation and execution were highly centralized. Although such centralization is no longer formally *approved,* subnational budgets are still scrutinized by higher levels of government. And tinkering with the sharing rates over the year, as has been happening, limits this new independence. This explains the strong control that some oblast finance departments—especially deficit oblasts—still seem to feel.

Under certain circumstances—for deficit oblasts, for example—the new Law on the Basic Principles of the Budget System and Budgetary Process allows the central government tight control over subnational budgets. If oblast or rayon revenues fall short of planned expenditures, or if a deficit is incurred during budget execution, the law lays down the specific means by which subnational governments should balance their budgets. Current expenditures take priority over capital spending (and social expenditures take priority over other outlays within the current budget). If a deficit remains after eliminating all capital spending, the oblast or rayon must then make monthly pro rata reductions in current expenditures (by 5, 10, or 15 percent, or whatever is needed) across the entire budget. The only exceptions are items designated as "protected" by the local soviet or by the upper level of government soviets.

These legal restrictions, together with other current practices, impose limits on the expenditure discretion of subnational governments—discretion that is essential if they are to increase efficiency in the delivery of public services. In some localities, an ex ante deficit may be best eliminated by cutbacks in current spending, rather than capital spending, and across-the-board cuts may not be warranted. Subnational governments are in the best position to judge which measure will be more effective. The imposition of protected items or budget categories by higher levels of government constitutes yet another mandate and is inappropriate unless the service affects other communities.

Unpredictability of revenues

Revenue uncertainty has also contributed to lack of expenditure autonomy. With budgets vulnerable to ad hoc changes based on negotiations with upper-level governments, budgetary outcomes depend more on bargaining power than on objective factors. The more transparent tax-sharing rates introduced in the second quarter of 1992 could provide some stability. So, too, could a new system of intergovernmental finances (chapter 5). Revenue uncertainty is as much a problem for rayon and city governments, which are directed by oblast finance offices, as it is for oblasts, which are dependent on decisions of the federal government. The recently introduced Law on the Budgetary Rights of Local Self-Governments seeks to address this issue, ensuring funding for 70 percent of oblasts' "minimum required budget."

Finally, the high rate of inflation (2300 percent in 1992 alone) has contributed significantly to the unpredictability of revenues of oblast and rayon governments and has worsened the impact of the financial arrears of the federal government on local budgets. Even though budgets in 1992 were formulated quarterly, the lack of indexation of federal funds significantly reduced predictability of revenues.

Expenditure needs and norms

In the old regime the expenditure budget was based on detailed norms, that is, minimum physical and value standards of provision—per student, patient, hospital type, and the like. The federal government, however, often interpreted these norms as maximum levels in negotiations with oblast governments. Norms were, in fact, no guarantee of either adequate provision or the elimination of fiscal disparities. Disparities in the provision of public services among oblasts were pronounced because norms were designed only to keep existing facilities running, not to make up for deficiencies where there was a shortage in such facilities. Oblast facilities' needs were to be considered in the capital investment budget; if these were equitably distributed (we have seen that they were not) the recurrent budget would follow suit. Thus, while norms alone were never designed to respond to the needs of the local population or to be equalizing, the fact that they finance the recurrent costs associated with inequitably distributed capital outlays has exacerbated the inequity.

Although the Ministry of Finance discontinued norms in 1988, oblast and rayon governments are still using them. The 1991 and 1992 budgets, at all levels of government, were mostly based on past expenditure levels, adjusted for inflation, and negotiations involved disagreements about proper inflation adjustment coefficients or so-called price norms. Given the scarcity of regional and subnational price indexes, it is hard to say just how adequate price adjustments have been. But almost without exception, subnational governments complain about big gaps between actual inflation and that allowed by the Ministry of Finance. This "incremental budgeting" may have exacerbated regional biases and past distortions in sectoral spending, so that regions with population growth or above-average inflation may be significantly underserved.

Incremental budgeting through price adjustment is not sustainable in the long term. There have been calls for a return to budgetary norms. But using these for the whole country will mean little in a system of subnational public finance with local budgetary discretion, and where costs and conditions of provision differ considerably across jurisdictions. Any equalizing effects that an improved system of norms may offer can be better achieved by an appropriate system of intergovernmental transfers (chapter 5).

In this context the Ministry of Finance needs to develop a methodology that could help determine the service needs of jurisdictions. There are two basic approaches to the estimation of expenditure needs, a crucial element in any formula-based system. One begins with concrete expenditure norms and then seeks to cost them out. In Russia this could be done by using existing (or modified) expenditure norms—for example, the per pupil cost of education, based on the standard cost of a teacher, classroom operation, and the like—to derive a cost figure in rubles. Performing this calculation for each oblast expenditure function, one can ascertain the oblasts' overall expenditure needs. The precision of this approach has much appeal (it is being applied successfully, for instance, in Denmark); its drawbacks are the degree of complication involved and the cost of keeping the indicators current.

A different and far simpler way of defining expenditure needs uses umbrella variables such as population, per capita income, city size, poverty rates, density, the centrality of a city, and the like. Such an approach is used in Germany and for some grant programs in the United States. The German approach weights the population figure higher for larger German cities to reflect their function as centers of economic activity for surrounding regions. The total weighted population and other indicators are used to distribute the available pool of equalization funds. In Russia simplicity would argue for using more aggregate data on population, per capita income (when it becomes available), and the relative importance of population groups with special needs (chapter 5). However, it might also be possible to adapt the existing norms. *Some* measures of needs are basic in any formula-based system of equalizing transfers from central government to oblasts. To address the divergent needs of rayons and cities, oblasts also need to develop similar methodologies.

Centrally fixed wage scales

Another important limitation on subnational budgetary discretion is that all public employee wages have to conform to a federally imposed national wage scale. This creates two big problems. First, the federal government can mandate wage increases across the board, regardless of subnational budgetary positions, wreaking havoc on subnational budgets. Witness the recent experience with pay raises for teachers and other local employees, in which delays in federal compensation imposed extra burdens on subnational budgets. The second problem is that national wage scales do not allow the flexibility to compensate public employees for different costs of living—or to attract people to a particular job or location.

Given the importance of stabilization in the Federation's transition toward a market economy, there is some short-term justification for keeping a national wage policy. In the longer run, however, oblasts and rayons should have independent compensation systems. This has started to evolve, as subnational governments add compensation supplements or bonuses to local salaries to soften the rigidity of wage scales. The money has come from various sources. For example, a 10 percent bonus paid to doctors by Nizhniy Novgorod oblast came from budget savings in health care.

Budgetary review and approval

Although rayon governments are supposed to have budgetary independence, in practice many rayons and *gorats* (villages) seem to have their budgets scrutinized, if not approved, by oblast finance and budget offices. This practice, not surprisingly, appears to be stronger in rayons that rely heavily on oblasts for operating funds. Nor is it surprising that poorer and rural rayons are likely to be more tightly controlled by the oblasts. In some cases rayon budgets are not only approved but proposed by the oblast.

One reason for such interference may be the traditional lack of confidence of upper government in the decisions of lower governments—in this case, the rayon soviet. Another reason is the traditional vertical structure of finance departments in Russia: all directors and deputy directors of oblast and rayon finance departments were employed and paid by the federal government, although their hiring and firing was by the local soviet on the recommendation of the federal finance officer. More generally, local administrations have dual accountability. They are accountable to their local soviet and to those higher-level executive and administrative departments governing their sphere of competence. In practice candidates for some jobs have to be approved by the upper-level government.

All of this diminishes the gains in efficiency from decentralization. The more hamstrung subnational authorities are, the less interest taxpayers will have in the local political process and the less likely it is that the subnational government will satisfy the needs and preferences of taxpayers. Yet this direct link between taxpayers' preferences and subnational officials' actions is the strongest argument for decentralization.

In truly decentralized fiscal relations, upper-level governments only oversee those activities of subnational governments for which they are financially liable. Subnational governments are free to form budgets, and all employees are paid out of local funds to avoid conflict of interest.

In Russia this goal would be served if all oblast and rayon finance officers were paid from local budgetary funds. The only exception should be the tax administration: employees of the State Tax Service should remain on the central government payroll.

Budgetary management

Despite many new laws addressing budget procedures, important budgeting principles are still being ignored. Field visits revealed much confusion about proper procedures, some of which can be explained by the newness and complexity of legislation. A frequent problem is oblasts' payment arrears. Some subnational governments are increasingly using unpaid balances to bring their budgets into apparent balance. The magnitude of oblast arrears is hard to establish; it would be clearer if subnational governments used accrual accounting. However, Russian accounting practices allow the use of cash accounting, which helps hide arrears and budget deficits. For example, one cash-strapped oblast visited had paid pensioners only a fraction of the minimum pension due and was in arrears in its payments to suppliers. The federal government also has been consistently in arrears (reportedly by an average of two months) in its payments and obligations to subnational governments, even though arrears are inconsistent with federal budgetary discipline.

Expenditure assignment at a crossroads

Four issues in expenditure assignment need to be reexamined in the Russian Federation:
* Reassignment of social expenditures
* Reassignment of capital spending responsibility
* Budgetary implications of ownership transfers
* Divestiture of public sector functions by state enterprises.

Reassignment of social expenditures

In 1992 the central government shifted to subnational governments the responsibility for most price subsidies, social protection programs, local transport (including subways), and other public activities. There was partial or no compensation. Many now think the decision on social protection was made too quickly. The shift was politically expedient, and it was hoped that the problem would soon solve itself because most subsidies would be phased out. In fact, although subsidies will be reduced after prices are freed, the underlying problem of financing social protection (for those most hurt by price reform and economic liberalization) will not.

The adequacy of the social safety net will be an issue of national priority during the hard transition ahead. Surprisingly, the process of economic readjustment has not yet resulted in massive layoffs and plant closings. The response of most enterprises to collapsing markets has been to retain employees, even with minimum or no wage payments. In 1992 the official unemployment rate was less than 1 percent, and the state unemployment fund remained in surplus. Nevertheless, a high unemployment rate and mounting social needs can be expected eventually, as the present situation is unsustainable. Clearly the social safety net should not be the sole responsibility of subnational governments. The central government could finance (but not necessarily administer) subsidies (most likely in cash) targeted to the needy. Recipients could be identified by rayons using self-targeting or other mechanisms. The rayons would continue to administer this social safety net, and actual costs would be reimbursed by the federal government.

Thus far social safety net budgeting has been haphazard, budgeted amounts insufficient, and necessary data uncollected. In the first quarter of 1992, R 1.3 billion from the Social Support Fund was reportedly allocated to twenty-three oblasts, the only ones to supply the required information to the central authorities. Significantly, sixty-five oblasts, including many of the poorest, received nothing. For the rest of 1992 no specific allocations were made to oblast budgets. Instead, social safety net funds have been denoted as an open reserve item of the federal government. This again puts poorer oblasts at risk, especially because the Ministry of Finance does not count the number of poor families in the oblast—or use any other welfare indicator—in formulating oblast budgets and subvention policies.

Shifting additional expenditure responsibilities to local governments, as was done with subsidies for food, medicine, and all capital investments in 1992, has reportedly created significant budget pressures on many local governments. One general concern in Russia and in the international community has been the impact that these underfunded expenditure mandates may have had—especially in combination with the overall fiscal austerity—on the ability of subnational governments to provide other services, in particular services in health, education, and social support.

Concerns about the possible crowding out of social services are already reflected in the special treatment granted to the social sector in the adjustment process. The Russian government declared the social sectors—health, education, and social protection—to be priority sectors for budgetary allocations since 1992. This meant that the social sectors were spared the drastic budgetary cuts suffered by other sectors, such as defense or the economic sphere. In addition to the priority given to the social sectors in the budget formulation process, the Law on the Basic Principles of the Budget System and Budgetary Process also gives the social sectors priority status when expenditures must be cut because of unforeseen revenue shortfalls and looming budget deficits.

Is there evidence that there has been a decrease in the supply of social services? Field visits did not reveal drastic cuts in services resulting in actual school or hospital closings. However, there are reports of numerous closings of kindergartens. Field visits to oblast and rayon governments also reveal budgets with practically no funds for new buildings or the replacement of old ones. Analysis of the composition of recurrent expenditures indicates that funds for supplies and operations in many cases have been cut to a minimum or eliminated.

Budget data show that real per capita oblast expenditures in the social sectors decreased between 1991 and 1992 (table 4.1). Note that federal government spending in the social sector is not included in table 4.1. However, because federal government responsibilities in the social sphere have decreased rather than increased (many having been transferred to oblast and rayon governments), the figures in table 4.1 should tell a consistent story about whether real current expenditures on social services have decreased over the past year. The results in table 4.1 show a significant decline—almost 40 percent—for the average oblast in per capita real expenditures on social services. For many oblasts the decreases have been more dramatic. The dispersion of real per capita expenditures, as measured by the coefficient of variation, appears also to have increased in the past two years.

Finally, a regression analysis of per capita social expenditures on wage income per capita for 1992 showed a significant positive relationship, indicating that richer oblasts had better social services.

Per capita social expenditures = 55.9 + 0.04 per capita wage income

(2.3)   (7.9)

F-statistic = 62.9, adjusted R^2 = 0.56, N = 48.

This result suggests that the distribution of social expenditures per capita is not equalizing.

Impact of fiscal constraints on social protection and infrastructure

How have oblasts adapted and responded to fiscal constraints? Field work in Yaroslav, which had a budget surplus in 1992, suggests social spending will come under severe pressure in 1993 because of the declining revenue base, increasing unemployment, and the divestiture of social assets by privatized enterprises.[2] The oblast has developed a three-point strategy to cope with the economic crisis and effects of transition (Le Houerou 1993). It includes:

• *Social protection* aimed at guaranteeing minimum needs. A laudable goal is to gradually shift from the present 167 different subsidies and benefits now administered to a more targeted system of cash benefits for the truly needy. Resources are included in the budget to define a local subsistence minimum. The lack of a means test is a major stumbling block.

• *Reorganization of ancillary social assets* now managed by the enterprise sector. Some of the social functions are to be provided on a contract basis between each enterprise and municipal authorities.

• *Development of privately funded social infrastructure* in the fields of health, education, sports, and culture by means of tax and other incentives.

This strategy is commendable. Moreover, the authorities have made an excellent effort to rationalize the unwieldy welfare system by categorizing existing benefits by recipient and source of funding. Nonetheless, during the transition to a new system, existing programs will remain deficient.

Planned activities, even if fully funded, are unlikely to meet both social needs and the demands of proactive programs. Pressure is notable in several areas. For one thing, funding at the oblast level is only available for 30 to 40 percent of estimated needs in social services (health and education). Priority will go to meeting the wage bill and to feeding programs. The new health insurance system (3.6 percent of the enterprise wage bill) will support current medical expenditures, but it is estimated that much more is likely to be needed. The budget will cover the difference, at the expense of capital investment. The uncertainty over funding has bred bargaining. Funds to complete the veteran's hospital, for example, came via the Supreme Soviet (at the personal direction of its chairman, Ruslan Khasbulatov). Only 40 percent of projected required social welfare spending for the oblast has been included in the consolidated budget; it is unclear whether the remainder can or will be fully met by rayon and municipal budgets. Social administration officials hope to secure funds from other parts of the budget, extrabudgetary funds, or tax increases on enterprises. Finally, some 20 percent of the Yaroslav municipal budget will support maintenance of divested enterprise social assets in 1993, triple the level in 1992. This is almost equal to the projected deficit in the Yaroslav budget for 1993. Firms report receiving only a portion of payments they are due for providing social services— as agreed under contract with oblast and municipal authorities—and this only at the end of the year. Without municipal financing, enterprises say they have no choice but to cease providing social services.

The outlook is serious: Yaroslav is an oblast with a rapidly changing labor market accompanied by widening income disparity and a falling standard

Table 4.1 Real per capita oblast expenditures on social and cultural services, by oblast, Russian Federation, 1991 to second quarter 1993

(in rubles, deflated using end-of-period prices)

			1993	
Oblast	1991	1992	First quarter	Second quarter
Arkhangelskaia oblast	459	298	288	35
Nenetskii AO	—	838	675	81
Vologodskaia oblast	538	334	271	33
Murmanskaia oblast	813	494	500	60
Republic of Karelia	646	378	320	39
Republic of Komi	678	420	426	51
St. Petersburg	619	190	230	28
Leningradskaia oblast	447	242	213	26
Novgorodskaia oblast	567	259	264	32
Pskovskaia oblast	548	269	304	37
Brianskaia oblast	490	183	189	23
Vladimirskaia oblast	409	219	218	26
Ivanovskaia oblast	—	217	179	22
Tverskaia oblast	—	185	193	23
Kaluzhskaia oblast	417	188	280	34
Kostromskaia oblast	510	239	235	28
Moscow City	620	321	290	35
Moskovskaia oblast	374	182	171	21
Orlovskaia oblast	512	209	224	27
Riazanskaia oblast	436	225	195	23
Smolenskaia oblast	460	210	210	25
Tul'skaia oblast	389	210	198	24
Yaroslavskaia oblast	394	272	256	31
Nizhniy Novgorod oblast	345	220	240	29
Kirovskaia oblast	471	239	241	29
Republic of Marii-El	581	304	285	34
Mordovian Republic	541	267	242	29
Republic of Chuvash	2,058	254	217	26
Belgorodskaia oblast	441	244	298	36
Voronezhskaia oblast	433	204	206	25
Kurskaia oblast	458	209	221	27
Lipetskaia oblast	435	249	196	24
Tambovskaia oblast	468	226	236	28
Astrakhanskaia oblast	482	197	206	25
Volgogradskaia oblast	428	205	185	22
Samarskaia oblast	—	278	287	35
Penzenskaia oblast	397	183	204	25
Saratovskaia oblast	403	219	205	25
Ulianovskaia oblast	—	235	250	30
Republic of Kalmykia	799	336	342	41
Republic of Tatarstan	475	287	272	33
Krasnodarskii krai	382	189	197	24
Republic of Adygeya	73	217	200	24
Stavropolskii krai	—	163	188	23
Karachai-Cherkess Republic	—	223	193	23
Rostovskaia oblast	377	179	196	24
Republic of Dagestan	457	198	165	20
Kabardino-Balkar Republic	—	206	207	25

	1991	1992	(1) 1993	(2) 1993
North Osetien Republic	507	209	164	20
Chechen Republic and Ingush Republic	403	20	16	2
Kurganskaia oblast	—	255	271	33
Orenburgskaia oblast	465	258	256	31
Permskaia oblast	449	308	266	32
Komi-Permyatskaia AO	—	276	276	33
Sverdlovskaia oblast	504	335	282	34
Cheliabinskaia oblast	488	352	307	37
Bashkortostan Republic	—	366	328	40
Udmurt Republic	545	267	270	33
Altaiskii krai	494	253	281	34
Republic of Altai	—	380	508	61
Kemerovskaia oblast	624	382	315	38
Novosibirskaia oblast	449	203	210	25
Omskaia oblast	515	297	290	35
Tomskaia oblast	615	329	332	40
Tyumenskaia oblast	290	382	419	50
Khanty-Mansiiskii AO	—	782	819	99
Yamal-Nenets AO	—	1,124	954	115
Krasnoiarskii krai	532	398	362	44
Republic of Khakasia	—	275	260	31
Taimyrskii (Dolgano-Nenetskii) AO	—	993	607	73
Evenkiiskii AO	—	752	913	110
Irkutskaia oblast	—	312	346	42
Ust'-Ordynskii Buryatskii AO	—	396	384	46
Chitinskaia oblast	547	284	249	30
Aginskii Buryatskii AO	—	377	353	42
Republic of Buryatiia	709	337	331	40
Republic of Tuva	1,034	466	462	56
Primorskii krai	—	273	255	31
Khabarovskii krai	—	370	404	49
Evreyskaya AO (Jewish)	—	308	311	37
Amurskaia oblast	368	286	330	40
Kamchatskaia oblast	966	529	535	64
Koryakii AO	—	1,539	1,300	157
Magadanskaia oblast	910	663	728	88
Chukotskii AO	—	972	763	92
Sakhalinskaia oblast	901	543	536	65
Republic of Sakha (Yakutia)	1,334	1,238	865	104
Kaliningradskaia oblast	—	214	205	25
Total		282	271	33
Average	547	344	330	39
Standard deviation	277	248	203	25
Minimum	73	20	16	2
Maximum	2,058	1,539	1,300	157
Coefficient of variation	0.5069	0.7198	0.6142	0.6288

— Not available.
AO Autonomous okrug.
AR Autonomous republic.
Source: Ministry of Finance of the Russian Federation; author's calculations.

of living. A household income survey conducted in April 1993 revealed that 38.8 percent of the Yaroslav city population of 640,000 lived below the federally determined subsistence level. The survey did not take in-kind income into account, and there are problems with the poverty line, so the figure may be somewhat inflated. However, the absolute poverty level correlates closely with respondents' view of their relative income level (40 percent consider themselves poor or poorer than average) (Le Houerou 1993).

Reassignment of capital spending responsibility

The assignment of public investment responsibilities among the different levels of government of the Russian Federation—central, oblast, and rayon— is going through a period of rapid transition. So are capital budget preparation and execution at all three levels of government. Currently, public investment is the most confusing and unsettled area in the public expenditure arena.

Two main factors have contributed to this confusion. First, the assignment of capital expenditure responsibilities has changed from a purely central government responsibility in the previous regime to a predominantly local and regional responsibility at the present time. This radical shift has most often been the result of budgetary pressures at the federal government level; thus, it has not been carefully planned. However, the recent changes should result, in many cases, in an improvement in the allocation of resources within the public sector if adequate funding is also available.

Second, the multiple sources of public investment financing and the difficulty of accounting for all of them in a system of intergovernmental relations with interdependent budgets also contribute to this confusion. The sources of public investment financing include not only the federal, oblast, and rayon budgets. They also include special programs and transfers engineered by presidential decree or at the initiative of the Supreme Soviet—not always reflected in the budget—and extrabudgetary funds, public enterprise surplus funds, and (of less importance recently) federal funds. Although oblasts and rayons are theoretically allowed to borrow for capital investment purposes, thus far there has been no substantial borrowing from banks or issuing of public debt by subnational governments. This multiplicity of funding sources for public investment has meant that there is no reliable information on the level of funds invested in each subnational jurisdiction.

Capital investment in the public sector before independence. In the former U.S.S.R., capital expenditures were fully centralized. Most of the capital investments were planned and frequently executed by the Ministry of

Economy (the former Gosplan). Other executing agencies were line ministries and their subordinate state enterprises. All requests from subnational governments and government agencies were channeled through the line ministries. The Ministry of Economy appraised those requests based on the recommendations of the line ministries and compiled the list of projects to be executed every period.

The list of projects put together by the Ministry of Economy of the U.S.S.R. contained the possible sources of funding for each. Toward the end of the regime the Ministry of Finance played an increasingly important role in selecting which investment projects were eventually funded. There were some exceptions to this pattern. In some cases the Ministry of Finance directly funded a project and in other cases enterprises directly financed a project without going through the Ministry of Economy.

The oblast and rayon governments did not have any responsibility in the capital investment area, although they occasionally acted as agents of the central government. In this period, therefore, capital expenditures were not part of the local government budget; they showed up only in the federal government budget and the income statements of state enterprises. (The exceptions were those projects funded directly by the Ministry of Finance, in which case both the transfer and the capital expenditure did appear in the budget of the oblast or rayon government.) However, the oblast and rayon governments were exclusively responsible for financing the current operations and maintenance of the facilities.

The separation of the investment decision from maintenance and operation decisions had several undesired effects. First, and most important, it led to inadequate maintenance of facilities by subnational governments. Clearly, subnational governments may have had less interest in maintaining facilities because their replacement was perceived to be a cost only to the central government. For many years there has been a shortage of funds for maintenance and repair of the existing social infrastructure. The increasing budgetary difficulties of recent years have accentuated the trend to sacrifice maintenance funds to "protected" items in the budget, such as salaries and wages. In so doing, Russia has been borrowing heavily against the future—current savings in maintenance funds in the thousands of rubles will in the future require replacement capital costing millions.

Second, the centralized approach eliminated any incentive for the mobilization of local resources for public investment purposes. Any locally financed public investment would have crowded out an identical amount financed with federal funds. This reality left local governments at the mercy of central decisionmakers with respect to the level and composition of local infrastructure. This dependency became all too obvious in the first quarter of 1992, when the central government suspended all investments in infrastructure and capital equipment, with the exception of some vital activities in the energy and agricultural sectors (see below). Local governments, for the first time, had to assume responsibility for investment in the local public sector. Financing for these investments in the first quarter of 1992 came from regular budgetary sources and in some cases from extrabudgetary funds. The actual level of investment was very modest, however.

Capital investment in the public sector: postindependence trends. Under severe budgetary pressure the federal government in mid-1992 shifted many types of responsibilities for capital investment to local governments. This shift in responsibilities unfortunately included not only the type of infrastructure that can be properly considered the responsibility of local governments, such as schools and hospitals, but also capital investments in areas that are clearly of national significance and should therefore not become the responsibility of local governments, such as airports, interoblast highways, and housing for military personnel.

The drastic reassignment of investment responsibilities in July 1992 was announced at the time as a permanent change. However, some of these expenditure responsibilities now have been shifted back to the federal government. Field visits reveal that for some items the benefit of this decision on local governments may not have been very significant because little investment was taking place.

However, not only is there still confusion about what level of government is responsible for certain types of public investments, but the overall picture of capital expenditure responsibilities in 1992 is very different from what it was in 1990–91. In the social sphere almost 100 percent of investment is now the responsibility of subnational governments. Even though the policy of the Russian government has been to emphasize investments in the social sector, in particular in health and education services, very little spending has taken place over the past two years in these sectors. For example, in Moscow oblast the entire investment budget for the social sector for 1993 is planned to be R 74 million for a hospital, R 55 million for a primary school, and R 25 million for the completion of one apartment building (totaling about US$154,000 at the prevailing exchange rate of 1,000 rubles to the U.S. dollar).

In the economic sphere there were also significant shifts in responsibilities in 1992. The most important sectors shifted to the local level were agriculture and aeroindustries. Until 1992 all investments in the agricultural sector were the responsibility of the federal government. These investments amounted, effectively, to free subsidies for the agroindustrial sector, both before and after 1992.

The importance of agriculture in capital expenditures at the oblast levels is illustrated by the expenditure figures for the Moscow oblast, primarily an industrial oblast. In 1992, investment in agricultural projects by the oblast represented 18 percent of all its capital expenditures. In 1993 this figure has risen to 56 percent of all investments in the Moscow oblast.

The other important capital projects in the economic sphere that are being financed by subnational budgets are equipment and infrastructure for public utilities. Before 1992 all investments of public utilities were financed by the federal government. Public utilities in Russia include not only what is understood by that term in Western countries—gas, electricity, and water and sewerage—but also communal services such as garbage collection and cleaning, and most notably housing services. Most of the fees and tariffs for household consumption of services for water, sewerage, heat, electricity, gas, and sanitation are set by the federal government at levels well below operating cost. Public utilities do, however, have more freedom in their dealings with enterprises.

Capital budgeting: institutional responsibilities

At the *federal* level the division of responsibilities for capital budgeting is still shared by the Ministry of Finance and the Ministry of Economy. The division of power between the two ministries has been shifting back and forth over the past year and has not been settled yet. Some proposals would eliminate the Ministry of Economy; others would subordinate the Ministry of Finance to the Ministry of Economy. At present both ministries help implement the government investment program. Budgetary limits for investment spending and, ultimately, investment priorities are set by the Council of Ministers and enforced by the Ministry of Finance. The role of the Ministry of Economy has been reduced mainly to maintaining a list of approved projects that have been reviewed by line ministries (for example, requests for school buildings are reviewed by the Ministry of Education). The Ministry of Economy currently appears to do very little planning or capital project evaluation and selection, and it clearly has nothing to do with financing. Some additional roles for the Ministry of Economy at the present time include developing expenditure norms for budget preparation and maintaining and tracking data.

At the *subnational* level the current reality is that the federal government has no control over use of subnational government investment funds that are approved as part of the overall funding for the oblast. In 1992 there were many cases in which oblasts diverted funds for capital investment in a particular sector—as agreed in budget negotiations with the Ministry of Finance—to capital investments in other sectors or even to recurrent expenditures. Draft legislation in the Supreme Soviet would prohibit this kind of intrabudget shifts by the oblasts. But this legislation would seem to clash with the budgetary autonomy given to subnational governments in the Law on the Budgetary Rights of Local Self-Governments and the Law on the Basic Principles of the Budget System and Budgetary Process.

The selection of capital projects and the formulation of capital budgets at the oblast level appear to be similar to the process at the central government level. For example, for 1993 Moscow oblast has a list of projects for each rayon (and for the oblast itself) compiled by the oblast committee on economy. Each project has attached to it a list of possible sources of finance. Sometimes rayon governments and, less frequently, enterprises participate in the financing. After the list of projects is finalized, the committee on economy works with the oblast department of finance to agree on what projects to finance within the overall limit provided by the budget. The department of finance makes the decision on the final list of projects to submit to the oblast soviet for review and approval for the next year. In Moscow oblast these recommendations were approved in 1993 without any major changes.

Capital budgeting and the need for reform

There is a clear need to reform capital expenditure responsibilities. Fundamentally, subnational governments should be assigned responsibility for capital investments that are in correspondence with the responsibilities they have been assigned for current expenditures. Thus, if the operation of schools, hospitals, and local roads is the responsibility of rayons, these governments should also have responsibility for financing these infrastructures. Expenditure responsibilities in capital investments that have a regional dimension should be transferred to oblast governments, and those with a national scope to the federal government.

There are significant gains in overall efficiency to be derived from the *appropriate* decentralization of capital investment in the public sector. Clearly, the assignment in the past of all expenditure responsibilities to the central government was an inferior strategy. It is unrealistic to think that the central government could have, now or in the future, the information or the resources necessary to make efficient expenditure choices on behalf of eighty-nine oblast governments and thousands of rayon governments. Local governments have much better information on the type and level of investment needed. Unifying the decisionmaking process for investment with that for operations and maintenance will also eliminate the perverse incentives that are present—such as low maintenance expenditures—when these decisions are made by different levels of government.

The federal and oblast governments should develop public investment programs for viable projects. The list of projects should include worthwhile unfinished projects, which should be ranked with new projects. The appraisal of these projects needs to be based on a rigorous cost-benefit analysis using realistic rates of discount. The appraisal techniques still used in Russia were better suited to the material product system of the former regime. Updated appraisal techniques need to be introduced through extensive training of budget officials in market-based project evaluation.

With respect to financing instruments, there are currently two initiatives to develop nonbudgetary financing for local government projects. First, a new State Financing Company has been created at the federal level, with the charge of providing long-term credit to subnational jurisdictions for selected capital investment projects. Second, the Draft Law on Subventions to Local Governments, which was under review for more than a year and was passed but had not yet been implemented as of 1993, envisages the formation of an extrabudgetary fund that would finance capital projects and would be based on selection criteria other than those used for the regular budget.

A preferred alternative would be to develop financial intermediaries and capital markets that would allow local governments to issue bonds with the appropriate maturity to finance long-term capital investments (chapter 3). Unfortunately these institutions will develop only in the longer run as the Russian economy stabilizes and matures as a market economy. Consequently, specialized lending institutions for local governments at the federal level may be one way to proceed at the present time, if strict market-based banking criteria are used in lending. The operations of the specialized institutions should *not* be seen as instruments for subsidizing desirable activities at the local level or supporting poorer oblasts. Both these policies should be implemented through budgetary channels. Specifically, the federal government could use targeted grants with a variable matching formula to stimulate more local investment and help poorer regions more (chapter 5).

Budgetary implications of ownership transfers

During transition there have also been new assignments of asset ownership to subnational governments. All housing ownership, for example, has been given to subnational governments or to local public enterprises. The division of government assets among the different levels of government has been remarkably smooth (chapter 2). These transfers should also help decide responsibilities for proper maintenance of capital structures. The shift of ownership responsibility has not eliminated this need. Reassignment, especially of housing, has added huge demands to subnational government budgets. Housing maintenance needs for 1992, which have been estimated at R 67 billion–R 100 billion by the Ministry of Economy, have not been budgeted by the central government, and subnational governments are likely to cover only a small portion of them. The recurrent budget implications of new assignments of asset ownership need to be explicitly considered in the new assignment or sharing of revenues and transfers.

Divestiture of public functions by state enterprises

Under the Russian enterprise system state enterprises are responsible for providing (or financing) many social services—especially infrastructure in education and health care. Their contributions to subnational budgets vary depending on the relative size of the public enterprise in the local jurisdiction. Although on average their contributions are estimated at no more than 3 to 5 percent of GDP, some recent estimates put them as high as 40 percent of the subnational social expenditure budget in some oblasts. In one-company towns *all* social infrastructure outlays may be undertaken by enterprises, and there may be no social expenditures on the oblast or rayon budget whatever.

Clarification is urgently needed on what is truly the enterprises' responsibility and what is the government's responsibility. Some enterprise directors consider expenditures in the social sphere to be concealed taxation. Some progress has been made toward divestiture of these activities because of the financial difficulties of many public enterprises. Their contributions have fallen dramatically with the reduction (or elimination) of state enterprise subsidies and pressures to become more efficient. Only housing maintenance and losses are tax deductible, while investment in schools, health, and housing are funded from after-tax profits. This net income is needed now, more than ever, for investment in plant and equipment.

In some cases enterprise worker collectives have voted for higher enterprise expenditures on social services, sacrificing salary raises and bonuses. In the final analysis the funding of public services does not belong in the private sector and should be transferred to subnational governments. Public enterprises will be unable to compete in a market economy if they remain so burdened. More generally, public enterprises should contribute to subnational finances as private enterprises do—through taxes and user fees.

When enterprises relinquish social responsibilities, another issue crops up. How should these expenditures be assigned among different levels of government? Traditionally, the central government was responsible for all matters relating to its own enterprises, and local governments for theirs. Thus, the central government would be indirectly responsible for a health clinic in a centrally owned enterprises even though health clinics are a "subnational sphere" of responsibility. In a redesigned system, in principle, responsibility for enterprises' social functions should be assigned without regard to former ownership.

The jettisoning of social spending by enterprises is, of course, disruptive to subnational budgets. The net impact will reduce the need for government subsidies to enterprises (or increase their after-tax profits). However, these savings or benefits may not accrue to the same level of government that picks up the expenditure tab. Concrete quantitative analysis of the budgetary implications of this divestiture is needed. Paradoxically, those regions of Russia that benefited most from the presence of enterprises are now most at risk because of the elimination of enterprises' social responsibilities.

Appendix 4.1

To reach an approximation of public service disparities within the Russian Federation, 1989 data for public service infrastructure of the eighty-nine oblasts were analyzed. (Data are taken from *The Statistical Yearbook of the Russian Federation 1989* and from the Ministry of Finance, March and June 1992 budgets.) An index for "fixed capital for public health, physical education, and social security" of oblasts was used and was considered as a proxy for accumulated past fiscal disparities. (The mean value of the index for 1989, 1990, and 1991 was 264.5, with a coefficient of variation of 0.30, a maximum value of 549, and a minimum value of 138.) This suggests a high variation for infrastructure. To explain this variation, we regressed the index on several characteristics of the oblasts. Income (as proxied by the average monthly wage in the oblast in 1989) explains a big part of the variance of "fixed social capital":

$$\text{Fixed social capital} = 82.70 + 0.695 \text{ monthly wage}$$
$$(3.03) \quad (6.90)$$
$$\text{Adjusted } R^2 = 0.41, \, N = 69.$$

Adding other variables (such as population, population density, percentage of urban population, and industrial output per capita) did not improve the equation. Only population density was marginally significant and took a positive sign.

Appendix 4.2

For the first quarter of 1992 oblast expenditure per capita was regressed on the oblasts' average monthly wage and other independent variables (using 1989 values) (see appendix 4.1 for source of data). The results were as follows:

Expenditures per capita = 5.47 + 12.30 monthly wage
                           (3.08)   (3.60)

−41.7 percentage urban
(1.81)

−47.6 number of rayons
(2.38)

F-statistic = 6.57, adjusted R^2 = 0.204, N = 69.

The results parallel those for fixed social capital: per capita expenditures are *positively* related to the average income in oblasts (as proxied by the monthly wage). Oblasts with more urban dwellers and more jurisdictional fragmentation (proxied by the number of rayons in the oblast) tend to have lower expenditures per capita, after controlling for income levels. Better-off regions receive higher budgetary expenditure allocations, and the urban areas are relatively underserved in expenditures.

Notes

1. As Bahry (1987) points out, subnational budget figures were published regularly but were incomplete. Investment data were more complete but were published less frequently, for only some jurisdictions, and with year-to-year gaps and inconsistencies. For example, no investment figures have been published for any Russian Federation oblasts since 1975.

2. This discussion draws on an unpublished World Bank report by Philippe Le Houerou (November 1993) on fiscal management in Yaroslav. We are indebted to Philippe Le Houerou for this background.

5

Revenues and revenue assignment: intergovernmental fiscal relations in the Russian Federation

Roy Bahl

There is no single best way to finance subnational governments—it typically depends on a country's history and objectives. Countries around the world have chosen widely differing paths, the most suitable depending on the objectives a country sets for itself. In most, however, it is a combination of the assignment of (or shares in) national taxes, local taxes (usually property tax and business tax), user charges and benefit levies, and transfers from higher-level governments. Where the central government is federal, the state or provincial governments are usually given broader taxing powers—often on sales and personal income. Whatever the fine print, this fiscal relationship between central and subnational governments, if mishandled, can be a source of future friction and political tension. Like much else in Russia the intergovernmental fiscal relationship is in transition, and the outcome, perhaps more than any other issue, will define the nature of the Federation, at least for the foreseeable future.

In early 1993 Russia's oblast and rayon governments were financed by a negotiated system of shared taxes and ad hoc grants—subventions, in Russian fiscal terminology. Of all taxes collected within their boundaries oblasts retained about 20 percent of the value-added tax (VAT), 60 percent of enterprise income tax, 50 percent of excise duty on vodka, and 100 percent of personal income and other excise taxes. If these revenues did not match spending needs as negotiated with the Ministry of Finance, then a "deficit grant" or subvention was made. Within an oblast the arrangements for tax sharing and the allocation of subventions with rayons were left to the oblast government. The present negotiated system, however, is not sustainable, and there are calls for reform from both central and subnational governments.

By some accounts the Russian government has decided how it wants to proceed with its system of intergovernmental finances. Under a 1992 law, the Basic Principles of Taxation, the present system should be replaced by a pure "tax assignment" system—that is, central government will define the tax bases, set all tax rates, and assign corporate and personal income taxes to subnational government and VAT to central government. But will that happen? Certainly there are no immediate plans to implement the Basic Principles, and some officials doubt whether they ever will take effect. More recently the Law on the Budgetary Rights of Local Self-Governments (1993) has legislated sharing of most taxes and has assigned a few others but has failed to specify the sharing rates.

Whether the government moves to this new assignment system, simply makes adjustments to the present transitional system, or designs a new model, some fundamental questions must be answered:

- How does the tax system of the Basic Principles compare with the one operating at present?
- Will tax assignment (versus tax sharing) provide subnational governments with enough revenue to meet spending responsibilities?
- Can subnational governments provide adequate services, under either the present system or under the Basic Principles?
- Is the federal government's macroeconomic policy compromised by either the Basic Principles or the present system?
- Do oblast and local governments have enough fiscal incentives to increase revenue mobilization and efficiency in delivering public services?
- Is either the proposed new revenue-sharing structure or the present system sustainable in the long run? If not, what other forms of intergovernmental arrangement might be considered?

In a real sense the resolution of the current revenue-sharing debate will define the nature of the Russian Federation, at least for the foreseeable future. One extreme is continued fiscal centralization, with relatively little subnational autonomy and continued central direction of the activities of the subnational government sector. The other extreme is a heavy involvement of oblast governments in establishing priorities for investment and social services and in raising revenues. In between are various forms of tax base sharing; schemes that make provision for special regimes where some regions will have more fiscal powers than others; and heavier use of grants to give subnational governments more autonomy on the expenditure side while continuing to keep the revenue instruments under the control of the center. This chapter is about how such options fit the Russian context.

Revenue sources for subnational governments

Intergovernmental relationships across the globe come in many shapes and sizes. Generally the system chosen will be the one that best helps central government's political ideology or economic aims. The government may, for instance, focus on the importance of economic efficiency or technical efficiency, equalization or macroeconomic control. In federalisms with heterogenous populations, and with ethnic or cultural diversity, autonomy may also be an issue. One system cannot simultaneously achieve all these aims, and governments must decide on priorities, which will dictate the system chosen. Each has its drawbacks. Tax assignment, for example, gives subnational governments fiscal sovereignty that may not be revoked. Tax sharing of the Russian variety, based on "derivation" of revenues, and in which revenues accrue to the regional government that has collected them, may be more flexible but could compromise equalization goals.[1]

Tax assignment

Taxes are assigned when one level of government has sole rights to collect and use the tax and, usually, to set its rates and define the tax base. Strictly speaking, if subnational governments cannot set the base or choose the rate of the assigned tax, the system is more akin to 100 percent sharing of a federal tax. Thus, for purposes of this analysis, we consider the Russian personal income tax (which is "shared" 100 percent with the oblasts) to be a shared tax, since the oblasts cannot adjust either its rate or base. However, one might also see it as 100 percent assigned. The distinction is to some degree grey.

Sometimes, in the United States for example, subnational governments have broad discretion to tax income, consumption, and wealth. But in industrial countries that are more centralized, and in most developing countries, central governments keep the income, sales, and international trade taxes (they may share some with lower levels), while subnationals are assigned taxes that yield less, such as property tax and certain excises. One advantage of this division of revenues (from the central government's viewpoint) is that local governments are kept on a short leash. One drawback is that revenue from these taxes is unlikely to cover subnational spending and extra transfers (grants for example) from central to subnational government are usually needed.

Revenue sharing

Even if the central government collects most taxes, some can be formally shared with subnational governments. This approach is simple and guarantees subnational governments a percentage of revenues. One method is retention according to where the tax was collected (the derivation principle). Another is for some fixed portion of revenues to be pooled and redistributed by formula or by cost reimbursement of eligible activities.

Tax base sharing (surcharges)

Subnational governments may be allowed to levy surcharges on national taxes, perhaps up to a ceiling. This piggybacking on the national tax base is simple and works best when a consistent definition of the tax base is used by all levels of government. Subnational governments can usually rely on the superior administrative machinery of the central government to collect these surtaxes. In the United States many (but not all) state governments use the federal income tax base and coordinate with the federal Internal Revenue Service, but assessment and collection are done by the state governments.[2] Some taxes lend themselves better to piggybacking than others. VAT is notoriously inappropriate; personal income tax is perhaps the best.

Concurrent tax powers

Both central and subnational governments may tax the same activity or tax base, but according to different definitions of the base. Switzerland is an example: both federal and canton governments tax personal income and corporate profits, but the exact definition of the tax base differs. A similar system is used in some U.S. states. This tends to complicate matters and can lead to overlapping and conflicting incentives.

Designing an intergovernmental system

In designing the best system of intergovernmental fiscal relations, the first step is to assign expenditure responsibilities to subnational governments. As noted in chapter 4 the considerations that go into assigning expenditures in a heterogenous federation such as Russia's may differ from those in a homogenous one. Only when expenditure responsibility has been assigned is it possible to select the financing structure that fits these expenditure responsibilities, based on the expenditure assignments and the objectives of the government. Unfortunately, the cart is often put before the horse and the revenue-sharing issue is taken up independently. Such is the case in Russia.

This being the reality, there are some principles of intergovernmental finance that offer useful guidelines for deciding on the division of revenues among levels of government.[3] One begins with a principle of correspondence between expenditure responsibility and revenue needs. Subnational governments must have a revenue base (and an ability to tap it) that generates enough funds to provide adequate services. Often central governments will offload deficits without consideration (or even knowledge) of the impact on state and local government budgets. Such was the case under the fend-for-yourself federalism of Presidents Reagan and Bush in the United States, and in Russia in 1992.

Appropriate assignment of taxes

Where taxes are assigned, it is good practice for central governments to keep and control those taxes that are crucial to macroeconomic stabilization policy or income distribution, as both of these functions are generally thought to be a more proper function of central than of subnational government (Musgrave 1983). These taxes usually include progressive personal income taxes, corporate taxes and taxes on capital gains, indirect taxes on luxury consumption, and payroll taxes to support social programs. Many countries have national sales taxes (the VAT is increasingly common) too.

Customs duties almost always are (and should be) national taxes because of their strategic importance to foreign trade policy and national industrial development. As a subnational tax (or a derivation-based shared tax), they would accrue to only a few jurisdictions, which would be unfair. Also, customs taxes may be too unstable to be a suitable basis for revenue sharing. The same would be true of natural resource taxes (chapter 6).

Which taxes make good subnational taxes?

Subnational governments, then, are left with sources of revenue that are neither principal macroeconomic stabilizers nor major instruments for changing the distribution of income. Subnational governments need stable revenues because they cannot finance extensive deficits through borrowing and must provide essential services. In principle, they should rely on taxes whose burden is not easily "exported" beyond local boundaries (Break 1980; Oates 1972). In other words the burden of local taxes should fall on the local population.

In the more centralized industrial economies and in the developing countries, the central government usually controls taxes that have important effects on national-level resource allocation. Thus, corporate income taxes are often central government taxes because of the importance of achieving standard incentives with respect to investment, technological change, labor practices, and so on. Location decisions should not be tax-driven. If subnational governments levy taxes on enterprise income in an uncoordinated way, the result may be tax exporting—that is, one region taxes enterprises whose goods are sold to another region. For example, subnational taxation of corporate profits can give rise to fairness concerns relating to tax exporting. If one assumes that most of the burden of profits taxes falls on shareholders, this tax would in effect hit shareholders living in many other jurisdictions. Tax "competition" can also result if localities compete with each other by offering tax incentives to attract enterprises. Thus, subnational governments should be given tax bases that are not mobile and do not distort location decisions in production or consumption. As Musgrave (1983, p. 19) eloquently put it ". . . income and profits taxes are least suitable to the local level, questionable at the middle and preferred at the central level."

Despite these problems some industrial countries (such as the United States and Canada) have given subnational governments the authority to levy company income taxes. The argument is that the economy can benefit from state and local governments competing for industrial development, that local governments are entitled to recoup the cost of public services used by business, and that, in any case, many companies do most of their production and sales within a single jurisdiction.

There is a related issue: taxation of natural resources (minerals, fuels, forests, and the like). One argument says that subnational taxation of these resources is fair because the local population deserves some of the bounty from its natural wealth and because extraction often imposes economic and environmental costs on the locals. Without local resource taxes these costs would go uncompensated. There is an equally convincing argument for federal taxation. Since natural resources are unequally distributed, subnational taxes would greatly benefit well-endowed regions at the expense of others. The issue is more fully discussed in chapter 6.[4]

Personal income tax is usually a central government levy because it is used both for stabilization and for redistribution. It is also a reasonable state-level tax. It is more difficult, however, as a local tax (city or county) because people may not live and work in the same area. If one accepts the notion that state and local governments cannot have a major impact on income distribution, then subnational government income taxes should be a simple flat rate tax (on payrolls, for example).

Single-stage retail sales taxes are a good subnational tax, because they yield relatively stable revenues. However, they are efficient only if the region is big enough to avoid leakages (that is, consumers crossing to provinces with lower taxes). Even so, sales taxes are better for states and big cities than for smaller local governments. The multistage VAT, however, is a different story. It is best levied nationally because of complications in inter-

state crediting of VAT payments and the difficulties of administering different rates for each subnational government. Canada is an example of a
country with a national VAT, as well as provincial retail sales taxes levied by
the provinces.

User charges and benefit fees, as well as motor vehicle taxes and
charges, are particularly attractive for local (city and county) governments.
Property taxes are a common local tax because revenue is relatively stable.
Moreover, since such taxes finance local services that help to increase property values, beneficiaries of this public spending are made to pay. Such taxes
can also be equitable, since the better-off have better housing and pay more
taxes, while the poor are often excluded. One possible arrangement of tax
assignment that reflects these principles is shown in table 5.1.

Intergovernmental transfers

Perfectly matching the revenues and spending of subnational governments
via assigned or shared taxes is virtually impossible. In most countries, therefore, fiscal transfers are needed to make up revenue shortfalls. Such fiscal
deficits may be closed in other ways: transferring tax powers to subnational
governments, transferring responsibility for spending to central government, or reducing subnational spending and service standards.

Even when taxes and transfers together finance the expenditures of
subnational governments in aggregate, not all of the individual subnational
governments will have balanced budgets. Some will have deficits; some will
have surpluses. Some localities will be at a disadvantage for reasons beyond
their control: few natural resources, a disproportionate number of young,
old, and poor people, lower per capita income. Differences will emerge
between large and small cities, urbanized and rural municipalities, rich and
poor regions. If it is agreed that poor regions should not provide their people
with worse services than rich ones, equalizing transfers can be used. One
risk of this is that it may reduce recipient governments' incentives to collect

Table 5.1 Possible tax assignments for each level of government

Central-level taxes	State-level taxes[a]	Local-level taxes
Value-added tax (VAT)	Individual income tax	Property taxes
Individual income tax	Surcharges on national taxes	Vehicle taxes
Corporate income tax	Retail sales taxes	User charges
Excise taxes	Excise taxes	Licenses and fees
Natural resource taxes	Property taxes	
Customs duties	Vehicle taxes	
Export taxes		

a. Some of these taxes may also be appropriate for large cities.

revenues—that is, their "tax effort." Transfers are thus at the heart of subnational finances. But designing a transfer system is difficult, not least because of the many goals that such systems might set out to achieve. One system cannot simultaneously achieve all of these ends, and governments must decide which are the most important.

So what are the requirements and pitfalls in Russia? First, transparency is paramount. Second, there could be a risk of excessive equalization in the system—if it leads the better-off oblasts to opt out in response. Third, special regimes, once granted, are almost impossible to reverse. So a comprehensive but flexible formula-based transfer with limited equalization may have much to offer.

Formula grants versus ad hoc approaches to transfers

Should Russia's transfer system be based on distribution rules, or should it be ad hoc? If only the federal government's ability to pursue macroeconomic policy were a consideration, an ad hoc approach would give the center the greatest flexibility. Indeed, this is done in many fiscally pressed countries. However, to allow subnational governments to plan fiscal operations, a formal, formula-based approach (both for the *volume* and *distribution* of grants) is preferred. Rules can, of course, be changed, and have been changed in countries as diverse as Canada, India and, recently, Germany. By contrast, where ad hoc approaches have been common (such as Nigeria, Indonesia and, of course, Russia) there have been political tensions and accusations of favoritism to favored regions (chapter 7).

Formulas and indicators. What indicators should be included in the formula? In other countries that use a formula-based approach, a broad estimate is made of expenditure needs and of subnational revenues available to finance these needs. Depending on how much equalization is wanted, transfers are used to fill all or part of any gap. The most difficult task is defining expenditure needs for each jurisdiction.

There are two basic approaches to the estimation of expenditure needs, a crucial element in any formula-based system. One approach begins with concrete expenditure norms, and then seeks to cost them out. In Russia this could be done by using the existing (or modified) expenditure norms, for example, the per pupil cost of education, as described in chapter 4. And, as pointed out earlier, since in Russia expenditures may be affected by elements such as transport costs, one cannot assume that the costs of providing a service are equal across all jurisdictions. Establishing norms may be both difficult and costly. A different and far simpler way of defining expenditure needs uses umbrella variables such as population, per capita income, city size, poverty rates, density, centrality of a city, and so on. Such an approach is used in Germany and for some grant programs in the United States. The population figure is weighted higher for larger German cities to reflect their function as a center of activity that goes beyond the urban district itself, and the like. These factors and the total weighted population are used to distribute the available equalization funds.

Many countries also include an estimate of the local government's "revenue capacity" in the formula. Revenue-raising capacity is important because if actual revenues and not tax *capacity* is used, an oblast could reduce tax effort and collections and receive correspondingly higher transfers. An appropriate indicator of taxable capacity might include any of the local tax bases over which the local government has discretion—in Russia these are (now) tax bases such as property values, business turnover, and local fees. To estimate the revenue potential of an oblast, the estimate of each tax base may be multiplied by the average oblast tax rate for each base. Undertaking this calculation for each tax and adding them up is one means of estimating "taxable capacity."

Other grants. In addition to general "gap-filling" transfers, many countries also provide other types of grants to local governments. "Specific grants" are designed to finance only those expenditures chosen by the grantor— and may sometimes finance all of the expenditure. If they finance only a part of the expenditure, they are known as "matching grants" and require a parallel contribution from the local government receiving the funds.

Matching grants have important advantages: first, they economize on scarce central government resources, since local governments share in the cost of financing the desired levels of certain services. Second, matching grants are an efficient way of encouraging local expenditures. From the local government's viewpoint the fact that the center pays part of the cost makes it seem cheaper to provide the service. As a result the local governments are likely to provide more of it. Matching grants are often used where expenditures in one locality benefit residents in another and where local government may consequently "underspend" on this item.

Unfortunately, clear guidelines are not available to assist the center in determining the precise matching rate for particular expenditure programs or how those rates should be varied in accordance with the characteristics of different local governments. The matching rate for each program may be thought of as having two components. First, the basic matching rate for each service should reflect the degree of central government interest in the provision of that service. Second, the rate applicable to any locality should be closely related to the need (income level or capacity) of the local government. The matching rate for any particular locality for any particular program would then be higher: (1) the greater the degree of central interest and (2) the lower the (expected) degree of local enthusiasm and ability to support that program or investment. The exact structure of the final formula for any service can likely be determined in any country only after a period—perhaps a prolonged period—of trial and error and of observing the results and adjusting the shares as necessary to approximate more closely the (centrally) desired outcomes (Shah 1991).

Transfer formulas in Russia

In Russia developing a transfer system is especially complex. Because all revenues are collected subnationally, one question is what share of aggregate national revenues should be retained by the oblast level *in aggregate* (the so-called vertical balance issue). Another is how revenues should be allocated among the oblasts—by formula or by another means (the horizontal balance issue). The present system of negotiated tax shares basically addresses both issues with one instrument—the negotiated tax-sharing rate—which differs across oblasts.

In Russia the basic ingredients of most revenue-sharing formulas—expenditure needs and revenue capacity—are not easy to define. It is hard to identify who is rich or poor in Russia—that is, where expenditure needs are high in relation to means. Also, compressed wages and distorted prices make it difficult to interpret statistics on per capita income. In some remote areas the costs of providing basic services may be high indeed: in the north, food and raw materials may have to be delivered by icebreaker. Some areas in Siberia are up to 1,000 miles from a railhead and are snowed in for many months of the year. On the revenue side a region's tax base and revenue capacity can change radically—for example, if energy and input prices change (Craig and Kopits 1993).

Thus, in Russia *simplicity* should be the watchword—at least for now. Russia may not be ready for a formula based on per capita income as an indicator of fiscal capacity, partly because existing measures of income are unreliable. However, it should be possible to identify some *broad indicators*. Some industrial countries, for example, use the size of the population, the concentration of high-cost citizens (pensioners, say), and urbanization. Others base formulas on key indicators of public service needs—miles of substandard roads, deficiencies in school and hospital space. A few, notably Denmark, quantify expenditures, item by item. In Russia, this could be done by using the existing (or modified) expenditure norms—for example, per pupil cost of education, given the standard cost of a teacher, classroom operation, and the like—to derive a cost figure in rubles. Performing this calculation for each expenditure function can build up each jurisdiction's expenditure need. The precision of this approach has much appeal; however, it is complicated and costly to keep current. In Russia, as in some other countries that have made major changes, a "transitional factor" will also need to be brought in to smooth the move from one system to another.

The initial construction of a revenue-sharing formula is an arbitrary process: a "grants commission" that develops the formula is the way that countries such as Australia and India have chosen to deal with this problem (chapter 7). One reason for this choice is that developing a formula, although technically complex, is not *only* a technical exercise. Political considerations often arise, and the "grants commission" is thought by many to be a relatively objective adjudicator of interests. Furthermore, its permanent secretariat is available to carry out the concrete and complex empirical work—including the ongoing data gathering—that such an exercise requires. In Russia, particularly, top-down executive decisionmaking may not receive much support from oblasts.

For this reason it would be premature to say which indicators or which formula(s) are appropriate for Russia, or to go beyond suggesting that the formula should include needs-based and capacity-based indicators. First, the overall system chosen for Russia must be the outcome of policy debate within Russia—following on from the work of the "blue-ribbon commission" · mentioned in chapter 1. Second, it is a complicated, data-intensive exercise, ultimately involving a census of governments (as outlined later in this chapter) and simulation of alternative options. Only then can the appropriate choices be made.

Equalization and sharing formulas

How much equalization is attempted through the intergovernmental fiscal system is a strategic decision in any country, more so in Russia. Equalization will penalize those better-off regions that have the greatest industrialization and growth potential. Many oblasts—those rich in natural and industrial resources, for example—resent the (perceived) cross-subsidies in the present system and would like to opt out (chapter 7). However, if any one oblast is granted an exemption, others may demand similar treatment, leaving only the poorer oblasts in the system. Ironically then, overemphasis on equalization could, at present, prompt the wealthier to withdraw and reduce the potential for implementing any equalization.

At this point in Russia's history it is probably best to let the intergovernmental fiscal system give significant scope to the initiatives and fiscal energies of the better-off areas, in the interest of more economic growth. This could be achieved by letting oblasts retain a relatively large share of the revenues they collect. Limiting the scale of resources shared by formula, while still using a formula-based system to distribute some revenues, can help address this tension.

Evaluating alternative revenue-sharing and tax-assignment models

How does a government take these pros and cons into account in structuring its intergovernmental fiscal system? Among the more important factors that enter into a government's decisions about how much taxing power to give subnational governments and which taxes to assign to which level of government are revenue adequacy, economic efficiency and local autonomy, equity, macroeconomic policy, and administrative feasibility. The weight a government gives to each factor determines the kind of fiscal decentralization that will emerge.

The principal lesson here is that there is no one best system of intergovernmental finance, in terms either of how much taxing power to assign to subnational governments or which taxes to assign. The right choice depends on the goals the central government most wants to achieve. Some general principles should, however, be taken into account in designing the intergovernmental system:

- Designing a tax-sharing or assignment system should begin with a full understanding of the budgetary implications of expenditures assigned to subnational governments. These costs determine both the level of revenue and the revenue elasticity subnational governments will need.
- If economic efficiency is an important goal and the central government wants to encourage subnational revenue mobilization and efficient state and local government operations, some taxing power must be delegated to subnational governments.
- If equity is a dominant goal, a formula grant should weigh more heavily in the system, and a premium should be placed on finding (or developing) formula indicators to achieve such equalization.
- Macroeconomic considerations suggest that countries with chronic deficits and unstable economies are less able to dedicate a significant share of their revenues to subnational governments.

The realities of Russia's system of subnational taxation

With the Russian economic and political system in turmoil, it is hardly surprising that intergovernmental fiscal relations are not running smoothly. Although a new intergovernmental financing arrangement is provided for in the Basic Principles, the system of negotiated tax sharing inherited from the previous regime has continued to operate. The retention rates for the various taxes have been changed in significant ways throughout 1992 and 1993. Up to the first quarter of 1992 retention rates for VAT varied across oblasts. Since then, fixed shares of VAT have been adopted and then given up again, and an increasing share of the corporate income tax has gone to subnational governments.[5] The rate of sharing still varies (by tax and across oblasts) but on average, subnational governments retained about 40 to 45 percent of taxes they collected (tables 5.2 and 5.3). When subventions and transfers are factored in, however, the share is probably closer to 50 percent.[6]

Table 5.2 Distribution of subnational government tax and nontax revenues, Russian Federation, 1992

(in billions of rubles)

Revenue source	Total revenue	Percentage of total
Personal income tax	431.3	16.7
Enterprise income tax	920.9	34.5
Value-added tax	498.1	18.6
Excise taxes	110.8	4.2
Land and property tax	108.6	4.0
Natural resources: royalties and payment	104.7	3.9
Stamp duties and other nontax revenues	—	—
Revenues from privatization	43.4	1.6
Other local taxes	125.6	4.7
Subventions	142.5	5.3
Federal transfers to autonomous regions	186.1	6.9
Total revenue	2,672.3	100.0

—Not available.
Source: Data provided by the Ministry of Finance of the Russian Federation, July 1993.

Table 5.3 Revenue structure and revenue sharing, Russian Federation, 1992

(in billions of rubles)

Revenue source	Total collections	Subnational amount	Subnational share (percent)
Personal income tax	431.3	431.3	100.0
Corporate income tax	1,566.8	920.9	58.8
Value-added tax	1,998.9	498.7	24.9
Excises	211.5	110.8	52.3
Foreign trade taxes	460.0	8.0	1.7
All other taxes[a]	565.0	312.0	n.a.
Total tax revenue	5,231.0	2,280.0	43.6

n.a. Not applicable.
Source: Data provided by the Ministry of Finance of the Russian Federation, July 1993.

Tax administration problems

If subnational taxation is to be effective, subnational governments must have capable tax administrations. Many countries argue that subnational tax administration is so weak that further decentralization of taxing powers would reduce revenue mobilization. In addition, skilled fiscal analysts, accountants, valuation experts, and tax collectors may be too scarce, nationally, to be shared between central and subnational governments. Moreover, because oblast and rayon politicians are closer to the local population and businesses, and because subnational governments compete with one another for economic activity, there is less incentive for good local tax administration. However, it can also be argued that assigning or giving the *right* taxing powers (property tax, business and vehicle taxes, licenses) to subnational governments can increase overall revenues (Bahl and Linn 1992, chapters 4 and 12).

In most Western market economies there are distinct central and subnational tax administration authorities. However, most economies in transition (China, Hungary, Poland, Romania, Viet Nam, and the former U.S.S.R. republics, Russia included) have only a *single* administration. In these countries tax assessments and collection are carried out by this single tax service, through its decentralized offices at the local government (rayon) level, and revenues are "shared up" to provincial and central governments. In China, the CIS, Russia, and Viet Nam the decentralized tax offices are formally part of the central government's administrative system. In these countries, however, the tax offices' "dual" responsibilities as parts of both the local government apparatus and the central administration give rise to substantial conflicts of interest, as outlined in chapter 2 (Bahl and Wallich 1992).

Although such a single nationwide administration eliminates duplication, it also makes it difficult to "assign" taxes exclusively to subnational governments. In such a case the central government tax administration would be in the uncomfortable (and incentive-incompatible) position of being asked to collect subnational taxes with the same vigor and efficiency as it collects central taxes, even though the central government does not share in those revenues.

Certainly the centralized approach administered by Russia's State Tax Service has not been overly successful in generating compliance. That there are tax administration problems during this transition period comes as no surprise. Not only are the tax structure and the system of tax sharing new, but the central State Tax Service is also relatively new. (It was formed in 1990, mostly with former employees of the local governments' finance departments, and it achieved ministerial status in 1991.) Moreover, some longstanding flaws in the system of tax administration have been magnified by economic liberalization. These flaws include the difficulty of taxing the newly emerging private sector, uncertainty about the tax laws (some local tax officers complained that they had little information on tax laws and had to rely on information published in the newspaper), inadequate staff to carry out duties assigned, weak recordkeeping and inefficient tax administration procedures, and an antiquated paper-based system and poor information flow. Strengthening the State Tax Service is a priority, as emphasized later in this chapter.

To complicate matters further, oblast and rayon governments are taking matters into their own hands. Some rayons in Nizhniy Novgorod, for example, are holding on to all taxes instead of sharing them with the federal government, as required. This case is still under review. The autonomous okrug of Khanty-Mansiiskii in 1992 unilaterally decided to retain 20 percent of the VAT instead of its 1 percent agreed entitlement. Other oblasts also are said to be withholding large sums.

Revenue adequacy and revenue-expenditure correspondence

Most transitional (and developing-country) governments are fiscally hard-pressed. Few of them give subnational governments access to broadly based income taxes (personal or corporate) or major consumption tax bases. This fiscal starvation of subnational governments ensures that they depend heavily on the center and on intergovernmental grants for finance. Developing countries with a federal structure rely more heavily on subnational governments to raise their own revenues and frequently empower states to collect sales or income taxes. Witness Brazil, India, and Nigeria. But this approach has not been without its problems, notably tax coordination and complexity (chapter 7).

In reforming socialist economies it is particularly important that subnational governments have an adequate revenue base, whether this comes from their own taxes, shared taxes, or grants. Otherwise, they may turn to economically undesirable sources of revenue, such as profits from direct public ownership of local businesses or the savings gleaned from pushing local public services onto enterprises. Another temptation to be avoided is giving local government only minor taxes on a wide range of products and activities. These are expensive to administer and unpopular and usually raise little revenue.

Subnational governments need an adequate—and "elastic"—revenue base; that is, one that automatically grows in step with incomes and spending needs. How does one define "adequate"? If demand for government services and the cost of providing them increase roughly in proportion with a region's GDP or income, a revenue-GDP elasticity of one would maintain that relationship.[7] The aim of government then would be to design a subnational revenue system whose base would increase along with GDP.

The same criteria must be applied to central government. If national revenue is more or less fixed in the short run, increasing the revenues assigned to subnational governments will weaken the budgetary position of the central government. Likewise, an increase in the elasticity of subnational government revenues may be met by a reduction in the elasticity of the central revenue base, leaving lower revenue growth to cover central spending.

Has Russia met these revenue adequacy tests? Despite the reassignment of spending responsibilities to subnational government budgets, oblast and rayon governments have not yet received a revenue adjustment that matches their new responsibilities. A look at the fiscal outcome for subnational governments in the first quarter of 1992 is revealing. Ministry of Finance data for early 1992 show that, of the eighty-nine oblasts, fifty-seven oblasts had a revenue shortfall (equivalent to R 99 billion) and thirty-two oblasts had a surplus (R 48 billion). Because the Ministry of Finance does not have the power (as it did in the past) to extract the surpluses and use them to finance deficit oblasts, the revenue cost to central government (the costs of funding the deficit grant) was the whole R 99 billion (not the net amount). This cost may be understated, because some deficit oblasts did not deliver adequate services to the population and some deferred payments. Moreover, the cash surplus of the thirty-two oblasts may not be money in the bank but a reflection of unfinished work and spending commitments made but not yet executed. Some Ministry of Finance officials say that the surplus simply reflects the oblasts' inability to spend more than 80 percent of what was planned.[8]

Another way to examine revenue adequacy is to look for a systematic relationship between revenues distributed to each oblast and that oblast's expenditure needs, as measured by such variables as population, density, and urbanization. A systematic positive relationship would be evidence that revenue allocations match the oblast's relative expenditure needs. No relationship or a weak relationship would suggest that revenues might not be distributed according to expenditure needs. (There are many ways to explain the absence of a systematic relationship between the distribution of revenues and the needs indicators used here. One possibility is that other, perhaps more important, needs variables were excluded from the regression.)

A multiple regression analysis was carried out for the sixty-four oblasts for which data were available, using first quarter 1992 data, with per capita retained revenues as the dependent variable. Expenditure needs were proxied by population, percentage of population living in urban areas (urbanization), and per capita value of gross industrial output (per capita GVIO). Similar independent variables were used to show the fiscal capacity variations among oblasts (equation 1 in table 5.4). An alternate specification replaces per capita GVIO with the average monthly wage, and urbanization with population per square kilometer (population density) (equation 2 in table 5.4). The same two specifications are reestimated with data for the first two quarters (equations 3 and 4 in table 5.4).

For the first quarter, four results stand out. First, less than half the variation in oblasts' retained revenues can be explained, suggesting that there are other important determinants of per capita revenues accruing to oblasts besides expenditure needs—or that the process of allocating revenues is random. Second, oblasts with a smaller population retain more revenues per capita. Third, oblasts with a higher average wage retain much *more* on a per capita basis. (There appears to be little relationship between per capita revenues retained and per capita gross industrial output.) Fourth, more highly urbanized oblasts retain more per capita. All this suggests that in early 1992, revenue distributions were driven largely by the strength of the economic base (wage levels and urbanization), not by expenditure needs.

When the same analysis is done for the first six months of 1992, the results are slightly different. (See chapter 2 for a discussion of policy changes between the first and second quarters of 1992 and beyond.) Even less of the variation in per capita retained revenues across oblasts can be explained by these factors, and only the average wage shows a significant (positive) relationship to the revenues received. This is important. It shows that none of

Table 5.4 Determinants of subnational government per capita revenues, by oblast, Russian Federation, first and second quarters 1992

(ordinary least squares estimates)

Per capita subnational retained revenues[a]	Constant	Per capita value of gross industrial output	Population (thousands)	Percentage of population living in urban areas	Population per square kilometer	Average monthly wage	R^2	N[b]
1. First quarter	400.99 (2.69)	-0.04 (-1.35)	-0.08 (-3.87)	8.01 (2.82)			0.22	52
2. First quarter	298.58 (3.01)		-0.60 (-3.36)		0.62 (0.61)	1.76 (6.16)	0.52	64
3. First and second quarters	-117.70 (-0.10)	0.09 (0.25)	-0.07 (-0.30)	42.79 (1.70)			0.09	73
4. First and second quarters	-905.04 (-1.00)		0.04 (0.18)		4.23 (0.49)	14.15 (4.36)	0.22	73

Note: t-statistics are shown in parentheses below the regression coefficients.
a. Data for the second quarter are revised budget estimates.
b. Some observations were dropped because data for all eighty-nine oblasts were not available.
Source: Estimated from data provided by the Ministry of Finance of the Russian Federation, March and July 1992.

the factors commonly thought to indicate demand for higher public spending (urbanization, population density, and population) are systematically
related to per capita revenues retained by an oblast. And it suggests that the
present allocation is not equalizing (see below). More recent analysis suggests that in 1993 similar results apply, which is not surprising since the
underlying system has changed little (Bahl, Martinez-Vazquez, and Wallace
1993).

Equalization

Ideally, central government transfers or grants, together with subnational
taxing powers or tax shares, should be such that all subnational governments
can provide basic services with the same level of tax effort. (Tax effort is
defined as the extent to which a jurisdiction exploits its tax base, or its taxable capacity. Thus, a poor jurisdiction with a weak tax base might be making better tax effort than a richer one, even though its actual revenue collections are much lower.) Under this model, where own revenues and tax
shares fall short for providing basic services, grants make up the difference,
enabling outlays to take place on a more or less comparable scale.

The advantages of this equalizing approach to subnational finance are
clear enough—by diverting resources from rich to poor regions, the quality of life for all can be evened out. But there can be disadvantages. Financing subnational governments by transfers (instead of by their own local taxes)
not only discourages subnational governments' tax effort but also reduces
local officials' accountability and inevitably brings on more central government interference in subnational spending. By contrast, under a system of
purely assigned taxes, those subnational governments with the strongest
economic base can raise more revenue with the same (or lower) tax effort
than their poorer neighbors. The goal of revenue mobilization would be
well served, but fiscal disparities between some regions would be greater.

These disparities can be offset with grants (or shared taxes) to the
poorest jurisdictions, but grants themselves are not without difficulties. One
problem is the appropriate scale of the grant—finding the right balance
between giving subnational governments tax shares or some taxing autonomy (and thereby encouraging revenue mobilization but increasing
disparities) and providing grants that equalize (but that may dampen tax
effort). Another formidable problem is finding an objective way to transfer
central resources to subnational governments. A shared tax, for example,
could be counterequalizing if it is retained (as in Russia) where the tax is
collected, that is, on a derivation basis. Even formula grants are not always
equalizing, because it is hard to find measurable indicators that reflect differences in fiscal capacity and spending needs. This may be especially the

case in Russia today (see below), although this will change as data become available.

In designing an equitable system, government planners must be able to measure and understand the disparities in fiscal capacity and expenditure needs across regions. They must also determine by how much these disparities would be increased (or reduced) by the various other ways of distributing central transfers or other forms of local taxing powers—or, in Russia, by changing administered prices (or freeing prices) of major inputs.

Equalizing aspects of Russia's new system

There is no a priori reason to expect that the tax sharing in effect in Russia before or since 1992 has been equalizing. The corporate income tax, shared on a derivation basis, will favor higher-income oblasts (with their more active economies) and areas where past government investment in enterprises has been heavy and therefore profits and tax revenues are higher. The same is true of the personal income tax, since areas with large industrial cities will have more employment and pay higher wages. The issue is a little less clear for the VAT, since central government's variable sharing rates are intended to favor poorer oblasts, hence some equalization might be expected. Indeed, VAT may have had an equalizing effect in the first quarter (and again in 1993) because its distribution by the federal government was on an ad hoc basis with negotiated sharing rates that varied across oblasts and presumably reflected needs. There were clearly wide variations in VAT retention rates in the first quarter (table 5.5) and again in early 1993. However, the switch to a fixed 20 percent VAT sharing rate in the second and third quarters of 1992 reduced any potential for redistribution from this source.

Table 5.5 Value-added tax retention rates, by oblast, Russian Federation, first quarter 1992

Retention rate (percent)	Number of oblasts	Percentage of oblasts
Less than 10	14	15.7
10–20	11	12.4
20–30	19	21.4
30–40	17	19.1
40–50	5	5.6
50–60	4	4.5
60–70	5	5.6
70–80	0	0.0
80–90	1	1.1
90–100	13	14.6
Total	89	100.0

Source: Data supplied by the Ministry of Finance of the Russian Federation, March 1992.

But just how equalizing (or not) has the Russian system been since its recent changes? Most analysts would agree that the objective of equalization is to subsidize oblasts whose fiscal capacity is not sufficient to support adequate levels of expenditures, even if the local area makes a reasonable tax effort. Because data constraints will not allow a thorough analysis of this issue here, general indicators of expenditure need and fiscal capacity are used to examine the distributional features of the present system. Higher levels of per capita GVIO and the average wage are used to indicate stronger taxable capacity; urbanization, population density, and population size are used to indicate greater expenditure needs.

The tax-sharing system in place in the first quarter of 1992 featured a variable VAT sharing rate and other shared taxes. Many analysts in Russia see variable sharing rates as a proper approach to dividing (regulating) revenues between the subnational and central governments, and there is some nostalgia for that system. The relationship between the retention rates of VAT and of total revenues and indicators of fiscal capacity and spending needs in oblasts is shown in table 5.6. (The retention rate, that is, the ratio of revenues retained by oblasts to revenues collected, ranged from 18 to 60 percent depending on the oblast. The average VAT retention rate was 24 percent, but ranged from zero, or no retention, to 100 percent, or full re-

Table 5.6 Simple correlations of tax retention rates with selected independent variables, Russian Federation, first quarter 1992

Dependent variable	Total retention rate	Percentage of population living in urban areas	Average wage	Population	Population per square kilometer	Per capita gross value of industrial output
1. Value-added tax retention rate, first quarter	0.77[a]	-0.60[b]	0.01[b]	-0.42[a]	-0.11[c]	-0.68[c]
2. Total retention rate, first quarter		-0.50[b]	0.07[b]	-0.57[b]	-0.14[c]	-0.51[c]
3. Percentage urban			0.40[b]	0.41[b]	0.23[c]	0.69[b]
4. Average wage				-0.13[b]	-0.30[c]	0.36[c]
5. Population					0.62[c]	0.26[c]
6. Population density						0.04[d]
7. Per capita gross value of industrial output						

Note: Retention rates are for first quarter 1992, and all other variables are for 1989. The retention rate is the amount of tax retained in the oblast expressed as a percentage of the amount collected in the oblast.
a. $N=88$.
b. $N=70$.
c. $N=68$.
d. $N=66$.
Source: Estimated from data provided by the Ministry of Finance of the Russian Federation, March and July 1992.

tention.) The average retention rate was found to be much higher in less urbanized and less populous oblasts and in those that have lower per capita GVIO. The retention rate for *all* revenues taken together is unrelated to either average wage or population density. The same pattern holds true for VAT shares. Moreover, the distribution of VAT retentions and total revenue retention are themselves highly correlated. Apparently, both were distrib-uted by roughly the same criteria in the first quarter.

These results do not make it easy to reach a conclusion about the im-plicit equalization in the first quarter. If per capita GVIO is taken as a mea-sure of the taxable capacity of an oblast, the tax-sharing formulas are equal-izing: oblasts that have a larger per capita GVIO retain a significantly *lower* share of the revenues they collect. If, however, average monthly wage is seen as a better indicator of income level, the data show no equalizing tendency for either total revenue or VAT sharing. Notably, there is no close correla-tion between the average wage and per capita GVIO (see table 5.6).

Another way to look at equalization is to measure the relationship be-tween tax retentions and expenditure needs, as proxied by income (per capita GVIO and the average wage), taking into account such things as population, population density, and urbanization.[9] The multiple regression results for the first quarter of 1992 give the same mixed results as the simple correlation analysis (table 5.7). Even allowing for variations in expenditure needs, tax retention is much higher where per capita GVIO is lower and where the average wage is higher. Moreover, both total retention rates and VAT-sharing rates tend to be higher in less urbanized and less populous oblasts. More than half of the variation in retention rates may be explained by this simple model.

Although these results suggest that first-quarter tax sharing did redis-tribute resources toward oblasts with a lower per capita GVIO and toward those with a higher average wage (the strength of this effect is greatest for the VAT-sharing scheme, in which the federal government made the dis-tributions on an ad hoc basis), this is not an equalizing scheme. Per capita GVIO is not necessarily an accurate indicator of fiscal capacity. (Ideally, one would want to include enterprise profits, value added, and wages, for example. And in Russia, where prices are distorted, GVIO does not prop-erly measure output.) The average wage is probably a fair indicator of the personal income tax base, and possibly of the household consumption el-ement of the VAT base. However, whether higher average wages in an oblast indicate that the local enterprises are more profitable, or that they produce with a higher value added, is debatable. If higher average wages do indicate a larger VAT and income tax base, then these results would seem to show that the Russian system of tax sharing in the first quarter was not equalizing.

Table 5.7 Determinants of subnational governments' total tax and value-added tax retention rates and per capita subventions, Russian Federation, first and second quarters 1992

(ordinary least squares estimates)

Dependent variable	Constant	Per capita value of gross industrial output	Population	Percentage of population living in urban areas	Population per square kilometer	Average monthly wage	$\overline{R}^2$	N
1. Total retention rate, first quarter	46.501 (14.950)	-0.002 (-2.920)	-0.002 (-4.180)	-0.113 (-2.070)	0.040 (1.630)	0.022 (2.809)	0.51	64
2. Value-added tax retention rate, first quarter	83.080 (6.135)	-0.013 (-5.225)	-0.003 (-2.100)	-0.699 (-3.126)	0.239 (2.370)	0.136 (4.163)	0.66	65
3. Per capita sub-ventions, first and second quarters	394.78 (1.45)	-0.28 (-3.44)	-0.30 (-5.23)	24.96 (4.18)			0.32	73
4. Per capita sub-ventions, first and second quarters	116.69 (0.51)		-0.24 (-4.12)		2.77 (1.26)	3.79 (4.61)	0.34	73

Note: t-statistics are shown in parentheses below the regression coefficients.
Source: Estimated from data provided by the Ministry of Finance of the Russian Federation, March and July 1992.

As the system changed in the second quarter, one would expect it to become (theoretically) less equalizing because uniform retention rates distribute revenues directly in proportion to taxable capacity and not expenditure needs. Even so, the system may have had an equalizing element. As the first quarter closed, it became clear that some subnational governments would run big deficits and would have to be subsidized. For the first quarter alone subventions totaled R 99 billion (about the same as estimated total subnational revenues). Subventions were not allocated by formula but were designed to fill ex post oblast deficits. These were estimated by taking normed expenditures (as determined by the Ministry of Finance) and subtracting revenues retained to arrive at the subvention. (By some accounts the normed level of expenditures is last year's amount adjusted by some proper level of inflation.) Among seventy-three oblasts studied the average subvention was 22 percent of revenues, ranging from 0 to 75 percent.

Were the subventions equalizing? To answer that we need to estimate the relationship between per capita subventions for the first two quarters and the independent variables that measure taxable capacity or expenditure need, as above. The regression results show that per capita subventions are much higher in oblasts with a lower per capita GVIO (equations 3 and 4 in table 5.7). Hence, they are equalizing to the extent GVIO is a measure of fiscal capacity. But they are also significantly higher in oblasts where the average wage is higher, suggesting they are not equalizing. Finally, per capita subventions tend to be much higher in oblasts with smaller and more urbanized populations. About a third of the variation among the seventy-three oblasts could be explained, suggesting that distribution is driven to a significant extent by other factors.

In sum, there is no strong evidence that either the first-quarter or the second-quarter system is equalizing, even if the subvention is taken into account. In fact, the distribution patterns for tax retentions and for subventions are similar. On the broader question of disparities among oblasts in resources available *after* revenue sharing, per capita revenues are much higher in oblasts where the average wage is higher (see table 5.4).

Efficiency and autonomy

An economically efficient system of intergovernmental finance (as outlined in chapter 4) is one in which local preferences determine the level and mix of public services offered, given the price that must be paid for these services, limited income, and externalities (Bergstrom and Goodman 1973). Thus, local residents will choose the service level they prefer and be taxed accordingly.

Efficiency depends on three conditions being satisfied. First, taxes can be adjusted up (or down) by the subnational government according to shifts in public spending. Second, subnational governments must have some control over the tax rate or base, and the burden of taxes must fall on local residents. Third, spending responsibility must be clearly assigned, and local government must be able to deliver efficiently any chosen level of expenditures. Obviously, these efficiency theories were developed for industrial countries, with a tradition of local self-governance. These conditions for efficient local self-government may not be satisfied in many developing or transition economies.

The present tax system in Russia gives subnational governments little revenue autonomy. All major tax rates and bases are decided by central government. And with borrowing rights strictly circumscribed, subnational governments have little scope to increase revenues to pay for more services. There are two exceptions: subnational governments may reduce revenues by opting for lower enterprise income tax, and they may levy some local taxes, although these have little revenue potential.

In a decentralized fiscal system, the revenue flow should also be certain enough to allow local governments to plan the use of funds. This is just another form of autonomy. Officials in Nizhniy Novgorod pointed out that fiscal planning is difficult because the sharing formula had been changed three times in the previous twelve months: "We do not know from one quarter to the next what the level of revenues will be." And the same uncertainty holds true for rayon and city governments.

Macroeconomic policy issues

When subnational governments are assigned taxing powers or a share in federal taxes, the central government's ability to use fiscal policy is weakened (chapter 3). For example, the greater the revenue guaranteed to subnational governments, the less the revenue available for the center's own macroeconomic stabilization purposes, for grants to backward regions, or for a subsidy or industrial location policy favoring certain regions. Does Russia's decentralized system of finance compromise its ability to formulate and implement macroeconomic policy? Russia's subnational governments clearly do not have enough fiscal autonomy to offset central government goals for the allocation of resources, since subnational governments have no control over the rates or the base of any taxes. But do present tax shares and assignments compromise the budgetary position of the central government? And are revenues dedicated to subnational governments so large as to mean a central government budget deficit?

Shared taxes are a big claim on federal revenues (table 5.8). Based on the first-quarter budget, the federal government spends 37.3 percent of GDP directly to meet its own needs. This compares with revenue (before sharing) equivalent to 37.8 percent of GDP. In other words the central government budget would be roughly balanced if *no* revenue were shared with subnational governments. After sharing, the central government has only 29.3 percent of GDP to meet its own needs, leading to a deficit of 8 percent. To this should be added any year-end subnational government revenue shortfall (ex ante subnational deficit) met by central government subventions. The situation in 1993 is broadly similar. Clearly, the central government's macropolicy objectives (including balancing its own budget) are compromised by the need to share revenues with the subnational level.

Table 5.8 Center-oblast revenue balance, Russian Federation, first quarter 1992

Federal revenue	Percentage of GDP
Total revenue collections	37.8
Shared with subnational governments	8.5
Estimated central budget deficit	8.0
Federal government direct expenditures	37.3
Estimated additional subnational shortfall	4.0
Amount available for direct central government expenditures	29.3

Source: Calculated from data provided by the Ministry of Finance of the Russian Federation, April 1992.

Revenue mobilization

Subnational governments need an incentive to increase revenue mobilization. Under the present system in Russia this could happen in two ways. Subnational governments might (indirectly) strengthen tax enforcement. They have some influence with local State Tax Service offices, and there is a close relationship between local governments and the state enterprises that make up the largest part of the tax base. Subnational governments might also help increase the profitability of their public enterprises.

Whether the Russian system has stimulated revenue mobilization or dampened it is an open question. On the one hand subnational governments have few incentives to collect aggressively since they retain only a fraction of tax collections. And since any shortfall will be made up by a deficit grant, why make a great effort? On the other hand subnational governments *do* have an incentive to increase tax collections because experience in 1992 and 1993 shows that oblasts can successfully negotiate larger retention rates on an ad hoc basis. So which describes their behavior better?

A wide variation in the tax efforts across oblasts (meaning that oblasts use their fiscal capacity to varying degrees) might be some evidence that there are revenue mobilization disincentives in the system. Indeed, there is a wide variation in the effective rates of tax collection among Russia's oblasts (we measure the effective tax rate as the ratio of tax collections to GVIO— see appendix 5.1). However, even if one takes other factors into account (such as the fact that a higher average wage or a more heavily urbanized oblast might have a greater capacity to tax), our studies show that there is, surprisingly, no significant relationship between the tax effort ratio and the tax-sharing rate. There is no evidence that an oblast with higher retentions makes a significantly greater tax effort—that is, that retentions provide an incentive to improve collections.

Possible impacts of the new tax and tax-sharing laws

The Basic Principles of Taxation Law would replace the present tax-sharing arrangements with a "pure" tax assignment system, without any transfers. Subnational governments are given the revenues from certain taxes, but not the power to set rates or bases. The Basic Principles also specify and assign some "local" taxes, over which subnational governments have full control.

Under the Basic Principles (or any other assignment-based system), the revenues assigned to the subnational government sector in total, and to the individual oblasts in particular, would be determined by the size of their taxable bases—primarily their capacity to raise corporate and personal income tax. This assignment will not necessarily be adequate to allow subnational governments (or the federal government) to meet their expenditure responsibilities at "normal" levels. The bases of the corporate and personal income tax may be quite unrelated to expenditure needs, either for individual subnational governments or for the subnational sector as a whole, depending on their expenditure responsibilities. If the new regime results in an overassignment of revenues to the subnational sector, there is no provision for an extraction back to the central government; if it results in underassignment, there is no provision for a subvention to make up the difference. No mention is made of a compensating system of intergovernmental transfers.

Clearly, under the Basic Principles the distribution of revenues would change significantly from the previous system. A simulation, based on 1992 first-quarter data, shows how selected oblasts would fare, in absolute and relative terms, under the current system and under the Basic Principles (table 5.9). For example, the Republic of Bashkortostan received R 627 per capita under the actual system of tax sharing but would receive only R 592 per capita from the taxes assigned under the Basic Principles. The loss, R 35 per capita, is equivalent to 5.65 percent of its first-quarter revenues. Bashkortostan, which received 2.46 percent of all shared taxes in the first three months of 1992, would receive only 2.19 percent under the Basic Principles.

What about the subnational government sector as a whole? On the revenue side the Basic Principles system seems to favor subnational governments with a greater net transfer when compared to the transitional (1992–93) system. Subnational governments would have given up about R 30 billion in VAT revenues but would have gained R 66 billion from personal and corporate income tax, to take the first quarter of 1992 as an example. Under the transitional system, 28.9 percent of total revenues went to subnational governments. Had the Basic Principles been in use, the figure would have been 31.3 percent.

The variations across oblasts would also be significant (tables 5.9 and 5.10). The median oblast would lose R 29 per capita, equal to 4.29 percent of revenues. Of the sixty-nine oblasts analyzed, forty-one (60 percent) would lose an average of R 118 per capita—fully 20 percent of their revenues. Some oblasts would lose as much as a third of their revenues. For twenty-eight oblasts revenues would increase under the Basic Principles. The median per capita increase would be R 139, about 18 percent of their revenues. Some oblasts' current revenues would increase by more than 30 percent. Oblasts with a higher average wage, a lower rate of urbanization, and a smaller population would, ceteris paribus, gain more revenue on a per capita basis with the switch to the Basic Principles (table 5.11). In some cases, the "wage

Table 5.9 Revenue impact of Basic Principles, estimated, by oblast, Russian Federation, first quarter 1992

(in rubles)

Oblast	Actual per capita oblast revenue	Estimated per capita revenue under Basic Principles	Difference per capita	Percentage difference	Revenue shares (percent)		
					Actuals, transitional system	Estimated, Basic Principles	Difference in share
Republic of Bashkortostan	627	592	-35	-5.65	2.46	2.19	-0.27
Republic of Buryatiia	890	525	-365	-41.02	0.92	0.51	-0.41
Republic of Dagestan	448	197	-251	-56.08	0.80	0.33	-0.47
Kabardino-Balkar Republic	652	415	-237	-36.35	0.49	0.30	-0.20
Republic of Kalmykia	883	268	-614	-69.59	0.28	0.08	-0.20
Republic of Karelia	835	837	2	0.19	0.66	0.62	-0.04
Republic of Komi	830	1,079	250	30.07	1.04	1.28	0.24
Republic of Marii-El	713	484	-230	-32.22	0.53	0.34	-0.19
Mordovian Republic	699	550	-149	-21.30	0.67	0.50	-0.17
North Osetien Republic	747	503	-244	-32.66	0.47	0.30	-0.17
Republic of Tatarstan	567	721	154	27.18	2.05	2.46	0.41
Republic of Tuva	—	—	—	—	0.19	0.06	-0.13
Udmurt Republic	686	550	-136	-19.81	1.09	0.83	-0.27
Chechen Republic and Ingush Republic	574	256	-318	-55.40	0.73	0.31	-0.42
Republic of Chuvash	664	586	-78	-11.73	0.88	0.73	-0.15
Republic of Sakha (Yakutia)	1,744	1,168	-576	-33.03	1.87	1.18	-0.69
Altaiskii krai	661	489	-172	-26.05	1.85	1.29	-0.56
Krasnodarskii krai	471	456	-15	-3.16	2.39	2.18	-0.21
Krasnoiarskii krai	603	810	207	34.42	2.15	2.72	0.58
Primorskii krai	—	—	—	—	1.54	1.51	-0.03
Stavropolskii krai	463	417	-46	-9.96	1.31	1.11	-0.20
Amurskaia oblast	772	536	-236	-30.62	0.81	0.53	-0.28
Khabarovskii krai	727	630	-97	-13.34	1.31	1.08	-0.24
Astrakhanskaia oblast	640	528	-113	-17.59	0.63	0.49	-0.14
Belgorodskaia oblast	659	584	-75	-11.44	0.90	0.75	-0.15
Brianskaia oblast	610	607	-4	-0.59	0.89	0.84	-0.06
Vladimirskaia oblast	538	814	276	51.20	0.88	1.26	0.38
Volgogradskaia oblast	581	604	23	3.97	1.49	1.46	-0.03
Vologodskaia oblast	649	773	125	19.23	0.87	0.98	0.11
Voronezhskaia oblast	564	501	-63	-11.21	1.38	1.16	-0.22
Nizhniy Novgorod oblast	529	775	246	46.58	1.95	2.69	0.75
Ivanovskaia oblast	591	884	293	49.55	0.77	1.09	0.32
Evenkiiskii AO	—	—	—	—	1.85	1.92	0.07
Kaliningradskaia oblast	334	322	-12	-3.45	0.55	0.50	-0.05
Tverskaia oblast	—	—	—	—	0.92	1.11	0.20
Kaluzhskaia oblast	594	477	-117	-19.64	0.63	0.48	-0.15
Kamchatskaia oblast	1,069	910	-159	-14.84	0.49	0.40	-0.10
Kemerovskaia oblast	768	815	47	6.11	2.42	2.42	0.00
Kirovskaia oblast	679	650	-29	-4.29	1.14	1.03	-0.11
Kostromskaia oblast	675	913	238	35.24	0.54	0.69	0.15
Samarskaia oblast	535	719	184	34.49	1.73	2.20	0.47
Kurganskaia oblast	690	461	-229	-33.14	0.76	0.48	-0.28
Kurskaia oblast	631	636	5	0.80	0.84	0.80	-0.04
Leningradskaia oblast	566	600	33	5.87	0.93	0.93	0.00
Lipetskaia oblast	637	648	11	1.76	0.78	0.75	-0.03

(Table continues on the following page.)

Table 5.9 (continued)

Oblast	Actual per capita oblast revenue	Estimated per capita revenue under Basic Principles	Difference per capita	Percentage difference	Revenue shares (percent)		
					Actuals, transitional system	Estimated, Basic Principles	Difference in share
Magadanskaia oblast	1,095	791	-303	-27.72	0.59	0.40	-0.19
Moskovskaia oblast	445	665	220	49.54	2.95	4.16	1.21
Murmanskaia oblast	979	640	-339	-34.58	1.11	0.69	-0.43
Novgorodskaia oblast	755	683	-72	-9.58	0.56	0.48	-0.08
Novosibirskaia oblast	616	514	-101	-16.44	1.70	1.34	-0.36
Omskaia oblast	673	592	-81	-12.09	1.43	1.18	-0.24
Orenburgskaia oblast	624	635	12	1.86	1.34	1.29	-0.05
Orlovskaia oblast	664	603	-61	-9.19	0.59	0.50	-0.08
Penzenskaia oblast	587	470	-118	-20.07	0.87	0.66	-0.22
Permskaia oblast	548	713	165	30.09	1.68	2.07	0.38
Pskovskaia oblast	723	490	-233	-32.27	0.61	0.39	-0.22
Rostovskaia oblast	493	595	102	20.69	2.11	2.40	0.29
Riazanskaia oblast	570	660	90	15.85	0.76	0.83	0.07
Saratovskaia oblast	543	519	-24	-4.39	1.45	1.31	-0.14
Sakhalinskaia oblast	1,180	902	-278	-23.56	0.83	0.60	-0.23
Sverdlovskaia oblast	630	787	157	24.92	2.95	3.48	0.53
Smolenskaia oblast	626	645	19	3.04	0.72	0.70	-0.02
Tambov oblast	592	528	-64	-10.77	0.78	0.65	-0.12
Tomskaia oblast	797	654	-144	-18.00	0.79	0.61	-0.18
Tul'skaia oblast	524	636	112	21.39	0.97	1.11	0.14
Tyumenskaia oblast	381	411	30	7.78	1.17	1.19	0.02
Ulianovskaia oblast	583	548	-36	-6.10	0.81	0.72	-0.09
Cheliabinskaia oblast	579	696	118	20.31	2.08	2.36	0.28
Chitinskaia oblast	667	407	-260	-39.04	0.91	0.52	-0.39
Iaroslavskaia oblast	532	764	233	43.75	0.78	1.05	0.28
St. Petersburg	828	1,008	180	21.73	4.12	4.73	0.61
Moscow City	1,132	1,398	266	23.47	10.07	11.73	1.66
Republic of Adygeya	—	—	—	—	0.26	0.21	-0.05
Republic of Altai	—	—	—	—	0.14	0.05	-0.09
Evreyskaya AO	—	—	—	—	0.21	0.10	-0.11
Karachai-Cherkess Republic	—	—	—	—	0.24	0.12	-0.12
Republic of Khakasia	—	—	—	—	0.37	0.42	0.04
Aginskii-Buryatskii AO	—	—	—	—	0.06	0.02	-0.04
Komi-Permyatskaia AO	—	—	—	—	0.11	0.05	-0.07
Koriakii AO	—	—	—	—	0.03	0.03	0.00
Nenetskii AO	—	—	—	—	0.03	0.02	-0.01
Taimyrskii (Dolgano-Nenetskii)	—	—	—	—	0.06	0.03	-0.04
Ust'-Ordynskii-Buryatskii AO	—	—	—	—	0.06	0.03	-0.04
Khanty-Mansiiskii AO	—	—	—	—	1.59	2.55	0.96
Chukotskii AO	—	—	—	—	0.26	0.11	-0.15
Evenkiiskii AR	—	—	—	—	0.03	0.01	-0.02
Yamal-Nenets AO	—	—	—	—	0.91	1.43	0.52
Arkhangelskaia oblast	682	565	-117	-17.21	1.06	0.83	-0.23

— Not available.
AR Autonomous republic.
AO Autonomous okrug.
Source: Author's calculations based on data provided by the Ministry of Finance of the Russian Federation, 1992.

effects" dominate and the big "winners" include large cities and higher-income oblasts, such as Moscow and St. Petersburg.

All this probably means that the change to tax assignment as proposed in the Basic Principles would so shock the present system that there would likely be calls for further adjustments. There would be no relationship between revenues accruing to an oblast and its expenditure needs. Compensating transfers, and perhaps a system of horizontal transfers, would be needed. Moreover, the Basic Principles would be less equalizing and would transfer resources to higher-income regions.

On the other hand, any change away from "ad hocery" would give subnational governments some budgetary certainty and would therefore allow improvements in fiscal planning. Moreover, the Basic Principles and tax assignment are more transparent than the transitional system with respect to which revenues belong to federal and which to subnational government, so its appeal in present-day Russia is understandable.

The Basic Principles may now be a dead issue, but the idea of tax assignment is not. This analysis, based on early 1992 data and on a plan that was not feasible for implementation, nevertheless can provide some basis for thinking through the pitfalls associated with tax assignment and the kind

Table 5.10 Summary of illustrative revenue impact, Basic Principles, Russian Federation, first quarter 1992

| | Gain (loss) from change | | |
Revenue impact	Difference per capita	As a percentage of current revenue	As a percentage of total shared taxes
Median revenue change (in rubles)	(29)	(4.29)	
Number of oblasts with a revenue reduction	41	41	62
Median revenue loss (in rubles)	(118)	(20)	(0.15)
Number of oblasts with a revenue increase	28	28	27
Median revenue gain (in rubles)	139	18	0.29

Note: Parentheses indicate negative values.
Source: Author's calculations.

Table 5.11 Determinants of differences in per capita revenues, by oblast, under transitional system and Basic Principles, Russian Federation

Dependent variable	Constant	Per capita value of gross industrial output	Average wage	Percentage of population living in urban areas	Population	Coefficient of determination	N
Difference in per capita revenues[a]	371.69 (4.08)	-0.11 (5.77)	1.43 (6.86)	-4.31 (-2.41)	-0.03 (-2.23)	0.68	64

Note: OLS regressions. t-statistics are shown in parentheses below the regression coefficients.
a. Difference in per capita revenues is taken from table 5.9, third column.
Source: Author's calculations.

of analysis that is necessary to support the development of a new inter-governmental financing system.

Options for further reform

The analysis above suggests that both the tax assignment model of the Basic Principles and the continuation of the present negotiated revenue-sharing system have weaknesses with respect to administration, macroeconomic consequences, revenue adequacy, revenue mobilization, and the granting of subnational autonomy. There are also some problems with a pure system of tax assignment that are peculiar to, and that may be fatal for, Russia. First, there are only three major taxes that can be assigned (VAT and the personal and corporate income taxes), and there are major pitfalls in earmarking any of these fully to any one level of government (see below). Moreover, a strict system of assignment may not fit the Russian system of tax administration because responsibility for tax collection rests with the decentralized State Tax Service offices, not an integrated federal government tax administration. The tax assignment of the Basic Principles would ask the State Tax Service to collect personal income tax, corporate income tax, and some minor local taxes (which accrue to subnational government) as efficiently as it collects VAT (which accrues to central government).

The choice of taxes for assignment

Have the right taxes been assigned to federal and subnational governments? Under the Basic Principles the corporate and personal income taxes will become revenue sources for oblasts, cities, and rayons. VAT will be assigned to the federal government.

The assignment of VAT. Assigning VAT to subnational governments is inappropriate. It is an origin tax, meaning that the tax is applied at the point of production, not the point of sale.[10] Thus, some oblasts would see their revenue bases enhanced (or compromised), depending on the stage of the production process in which their enterprises are specialized: whether, for instance, they import raw materials. Those oblasts heavy in export industries could also have a weak base because exports are zero-rated under Russia's VAT. Moreover, it could (and probably would) be disastrous if subnational governments were allowed to make discretionary changes in VAT rates and bases.

Any discretionary changes to the VAT by the federal government also could be a problem and affect the revenue yield of oblasts. Such changes are in fact contemplated as a part of the general and ongoing tax reforms in

Russia. These would have important revenue effects for different regions in different ways, depending on their economic structures. Thus, assigning VAT to subnational governments would likely cause them much revenue uncertainty.

The assignment of corporate income tax. Assigning corporate income tax to subnational governments raises major concerns about resource allocation. Income taxes in Russia come mostly from enterprises, and the regulation of enterprises is the responsibility of oblast, city, and rayon governments. Assigning corporate income tax subnationally is therefore likely to lead to substantial differentiation in enterprise taxation. While such differentiation exists in many industrial countries (such as the United States), it may be especially damaging in Russia at the present time. Differentiating the corporate income tax will not help to establish the common market desired across Russia and could create a tax jungle. It may influence enterprise location in ways that are inconsistent with national policy, and it may cause enterprise location decisions to be tax-driven. Tax competition has its virtues, but in present-day Russia (where there are substantial barriers to entry and distorted prices, as well as price decontrol and privatization) such competition may not be desirable.

Most countries with subnational corporate taxes have also had to address the issue of how to prorate revenues when the company operates in more than one jurisdiction. As Russian enterprises enter the market system, multiplant firms (operating in different oblasts and without separate accounts) will be more common. Subnational company taxes are applied in other countries, but they have more of a tradition of local governance and more experience in the administration of the complexities. Russia can do without such complications at the present time.

The assignment of the corporate income tax is, however, still a problem if the rate and base are decided centrally. As with VAT, subnational revenues may be vulnerable to discretionary changes by the central government. If the federal government changes the corporate income tax, subnational governments could face a revenue cut (or windfall) that bears no relation to changes in their expenditure needs. In addition, the enterprise income tax base is very sensitive to changes in federal industrial policy, and changes in such policies would put subnational revenues at risk. For example, central decisions (about, for example, wage rates, commodity and input prices, foreign exchange restrictions, and interest rates) could lead to direct reductions or increases in subnational government revenues, and the impacts could vary greatly across oblasts. This may be especially important in a transition economy, where input and output prices are still being liberalized and large-scale privatization is ongoing.

Moreover, the profits of many companies tend to be cyclical, and so are taxes on those profits. Assigning more stable revenues to the subnational government sector is preferable, if only because many essential services (health and education) are financed and delivered locally. Spending on these services should be supported by stable revenues. Finally, a subnational corporate tax is likely to be highly counterequalizing and would mean a greater need for some mechanism, such as grants, to offset this. In the much longer run, it may be feasible to consider some form of subnational corporation tax.

The assignment of personal income tax. The personal income tax is probably the best candidate for assignment to oblasts (the law "shares" it 100 percent with oblasts). Workers are more or less immobile (for the time being), and there is little taxable income outside wages and salaries. However, assigning personal income tax to the subnational level is inherently counterequalizing. As wages are liberalized, the tax base will grow faster in some areas than in others and the revenue disparity will widen. It is likely, too, that many low-income workers will ultimately be outside the tax net. As Russia moves more fully to a market economy, there will also be more cyclical instability in the tax. On the other hand the personal income tax is inherently elastic and, in a market economy, will grow in line with inflation and real income.

As in the case of VAT and corporate income tax, subnational revenues are vulnerable to discretionary changes in personal income tax by federal government. Personal income tax is an important instrument of social and macroeconomic policy in many countries and its rate and base can change often. Such changes are almost certain to occur in Russia, with a big impact on subnational government revenues.

One of the major problems with subnational assignment of personal income tax has to do with the intraoblast distribution of revenues. At present, personal income tax is distributed among subnational governments according to place of work. In the case of workers who commute this seems unfair because the rayon of *residence* provides basic services (health, education) to the workers but is not compensated.

Tax assignment and tax sharing: pros and cons

Much depends on *which* taxes are chosen for assignment to local government. There is typically little debate that property taxes and land tax, vehicle taxes, and some excises, business licenses, and fees are appropriately assigned to subnational governments. The discussion above suggests that of Russia's major taxes—VAT, corporate tax, natural resource tax, and personal income tax—only the personal income tax would make a good candidate for assignment. More generally, despite the appeal of transparency—each tax "belongs" to one level of government—the disadvantages of a system such as the Basic Principles, which relies wholly on tax assignment, seem overwhelming.

Given the many shocks, both external and internal, now besetting Russia's economy, the time is not right for another radical change. The fact that the Basic Principles Law was never implemented (and that the Law on the Budgetary Rights of Local Self-Governments, passed only in June 1993, codifies a modified sharing of major taxes and assignment of minor ones) hints at the problems and suggests that Russian policymakers are also searching for a new approach. Why is complete reliance on assignment of Russia's major taxes unwise in present-day Russia? First, the Basic Principles assign corporate income tax and personal income tax revenues to the subnational level but leave the authority to adjust the rate and base of each tax with the central government. The result is that all tax policy changes made by the central government—whether for macroeconomic or social policy reasons—could make the revenue position of subnational governments vulnerable. The recent changes in the VAT and personal income tax, which took effect in early 1993, are examples of policy changes that had critical and unintended impacts on subnational revenues.

Second, there is no necessary correspondence between the expenditure needs of a subnational government and the size of its tax base under this particular tax assignment system. The Basic Principles do not link resources with expenditure assignment, nor is there provision for a grant or subvention system to offset disparities.

Third, the corporate income tax and personal income tax would give subnational governments an unstable revenue base. More generally, the concern here is the unstable and unpredictable nature of these individual revenue sources and what this means for subnational and central governments in the transition. As the results of the first quarter of 1992 show, one tax (VAT) significantly underperformed, while two taxes (the personal and enterprise income taxes) overshot revenue estimates by substantial margins. (While these taxes have performed differently in subsequent periods, the basic point—revenue volatility—remains.) The experience of Hungary, Poland, and other Eastern European countries suggests that this volatility of tax bases and revenues is not the exception but the rule in economies in transition. A system that pools revenues (the volatility of the pool will be less than that of individual taxes) and then shares them, or that shares the major taxes, will avoid this. In addition, the State Tax Service might not collect federal and subnational taxes with the same level of efficiency.

Finally, enough taxes will have to be assigned to bring about revenue-expenditure correspondence, based on the oblasts' expenditure responsibilities. Given the magnitude of their expenditure responsibilities, oblasts will need access to about half of all revenue collections—that is, access to more than just one major revenue source—and there are only four taxes to choose from: VAT, corporate tax, personal income tax, and perhaps excises. It is not clear that the federal budget would be willing (or should be willing) to part in full with most of these revenues. In fact, it is likely that it would not, as its revenue needs are such that giving away a major tax—in toto—may not be an option. More generally, the overwhelming importance of macroeconomic stabilization in Russia today argues for protecting the integrity of the federal budget, and against depriving the center of major tax sources for the time being. Finally, giving oblasts rate-setting autonomy on some of these taxes is not easily workable in the case of VAT.

Most important is that the timing of this change might not be right: this major reform would be introduced at a time when there is an ongoing process of price liberalization and privatization and when the political and constitutional structure of the Federation and the government is not yet settled. The time may not be right to introduce fixity—in fiscal regimes—until a larger political change takes place.

In sum, the shift to a pure assignment system, as proposed in the Basic Principles, would provide few of the advantages normally ascribed to this approach. In particular, because no subnational rate or base setting is proposed in the Basic Principles, there really would be no true subnational component of the personal income tax, corporate income tax, or VAT. Transparency, in this case, means only that revenue sharing is less ad hoc. But "ad hocery" can be removed as easily under a shared as under an assignment system. Continuation of an (improved) tax-sharing-cum-grant system—building on the Law on the Budgetary Rights of Local Self-Governments—is the best path for providing the bulk of oblast finances over the next few years. In addition, there may be room for assignment of some taxes to Russia's oblasts, as discussed below.

Reforming the revenue-sharing system

The flaws in the present system might be sufficient for the Russian government to reconsider introducing reforms. If so, a new system of intergovernmental finance is needed. Where to begin? First, by identifying and prioritizing the objectives of the government. The determination of these priorities is a political decision. It is possible, however, to outline various objectives and suggest intergovernmental financing schemes that meet them. Most countries would have the following objectives:
- Correspondence between expenditures necessary to finance a minimum level of services and revenue assigned to the subnational governments.

- Equalization to offset fiscal capacity differences or to reflect differences in expenditure needs.
- Incentives for increased subnational revenue mobilization.
- Involvement of the local population in subnational budget decisions and increased accountability of subnational officials to their constituents.
- Minimization of the cost of administering the system.
- Gains in public acceptance and confidence through a system that is transparent, objective, and understandable.

One option for reform is an intergovernmental financing system that retains many of the good features of the present one, but attempts to remove weaker ones as well as ambiguities. The system would have four dimensions. First, the national revenue pie would be notionally divided between the federal and subnational governments based on their respective expenditure assignments. As for the oblast revenue portion, some would come (as now) by way of shared taxes, allocated on a derivation basis; the remaining oblast revenues would be distributed more or less as a grant, according to a transparent and fixed formula. In addition, oblasts would have some assigned local taxes and surcharges. A separate feature might be specific regimes to deal with the problems of ethnic minorities, natural resource–generating regions, and other special cases (chapters 6 and 7).

The subnational share. All revenues from the four major federal taxes would be notionally considered as a common pool. The central and subnational shares would be determined according to pre-agreed expenditure assignments. The Ministry of Finance's 1992 and 1993 budget estimates imply that about 55 percent of the national fiscal resources would have been allocated to the federal government and 45 percent to the subnational governments. Such clarity and transparency in establishing the size of the subnational pool are preferable to ad hoc decisions by the Ministry of Finance. They allow subnational governments to budget and plan.

Sharing on a derivation basis. Part of the oblasts' portion of the national revenue pool would be shared, as at present, according to derivation (or origin). That is, oblasts where taxes are collected would receive a share (which could range from 0 to 100 percent) of the taxes raised in their jurisdiction. (It should be noted that where the tax-sharing rate is 100 percent some would say that the distinction between tax sharing and tax assignment is to some extent semantic and relates only to rate-setting authority.) The sharing rate would be uniform for all oblasts and fixed for an agreed period. The rule could be simple. For example, suppose it were decided that half of subnational revenues should flow to them on a derivation basis. A portion of each major tax collected would be retained by the oblasts, with these proportions calculated to exhaust, in aggregate, the derivation-shared portion. The (uniform) tax shares (which might be different for different taxes) should be fixed for three to five years. The more the revenues that come to subnational governments by way of derivation-based sharing, the more the resources that will be channeled into (better-off) regions that have a larger taxable base.

This derivation-sharing aspect of the proposal is easily understood since it is similar in concept to the existing system. It differs only in that sharing rates are uniform and that only a portion of oblasts' revenue needs would be met this way. Moreover, it is not costly to administer and monitor. And as long as the retained shares do not differ too much by tax, it does not give the State Tax Service an incentive to collect one tax more efficiently than another. It would reward oblasts that are successful in attracting and promoting industry, and (with uniform sharing rates across oblasts) it would remove the negotiation and bargaining in today's sharing system. It would also provide subnational governments with a more certain flow of revenue and promote efficient budget planning. One possible drawback is that since taxes are assigned to the jurisdiction where they are collected, higher-income territories will receive more. This will be counterequalizing and will require an equalizing ("grant") component in the distribution formula (see below).

Another issue is that VAT may not easily lend itself to derivation sharing as the Russian economy changes in the next few years because oblasts with industries with a high value added will be at an advantage. This problem can be solved by removing VAT from the derivation-sharing system. The tradeoff is that eliminating VAT from the subnationals' revenue pool would make the derivation-sharing revenue pool more vulnerable to the business cycle (VAT revenues are relatively more stable than income taxes), and it would mean that personal income tax and corporate income tax sharing rates would have to be set higher, possibly increasing the State Tax Service incentive problem. That being said, the revenues for derivation sharing could consist of these two or three taxes, and some of the VAT could be used for the equalization-sharing portion (see below).

A derivation-shared (or locally assigned) corporate income tax will also eventually have to be allocated among jurisdictions for enterprises with branch operations. This is not yet a major problem because in Russia there are relatively few enterprises operating in more than one oblast. But the government must begin planning for an economy where these are commonplace. The solution will inevitably require a more complex tax system, yet the tax administration is already overburdened. Adjustments will also need to be made for the present assignment of all personal income tax revenues to the rayon of employment, and none to the rayon of residence.

Sharing through a transfer formula. If it is decided that VAT does not lend itself to derivation-based sharing, an appropriate portion of it could go into the revenue pool designed for equalization (which would also contain some fraction of other major national taxes). This part of the subnational revenue pool would be allocated using an equalizing transfer formula that explicitly takes into account expenditure needs and tax capacity. This would play the role of the "grant" in most revenue-sharing systems. The distribution formula would provide sufficient funds for all subnational governments to provide "minimum" levels of service (which are far from being defined in Russia). Such a formula-based sharing system, or grant, also makes receipts for subnational governments more certain, and therefore makes planning more efficient. If equalization is desired, distributions via the equalization formula can be designed to direct resources toward oblasts with low fiscal capacities or high levels of need or both. The more of the subnational revenue share that is allocated via the formula grant component (and the less via derivation), the more equalizing the system could be (assuming the formula is equalizing).

What indicators should be included in the formula? In most countries using this approach, the formula consists of (1) an estimate of expenditure needs; (2) an assessment of revenues to finance these needs; and (3) a rule about how much of the remaining gap is to be filled, that is, how far the equalization is to go. The formula typically looks something like this: *grant* equals *expenditure need* minus *revenue capacity at a constant level of tax effort.* The most difficult part is defining expenditure needs for each jurisdiction. As outlined earlier in this chapter, the overriding concern in designing such a formula for Russia today should probably be simplicity. Population-based indicators or physical indicators (number of students, hospital beds) have the advantage of being both simple and equalizing in their effect. But once expenditure needs and revenue capacity are estimated, the formula-based distribution would be allocated across oblasts, as would any transfers to fill (or partially make up) the estimated shortfall.

Accommodating special regions and special demands within a formula. The design of fiscal federalism is made more complex in Russia because some territories are demanding greater political and fiscal autonomy, greater devolution of responsibility for expenditures, and special tax regimes. These include Russia's ethnic oblasts and republics, which claim such rights based on their different culture and history. They also include areas rich in natural resources, which view themselves as entitled to a share in what they perceive as their heritage (chapter 6). Finally, some well-developed regions with good growth potential feel they are being held back by the current fiscal system, which appears to them to redistribute resources to the poor.

Oblasts in each of these groups have sought out special fiscal treatment and special regimes, often unilaterally (chapter 7). Once given, these are hard to "claw back." So far, Russia has responded to these demands in an ad hoc and piecemeal manner.

Demands for special treatment could be addressed through the formula, with any number of specific factors and any choice of weights built into the design of the formula. For example, the politically sensitive state of Punjab in India receives additional funding through a component of the sharing formula that recognizes the difficulty of being a border state. Also, as part of India's grant formula, "backward" areas are assigned a special weight that gives them extra compensation. Australia incorporates the special needs of the Northern Territories into the expenditure-needs equation. Similarly in Russia, a high concentration of ethnic minorities could be assigned a weight in the formula-based pool, in line with the arguably greater needs of ethnic areas. Areas rich in natural resources, but which have suffered underdevelopment and environmental degradation, could also be targeted in an objective way through a formula.

The idea of meeting special needs through a formula is appealing for several reasons. While the formula is uniform for all oblasts, its component parts permit special treatment of certain areas where deemed appropriate by policymakers. It can appease disgruntled groups by incorporating special circumstances in the grant formula while maintaining the transparency necessary to prevent a sense of injustice. Chapter 7 provides more discussion of this approach in other countries and its relevance for Russia.

Derivation sharing and formulas: some issues. How large should the derivation and formula portions be? Because some equalization is appropriate, a sizable formula-based component may be needed, especially if there is a national consensus that service provision should not differ much across oblasts. And if responsibility for the social safety net is passed to subnational governments, there may be more of a case for equalization. (For example, the current deterioration of Russia's health system, with numerous outbreaks of communicable diseases in 1993, suggests that poor, underfunded oblasts may no longer be able to provide basic health infrastructure to an acceptable standard.) But there are tradeoffs, as noted earlier. At this time in Russia's history the intergovernmental fiscal system should probably give more weight to the initiatives and fiscal energies of the better-off areas, in the interest of more rapid economic growth. This could be achieved by allocating more revenues on a derivation basis. It could also be supported by giving oblasts and larger cities powers to set some tax rates, possibly through surcharges (described below).

The scope for tax assignment: enhanced subnational taxes

Until subnational governments make tax as well as spending decisions, they will not be fully accountable to local taxpayers. Moreover, local populations should have the opportunity to pay more taxes if they want better services. Both birds can be killed with the same stone—enhanced subnational taxes, which in effect assign a subset of taxes to subnational governments. There are three subnational taxes that Russia could reasonably assign oblast and rayon governments at the present time and that could yield significant revenues at the margin:

- A surcharge on personal income tax, up to a federally prescribed limit
- A tax on land values in urban areas
- A tax on motor vehicles.

All have the advantage of falling only on local citizens (thereby increasing accountability of local officials). And they might also have a lower compliance cost and reap more revenue than the twenty-one local taxes proposed in the Basic Principles or the Law on Budgetary Rights. The disadvantages are that property and vehicle taxes would require some investment in setting up an administration; and both would be collected, in the near term at least, by the State Tax Service, which would not share in revenues.

Tax-base sharing (that is, surcharges) gives subnational governments some power to set tax rates through, say, a surtax on the national personal income tax or, less desirably, the enterprise income tax. This surtax would allow oblast and local governments to undertake some incremental spending, and it would make them more accountable to their constituents, since the surtax would be paid only by citizens of that oblast, who would want to know what they are paying for. A surtax on the personal income tax could easily be implemented through the State Tax Service and the added administrative burden imposed would be small. Each year the oblast would establish the rate for the following year. Subnational tax offices would apply it (together with the federal tax rate) to the income tax base. The amounts collected would then be remitted to central and subnational government in the usual way.

VAT should not be surtaxed. An oblast specializing in intermediate goods sold mostly outside the oblast would almost certainly prefer to "export" taxes to other oblasts (putting on high surcharges) rather than to tax its own citizens. A true *destination* VAT (levied at the point of sale) would require some adjustment for taxes on "imported" goods, as is now the case in the European Union (EU). However, it is doubtful that subnational governments would wish to give credit for "foreign" import taxes on purchases from suppliers in other oblasts. In Brazil, where VAT is a provincial tax, there are huge problems in administration, collection, and fairness, even though federal government sets maximum rates. It is doubtful that a regional VAT could operate much more satisfactorily in Russia.[11]

Candidates for tax assignment in the longer run. In many countries excise taxes and retail sales taxes are thought to be good local taxes. In Russia in the near term excise taxes (those on oil and liquor are the most important ones) would not make good local taxes because both are collected at the point of production (not sale) and produced in only a small number of oblasts, and revenues would therefore accrue very unevenly. Moreover, since both goods are exported, either domestically or internationally, their assignment to the oblast level would violate the principles of a good local tax. However, as these excisable goods become more widely produced, they are good candidates for assignment to subnational governments. Retail sales taxes do not exist at present in Russia, and none are planned. Were they to come into existence, they could in principle be oblast taxes, although coordination with VAT would be necessary and possibly problematic. (Canada has a national VAT and regional sales taxes, for example.)

Increasing revenues from local property, land, vehicle, and other taxes at the subnational level in Russia is crucial because other sources of revenue are shrinking. The local tax base is weak. Many subnational governments still receive revenues from the profits of enterprises, including some new joint ventures. With privatization, they may also receive revenues from enterprise sales. But both will decline (and eventually disappear), since privatization will leave all earnings in private hands. Most cities have huge amounts of taxable real estate (so a property tax has a broad base), but most subnational governments do not raise much from the tax. This is because valuations are out of date and have been eroded by inflation. Moreover, cadastral surveys and registration are poor. So, too, are collection and enforcement, and thus arrears are high.

Currently assigned local taxes. The Basic Principles of Taxation prescribes a long list of taxes assigned purely to subnational government. Except for land and property taxes, the time may not be right to push ahead with these twenty-one local taxes. They are unlikely to raise much revenue, even in the best of circumstances. They will also strain the collection capacity of the State Tax Service. And some of these taxes have high compliance costs that slow the workings of the economy. Moreover, they are likely to divert the attention of policymakers from more productive potential sources of revenue, such as surcharges, tax-base sharing, and increased user charges.

The flexible sharing framework
and its advantages in present-day Russia

The four-dimensional structure outlined above provides a flexible framework for Russia's intergovernmental finances. It permits using a combination of strategies that can change over time. First, it is compatible with shifts in expenditure responsibilities between the federal and subnational governments: if additional expenditures are shifted downstairs, the subnational portion of national revenues can be increased. Second, it is compatible with the changing emphasis on growth versus equalization over time: if greater emphasis on equalization is desired at some later stage, the portion of subnational revenues distributed on a formula grant basis can be made larger; if the decision is made to allow the better-off areas to reap the benefits of their larger fiscal capacities, the derivation sharing could be enlarged. The choice of "how much equalization" is essentially a political judgment, made differently in different countries, and is changeable over time. Third, by assigning a more robust set of taxes (surcharges and land and property taxes) to subnational governments and giving them greater rate-setting discretion on their assigned taxes, the system is also compatible with increased local fiscal discretion and autonomy.

Finally, it is compatible with regional diversity. As will be argued in chapter 7, the special needs (or demands) of Russia's regions can be better met via a formula-based approach that takes their needs into account than via the present ad hoc approach to responding to their demands. More generally, there would be no need for special regimes that could become very risky.

Such an intergovernmental system, if it is seen to be based on fair criteria and to be equitable, can defuse other difficult resource allocation issues—such as the sharing of revenues from natural resources and the demands for fiscal autonomy by some oblasts. A transparent and objectively managed system means that oblasts need not hold on to these few bargaining chips. In sum, at a time when nation building is paramount, a well-designed intergovernmental fiscal system is essential.

Designing the new system: concrete requirements

Further development and quantification of any options for redesigning Russia's system of intergovernmental relations will require detailed empirical work. The design (and later the monitoring of the performance) of the new system of intergovernmental relations will be a long-term, data-intensive exercise. But the data required are not readily available at present. For example, investment data for Russia's oblasts have not been published since 1975. Although a formidable task, it should be a priority for the central government, the oblasts, and the League of Russian Cities to begin developing data bases, such as a "census of governments." These should include tax collection and tax-base statistics, expenditure composition and expenditure-needs measures, socioeconomic characteristics of the population, and the stock of physical infrastructure and its state of maintenance. Subnational governments' poor record in data collection and the lack of tradition in this area point to a need for bold action at the highest level of government.

To complete the design of the new system, there has to be detailed accounting of the costs to subnational governments of the newly transferred responsibilities, as well as for traditional services. Without a rigorous effort on this front, the adequacy of subnational revenue needs will simply remain a matter of conjectural discussions. Similarly, the design of a system of intergovernmental transfers, with the objective of equalizing opportunities across oblasts, will require accurate information on expenditure needs, tax bases, and subnational tax effort. In contrast to Russia most industrial countries have standardized tax data that are regularly used for policy and research purposes.

Technical assistance could assist Russia in this complex area. This would focus both on the data-gathering side and on developing and designing the complex simulations that go into any revenue estimation model or expenditure system. This is not likely to be a quick or easy exercise. China has been modeling its revenue-sharing system (with foreign assistance) since 1988. The data collection and analysis underlying the development of Hungary's (much simpler) formula grant system took an initial two years of intensive preparatory work, and continued revisions to the system are still ongoing two years later. In Russia, while work on both data collection and modeling can and should begin, the important first step—making concrete assignments of expenditures—has yet to be taken. Thus, any "quick estimates" are likely to be as flawed as the Basic Principles. The need for the concrete exercise to begin soon cannot be overstated.

Additional dimensions of the intergovernmental framework

In addition to the major task of determining the adequate oblast revenue base, complex questions also arise with respect to tax administration (see below) and the special needs of Russia's large cities. Hitherto, little mention has been made of user charges, often thought to be the mainstay of local finances. Their role in Russia clearly needs to be expanded (as outlined below), but doing so will not be without problems.

Tax administration responsibilities

The tax assignment of the Basic Principles requires the State Tax Service to collect both taxes that accrue to subnational governments and minor local taxes (from which the central government derives no revenue) with the same efficiency as it collects taxes accruing to central government. A reasonable fear is that since local-level State Tax Service offices have scarce resources, they might devote these more heavily to collection of central taxes.

A switch to separate subnational and central tax administrations would, however, be ill-advised at the present time. Russia's scarcity of administrative resources makes it hard to argue for a separate tax service in each of the eighty-nine oblasts and 2,000-plus rayons. Rather, administrative constraints argue strongly for a continuation (and significant strengthening) of the single State Tax Service. Even so, government should move to eliminate the implicit "dual leadership" of the State Tax Service. This could be done by rotating top officials, as in many other countries; by federal assumption of financing responsibility for all the fringe benefits and noncash compensation of State Tax Service officials; and by providing office arrangements and the like. The elimination of this dual loyalty is essential, since the State Tax Service is taking on a larger role in collecting and remitting taxes to the central government. In Tyumenskaia oblast, for example, the State Tax Service has taken on the previous role of commercial banks in remitting taxes to the federal budget; conflicting loyalties are sure to create additional difficulties.

Over the longer run one might envisage some local collection and administration of taxes such as the property and vehicle taxes. However, international practice is mixed here also. In Canada and Australia provincial governments are responsible for property valuation and administration. In Germany and New Zealand valuation is national and rate setting and administration local. In the United States both rate setting and valuation are undertaken locally in most states.

Fiscal discretion for large cities

Special treatment could be given to large cities in the Russian system. In Russia, as in most countries, big cities have a greater taxable capacity—and more complex (and, it can be argued, expensive) spending needs. They could be given additional taxing powers (a bigger surcharge on central taxes, for instance); special support in implementing the property tax; or the right to set prices (user charges) for municipal services. Special investments could be made in better tax administration for big cities, and in the future these cities could be accorded greater borrowing powers. In Russia such special treatment could be given to all oblast seats, or other large industrial centers, where expenditure needs are high and where there is a willingness to tax citizens to provide better services.

User charges

Russia has not made much use of fees or user charges for services provided by subnational governments or subnationally owned utilities and enterprises. In 1990 nontax revenues, such as charges, fees, and fines, accounted for about 3 percent of their total revenues. Little seems to have changed since then on this score. For both industry and households, much greater use should be made of user charges (transport fees, charges for water, gas, and the like). Sometimes, weak accounting leads to underpricing of these services and needs to be strengthened. Sometimes, central government sets ceilings on any such fees or prices, and its record is less than impressive. The ceiling on urban transport fees, for instance, was recently raised by the Ministry of Finance from 10 kopecks (the original 1956 price) to 50 kopecks—only about 30 percent of operating costs in early 1992. Many housing rents are still at nominal levels (set in 1928) of 13 kopecks per square meter, although recent law allows subnational governments to fix rents at any level. It would be more appropriate to allow subnational governments to set rents at cost-recovery levels, since fiscal autonomy is an objective.

However, the extraordinarily low level of most such charges at present means that a move toward greater cost recovery (for example, through long-run marginal cost price setting in the case of utilities) could imply significant price increases. (In one Eastern European country it was estimated that cost-recovery electric power rates would absorb 40 percent of household disposable income, assuming no change in power demand.) Clearly, the phasing of changes in such prices and their structure (lifeline rates and the like) requires careful thought. Another approach might be to emphasize allocative efficiency by raising prices to appropriate levels and rebating a lump sum to consumers to partly offset the impact on household incomes (although this would compromise revenues [Bird and Wallich 1993]).

Intraoblast fiscal relations: oblasts and their rayons

The oblast soviet is responsible for the allocation of financial resources among its rayons and municipalities. It determines the share of taxes retained by each, and it may allocate extra subsidies, thus determining spending by each subnational government.

There are some constraints, however:

- Tax rates and tax bases are fixed by the center and may not be adjusted.
- Some minor taxes and charges are prescribed as fully local.
- A national law, passed in April 1992, prescribes revenue sharing from oil and specifically mandates the local (rayon) share to be 30 percent for oil and 50 percent for nonhydrocarbon minerals (chapter 6).

Should the federal government allow oblasts to have full control of and responsibility for all affairs within the oblast? There are advantages. First, it gets the central government out of the business of having to make fiscal decisions concerning the revenue needs of thousands of subnational governments. Second, it makes the oblast soviet more accountable to the local population. Third, it is clearly a step toward fiscal decentralization, bringing government decisions closer to the people. However, there also are some problems raised by this approach.

Issues and problems in oblast-rayon finances

Designing a system of intraoblast fiscal relations will require coming to grips with a number of important issues, notably, the fiscal disparities *within* oblasts, which are, some argue, greater than those between oblasts. How much revenue autonomy, and which revenue sources, should be accorded to oblasts are also important questions.

Disparities among oblasts. There are wide variations in economic well-being and fiscal capacity within each oblast. This means that each oblast must make difficult decisions about fiscal equalization. The oblast soviet cannot simply extend the central-oblast revenue-sharing scheme, which is based on the derivation principle, because that would exacerbate the economic disparities among the rayon governments. For example, within Riazanskaia oblast (which has thirteen rayons and two cities) per capita spending in the highest-spending locality was more than three times that in the lowest. Per capita expenditures were 50 to 100 percent greater in the cities of Riazan (the oblast capital) and Skopin than the average of all of Riazanskaia's rayons.

The oblast government must also allocate to itself some retained revenues. This leads to the enactment of equalization features in the revenue-sharing system by the oblast soviet but also raises tensions with the better-off local governments—particularly the urban centers, which feel they are unduly discriminated against to underwrite equalization. The situation is made more complex by the great public servicing needs in the urban areas. At present at least some oblast governments have opted to use uniform-rate tax sharing (which is counterequalizing) along with equalizing subventions (box 5.1).

Box 5.1 Intraoblast revenue sharing

Based on field work in Tyumenskaia, Nizhniy Novgorod, Riazanskaia, and Moscow oblasts and in Khanty-Mansiiskii okrug, it appears that oblast governments vary widely in how they allocate revenues among local governments. These oblasts are similar, however, in that all use a derivation principle as the primary instruments of revenue sharing.

After the central government changed its revenue-sharing program on VAT to a flat 20 percent and increased the corporate income tax locally retained share from 15 to 19 points on the 32 percent rate, all the oblasts visited in the course of field work also adjusted the oblast-rayon sharing formulas. All three of the oblasts visited after the change switched to uniform-percentage sharing for all local governments. These shared taxes were supplemented with various types of subventions. The examples in the table below give some idea of the variety in sharing arrangements as of July 1992.

Revenue sharing in three oblasts, Russian Federation, July 1992
(percentage of revenues accruing to each level)

	Moscow oblast		Tyumenskaia oblast		Khanty-Mansiiskii okrug	
Tax	Rayon	Oblast	Rayon	Oblast	Rayon	Okrug
Personal income tax	100	0	100	0	92.5	7.5
Corporate income tax	63	37	74	26	53	47.
Value-added tax	0	100	75	25	75	25

Source: Ministry of Finance of the Russian Federation.

Revenue-raising efforts. A second, and closely related, problem is that the need to equalize may dampen efforts to increase the rate of revenue mobilization. The State Tax Service staff is closely linked with the subnational governments (rayon and cities), and assessment and collection efforts may be less successful if the local community sees that it will not receive an adequate return from its increased revenue effort.

Both of these issues point to a major underlying concern—that oblast soviet decisions may not reinforce central government economic policy. An example: suppose that the central government decided to base its economic strategy for the next ten years on the development of urban centers and on the development of industries that require skilled labor and call for infrastructure at a certain level of provision. Under the present system the central government could not easily implement this strategy. The oblast soviet could still choose to allocate resources away from urban areas (toward rural areas) and could choose whatever focus on education it wanted. Thus, in truly decentralized systems the central government loses control over the implementation of national programs.

Planning certainty. Oblast and other subnational governments need to know their revenue flow with enough certainty to plan budgets. The present revenue-sharing system changed markedly and frequently in 1992, and efficient fiscal planning has been nigh impossible. And because the tax sharing is done on a derivation basis, the oblast soviets have also changed the intraoblast fiscal arrangements each quarter.

Subnational autonomy. Even leaving decisions on fiscal distribution to the oblast soviet is not enough for those who are the strongest advocates of fiscal decentralization. They would argue in favor of giving more autonomy to local (rayon and municipal) soviets. After all, the oblast may have millions in population, and the oblast soviet is far removed from the needs of the local populations. The local soviets are closer to their people and problems. Thus far, the lowest-level soviets have not been given much say in determining their local budgets.

Reform possibilities for oblast finances

The government is at a crossroads in intraoblast relations. The Basic Principles Law is ambiguous and so is the Law on Budgetary Rights. At present, revenue allocation choices rest with the oblasts, and some have opted to redistribute substantial amounts of revenues away from the urban centers to less-developed rayons. The issue is contentious, and calls have been made for a federal formula that identifies the share of each subnational government, either to enhance the position of the rural rayons or to protect the larger revenue base of the cities.

In general, there are three strategies. The first is complete centralization—making intraoblast relations a responsibility of the central government. The second is to maintain the status quo and let each oblast work out its own difficulties. The third is to leave the oblast soviet to decide on the basic fiscal structure, but to prescribe central mandates to constrain the decision so that it better matches central objectives. There appear to be advocates of each.

Centralizing oblast finances. Centralization may be the least desirable. In a country as large and diverse as Russia, it is unrealistic to believe that public servicing needs for every local area can be properly assessed from the center. There are no data that describe the fiscal situation in subnational government areas, and there is no capability to monitor the fiscal outcomes in subnational areas. Perhaps the greatest drawback is that this would be a step away from fiscal decentralization and would make local-level officials less accountable for fiscal decisions.

Federal-subnational fiscal relations should *not*, in fact, go below the oblast level, for two reasons. First, this would imply a federal program that purports to manage and equalize Russia's 2,000-plus rayons. Second, such an approach would have to apply the same formula to all suboblast equalization. A better route would be to leave the distribution to each oblast. If Russia sees itself as a federation, such center-rayon relations would be inappropriate. The federal government should concentrate on finding a proper relationship with its oblasts and regions and leave intraoblast matters to the subnational councils.

Maintaining the status quo. Continuing with the present framework would seem an option. It would involve less shock to the system at a time when the system is fragile and undergoing major changes. It would continue to leave accountability for fiscal decisions with the oblast soviet. It would be consistent with the reality that some republics will be given greater autonomy. Oblast soviets can shape an equalization program for the rayons and assign the oblast governments those services where there are major externalities or economies of scale.

A framework and central guidelines. The central government may feel that the problems with oblast autonomy in this area are great enough that some adjustments are necessary. The new Law on the Budgetary Rights of Local Self-Governments proposes important changes in revenue sharing and expenditure autonomy. One basic principle in this law is to give "structure to the relationship between the rayon government and its oblast government." The proposal is that the oblast guarantee funding for 70 percent of the amount required for a "minimum" level of public services in each rayon (but these minimum expenditures are not defined). The advantage is that it allows the central government to set minimum standards in the delivery of services. It also gives the rayon and city governments some certainty in planning budgets, since the 70 percent guarantee would be for five years. The disadvantages are that such mandates restrict the autonomy of the oblast in planning its own economic development and that the minimum needs of oblasts may not be defined in a reasonable manner.

The problem of finding the right fiscal relationships between central and subnational governments plagues countries around the world, not just Russia. Many different solutions have been found. The United States gives autonomy to the states to decide on the proper relationships between state and local governments, much as the present-day Russian system does. Both Nigeria and Brazil have defined the specific roles of local versus state governments, and many European countries (France, United Kingdom) take a unitary approach, whereby the central government plays a direct role in determining local fiscal outcomes.

For Russia some "framework law" (perhaps a variation on the Law on the Budgetary Rights of Local Self-Governments) may be appropriate, in which oblasts are required to pass through some revenues to the rayon or city, according to agreed guidelines. One alternative is to specify guidelines, for example, on the minimum amount of the shared taxes that must be passed through to the subnational governments. This approach was used by the United States in the distribution of revenue-sharing assistance to state and local governments in the 1970s and early 1980s.

Appendix 5.1 Empirical estimates of tax effort in Russia's oblasts

Whether the Russian system has stimulated revenue mobilization or damp-ened it is an open question. On the one hand subnational governments retain only a fraction of what is collected; hence, they have some *disincentive* to promote collections aggressively. And if any shortfall will be made up by a deficit grant, why make a greater effort?

On the other hand local governments *do* have an incentive to increase tax collections because they retain a significant percentage of what is col-lected. Moreover, the experience in 1992 shows that oblasts can be success-ful in negotiating larger retentions on an ad hoc basis.

The issue is treated here as an empirical one. We attempt to estimate the variation in tax effort among the oblasts. A wide variation (that is, a find-ing that oblasts use their fiscal capacity to varying degrees) might be some evidence that there are revenue mobilization disincentives in the system. Indeed, there *is* a wide variation in the "effective rates" of tax collection among the oblasts (where the effective tax rate is measured as the ratio of oblast tax collections to the value of oblast gross industrial output, or GVIO).[12] But this measure does not give a fair comparison of tax *effort* varia-tions across oblasts, because GVIO alone is probably not a proper measure of taxable capacity. Even for a given per capita GVIO, an oblast with a higher average wage for its workers and a more heavily urbanized population might have a greater capacity to tax. We attempt to take such factors into account in this analysis.[13] We have estimated:

$$T/\text{GVIO} = f(\text{GVIO}_p, W, U, P)$$

where T/GVIO is the ratio of total taxes collected in the oblast to gross value of industrial output, GVIO_p is the per capita gross value of industrial out-put, W is the average monthly wage, U is the percentage of population liv-ing in urban areas, and P is the population size.

The results for the first quarter of 1992, presented in equation 1 of appendix table 5.1, show that the ratio of tax collections to annual GVIO is significantly higher in oblasts with a higher average wage and a lower per capita GVIO. About half the variation across the sixty-four oblasts for which data are available can be explained.

The same regression analysis is repeated for the combined data for the first six months of the fiscal year, with the results reported in equation 3 of appendix table 5.1. The results are similar: the shares of taxes in total output are higher in oblasts where per capita output is lower, and where the average wage is higher. However, a much smaller proportion of the variation in the tax ratio can be explained for this period. This might be interpreted as showing some weakening in the relationship between tax collections and taxable capacity.

The regression-estimated value of the dependent variable from this equation, $\hat{T}$, is a measure of taxable capacity, that is, the amount that an average oblast with a given endowment of $GVIO_p$, W, U, and P would raise. The amount actually raised is T. The equation $E = T/\hat{T}$ is an index of tax effort, E, and can be computed for each oblast. An index of 1.0 would describe an average tax effort. An index below 1.0 would describe a low tax effort, and so on.

The results of this analysis for sixty-six oblasts for the first two quarters are presented in appendix table 5.2. Komi autonomous republic, for example, has a tax effort index of 1.27, that is, it raises 27 percent more taxes than we would expect given its taxable capacity. It is ranked fifth-highest among the oblasts compared here. The tax effort indexes range from

Appendix table 5.1 Determinants of tax collections, for oblasts, Russian Federation, first and second quarters 1992

(ordinary least squares estimates)

Dependent variable	/Constant	Per capita value of gross industrial output	Average monthly wage	Percentage of population living in urban areas	Population	$\overline{R}^2$	N
Taxes collected, as a percentage of GVIO, first quarter	0.57 (5.48)	-0.14 (E-03) (-6.56)	0.63 (E-03) (2.66)	0.37 (E-02) (1.81)	-0.12 (E-04) (1.26)	0.48	64
Per capita tax collected, first quarter	-73.43 (-0.30)	0.08 (1.46)	1.16 (2.08)	15.87 (3.32)	-0.04 (-1.23)	0.47	64
Taxes collected, as a percentage of GVIO, first and second quarters	0.74 (2.75)	-0.22 (E-03) (-3.71)	0.14 (E-02) (1.98)	0.61 (E-02) (1.11)	1.47 (E-05) (0.40)	0.21	72
Per capita tax collected, first and second quarters	-487.50 (-0.72)	0.31 (2.11)	1.64 (0.93)	22.30 (1.62)	0.07 (0.73)	0.35	72

GVIO Gross value of industrial output.
Note: E numbers in parentheses are exponents. t-statistics are shown in parentheses below the regression coefficients.
Source: Estimated from data provided by the Ministry of Finance of the Russian Federation, March and July 1992.

Amurskaia and Ivanovskaia oblasts (each more than twice the average) to Tyumenskaia oblast and Khabarovskii krai (60 percent below the average). In Tyumenskaia oblast, for example, this low effort may be accounted for by its (relatively) high level of GVIO, combined with low taxes on its major tax base—the natural resource sector. Surprisingly, there is no significant relationship between the tax effort ratio and the tax-sharing rate. The simple correlation between the total sharing rate and the tax effort index is -0.21. We cannot say that an oblast with a higher retention rate acts on this incentive to make a significantly greater tax effort.

Appendix table 5.2 Summary of tax capacity and tax effort, estimated by oblast, Russian Federation, first quarter 1992

Oblast	Tax effort ratio	Tax effort ranking	Oblast	Tax effort ratio	Tax effort ranking
Ivanovskaia oblast	2.53	1	Rostovskaia oblast	1.00	35
Republic of Kalmykia	1.79	2	Belgorodskaia oblast	0.99	36
Sakha Republic (Yakutia)	1.33	3	Sakhalinskaia oblast	0.99	37
Kostromskaia oblast	1.28	4	Orlovskaia oblast	0.98	38
Republic of Komi	1.27	5	Brianskaia oblast	0.97	39
Vladimirskaia oblast	1.25	6	Omskaia oblast	0.97	40
Vologodskaia oblast	1.21	7	Republic of Buryatiia	0.97	41
Amurskaia oblast	1.21	8	Republic of Marii-El	0.96	42
Nizhniy Novgorod oblast	1.20	9	Pskovskaia oblast	0.95	43
Cheliabinskaia oblast	1.20	10	Volgogradskaia oblast	0.95	44
Samarskaia oblast	1.19	11	Tambovskaia oblast	0.94	45
Krasnoiarskii krai	1.18	12	Kamchatskaia oblast	0.92	46
St. Petersburg	1.16	13	Altaiskii krai	0.91	47
Republic of Tatarstan	1.15	14	Kurganskaia oblast	0.90	48
Novgorodskaia oblast	1.09	15	Tul'skaia oblast	0.90	49
Moscow City	1.09	16	Voronezhskaia oblast	0.90	50
Iaroslavskaia oblast	1.08	17	Penzenskaia oblast	0.88	51
Lipetskaia oblast	1.08	18	Stavropolskii Krai	0.87	52
Orenburgskaia oblast	1.08	19	Saratovskaia oblast	0.86	53
Kurskaia oblast	1.07	20	Udmurt Republic	0.86	54
Republic of Bashkortostan	1.06	21	Ulianovskaia oblast	0.85	55
Kemerovskaia oblast	1.05	22	Novosibirskaia oblast	0.83	56
Riazanskaia oblast	1.05	23	North-Osetien Republic	0.81	57
Permskaia oblast	1.04	24	Arkhangelskaia oblast	0.81	58
Tomskaia oblast	1.04	25	Kaluzhskaia oblast	0.80	59
Republic of Karelia	1.04	26	Khabarovskii krai	0.77	60
Chitinskaia oblast	1.03	27	Magadanskaia oblast	0.76	61
Astrakhanskaia oblast	1.03	28	Kabardino-Balkar Republic	0.74	62
Republic of Chuvash	1.02	29	Republic of Dagestan	0.71	63
Smolenskaia oblast	1.01	30	Murmanskaia oblast	0.71	64
Kirovskaia oblast	1.01	31	Tyumenskaia oblast	0.69	65
Mordovian Republic	1.01	32	Chechen Republic and Ingush Republic	0.65	66
Leningradskaia oblast	1.00	33			
Krasnodarskii krai	1.00	34	Kaliningradskaia oblast	0.49	67

AO Autonomous okrug.
AR Autonomous republic.
Source: Author's estimates.

Notes

1. For a discussion of the intergovernmental arrangements in industrialized market economies, see Bird (1986) and Fisher (1989). For a review of arrangements in the developing countries, see Bahl and Linn (1992), chapter 13.

2. The income tax base for all American states is described in ACIR (1992).

3. Good discussions of the principles for dividing fiscal responsibilities among levels of government can be found in Musgrave (1961) and Oates (1977).

4. A good discussion of the case for federal taxation of natural resources is found in Mieszkowski (1983).

5. It was noted in several interviews with government officials that the Supreme Soviet felt uncomfortable with a system where the Ministry of Finance made an ad hoc distribution to the oblasts in the form of variable VAT sharing rates. The move to a uniform VAT retention rate was an attempt to make the system more transparent.

6. Tabular data have been made available to the authors by the Ministry of Finance of the Russian Federation and have not hitherto been published. Data may not correspond fully to other sources or to data from the same source obtained at a different time as revisions are ongoing (dates have been specified whenever possible). This is especially so for oblast-level data. Furthermore, categories undergo definitional changes and may not correspond from source to source.

7. The revenue-income elasticity is defined as the percentage increase in revenues divided by the percentage increase in income. The numerator does not include increases brought about by discretionary changes, but only automatic revenue increases due to changes in the tax base (income).

8. This information was provided to a World Bank mission during interviews with Ministry of Finance officials from the Territorial Department in July 1992.

9. The reason for doing this is to find the association between the retention rate and the income level (fiscal capacity), while adjusting for interoblast differences in expenditure needs. Simple correlations, as shown in table 5.6, indicate only gross relationships. Of course, the normal caveats hold in this regression analysis: the independent variables are assumed to reflect expenditure needs and not to be highly correlated, and the direction of causation is assumed to run from the independent variables to the retention rate.

10. Although in principle this could be overcome by switching to a "destination-based" VAT, there are no plans to do so in Russia at present.

11. See Tait (1988) for a discussion of the problems with VAT rate differentiation.

12. Another problem is that the numerator is a first-quarter estimate for 1992, while the denominator is an annual value for 1989. The absolute values of the dependent variable, therefore, have little meaning, but we assume that the variation in this index approximates that in the true tax ratio. It would have been possible to inflate the denominator using a national index and to annualize the numerator for purposes of presentation, but this would not have changed the pattern of variation in the dependent variable and therefore would not affect the significance levels or the explained variation in the regression.

13. This approach to tax effort analysis is described in Bahl (1971).

6

The sharing of taxes on natural resources and the future of the Russian Federation

Charles E. McLure, Jr.

One of the few bright spots on the bleak economic landscape of Russia is natural resources. Operating efficiently and selling at world prices, this sector could produce significant value added, earn badly needed foreign exchange and resources for the budget, and generate substantial wealth. Much, however, depends on the tax policy and the intergovernmental fiscal regime. Natural resources, of which oil and gas are the most important, must be taxed in a way that does not distort economic choices and induce wasteful exploitation, whether development is in private hands or is left to state-owned enterprises. Economic rents—that is, profits in excess of those needed to induce investment—would be an ideal base for taxation. Taxes on production should generally be avoided, as they distort economic choices. One possible exception: taxes or fees to compensate for environmental damage.

The division of revenues from natural resource taxes between the central and subnational levels of government, and among Russia's producing and nonproducing oblasts, is crucial to the future of the Russian Federation. The geographic concentration of resources is such that primary allocation of revenues to the jurisdictions where production occurs would create enormous fiscal disparities among subnational governments. These disparities could threaten the viability of the Russian Federation.

The Siberian oblast of Tyumen is home to only 2 percent of Russia's population but produces about two-thirds of its oil (see map). Indeed, almost all of Tyumen's oil comes from the autonomous okrug of Khanty-Mansiiskii, which contains about half of Tyumen's population and about 1 percent of Russia's population. In other words, oil production is about seventy times as concentrated as population in this region. Thus, if Tyumen or Khanty-Mansiiskii were to receive the lion's share of the revenues from taxes on oil, the fiscal disparities that would emerge would be very large indeed. What would that mean? Such heavy concentrations of oil wealth have caused social and political tensions even in Western industrial market economies.

Alaska has roughly 0.2 percent of the population of the United States and produces about a sixth of its oil; Alberta has 9 percent of Canada's population and 85 percent of its oil production. During the energy crisis of the late 1970s and early 1980s, when oil prices quadrupled, fiscal disparities created talk of "blue-eyed Arabs" in Alaska and Alberta and of a "new war between the states" in the United States. Of course, these two well-established federal systems survived the jealousy and acrimony, despite some talk of secession by the western provinces of Canada. In Russia today, the situation is quite different. The political situation is very much in flux and the Federation is weak. Moreover, some oil-producing areas (for example, the republics of Tatarstan and Bashkortostan) have large non-Russian populations, who for ethnic reasons may prefer not to be part of the Russian Federation. This creates problems of separatism and demands for fiscal sovereignty, among others (chapter 7).

Russia will have to address a number of issues as its natural resource sector develops. First, it must answer the "tax assignment" question—who should tax what in a federal system? Second, it must develop a strategy for distributing the potentially huge resource rents that could emerge as prices rise to world levels. During the transition to a market economy many groups will attempt to lay claim to resource rents. To the extent they are successful, resource rents available to be taxed by the government itself may not be large. Among those who will attempt to claim rents are consumers, workers, and managers in the resource sector and potential owners of enterprises. Another potentially important claimant to rents is the native population of resource-rich areas. Finally, if a few jurisdictions are able to appropriate a large fraction of natural resource taxes, or if small groups of native peoples are able to capture a large portion of rents, these areas (or groups) will face the important question of what to do with the money.

Why natural resources are special

Depending on the quality of resources, their accessibility, and the market price of the resources, resource rents can be enormous, and they can exist for considerable periods. Rents from oil and gas are by far the greatest, and not only in Russia. The value of Canadian oil and gas production in 1980, for instance, was estimated at roughly US$30 billion or 12 percent of GNP; of this about two-thirds (US$20 billion or 8 percent of GNP) was estimated to be rents (Heaps and Helliwell 1985, p. 461).

Many important rent-producing resources are concentrated geographically, and unlike other economic activities such as manufacturing and commerce, their exploitation is not mobile; it must occur where the resources are located. This implies that there are locational rents that can be appropriated by the producing subnational government, rather than rents that can be realized anywhere. For these reasons, the question of which level(s) of government should tax natural resources is an especially important and controversial one.

Political considerations also help explain the attention given to the division of revenues from natural resources. Consumers spend sizable fractions of their incomes on natural resources (including energy) or their by-products. In addition, demand for oil and gas is relatively price-inelastic—it does not change much even if prices rise—at least in the short run. Consumers react very strongly when the same increases in energy prices that squeeze them allow producing jurisdictions to collect large amounts of revenues from taxes and royalties.

Heightened awareness of environmental degradation should also increase interest in the division of tax revenues from natural resources. Indeed, those who live where oil is produced may see future payments for natural resources as indemnification for past abuses suffered under the Soviet system—poverty, environmental degradation, and despoiling of areas traditionally used by indigenous people for hunting and fishing and for religious ceremonies.

Natural resource issues in a socialist economy in transition

Prices of most natural resources in Russia, including especially those of energy, have been controlled by the state and set well below world market prices. This policy is equivalent to taxing domestic production and subsidizing domestic consumption. In July 1992 the domestic wholesale price of crude oil was about R 2,000 a ton, compared to a world price of US$120 a ton—a notional price of R 12,000 a ton at the then-prevailing exchange rate of R 100 to the U.S. dollar.[1] Thus, the domestic price of oil was only about 17 percent of the world price in rubles. Stated differently, the price control was equivalent to a tax of 83 percent of potential proceeds from the domestic sale of oil. Because of this policy, state enterprises in the natural resource sector in the former U.S.S.R. and now in Russia appear to have incurred losses and been supported by subsidies from the state.[2]

Distortion of relative prices

Controlled prices of energy mask a deeper problem. Under socialism, prices are not determined by market forces; they are fixed by planners. As a result, price liberalization may be followed by dramatic and erratic price move-ments, as market forces attempt to move from disequilibrium in relative prices to equilibrium. This process is complicated by many factors, includ-ing thinness of markets, concentration of production (monopoly or near monopoly), inadequate transportation and distribution, bureaucratic re-sistance, inflation, and shortages resulting from the transition process.

Role of state enterprises

Under socialism, ownership of natural resources is vested in the state and resources are extracted and exploited by state enterprises. Although the first of these facts is unlikely to change as Russia moves to a market economy, the second will.[3] State enterprises will be privatized, and foreign companies are being invited to participate in joint ventures to exploit natural resources. Until privatization comes there may be little incentive for managers to minimize costs and maximize profits. Managers' compensation is not based on profits. Even if it were, the results might not be satisfactory, because relative prices are distorted, and profits do not have the same meaning as in a market economy.

This could change dramatically with privatization and prices moving toward world market levels, which in July 1992 were roughly six times as high as domestic prices and in 1993 still remain very low. Certainly foreign direct investors would not be much interested in making big investments in natural resources if they did not expect to earn substantial profits.

Investment decisions

Investment capital for all state enterprises is provided from the budget. Recent budgetary stringency has reduced government funding of invest-ment, including that for natural resources. Future production of oil and gas is dependent on adequate investment. That should be forthcoming without state assistance, provided prices are liberalized and enterprises can retain enough earnings.

Enterprises' provision of social services

In Russia more social services are provided by the state (or state enterprises) than is the case in market economies. This extends far beyond such services as education and health care, commonly provided publicly in Western market economies. Housing, hospitals, schools, and child care, for instance, are provided by many employers in Russia. Enterprises will want to transfer many of these services to governments as subsidies to them are reduced.

This can be expected to affect how subnational governments in producing regions will use resource revenues.

Poverty in resource-rich areas

Because the natural resources of Russia have been exploited by state enterprises, the residents of resource-rich regions have not shared, and still do not share, in resource wealth, as they do in Western market economies. Indeed, they have been among the poorest in Soviet, and now Russian, society. Like enterprises in the resource sectors, they (or subnational governments) have until recently received only subsidies and subventions from the central government.

Depending on how resource rents are shared among republic, oblast, okrug, krai, and rayon governments and the restrictions placed on disposition of those rents by subnational governments, this situation also could change dramatically, especially as oil and gas prices rise to world levels. In particular, if subnational governments in the resource-rich areas receive substantial shares of resource rents, they could make (probably large) cash payments to local inhabitants. But, at the very least, there could be substantial increases in public services in resource-producing regions.

Taxing natural resources

Russian taxation of oil and other natural resources is based (either directly or indirectly) almost entirely on the value of production.[4] In addition to the taxes implicit in price controls, and the standard array of taxes that all enterprises in Russia are subject to (such as the value-added tax, the enterprise income tax, and the personal income tax that enterprises withhold on behalf of their employees), the resource sector is subject to a wide array of special levies.

• *Production payment.* A payment for the use of the subsoil (a sort of royalty or severance tax) of 8 to 21 percent of the value of production is levied on crude oil, gas, and coal.[5] This 8 percent minimum rate can be reduced if it is shown that the tax would render exploitation of a field uneconomical. The tax base is calculated by multiplying the output by its official wholesale prices. So if the domestic price of oil is R 2,000 a ton, the tax is R 160 a ton. The production tax is a shared revenue for the subnational and federal governments and would be an important source of revenues in producing regions.

• *"Reproduction of resources" fee.* A fee of 10 percent on the value of production has been set aside for a fund for the so-called "reproduction of resources," in other words, for new capital investment. This fee is based on the export price, and only state enterprises automatically have access to this exploration fund. They need such a fund, it is argued, since they do not have profits to finance exploration. Private enterprises are eligible only if they have an exploration contract with the government; if they have only a license to explore they are not eligible. Joint ventures are not eligible.

It is difficult to establish how this tax affects the petroleum sector. If the state-owned enterprise in question would have invested at least 10 percent of the value of its output in exploration and is allocated this much from the fund, the "tax" imposes no burden and should be ignored. If, however, such investments would not otherwise have been made, the whole amount should be treated as a tax. For those firms that must pay but do not have access to the fund, the full payment is a tax.

• *Exploration fee.* An exploration fee of 1 to 3 percent of the value of exploration expenditures—accruing fully to the subnational level—is being considered, although details have not been finalized.

• *Continental shelf exploitation fee.* A fee for exploitation of the continental shelf is currently being studied. This would be a charge for the risk of ecological damage caused by exploitation of the continental shelf. There are two options: one based on output and the other on the area of seabed exploited.

• *Export tax.* Since July 1, 1992, the export tax has been 38 ECU (European Currency Units) (roughly US$49.40) per ton of oil exported.[6] Formally a fully federal tax, it has recently come to be shared between federal and producing governments. (Sharing rates for producing oblasts as of early 1993 range from 25 to 65 percent depending on the oblast.)

• *Excise tax.* Since September 1992 there has been an 18 percent excise tax on petroleum, levied at the wellhead. In principle, this tax accrues to the central government. Since 1993, with the first-quarter budget, it is shared with the oblasts.

Overreliance on production-based taxation

The tax regime applied to natural resources in Russia is ill-suited to the extraction of economic rents. Taxes based on production, including the implicit tax that results from price controls on domestically sold oil, take more than 90 percent of the world market value of oil sold on the domestic market, even before a profits tax is levied (table 6.1).

This leaves little likelihood that any but the most productive fields would show any profit, even before profits tax. With oil that is exported, the situation is a little better; taxes related to production and export take just over half of the proceeds, although the export tax is still very large relative to other taxes on exported oil.

Table 6.1 Implicit and explicit taxation of the oil sector in the Russian Federation, 1992

(in rubles per ton)

Type of tax or revenue	For sales to domestic market	For sales to export market
Free market value of oil	12,000	12,000
Tax implicit in price controls	10,000	0
Production tax (8 percent)	160	160
Export tax (38 ECU per ton)	0	4,940
Reproduction tax (10 percent)	200	1,200
Net revenues, before expenses	1,640	5,700
Combined implicit and explicit "tax" rate (percent)	91.8	52.5

Source: Author's calculations, based on the tax rates prevailing in mid-1992 and on domestic petroleum prices as of July 1992 of R 2,000 per ton.

A recent World Bank study suggests that "present levels of taxation (80 to 85 percent of gross revenue valued at world prices is absorbed by taxes and subsidies) are unprecedented in the international petroleum industry, will stop new investment and may even reduce current production. Taxes on new development projects should be lowered significantly, ideally through exemption from export taxes. The structure of petroleum taxation in Russia must be changed from one that is revenue-based to one that is profits-based" (World Bank 1992b, p. 180). Since that analysis the exchange rate has been unified, eliminating most of the tax implicit in mandatory conversion of exchange receipts. On the other hand, the export tax has been increased from 26 ECU a ton to 38 ECU. On balance, production for export is improved by this combination of changes but the situation remains highly problematical.

This analysis also shows another defect inherent in a system that relies heavily on price controls and taxes on gross revenues or production: both are completely insensitive to the underlying profitability of a project. The burden on high-cost production is especially heavy; similarly, the tax is onerous when the world market price is low. Risk taking and production that would be economical in the absence of taxation are discouraged. Conversely, the tax yield on low-cost, high-yield output is small.

Sharing natural resource revenues between levels of government

In Russian federalism some taxes are assigned to the central government, some are assigned to subnational governments, and some (the so-called "regulating" taxes) are shared between the two levels. As outlined in chapter 2, the regulating taxes, with their differentiated sharing rates, are designed to fine tune the revenues that accrue to different oblasts and make them consistent with their expenditure needs. The sharing system as it applies to the natural resource sector is described in box 6.1. The tax shares

---

Box 6.1   The sharing regime for natural resource revenues

Export tax
100 percent to Russian Federation (as implemented in mid-1992, 30 percent
to the producing oblast; as implemented in the 1993 first-quarter budget, 25
to 65 percent to the producing oblasts).

Exploration fee
100 percent to producing rayons and cities

Petroleum production royalty[a]
- On production not in an autonomous national region (okrug):
  40 percent to Russian Federation
  30 percent to producing republic or oblast
  30 percent to producing rayon or city
- On production in an autonomous national region (okrug):
  20 percent to Russian Federation
  20 percent to producing republic or oblast
  30 percent to producing okrug
  30 percent to producing rayon or city
- On production from the continental shelf:
  40 percent to Russian Federation
  60 percent to bordering or producing republic, oblast, or okrug

Excise tax on petroleum
  30 percent to Russian Federation
  70 percent to producing republic, oblast, or okrug

---

a. These shares are given in Article 42 of the Russian Federation Law on the Subsoil,
adopted February 21, 1992. In the case of minerals other than hydrocarbons the shares
are 25 percent to Russian Federation, 25 percent to the producing republic or oblast,
and 50 percent to the producing rayon or city. In the case of production in okrugs the
oblast share is paid at the expense of the federation share. All revenues from generally
disseminated minerals accrue to the budgets of rayons and cities.
Source: Law of the Russian Federation on the Subsoil (1992).

---

that apply will have implications for the absolute levels of revenues received
by the federal and subnational levels and, both directly and indirectly, for
the fiscal disparities between oblasts.

Fiscal disparities between oblasts

As elsewhere, natural resources are not uniformly distributed in the Russian Federation. As a result, either subnational taxation of such resources
or the sharing of federal resource revenues on an origin (derivation) basis
could create large fiscal disparities among subnational jurisdictions.
Tyumen, for example, is expected to account for almost 65 percent of all of

Russia's oil production in 1993—a share that is thirty times its share of population. Of the other fifteen republics and oblasts that produce oil or gas, only eight have shares of production exceeding their shares of population by more than 10 percent; the ratio of production shares to population shares in these eight range from 1.4 to 5.6. Other than Khanty-Mansiiskii the ratio exceeds 3.0 in only Tomsk (5.6), Komi (4.5), and Tatarstan (3.1). Thus, the present potential for huge fiscal disparities involves primarily the extraordinary wealth of Tyumen in the case of oil. In the case of other resources there are similar disparities.

What are the potential magnitudes of such disparities? The present arrangements for sharing revenues from the 8 percent production tax could yield dramatic results, depending on how prices move. Based on projected 1993 production for thirty-one "production associations" (the name for the Russian state-owned enterprises active in the petroleum sector), twelve of which operate in Tyumen (table 6.2), one can calculate per capita shared revenues received by each republic or oblast (including its okrugs, rayons, and cities). We assume an 8 percent production royalty based alternatively on (1) the domestic price of R 2,000 a ton prevailing in mid-1992 and (2) the international price (in rubles) of R 12,000 a ton and use the sharing rates of 80 percent for Tyumen and 60 percent for other republics and oblasts (table 6.3). Under this scenario Tyumen would receive R 8,912 per capita if the price were R 2,000 a ton and six times that at a price of R 12,000 a ton. At the then-prevailing exchange rate this amounts to US$89–US$550 per capita. (In the other eight oblasts with production/population share ratios in excess of 1.1, the per capita figures would range from R 304 to R 1,232.) Tyumen would receive 71.6 percent of shared revenues.

These are not small numbers. Tyumen would receive per capita shared revenues from petroleum equal to almost 80 percent of the annualized minimum wage of R 10,800 prevailing in mid-1992. With oil at world prices Tyumen's per capita revenues would be almost five times the (then-prevailing) minimum wage. There are caveats. First, depletion of reserves in Tyumen will reduce the present disparities.[7] Second, this analysis covers only oil. Once all natural resources are added, other jurisdictions will join Tyumen in the list of resource-rich oblasts (although the addition of gas will accentuate the disparities, given the huge reserves of gas in Yamal-Nenets). In 1980 Russian gold production was concentrated in the Northeast (39 percent); Yakutia (22 percent); Transbaikal (13 percent); Maritime (8 percent); Lena (7 percent); other areas of Siberia (6 percent); and the Urals (5 percent). Nickel is mainly located in Norilsk in Siberia (Russia's biggest producer), Monchegorsk in the Kola Peninsula, and the Urals. The third caveat is that oil and gas development in other areas (for example, the Sakhalin Islands) will also eventually reduce disparities.

Table 6.2 Shares in population and projected oil production, by republic, oblast, or krai, Russian Federation, 1993

Republic, oblast, krai	Population		Production		Ratio of production share to population share
	Number of people (thousands)	Share of total population (percent)	Tons of oil (thousands)	Share of total production (percent)	
Tyumen[a]	3.16	2.13	220.04	64.63	30.34
Tomsk	1.01	0.68	12.96	3.81	5.60
Komi	1.27	0.85	13.08	3.84	4.52
Tatarstan	3.68	2.48	26.10	7.67	3.09
Bashkortostan	3.98	2.68	19.80	5.82	2.17
Udmurt	1.63	1.10	6.80	2.00	1.82
Orenburg	2.19	1.47	7.65	2.25	1.53
Kuibyshev (Samarskaia)	3.29	2.21	11.08	3.25	1.47
Perm	3.11	2.09	8.85	2.89	1.38
Chechen and Ingush	1.31	0.88	3.23	0.95	1.08
Sakhalinskaia	0.72	0.48	1.70	0.50	1.04
Kaliningrad	0.89	0.60	0.84	0.60	0.42
Saratov	2.71	1.82	1.13	0.33	0.18
Stavropol	2.93	1.97	1.13	0.33	0.17
Krasnodar	5.18	3.49	1.51	0.44	0.13
Dagestan	1.85	1.25	0.58	0.17	0.09

a. Includes Khanty-Mansiiskii.
Source: Ministry of Fuels and Energy of the Russian Federation.

Within republics and oblasts, some okrugs and rayons will have substantially more resources than others if republic and oblast revenues are shared on a derivation basis, that is, where they are collected. In Tyumen, for example, most oil is produced within the autonomous okrug of Khanty-Mansiiskii, whose ratio of production share to population share will exceed 70.[8] Whether Khanty- Mansiiskii is a part of Tyumen or a separate oblast, its per capita production tax payments (assuming a sharing rate for the okrug of 60 percent) would be R 17,200, even at a domestic price of R 2,000—160 percent of the annualized minimum wage rate in 1992.

The Khanty-Mansiiskii okrug administration estimated in July 1992 that its newly acquired royalty revenues for only the last seven months of 1992 would amount to R 11 billion, or one-quarter of the total 1992 okrug budget of R 43 billion. At world prices, estimated production tax revenues of R 70 billion would enable an almost doubling of the okrug's budget—from this source of revenue alone. This suggests that Khanty-Mansiiskii would benefit greatly from the combination of liberalized prices and its 60 percent share in resource revenues.

Other distortions and disparities from the present system are also likely to emerge. For example, the present practice of derivation-based export rebates for the value-added tax may have important and unrealized intergovernmental implications. (As a consumption-based tax, the value-added

Table 6.3 Shared revenues from production payments, at prices of R 2,000 and R 12,000 per ton, by republic, oblast, or krai, Russian Federation, 1993

(in revenue per ton)

Republic, oblast, krai	Shared revenue		Shared revenue per capita	
	At R 2,000	At R 12,000	At R 2,000	At R 12,000
Tyumen[a]	28,164	168,984	8,912	53,475
Tomsk	1,244	7,465	1,232	7,390
Komi	1,256	7,534	989	5,933
Tatarstan	2,506	15,034	681	4,086
Bashkortostan	1,901	11,405	478	2,866
Udmurt	653	3,917	401	2,404
Orenburg	734	4,406	335	2,011
Kuibyshev (Samarskaia)	1,064	6,382	323	1,940
Perm	946	5,674	304	1,825
Chechen and Ingush	214	1,284	237	1,420
Sakhalinskaia	163	979	226	1,358
Kaliningrad	81	484	91	546
Saratov	108	651	40	239
Stavropol	108	651	37	221
Krasnodar	145	870	28	168
Dagestan	56	334	30	182

a. Includes Khanty-Mansiiskii.
Source: Author's calculations, based on table 6.2.

tax ordinarily would not deserve much attention.) If oblasts containing the Russian terminals of export pipelines are required to make export rebates of value-added tax on oil, they could find themselves in dire straits, especially if the oil is valued at world prices.

Some general principles for taxing natural resources

Governments use a variety of taxes and other instruments to appropriate income from natural resources.[9] First, they may simply own the resources, receiving compensation in royalties, production sharing, lease payments, and bonus bids when others exploit their resources. Second, they may also receive dividends if state-owned enterprises exploit the resources.[10] Governments can also use taxes to appropriate some of the income from resources, whether they are exploited by state enterprises, private enterprises, or joint ventures. Among the taxes used are severance taxes (based on either volume or value of production), income taxes, rent taxes, property taxes (on resource reserves), and export duties. Finally, governments use such techniques as price controls and export restrictions to transfer income potentially received by owners of natural resources to the consumers of the resources (or of products incorporating them).[11]

It is crucial that national and subnational governments agree on consistent rules of the game for the taxing of natural resources. Otherwise, gaps and overlaps in taxation can create undesirable incentives for uneconomical behavior. This does not only involve the question of tax assignment—protecting both foreign and domestic producers and investors from central-local tensions over which level of government should tax what. It also includes the tax treatment (for example, deductibility or creditability) of payments made to other (foreign) governments in calculating liability for income tax.

The case for taxing economic rents in the resource sector

The exploitation of natural resources often produces economic rents—that is, returns greater than needed to induce investment. Taxing these rents is often superior to other forms of taxation because it merely reduces surplus and does not affect decisions on investment, production, or the timing and quantity of output. By comparison, most other forms of taxation affect these decisions and can result in suboptimal exploitation of resources.[12] A nontechnical description of the concept of economic rents might read as follows: "In producing and selling [ore], the [producer], after covering all necessary costs, may have a surplus. These costs include . . . labor payments, minimum interest and other capital payments, purchases of equipment and supplies, and charges levied by governmental authorities for services and facilities provided to the mine and the industry. Necessary costs also include 'implicit' payments or opportunity costs for management, risk-bearing, and 'normal profit' or capital return. . . . Any surplus of revenue over all such public, private, explicit, and implicit costs is 'economic rent'" (Scott 1978, p. 11).[13]

The concept of economic rent can be illustrated in the context of a competitive closed economy in figure 6.1, where S is the supply curve for oil, D is the demand curve, and P is the price in competitive equilibrium. The shaded area represents economic rents. The rent represents the gain to sellers because oil is being sold at a price above that required to induce its supply, as represented in the supply curve, S.

Being a tax on surplus, a tax on rents does not affect the equilibrium price or quantity. But a tax on output does affect these variables, and thus induces suboptimal allocation of resources. Suppose, for example, that a tax of T per unit of output were to be imposed. This would shift the supply curve to S' and price and quantity to P' and Q' respectively. Rents would fall to equal the amounts contained in the cross-hatched area.[14] (An alternative and equivalent way of showing this is as a fall in the demand curve, as seen by producers.)

If taxation is designed to capture all (or most) rents, incentives for efficiency and cost consciousness will be dulled, so moderation in setting rates

Figure 6.1 Economic rent in a competitive closed economy

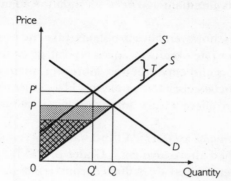

is needed. It is important, also, to design tax instruments carefully, so that economic rents actually constitute the tax base.[15] While easy in theory, this is difficult in practice. The three main approaches—the profits tax, the resource rent tax, and the simplified alternative tax—each have difficulties.

Profits taxes to tap rents. Using a profits tax as a starting point for tapping into resource rents may be especially hard. Its base is the difference between receipts and expenses in the current year, both calculated on an accrual basis. It differs from a corporate income tax because it provides deductions for the normal return to equity capital (the rate of return that can be earned on alternative investments) as well as for interest expense.[16] Thus, to calculate profits it is necessary to know the normal return to capital. This is inherently impossible and any attempt is arbitrary. To the extent the assumption used is inaccurate, calculated profits will over- or understate economic rents.

Resource rent tax (RRT). The tax base here is the difference between accumulated receipts and expenditures, both measured on a cash flow basis and adjusted by an interest factor to state them in present-value terms ("compounded net cash flow"). Financial receipts and expenditures (for example, interest) are excluded. Tax falls due when the present value of receipts exceeds expenditures. Once tax has been paid, the base that has been taxed is eliminated from future calculations. The RRT effectively taxes only income exceeding the interest rate used to adjust past receipts and expenditures. If that threshold interest rate exactly equals the normal rate of return earned on alternative investments (the minimum to induce investment) the tax base is exactly economic rents.

There are two major advantages of RRT. Because prior expenditures are simply accumulated, with interest, the proper time pattern of allowances for depreciation and depletion does not matter. Similarly, the exclusion of financial payments eliminates the need for inflation adjustment of interest payments.

The RRT does, however, have problems. Like the profits tax, it is hard to know the proper rate of return. This is crucial, given the interest adjustment of all receipts and expenditures. Moreover, in an inflationary environment, it may not be satisfactory simply to add together receipts and expenditures occurring in different years, unless the interest rate varies with inflation.

Simplified alternative tax (SAT). A third way to tax rents is a cash flow tax called the simplified alternative tax.[17] Under the SAT, expenditures (except financial expenditures) are deducted from receipts on a cash flow basis. The SAT is equivalent to the RRT if the threshold rate under the RRT is the normal rate of return. The SAT has advantages over profits taxation and the RRT. First, there is no need for inflation adjustment in measuring the tax base, since transactions have tax consequences only in the year they occur. Second, since there is neither a deduction for financial costs nor compounding of earlier receipts and expenditures, there is no need to choose a normal rate of return for calculating the tax base. Third, timing problems do not arise because of the use of cash flow accounting.

Competitive bidding. Another method of extracting rents is competitive bidding (or auction), provided there are enough independent bidders and no collusion. The huge size of projects in the natural resources field often precludes many bidders. For example, only three consortia have been interested in developing petroleum on the Sakhalin Islands; each includes some of the world's largest companies. Moreover, potential bidders may not trust the governments; for example, there may be concern that the government may go back on a contract if it proves more lucrative than expected. "As long as firms expect this behavior to be possible, and governments cannot commit themselves to forswear it, firms will underbid on the competitive auctions and revenues from resources will not be maximized" (Gramlich 1984, p. 269).[18] Such improper use of discretionary power was one of the problems of the Soviet economy (Litvack 1991), and recent experience suggests that these have not been eliminated and indeed may have been exacerbated by the weakening of the system of commands that formerly governed the economy.

Benefit taxes and fees for environmental damage

Exploitation and processing of natural resources in Russia has been conducted without much concern for the environment. Indeed, devastation has been enormous.[19] A recent study noted that "Norilsk is probably the most heavily polluted area in the U.S.S.R. The worst pollution problems in the area are caused by the emissions of sulphur. . . . Furnace gases containing about 3 percent sulphur are simply released into the atmosphere. In this way, the Norilsk complex emits about two million metric tons of sulphur dioxide into the air each year. The effect on the Arctic tundra and vegetation is disastrous. Acid snow and rain spreads for many kilometers from the smelters. When snow melts in the spring, sulphur is released onto vegetation, rivers and lakes, causing serious damage" (IMF and others 1991, vol. 3, p. 268).[20]

In oil and gas the problems include damage to the permafrost from heavy oil field equipment, spillage of oil, emissions of hydrocarbons from flaring of gas, and discharge of waste water from refining and petrochemical industries. Enterprises exploiting natural resources and creating such damage should pay taxes that are related as closely as possible to the costs of environmental degradation. Rents should be measured only relative to costs that include all social costs. The "polluter pays" principle has been legislated, and in 1991 alone more than R 2 billion in fines were assessed. In September 1992 pollution fines and taxes were increased by an average of 500 percent, with further increases to be indexed to the inflation rate (World Bank 1992b, p. 164).

Taxes intended to cover social costs of exploitation of natural resources should be based on estimates of social costs (for example, the cost of transportation infrastructure or the increased health and other costs attributable to environmental degradation). Indeed, payments intended to defray social costs are most appropriately seen as fees, rather than taxes. Ordinarily, taxes based on economic rents are not appropriate for this purpose, since rents do not bear a close relationship to the social costs of exploitation. In fact, being levied on surplus, rent taxes do nothing to reduce environmental damage (Muzondo 1992). Moreover, where rich deposits of resources are involved, and rents are large, the taxes (or fees) needed to defray social costs generally may not be a large part of resource rents.

Unfortunately, it is often difficult to measure environmental degradation or quantify its costs. In some cases, taxes or royalties on the volume (not the value) of production may be a reasonable surrogate for charges related more precisely to environmental damage.[21]

Which level of government should receive resource rents?

Some argue that subnational taxation of resources is appropriate. There are, however, good reasons for allowing national governments to take most revenues from taxing natural resource rents.

Arguments for national-level taxation of natural resources

Some arguments favoring national taxation of natural resources depend crucially on the geographic concentration of the resources. There are strong reasons that a "good tax for subnational authority would have a tax base that is widely and evenly distributed throughout the country. Taxes on natural resources may be the most uneven of all" (King 1984, p. 211).

Economic stabilization and instability of revenues. Revenues from resource rents are sometimes extremely unstable and unpredictable. They vary with output and, especially, price (both of which are generally beyond the control of a country, region, or government) and can cause budgetary problems for subnational governments, which need stable and predictable flows of revenues. "A state that depends on revenues from a particular extractive resource may find itself in a dangerously unstable fiscal position" (Scott 1978, p. 8). National governments are likely to be better able to deal with this potential instability.

Moreover, assigning unstable revenue sources to subnational governments can exacerbate the difficulty of maintaining macroeconomic stability, if their expenditures are based primarily on current (not long-run) revenues. National governments, by contrast, are better equipped to have revenue sources that vary directly with macroeconomic conditions and can better deal with variability in revenues through their superior taxing and borrowing powers.[22]

Economic efficiency. The standard economic argument for taxation of economic rents is efficiency: rent taxes do not distort economic choices, and they avoid the need for other sources of revenue that do. This is correct, as far as it goes. If natural resources are assigned to or flow to subnational governments, differences in fiscal resources available across the subnational jurisdictions can be enormous. Subnational taxation of geographically concentrated natural resource rents can lead to inefficient migration to resource-rich jurisdictions, wasteful spending by those jurisdictions, or both.[23] In the United States in 1980 the "energy-rich" states had 115 percent the per capita tax capacity of other states; for Montana it was 200 percent and for Alaska 515 percent (Cuciti, Galper, and Lucke 1983, pp. 38–39). In 1978, 55 percent of gross general revenues of the government of Alberta were from natural resources, compared with 10 percent for the whole of Canada (Cairns 1982, p. 286). Even in 1987–88, when oil prices had fallen, Alberta's fiscal capacity was estimated at 145.6 percent of the national average (Dahlby 1992, p. 121).

Resource-rich subnational governments with the power to tax resource rents can endow residents with huge benefits—lower income taxes, cash payments to residents, high levels of public services, and subsidized business activity. Any of these can induce inflows of capital and/or labor that are not justified by the relative productivity of factors, thereby reducing national output. This is not speculation: during times of high oil prices Alaska eliminated its personal income tax and made cash payments to residents— ranging from US\$300 to US\$1,000 a year (Pretes and Robinson 1989). At the height of the energy crisis in the late 1970s to early 1980s, the resource rents of the Alberta government were estimated to have a present value of roughly US\$100,000 per capita, a powerful stimulus to in-migration (Helliwell 1982).

Resource-rich jurisdictions may also waste money, and certainly, they are more likely to undertake lower-priority expenditures than regions with cash-strapped budgets. Governmental investment in (or subsidization of) uneconomical business activity is common, for example.[24] A particularly pernicious kind of waste in some countries is investment in industries processing natural resources, with little regard to the economics of such investments. This is sometimes an undesirable consequence of the understandable desire to replace wealth in the ground with invested capital. Heaps and Helliwell (1985, p. 426) note that "the use of tax allowances to encourage further processing can involve an effective rate of subsidy, and a loss of potential revenues, that far outweighs any possible economic gain conferred by the processing activity."[25]

While theoretically important, these inefficiencies may not be large. The maximum welfare loss from uneconomical attraction of capital and labor to resource-rich states of the United States in 1980 was between 2 and 9 percent of resource revenues, as estimated by Mieszkowski and Toder (1983).

In Russia, however, there is another possible inefficiency if resource rents flow to subnational governments. There may be a strong tendency to use them to continue government provision of housing and other services that would be provided privately in a Western market economy. This impedes labor mobility and increases the power and influence of local politicians in a way that cash grants would not. Whereas any deviation from strict per capita cash payments would be obvious, public officials would have greater latitude for favoritism in providing public services, housing, and other income in kind. This may be a source of economic inefficiency, as well as political conservatism.

Equity considerations. The same fiscal disparities that cause economic inefficiencies can also create inequity. Many believe it unfair that some residents pay markedly lower taxes or enjoy substantially higher levels of public spending than others, simply because of where they live. This suggests that resource revenues should flow to the central government. Regional disparities have led to much conflict in some countries (for example, between resource-rich U.S. states (and Canadian provinces) and consuming states (or provinces) in times of high oil prices in the 1970s and early 1980s.[26]

Tax exporting. Finally, consuming states often argue that their residents are being exploited by the resource-rich states, which export resource taxes to them.[27] This issue is commonly overstated, partly because of faulty economic analysis.[28] In market economies most taxes cannot be exported to consumers in other states:[29] by definition, taxes on economic rents do not affect product prices and thus cannot be exported to out-of-state consumers. Second, virtually no subnational jurisdiction enjoys the market power to affect the market price of natural resources; they are essentially "price-takers." As a result, higher production taxes, like taxes on economic rents, would be borne by owners of resources, and not consumers. For example, prices of oil are determined by the forces of supply and demand operating in world markets (perhaps as conditioned by the actions of the Organization of Petroleum Exporting Countries, OPEC). An increase in the Texas severance tax would be borne by owners of Texas resources, not by consumers (who have access to suppliers not affected by the Texas tax).

One important exception is particularly relevant to Russia: government control of prices for natural resources sold in domestic markets. If controls are binding and controlled prices are set to allow the pass-through of production taxes, these would be borne by consumers and thus could be exported.

Arguments for subnational taxation of natural resources

Whereas arguments favoring national taxation of natural resources tend to be based on economic analysis, those for subnational taxation are generally political and emotional. They call into question the very nature of federalism.

Social and environmental costs of exploitation. Some social costs of exploiting natural resources are localized. These include demands for special transport infrastructure, increased costs of health care, and environmental degradation. For equity and economic efficiency, subnational governments should receive enough in tax revenues (or fees) to defray these localized costs. Of course, where costs are not localized (such as pollution across boundaries), it may be more appropriate for national government to levy charges. As important as these arguments are, they do not address the primary issue: the assignment of taxes or rights to revenues not related to social or environmental costs.

Subnational entitlement to rents. Any nation whose natural resources are exploited would justifiably argue that it has the right to tax international flows of income from natural resources because it is "entitled" to a share of such income.[30] This argument is sometimes used to justify taxation by subnational governments in which exploitation of those natural resources occurs. The validity of this argument depends on the nature of the federal system. The argument has force only if primary allegiance is to the subnational government, as it might be in, say, a confederation, or in the case of special regimes for certain subnational jurisdictions. If, on the other hand, primary allegiance is to the national government, this argument is not persuasive.

The "heritage" issue. Subnational governments have argued strongly that they have the right to tax natural resources located within their boundaries, to convert resource wealth (their "heritage") into financial capital—to turn "oil in the ground into money in the bank." For example, the former governor of North Dakota describes his state's severance tax as "just compensation for losing forever a one-time harvest" (Link 1978, p. 264). This argument begs the question, since it assumes implicitly that the power to tax should be vested in subnational governments—that the heritage is that of the state, not the nation. Once again, the validity of this view depends on the nature of the federal system.

Increased national saving. If a small group of people or the government of a small population realizes resource rents, they are more likely to set up a trust fund or otherwise save and invest the rents than is a large group or its government. Kuwait and Saudi Arabia support this argument; but some oil-rich developing countries, which borrowed against future oil revenues to finance current spending, do not. Even so, this is a potentially important consideration, given Russia's need for capital. Much, however, depends on what is done with resource wealth saved by subnational governments.

There are three obvious alternatives: investing in the resource-rich area, investing throughout Russia, and investing abroad. The first (probably the most likely) may be the least productive. The third (probably the most sensible) would likely be politically unpopular, both in Moscow and in subnational jurisdictions. The second (investing throughout Russia) is consistent with the argument for subnational taxation but seems unlikely, partly because of the lack of well-developed capital markets. On balance, this line of reasoning does not appear to add much to the case for subnational taxation.

Survival of the Federation. The last argument for subnational assignment is simple, essentially political, and powerful. There is a question "whether subnational jurisdictions will in fact be willing to join the Federation (or will be willing to remain there) unless their patrimony in natural resources is protected" (Musgrave 1983, p. 13). Will the Russian Federation survive if subnational governments of resource-rich regions do not receive a substantial share of the revenues from taxes on "their" resources?

How, then, should Russia share natural resource revenues?

This question places in bold relief a fundamental issue: what is the nature of federalism in a particular country? It is useful to distinguish three views.

The "federation" view. If citizens of Russia see their primary political allegiance as being to the Russian Federation, rather than to the subnational entities (if, for example, they think of themselves as Russians, rather than as Siberians or citizens of Tyumen), there is much to be said for the federal government having primary access to fiscal revenues from important natural resources that are unequally distributed throughout the Federation. This is true as a matter of both equity and economic efficiency—to prevent the inequities and locational distortions that result from large differences in the fiscal resources available to the various subnational entities. Such differences in fiscal capacity are translated into differences in ability to supply public services with a given tax burden on activities other than natural resources or different tax rates on nonresource activities. In addition to causing undesirable migration to resource-rich jurisdictions, it can be argued that the inequity is unfair.

Implicit in this view of equity is an underlying view that the proper "domain of concern" is all of Russia, not part of it (McLure 1992b). This means that large discrepancies in incomes (or in the level of public services) across oblasts is undesirable and should not be aggravated by allocating resource revenues to these entities. Those who hold this view of the domain of concern, based on their view of federalism, do not place much weight on the entitlement and heritage arguments for subnational taxation, since they see the heritage to be that of the nation, not that of the subnational government.

The "confederation" view. If, on the other hand, primary allegiance is to the subnational entities, it is natural that these entities have primary access to fiscal revenues from natural resources. Under this more limited view of the domain of responsibility, differences in the average incomes in the various subnational entities are not a matter of major concern.

The academic consensus. Although there is certainly some disagreement on the issue, academic opinion is in substantial agreement that, aside from the taxes needed to offset the social costs of exploiting natural resources, taxes on natural resources, and especially those on rents, should be assigned to national governments and not to subnational ones. This is true for both distributional and efficiency reasons. As Musgrave (1983, p. 11) notes, "tax bases which are distributed highly unequally among subjurisdictions should be used centrally."[31]

A compromise view. There is no inherent reason that particular taxes must be assigned solely to one level of government; in many cases it would be quite possible for both the Federation and subnational entities to tax the same base or to share revenues. As suggested earlier, in such cases it is desirable to have substantial cooperation, both horizontally (that is, between oblasts or other subjects of federation) and vertically (between the Federation and the various subnational entities) to avoid administrative chaos and economic distortions.

How other countries share resource revenues

Throughout the world, nations with federal systems of government have done poorly with respect to revenue sharing, as judged by the normative considerations presented thus far.

The United States. In the United States, federal, state, and local governments are each responsible for collecting their own taxes. The Constitution does not assign any taxes, and there are few (if any) examples of shared taxes.[32] Both the federal government and state governments can levy any tax not prohibited by the Constitution or, for states, by federal law. Natural resources are taxed under federal and state income taxes (levied on corporations by about thirty-six of the fifty states), state severance (production) taxes, and local property taxes.[33] In addition, Alaska obtains enormous amounts of revenue from oil and gas produced on state lands, Texas less so. The federal government and states also receive royalty payments from natural resources produced on federal lands within their boundaries. Only in the 1980s did the federal government impose a temporary windfall profits tax on the oil industry.

Canada. Under the Constitution of Canada, natural resources belong to the provinces.[34] As a result, the provinces have access to royalties as well as tax revenues, and set production targets. They are allowed to levy "direct taxes within the province," but not indirect ones.[35] Under the Constitution, the federal government also has authority to tax natural resources. The federal government's primary source of revenue from oil and gas has traditionally been the corporate income tax. This division of powers (provincial ownership and federal regulation) inevitably causes intergovernmental conflicts.[36] Moreover, extreme geographic differences in resource endowments created large disparities in resource revenues in the 1970s and early 1980s. Roughly 85 percent of all oil and gas is produced in one sparsely settled western province, Alberta. Because of the differences in the fiscal capacity of provinces—and natural resources are a contributing factor here—equalization has been an important part of the Canadian landscape.[37]

Australia. In Australia the federal government can impose any tax, but the states cannot levy sales tax or other indirect taxes, nor the individual and company income tax. The states were, however, given exclusive right to payroll tax in the 1970s. As late as 1981–82, the central government collected 80 percent of all taxes.[38] The Australian Constitution gives to the states all powers not mentioned in the Constitution. Its silence on natural resources thus gives the states title to the resources within their borders and the right to tax them. But the federal government also has wide-ranging revenue powers, including leasing offshore drilling rights, export duty on coal, levies on natural gas and crude oil, and company income tax. It collects a 10 percent royalty on offshore minerals, 60 percent of which it passes to the states.

As in Canada and the United States, uneven geographic concentration of resources has led to disparities in state revenues from resources. For example, in 1978–79 Australian states raised between US$3 and US$43 per capita (from 2 to 20 percent of total revenues) from resource taxes. (The federal government raised US$137 per capita, or 9 percent of all taxes, from resource taxes.) These disparities are less troubling than in the United States, or even Canada, because of the extensive use of federal grants to the states. As one observer has noted, "Australia has the most equalizing federalist system in the world" (Gramlich 1984, p. 231).

Implications for Russia

The taxing arrangements in the three industrial countries surveyed do not accord with the views of academic authorities on tax assignment surveyed above. Subnational governments in these three federations have considerable latitude—which they use—to levy taxes on natural resources, despite the geographic unevenness of this tax base.[39]

One can only speculate about the reasons for such marked divergence between theoretical principles and reality.[40] One important cause for the divergence must certainly be that the academic analysis of the tax assignment problem summarized above did not exist at the time the Constitutions of Australia, Canada, and the United States were written. "The theoretical literature on taxation in federal systems is largely a product of the period after the Second World War. The development of normative rules on these subjects occurred well after the events on which they were supposed to shed light" (Groenewegen 1983, p. 293). In addition, it seems unlikely that anyone could have realized the importance of the issue at the time these three countries were established.

Perhaps constitutional assignment of powers to tax natural resources would be different if done now, *if* the literature on tax assignment and the geographic diversity of resource endowments, but not the actual location of resources, were known to the drafters. In Russia the location of many resources, as well as the stakes involved, are fairly well known. There is little reason to believe they will be ignored. As indicated earlier, if resource-rich regions do not get much of the revenues from taxes levied on "their" resources, the Russian Federation may not survive.

Dividing the spoils from resource revenues

Governments are not the only ones who want a share of income from exploitation of natural resources. Who are the other potential claimants to Russian resource rents?[41] And how do they influence the policy decisions that determine the division of rents?

Claimants to resource rents

The Russian Federation and subnational governments could share resource rents in many ways (providing prices are liberalized). There are revenues from public ownership of resources (including bonus bids and royalties) and taxes on the exploitation of resources. Then, there are income taxes on the recipients of rents discussed below—indigenous peoples, domestic shareholders, foreign investors, monopolistic enterprises providing services to the energy sector, managers, and workers. Under present law, specific fractions of these revenue flows would go to particular levels of government.

It is useful to distinguish (1) those who can extract some rents by artificially suppressing the price they pay for resources and those who increase prices for what they sell to the resource sector from (2) those who may share

in the residual rents of the sector. Among those who can claim a share of
the rents by suppressing prices or increasing costs are consumers, workers
and managers, and certain related industries.

Consumers. At present, through price controls, consumers are appro-
priating most rents. As long as price controls continue, there will be little
for anyone else to appropriate. Conversely, if (when) domestic energy prices
are increased to world prices, rents will be large.

The effects of rent seeking are readily illustrated using the type of dia-
gram used earlier to explain the concept of rent (figure 6.2). Consider first
the effects of price controls on oil. If the fixed price for petroleum is only
P_f, rents are reduced from the shaded area to the cross-hatched area. Rents
may even be negative, if the controlled price is low enough (that is, if it is
below the lowest point on the supply curve), and yet production occurs
because it is mandated and the state covers losses.

Workers and managers. Workers and managers will try to capture some of
the rents. Before privatization, they may use labor management to grant
themselves higher wages. Under labor management, labor councils participate in decisions to hire and fire managers and help set the compensation
and working conditions of both management and workers. Where such
powers are comprehensive and unlimited, the results can be disastrous
because labor has some of the benefits (but not responsibility) of ownership. Labor can demand (and force management to provide) higher wages
or better working conditions (measured relative to a norm of competitive
wages). But it may have little interest in reinvestment of profits because it
cannot sell this "ownership" right or leave it to its heirs. The desire for higher
real wages and the relative lack of interest in reinvestment may lead to the
decapitalization of enterprises. In industries where there are resource rents
labor can set compensation to confiscate for itself a large share of rents.

Figure 6.2 Effects of price controls on rent seeking

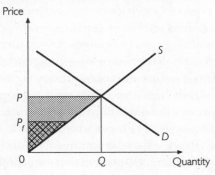

After privatization occurs, workers will presumably attempt to maintain or increase their share of rents through collective bargaining for high wages, fringe benefits, and favorable working conditions. This may be achieved more readily in existing oil fields than in fields developed by foreign investors. Labor unions attempt to achieve similar goals in market economies but are constrained by the contrary incentives of managers and the forces of competition. Russia's legislation on labor relations will be crucial.

Related industries. The oil industry is dependent on many related industries for realization of potential rents. For example, it must have oil field equipment and move its products through pipelines. Depending on the policies pursued in such areas as privatization, demonopolization, liberalization of international trade, and regulation of pipeline charges, these service enterprises may capture some rents arising in the petroleum sector. A monopolistic supplier of oil field equipment may, for example, charge more than a competitive price. That will depend on whether there is a domestic monopoly after the transition to a market economy and the extent of competition from imports. Similarly, whether a pipeline could extract rents properly attributable to the exploitation of oil and gas depends on competition and the nature of any public utility regulation.

Increased costs for labor or for other inputs can be modeled in a chart similar to that used in figure 6.1 for the tax on output. Thus, T can be reinterpreted as the increased labor or other costs per unit of output of oil.[42] Rents are reduced to the cross-hatched area. But here, the transfer of rents is to those supplying higher-cost labor or other inputs, rather than to the government. Increased costs of pipeline services, like taxes on output, can be modeled either as an increase in cost or as a reduction in the demand curve, as perceived by the supplier of oil. In either event the result is a reduction in output and reduced rents in the resource sector.

Claimants to residual resource rents

In addition to those who can extract resource rents via manipulation of relative prices, residual rents can also be claimed by a number of agents.

New owners. Privatization is crucial for successful transition to a market economy; only privatized firms are likely to provide managers with the incentives needed to induce efficient operation. The techniques used to privatize state enterprises will have important implications for the size and distribution of resource rents. Workers and managers are sometimes given preferential access to shares. To the extent that citizens are allowed to buy shares (perhaps using vouchers) or invest in new enterprises, they may share in resource rents. Also, the treatment of existing enterprise debt is important. If such debt is simply canceled, the results will be very different than if new enterprises take responsibility for it.

Foreign investors. Foreigners who invest in Russian natural resources do so in the expectation of earning profits. Some of what may appear ex post to be extraordinary earnings may reflect returns required on an ex ante basis to compensate for the substantial political and economic risks (in addition to the geological risks) of investing. Even so, successful foreign investors may enjoy substantial rents.

Indigenous peoples. The Russian debate on the disposition of resource rents is not unlike the debate in parts of North America. Some resource-rich regions (for example, Khanty-Mansiiskii, Yamal-Nenets, and the Sakhalin Islands) have populations ethnically different from the rest of the Federation. The Supreme Soviet of the Federation has considered legislation that would give indigenous peoples a veto over the development of natural resources. The native people of Khanty-Mansiiskii already ostensibly have such power, under a decree (The Rights of Ethnic Minorities) signed by the president of the Russian Federation in 1992. Such veto power could, if upheld, allow native peoples to appropriate much of the residual resource rents from production on their traditional lands.

The native population of some resource-producing areas is small. For example, the indigenous population of Khanty-Mansiiskii is only 54,000, or 1.7 percent of the population of Tyumen and well under 1 percent of the population of Khanty-Mansiiskii. If they were to extract a substantial portion of the resource rents produced on their traditional lands, they could become wealthy, at least by Russian standards. How wealthy?

Suppose, for example, that natives of Khanty-Mansiiskii had title to land accounting for 10 percent of oil production in Tyumen. Suppose also, for argument's sake, that they negotiated oil leases granting them an 8 percent share in the value of this hypothetical 10 percent of production. At (July 1992) domestic prices and exchange rates their share would have been in excess of R 52,000 per capita (US$520), or almost sixty times the (then-prevailing) minimum wage. More to the point, at world prices per capita revenues would have been more than R 300,000, or more than US$3,000 annually. This may not sound like much by Western standards, but it is large indeed by Russian standards.

A strategy for dividing rents

The issue of potential claimants of resource rents in Russia is more complex than in Western economies. It involves price liberalization, privatization, demonopolization, regulation of public utilities (pipelines), labor relations law, the inadequacies of domestic capital markets, and liberalization of international trade—in short, most issues of transition to a market economy, as well as the rights of indigenous peoples. Depending on how these issues are handled, there may not be much rent to divide among governmental claimants. If they are handled in a way that produces a competitive environment, there should be substantial resource rents. Unless these are captured by indigenous peoples, tax assignment will be crucial.

Russia must act quickly to put in place a carefully considered legal and economic system for the fair and efficient sharing of resource rents. Delay does not mean that the rents will not be appropriated; they will be, but not necessarily in a way that is fair or economically sensible. Experience in market economies suggests that, once the distribution of rents is in place, it may be difficult to revise, since the concentration of wealth can provide political influence that impedes reform.

Natural resources and the treatment of native peoples

Two economic issues are important: native peoples' control over resource exploitation on their lands and the tax treatment of native peoples and the organizations representing them.[43] In particular, if indigenous peoples do obtain substantial rents, it may be crucial to decide whether these payments are to be nontaxable capital transactions (as in Canada and Alaska) or taxable income. Experience in Alaska and northern Canada is relevant for Russia in dealing with claims of native peoples to rents.

Sovereignty and land claims settlements. When the European settlement of North America began, the continent was occupied by native peoples organized as "nations" that had the attributes of sovereignty. Any sovereign nation has an inherent right to determine the terms under which (and, indeed, whether) its natural resources are to be exploited. Second, such a nation cannot be subject to taxes of another sovereign nation.[44]

Of course, European settlers systematically and consistently violated the sovereignty of native North Americans. They aggressively and without compensation settled the lands of native peoples, concluded treaties (thus ostensibly recognizing sovereignty), and then repeatedly broke them (again violating sovereignty). In the end, they forced native peoples on to reservations and tried to assimilate them, attempting to annihilate both political sovereignty and cultural identity.

Several land claims have been settled in Canada, and others are in various stages of completion. These settlements will finally and comprehensively extinguish all aboriginal rights.

Taxation of native peoples. Canada provides native peoples with exemption from taxation under certain circumstances.[45] Essentially, income earned on reservations and income from property located on reservations are exempt. Only Indians are exempt; a corporation is not, even if its headquarters, assets, and activities are located on a reservation and all its shareholders would (individually) be exempt. Compensation paid for the extinguishment of aboriginal claims is regarded as a capital transfer and therefore exempt from tax. Income from reinvestment of compensation is taxable.

Nonetheless, several recent agreements have provided tax exemptions for so-called settlement corporations created to hold and invest financial compensation received in settlement of claims. Providing certain rules are met, the income of these corporations will not be taxed for fifteen years. Their permitted activities include many social activities (child care, adoption, alcohol and drug abuse treatment), housing finance, education and training, economic development loans, and per capita distributions to elders and low-income native people.

Managing the resource heritage: trust funds and investment policy

Natural resource–rich jurisdictions often have windfall gains—budgetary inflows that far exceed current budgetary outlays or immediate investment opportunities. In Khanty-Mansiiskii, for example, the okrug government estimated that production tax revenues for the last seven months of 1992 would be about to R 11 billion; when annualized, this amounts to about half of the total okrug budget for 1992 (R 44 billion). At world prices for oil, these revenues would be R 113 billion, or four times the annual budget. Khanty-Mansiiskii okrug will benefit greatly from even its modest (30 percent) share in the production tax revenues.

Alternative uses

Options for using these windfalls include spending on current outlays; investing the excess revenue in a "heritage fund"; giving away the revenue to local citizens by means of "demogrants"; and taking advantage of the additional revenues to reduce the tax burden on local citizens. In Russia increased subnational revenues from natural resources could not be used to reduce or minimize nonresource taxes of subnational governments, as they have in North America, since subnational governments levy no important taxes. (Increased resource revenues could result in the reduction of federal subventions and the reduction of federal tax shares, if these continue to be negotiated.) The most likely use of such revenues would be to finance increased public services or to establish heritage funds. They might also be used to finance cash grants.

Given Russia's present budgetary stringency, it is probably realistic to expect any resource revenue obtained by the federal level to be spent on current budgetary outlays. It would be unwise for the okrugs to spend these huge amounts on current outlays. While there may be a case for using some of the revenues to bring public service levels up to some agreed standard, spending amounts that are multiples of present oblast budgets can only imply low-productivity outlays. The establishment of a trust fund or "heritage fund" to convert the nonrenewable natural resource into "renewable financial capital" has much to recommend it.

If the governments of resource-rich and sparsely settled subnational jurisdictions (or indigenous peoples) obtain substantial shares in resource rents, what should they do with them? Governmental officials in Khanty-Mansiiskii and in Tyumen said they wish to use oil revenues to create an investment fund for the future, once oil production has declined. This raises at least two questions: whether trust funds should be used, and how trust funds, subnational governments, or tribes of native peoples should invest their money.

The use of trust funds seems to be a sensible policy, once the existing deficit in public services has been met. But caution should be exercised in investments. The experience of many oil-producing countries, and even subnational governments and Indian tribes in the United States and Canada, indicates that it would be unwise to succumb to the natural temptation to pour resource revenues only into local projects. A recent study of the wind-fall gains from oil in the post-1973 period in the developing world suggests that "the overall performance of RBI [resource-based industrialization] projects seems to have been very poor. . . . Some public manufacturing projects have been unable to cover even their *wage* bills, let alone the costs of other inputs and a market return to investment. . . . Loss-making public investments have left governments facing a difficult choice—to subsidize directly, to protect and to shift costs to other sectors, or to close plants and write off the losses" (Gelb and associates 1988, p. 109).

Strategies for investing windfalls

Several resource-rich states and provinces of North America have established "trust funds" or "permanent funds." Some trust funds also have been established for the benefit of native peoples. Iran, Kuwait, Oman, Saudi Arabia, and Venezuela have also created trust funds. Although the rhetoric differs from place to place (and practice has not always matched the rhetoric), the same general idea has motivated the creation of these funds. "First, the fund strategy assumes that natural resource revenues should not be used for current consumption alone, but rather should be extended across several generations or in perpetuity. Second, trust funds provide a means to replace resource rents, which will eventually decline and ultimately cease to exist altogether. Trust funds transform a non-renewable energy or mineral resource into a renewable financial resource" (Robinson, Pretes, and Wuttunee 1989, p. 270). Finally, "the dire 'boom and bust' consequences that stem from resource dependence can be mitigated by preserving a portion of resource rents for use during bust periods" (Pretes and Robinson 1990, p. 301).

The two very different strategies that have been followed by trust funds in North America can be characterized as primarily the pure "trust" model and the "developmental" model. Whereas the governmental Alaska Permanent Fund has followed the former strategy, the regional corporations (the legal devices utilized in lieu of trust funds) established under the Alaska Native Claims Settlement Act (Alaska Native Claims SA) and the Alberta Heritage Savings Trust Fund have followed the latter.

Robinson, Pretes, and Wuttunee (1989, pp. 270, 271) characterize the two strategies as follows: "The trust model emphasizes security of principal, avoidance of risk, and generation of income. Fund managers will select investments based on financial criteria alone. They will search for the best investment, that providing a high return with a low risk, whether or not the investment is located inside or outside the region. Trust models emphasize stability, diversification of the portfolio and guaranteed return."

By comparison, the developmental model "also takes into account social criteria when investing. A developmental fund will maintain investments within the region in the hopes of stimulating employment or providing local capital. Some low-risk, high-income investments will be sacrificed in favor of those with a direct local impact. Developing infrastructure and diversifying the local economy are two paths open to developmental funds. Their investments may not produce a financial return, but they may provide some intangible benefit to the community."

The experiences of three investment funds

The experiences of investment funds in Alberta and Alaska have been radically different with respect to both policies and results and are explored below.

Alaska Permanent Fund. The Alaska Permanent Fund was established in 1976 to prevent US$900 million in lease receipts from being spent quickly on state projects of questionable merit. Twenty-five percent of state mineral royalties and other resource revenues are deposited in the fund. The fund is required to invest so as to maintain the real value of the fund. The purpose of the fund is threefold: to save part of the state's oil wealth, to invest these savings, and to use the savings to produce income.

Reflecting the fund's investment objective, investment targets for 1987 were 83 percent bonds, 12 percent stocks, and 5 percent real estate. Only 5 percent of all investments were made within Alaska, on the assumption that if a project is worthy of investment, outside capital will support it. Indeed, local investments—which are not only risky but also subject to political bias—are eschewed.

As a result of this policy, 11.5 percent was the nominal realized annual return over the five-year period ended in 1986. By the late 1980s the principal of the fund was nearing US$10 billion, and income was roughly US$1 billion annually.

Beginning in 1982 the fund has paid dividends to residents of the state. Following an initial dividend of US$1,000 per capita, dividends have ranged from US$331 in 1984 to US$708 in 1987. The payment of dividends reflects the view that income from the fund will be spent more productively by individuals than by government. These payments give Alaskans a stake in the successful management of the fund and thus increase the accountability of the fund managers.

Alberta Heritage Savings Trust Fund. From 1976 until 1987 a portion of all provincial revenues from petroleum, natural gas, and coal were deposited in the Alberta Heritage Savings Trust Fund. In 1988, when the fund reached Can$13 billion, a cap was placed on the fund and no more money was deposited in it (Pretes and Robinson 1989, p. 304).

Unlike the Alaska fund, the principal of the Alberta fund is not inviolate; it can be appropriated by the provincial cabinet at any time. This allows the provincial government considerable latitude and opens the way for the use of the fund for political purposes. In fact, the Alberta fund has been used to achieve both social and economic objectives. Its investments include "loans to other provinces, equity investments in capital development projects, common stocks, as well as nonfinancial investments such as irrigation projects, recreation facilities, hospitals, and scholarship funds" (Pretes and Robinson 1989, p. 1990). Almost all the Alberta fund's investments are within Alberta.

Alaska Native Claims SA Corporations. These corporations were capitalized with surface and subsurface rights to 18 million hectares of land and a one-time cash settlement of US$962.5 million, for the benefit of Alaska's native persons (who numbered 78,436 in 1971).

The developmental strategy followed by these trusts has produced a dismal profit performance. Over the ten-year period 1974–84, the average return on equity has been a *negative 4 percent.* Moreover, the trusts have done this with a 30 percent ratio of debt to total assets, increasing their vulnerability to loss of principal—and even bankruptcy—resulting from bad investments. "Superior investment results would have been achieved by simply investing in U.S. government savings bonds" (Robinson, Pretes, and Wuttunee 1989, p. 10).

To some extent, the performance of the regional corporations reflects a conflict in their stated objectives. It is impossible simultaneously to improve health, education, and social and economic welfare; to provide employment and business opportunities; and to preserve and increase the value of corporation assets for future generations. To achieve these objectives, direct investments were made in a number of Alaskan resource-based industries, including sand and gravel, timber, minerals, fishing, and petroleum exploration, as well as in support services.

The corporations have made few, if any, dividend payments to beneficiaries. Since the corporations were created and sustained under the forced draft provided by large sums of money to be invested locally, and not by the stimulus of business opportunities, their poor results are not surprising.[46]

Lessons for Russia

It would be troubling if Russia's subnational governments were to use revenues from taxation of natural resources to concentrate on local investment, including resource-based industrialization. This would neglect both the potential risk of such a policy and the possible benefits of investment in the rest of Russia, in other parts of the former U.S.S.R. or in world capital markets. It would be all too reminiscent of the unfortunate experience of the Alberta Heritage Savings Trust Fund.

Conclusion

As prices for natural resources rise to world levels, the revenues from resource taxes could be huge. This raises important issues of public policy. First, it is important to shift reliance from taxes on the value of production to taxes on economic rents. Continued heavy reliance on production taxes will discourage investment and induce suboptimal exploitation of resources.

Second, in the transition to a market economy, many groups will attempt to appropriate part of the economic rents. Consumers will demand ceilings on prices; workers and suppliers will try to increase wages and charges for goods and services; workers, managers, and citizens will seek to acquire (on favorable terms) shares in enterprises being privatized; foreigners will try to negotiate attractive terms for exploitation of resources; and native peoples will seek a veto over development of resources located on their native lands. The distribution of resource rents, including the amount left for governments to tax, will depend crucially on laws on price liberalization, monopolization, liberalization of international trade, labor laws, regulation of pipelines, privatization, foreign trade, and the claims of native peoples.

Third, how revenues from taxes are shared among the Federation, republics and oblasts, and localities will be contentious. Regions producing oil and other natural resources feel that in the past they have been neglected by the central government in Moscow and have suffered environmental devastation. They may not want to share revenues from "their" resources with the central government, especially if they are not compensated to their satisfaction. But resources are so unequally distributed throughout the Federation that, if all resource revenues went to producing areas, there would be large fiscal disparities. Moreover, in the short run resource rents may be the only reliable and adequate source of finance for the central government. The division of resource rents among the many claimants, both governmental and nongovernmental, will pose a stringent test of the viability of democratic government in Russia and of the nature of Russian federalism.

Notes

1. In May 1992 the maximum price was R 2,200 a ton. The average price was about R 1,700–R 2,000 a ton in July 1992.

2. It is difficult to provide unequivocal support for statements such as this in an environment in which all prices are distorted and investment funds are provided by the government.

3. See the Law of the Russian Federation on the Subsoil (adopted February 21, 1992). The formal statement of state ownership should not be overemphasized. As noted in the text, indigenous peoples are being given rights in determining the use of natural resources that involve important attributes of ownership.

4. This discussion is based on World Bank (1992c).

5. Decree No. 478, dated July 9, 1992.

6. Presidential Decree No. 629 of June 14, 1992. Previously there was a requirement that 40 percent of foreign currency earnings must be surrendered at 50 percent of the free market rate; this constituted another substantial tax on exports. Since the unification of the exchange rate this requirement implies an implicit tax of only one-half the spread between the buying and selling rates for rubles.

7. Tyumen's share in actual 1991 production was 68.35 percent; for 1992 its projected share is 66.75 percent.

8. This figure and the statements that follow are based on attribution of all Tyumen oil production to Khanty-Mansiiskii.

9. See Boadway and Flatters (1991) for a more comprehensive description of instruments that can be used to tax natural resources.

10. The government may receive business income if it exploits the resources itself, instead of employing a state-owned enterprise for the purpose. This distinction is not considered further.

11. Canada followed a policy of pricing oil and gas below the world price for many years, as did the United States for natural gas sold in interstate trade. Nellor (1983, p. 296) and Gramlich (1984, p. 269), writing about Australia, note state use of excess freight charges and below-cost use of coal in state-owned electric power plants.

12. For more on this crucial topic, which is beyond the scope of this chapter, see Heaps and Helliwell (1985) and Boadway and Flatters (1991, pp. 6–10 and 13–35) and literature cited there. Conrad, Shalizi, and Syme (1990) note that there may be good reasons (including greater risk aversion by the taxing jurisdiction than by the firm exploiting the resource) for not designing resource taxes with the single-minded goal of taxing rents.

13. See also Cairns (1982, pp. 277–80).

14. Consumer surplus is shown by the area below the demand curve and above *P*. Note that the sum of consumer surplus and rents falls by more than the amount of tax revenues. The difference is the loss of value induced by the distorting tax on production.

15. Helliwell (1982) suggests, however, that this point can be overstated.

16. Note that the terms "income tax" and "profits tax" are being given their normal Western meanings. In Russia the second term is commonly used for what is an income tax in the West. The first is commonly used to denote a tax that allows no deduction for labor payments; it has no common analog in the West.

17. In other contexts such a tax has been proposed, for example, in Institute for Fiscal Studies (1978), Hall and Rabushka (1983, 1985), Bradford (1986), Zodrow and McLure (1991), and McLure (1992a).

18. Helliwell (1984, p. 123) and Nellor (1983, pp. 306–7) make the same point.

19. See generally IMF and others (1991), chapter 5.1. On environmental issues in the energy field, see vol. 3, pp. 204–9. Environmental issues in mining are discussed in vol. 3, chapter 5.7, passim.

20. "The smelting center at Norilsk produces about 10 percent of the country's *total* hazardous emissions, including 1.2 million tons of sulphur dioxide (SO_2) per year" (World Bank 1992b, p. 163).

21. Muzondo (1992, p. 28) notes that "output taxes could be viewed as proxies for static Pigovian taxes." He also suggests that taxes on remaining reserves may substitute for taxes intended to be related to accumulated environmental damage.

22. This is not to say that national governments could easily deal with revenue instability—or that they commonly do. See Gelb and associates (1988), chapter 8, on the adjustment problems experienced by oil exporters following the oil shocks of the 1970s and 1980s. The conventional wisdom on managing instability in revenues is to assume that public expenditures would be relatively stable over the cycle—or at least not procyclical—and that swings in revenues from natural resources would be neutralized. This theory does not accord well with history; Gelb and associates (1988, p. 132) observe that "oil exporters should have saved a far larger proportion of the windfall abroad than they actually did."

23. McLure (1984) presents this argument in detail. Scott (1978) and Cairns (1982) make the same point. For a more rigorous theoretical presentation, see Flatters, Henderson, and Mieszkowski (1974).

24. Pretes and Robinson (1989) note that the trust funds of Alaska and Alberta have followed very different strategies. They write that the Alaska Permanent Fund was built around the concept of a "trust." Most of the fund's investments—mainly in high-quality U.S. government securities—are outside Alaska. The fund's emphasis is on protecting and enhancing principal, rather than on development. By comparison, the Alberta Heritage Savings Trust Fund is clearly a "development fund," according to the authors. Excepting only loans to other provinces, the Alberta fund's investments are inside Alberta.

25. Brown (1982, p. 292) identifies yet another risk, the "balkanization" of processing activities.

26. It is interesting to note the terminology used in this debate. Scott (1978, p. 2) refers to the "central and provincial share of the spoils." During the energy crisis of the late 1970s and early 1980s references to "blue-eyed Arabs" were rampant in the American and Canadian debates. The subtitle of Leman (1981) is "Beyond Greed and Envy."

27. See Hellerstein (1986) for a sample of these views.

28. The U.S. Supreme Court has rejected the argument that tax exporting is relevant in determining the constitutionality of facially nondiscriminatory taxes on natural resources; see McLure (1983d) and references cited there. The question of tax incidence could, in principle, also arise in judging the constitutionality of taxes levied by the provinces of Canada, which are limited to the use of "direct taxation within the province." In fact, Cairns (1982, p. 265) notes the Canadian courts have eschewed sophisticated analysis of tax incidence and tax exporting in favor of simple rules of thumb.

29. For further development of this theme and for exceptions to this generalization, see McLure (1983d).

30. See Musgrave (1984) for a statement of this view.

31. See also Ip and Mintz (1992, p. 86).

32. The federal government has been authorized to collect income taxes for the states, but no state has availed itself of this service. There are no examples of taxes shared between the federal and state governments.

33. See the appendix in Hellerstein (1986) for a description of state taxation of natural resources in the early 1980s; the broad details have not changed dramatically since then.

34. This was provided in the British North America Act (BNAA) of 1867, the act of the British Parliament that served as Canada's Constitution until 1982, when it was patriated with little change. The prairie provinces of Canada, Saskatchewan and Alberta, were originally not allowed to retain ownership of natural resources, although provinces joining Canada earlier had done so. Similar treatment was eventually accorded the prairie provinces. For an analysis of constitutional issues in the taxation of natural resources in Canada, see Whyte (1983).

35. Since at the time of the original prohibition, excises and customs duties were the important sources of revenues, the apparent intent was to assign to the provinces only minor and "unpalatable" taxes; see Dahlby (1992, p. 115). This restriction has been interpreted as outlawing royalties on alienated resources, but not on unalienated ones. That is, the provinces can collect royalties as landowners, but not as tax collectors.

Ip and Mintz (1992, p. 84) note that only British Columbia utilizes a cash flow tax. Other provinces, particularly Alberta, have used forms of taxation that deter investment.

36. Canadian experience of the early 1980s was dominated by the National Energy Program (NEP), an interventionist program adopted by the federal government which, while largely eliminated by the Western Accord signed in March 1985, still casts a long shadow over Canadian policy in this area. The NEP was introduced unilaterally by the federal government in October 1980, following unsuccessful negotiations with the government of Alberta concerning pricing and revenue sharing. The stated objectives of the NEP were increased federal revenues, greater Canadian participation in the oil and gas industry, greater security of energy supply, and a uniform price for consumers. Among the original policies comprising the NEP were a tax on production revenues in excess of operating costs, a tax on all consumption of oil and gas, and a refining levy (to be used to subsidize oil imports); the NEP also continued the practice of using export controls and export taxes to hold wellhead prices below world prices. On the NEP, see McRae (1985) and Helliwell, MacGregor, McRae, and Plourde (1989) and references given there. Some, but not all of the policies that comprised the NEP would be prohibited by the Free Trade Agreement with the United States; see Plourde (1991).

37. See, for example, Boadway and Flatters (1983) and Courchene and Melvin (1980).

38. Much of this description is from Nellor (1983), Gramlich (1984, pp. 259, 266–73), Groenewegen (1983), and Helliwell (1984, pp. 117–24). For a detailed description of natural resource taxation in Australia, see Stevenson (1976). James (1992) provides a recent description and analysis of tax assignment in Australia.

39. By comparison, Gandhi (1983) concludes that in the four less-developed countries he surveyed, tax assignment is "rational and consistent with theoretical principles"; state taxation of natural resources in Malaysia is an important exception to this generalization. This may simply reflect a general tendency for government finance to be more highly centralized in developing countries than in industrial countries.

40. This discussion draws on McLure (1983c, pp. xvi–xviii; 1992b).

41. McRae (1985, p. 53) provides a description of producers' rent, provincial governments' rent, and rent of the federal government and consumers.

42. Strictly speaking, this modeling is appropriate only if the increased cost of labor (or other inputs) does not induce substitution of other factors for labor (or other inputs whose price rises).

43. Noneconomic issues, such as the desire to recapture and preserve a nearly lost heritage, are also important but are beyond the scope of this chapter. Such issues can have important economic implications, for example, when the desire to return to hunting and fishing is inconsistent with exploitation of natural resources.

44. Strother and Brown (1991, pp. 4–6 and 19–22, respectively) discuss whether Canadian courts are likely to recognize this aspect of sovereignty and the Native American view that aboriginal sovereignty inherently carries with it exemption from the taxation of Canada and its provinces.

45. Strother and Brown (1991, p. 3), citing Bartlett (1978), note that the exemption from taxation is the outgrowth of a two-pronged Canadian approach to policy toward Indians: (1) to civilize, assimilate, and integrate the Indian population and (2) to protect the Indians until they were civilized and protection was no longer necessary. Exemption from taxation was seen as part of the second objective of protecting Indians from market and other intrusions. It has been argued that the government has a fiduciary responsibility to protect the Indian population.

46. Moreover, by law only shareholders in the corporations could serve on the boards of directors of the corporations. Since there was not a large pool of native people with business experience from which to draw, non-native managers were required in the early years of the corporations. Another source of disincentives for effective management deserves attention. By law regional corporations are required to share 70 percent of revenues earned from timber and subsurface resources with the other regional corporations; there is no equivalent requirement for the sharing of losses (Robinson, Pretes, and Wuttunee 1989, p. 267). This is tantamount to a 70 percent income tax, with no loss offset. These authors estimate that these revenue-sharing provisions have produced US$35 million in litigation fees.

7

Regional demands and fiscal federalism

Jennie I. Litvack

Before the dissolution of the U.S.S.R., experts had said that "fiscal arrangements [in the U.S.S.R.] were very much in flux, and appeared to be headed in the direction of looser federation" (Hewitt and Mihaljek 1992). Today, fiscal arrangements in Russia continue to be in flux, pose great challenges to the central government, and also appear to be leading Russia toward a looser federation. The U.S.S.R.'s unsuccessful effort at maintaining unity while undergoing the multitude of changes associated with economic and political liberalization provides cautionary evidence to the current Russian Federation regarding the need to address regional demands. Indeed, the Russian Federation's ability to prevail, under its current administrative borders, is seriously threatened today as the ever-weakening center continues to grapple with the demands of autonomy-seeking regions. The importance of designing a system of intergovernmental fiscal relations that is acceptable to both the center and the periphery is urgent.

This chapter describes Russia's volatile situation with regard to regional demands and addresses the questions: Why are regions demanding greater autonomy? What are they demanding? How can these demands be addressed? What is the role of intergovernmental fiscal relations?

Russia's transition toward a market economy and democratic government during a time of tremendous economic and political instability certainly provides as great a challenge to policymakers as one can imagine. Nevertheless, international experience provides valuable lessons concerning issues relevant to Russia as it attempts to address regional demands. Some of these lessons are highlighted in this chapter as country experiences are described. Suggestions as to what Russia can draw from this experience form the basis for recommending a flexible framework for the design of inter-governmental fiscal relations in Russia.

Regional demands in Russia

Fiscal federalism is particularly complicated in Russia because many regions are demanding political autonomy, greater devolution of responsibility for expenditures, or special tax regimes. Who is making these demands? Areas inhabited by non-Russian ethnic groups (which are in a majority only in Tatarstan) claim autonomy because of their different history and culture. Several areas rich in natural resources want special financial arrangements that allow greater local benefits. Some of these regions say that they have not benefited from the presence of natural resources; on the contrary, they allege that they have suffered severe environmental damage from resource exploitation. Claims are compounded in a few resource-rich territories that also have sizable ethnic minorities (for example, Yakutia, Khanty-Mansiiskii, and Tatarstan). Other developed regions that have the potential to grow more rapidly—that is, those that are industrially well endowed—also want greater fiscal autonomy so they can benefit from their stronger economic base. Finally, throughout Russia, other regions that perceive a lack of cen-tral leadership and are frustrated with a macroeconomic stabilization pro-gram that has been unsuccessful are also demanding greater autonomy. The economic rules of the game change too often, and these regions want to create and manage their own policies.

Ethnic separatism

Separatist sentiments in regions with ethnic minorities have manifested themselves in disturbing ways. In early 1992 some twenty oblasts unilater-ally instituted a single channel tax collection regime, whereby all tax rev-enues were collected subnationally and a portion (determined by the oblast itself) was remitted to the center. (In 1993 the number of oblasts taking this measure reportedly rose to thirty.) When subnational governments (rather than central government agencies) are responsible for collecting revenues (as is the case in Russia), the potential for only partial remittances to the center can be a serious issue. Because of the "free rider" problem, a region may not have the incentive to remit all that is due, since critical federal ser-vices (for example, foreign defense and macroeconomic objectives) will con-tinue to be delivered, even while the region retains funds (Hewitt and Mihaljek 1992). Experience in other countries, including the U.S.S.R., Yugoslavia, and China, shows the vulnerability of the central government when it depends on remittances from subnational governments (chapter 3). In Russia the center threatened to force compliance by halting all central expenditures in the troublesome oblasts and denying them export and import licenses, central bank credit, material supply from the central supply system, and cash or currency provision. This was sufficient to persuade all regions, except Chechenya, to resume some regular payments—for the time being. Yakutia, however, has decided to take on federal expenditure responsibilities *and* to retain all the revenues.

Although the single channel system is no longer a palpable threat, disgruntled and rebellious regions persist. The Federation Treaty, which defines relations between center and periphery and confirms the "federal relationship" pending the introduction of the new constitution, was signed on April 10, 1992, by all oblasts except Tatarstan and Chechenya. Under this treaty, Russia's oblasts are all "subjects of federation" under the federal government. However, under Tatarstan's own Declaration of State Sovereignty (1990), its laws take precedence over Russian laws. Chechenya's president has stated his region's position clearly: "Chechenya's stance is unequivocal—it wants complete sovereignty and independence from Russia" (Foreign Broadcast Information Services [FBIS], December 17, 1992). Russia is using all means at its disposal to force Chechenya to comply. It has imposed a banking blockade, canceled all flights to Chechenya's capital, halted all federal wage payments, and banned Chechen exports. Nevertheless, Tatarstan and Chechenya continue to resist participation in the Russian Federation, while maintaining their vision of a confederation based on "economic, scientific, technological and cultural cooperation" (FBIS, December 17, 1992). Other areas, too, want greater independence because of their ethnic composition and dissatisfaction with their economic relationship to the center.

In these oblasts the traditional responsibilities of central and local government have become blurred, as each tries to tip the balance in its favor. Disgruntled regions want to minimize their dependence on the center by reducing reliance on national public goods—that is, nonexclusionary services whose provision benefits all citizens and are traditionally provided by the central government. For example, although foreign affairs is the domain of central government in most federations, many Russian regions have established "ministries of external affairs" and initiated contacts with foreign governments.[1] The Republic of Bashkortostan has signed treaties with most Russian regions, as well as countries in the CIS, and plans to extend ties to China through Kazakhstan. In December 1992 the predominantly Muslim Chechen Republic mobilized its local militia and formed Muslim paramilitary groups in the mountains to defend the region without relying on the Russian military. Tatarstan refused to contribute to national food stocks but has assumed responsibility for paying for federal troops and correctional labor institutions on its territory.

While regions are trying to increase autonomy, the center is using expenditure policy to strengthen vertical links with subnational governments. It has shifted budgetary priorities across oblasts to provide extra services to politically troublesome areas. For example, the Ministry of Transportation is building a civil airport in Ingushetia, while the Ministry of Education and the administration of Ingushetia are developing a training school program. These are concrete strategies to maintain unity. Unfortunately, the recent tendency to shift spending responsibilities downstairs to subnational governments to meet national budget targets is creating difficulties (and frustration) in oblasts that have been left with inadequate resources (chapter 3). Ironically, as the center tries to address the political threat in one region it is creating problems in other areas where before there were none. Indeed, in recent constitutional debates many oblasts have expressed strong disapproval of the preferential treatment provided to the ethnically based autonomous republics. Further concessions (via the constitution or other channels) to the ethnic areas may lead to greater resistance by the other oblasts.

Resource-rich areas

Another extremely sensitive issue that is driving a wedge between central and subnational governments is the sharing of natural resources. Resource-rich areas are aggressively trying to take what (they feel) is theirs, but the center relies on these geographically concentrated resources for revenues to meet national objectives such as macroeconomic stability, provision of national public goods, and regional equalization. Whether resource-rich regions should be allowed a big share of resource taxes depends really on Russian self-identity—that is, whether "we" are the citizens of the Russian Federation or the citizens of the smaller, local jurisdiction (chapter 6). The draft Law on Ethnic Minorities (1992) seems to give substantial property rights (the right to veto mineral exploitation on their lands) to the natives of resource-rich areas, although it is not obvious which subnational governments should benefit from resource rents and which should not. Nonetheless, natural resource–rich regions are demanding greater local benefits from "their" resources than they have received in the past.

Because the future of the Russian Federation depends greatly on its natural resource wealth, the central government is moving carefully. For example, in January 1993 the federal government said that it wanted to stabilize the Russian economy by developing fuel and energy in the Tyumen oblast in Western Siberia. Knowing that this would be unpopular there (more of Tyumen's "heritage" would be taken by Russia), the Russian minister of security, Viktor Barannikov, went to Tyumen to maintain calm. As the center focuses its efforts on obtaining greater natural resource revenues, regions are aggressively taking control of resources within their own borders. The president of Tatarstan said in early 1993 that the oblast plans to double foreign oil sales and that if Russia does not allow it to determine the amount of oil sold abroad autonomously, it will "adopt retaliatory sanctions against the center." Both the center and the periphery have forcibly expressed their claim on natural resource revenues and both have implicitly or explicitly threatened action to achieve their aims. The region of Yakutia, home to an ethnic minority as well as to 99 percent of Russia's diamond production (25 percent of the world's), also demands greater autonomy and retention of *its* natural wealth. This area, which contains less than 1 percent of Russia's population, has threatened to break away from the Federation: it has its own president, its own ministry of external affairs, and a written constitution with laws that claim to take precedence over Russia's (*New York Times,* November 1, 1992, "Poor Region in Russia Lays Claim to Its Diamonds"). In late 1993 it reportedly negotiated permission to retain all revenues from gold exports.

Industrially well-endowed regions

Almost as difficult as resource-rich regions are territories with large industrial bases, such as Nizhniy Novgorod. Should the people of these particular oblasts or the whole of Russia benefit from this endowment? This issue is complicated somewhat because areas with strong industrial bases might be best able to use public revenues to invest in infrastructure, which makes for productive and fast-growing enterprises. Because of the present system's nontransparency and the perception that tax sharing works against better-off oblasts, many rich oblasts see themselves subsidizing the poor.

It is the *perception* of net flows that determines regional attitudes toward the center, not actual flows (Bookman 1991). This is particularly important for Russia since empirical evidence of equalization shows that, in fact, there is less equalization between oblasts than commonly perceived (chapters 4 and 5). Zimmermann (1992) points out that a simple net assessment of revenues, which compares outflows (that is, regional remittances) and inflows (central transfers and expenditures in the region), is an oversimplification since the multiplier effect for various flows differs. Nevertheless, the perception of greater equalization in Russia may lead wealthier republics or oblasts to demand that they benefit more fully from their endowments.

Other regions

In general, regions are reacting to the lack of central direction from Moscow and are demanding and assuming greater autonomy than envisioned under the Federation Treaty. The communist system encouraged regional nationalism by making regional politics the only acceptable form of political participation in a one-party state (Milanovic 1993). Regions could compete (on the basis of nationalism) for scarce resources. As a result, dynamic local leaders played an important role in subnational government and finance and are now speaking up about lack of central government guidance and proposing alternative structures. Since Russian independence in 1991, economic policies have changed almost quarterly. This uncertainty has meant extremely disappointing foreign investment as well as economic disarray and has inspired regions to rely less on the center and (from their perspective) to assume more control of their own destiny. According to one analysis, Russia's eighty-nine oblasts now have 14,000 regulations that directly contradict Moscow's legislation (*Economist* 1993). The fact that the center cannot be relied on to create and implement acceptable polices was underscored to the regions during President Yeltsin's bitter confrontation with members of Parliament in September 1993.

Central government response to regional demands

Politics and economics are intertwined in fiscal federalism. Regions that perceive unjust or undesirable economic treatment by the center express themselves politically—that is, they demand greater autonomy to reap the economic benefits to which they feel entitled. The "whither Russia" theme presented throughout this book is perhaps most apparent when this issue of regionalism is examined. The existence of the Russian Federation depends on the union of oblasts and their acceptance of national identity. But in many parts of the country the notion of nationhood is weak. The central government's economic and, particularly, budgetary policies have further eroded the concept of nationhood. With the trend in Russia being to push expenditures downstairs and retain revenues upstairs, subnational governments are increasingly rethinking ties with the center. They are weighing gains and losses from participation in the Russian Federation. Regions that feel ethnically or culturally different have particularly questioned their national allegiance and have demanded greater autonomy. How the federal government addresses regional demands will determine the willingness of disgruntled (and sometimes rebellious) areas to remain within the Federation, as well as the ability of the central government to continue essential functions.

Hewitt and Mihaljek (1992) discuss the concept of "minimum powers" of a central government in a federation. There is no scientific method for determining these powers, but they are linked to the advantages of maintaining a federation, as opposed to separating into fully independent countries or forming a confederation. Some activities increase collective welfare significantly when conducted by the central government and would result in welfare losses if decentralized. These include promoting internal free trade, international trade, and foreign relations; maintaining macroeconomic stability; and providing public goods that benefit the whole country. The Russian central government must be able to perform these minimum functions to justify its existence to the many disparate oblasts. How the central government resolves intergovernmental fiscal issues, including the sharing of natural resource revenues, will largely determine its ability to function and, ultimately, its survival. Whether it is economic or political differences that inspire demands for greater autonomy, a sound fiscal system lies at the heart of any solution.

The demands for greater autonomy have spread and grown throughout Russia. The central government has met these demands in an ad hoc fashion, striking deals to keep disgruntled areas within the national fold. The disintegration of the U.S.S.R. occurred when fiscal relations broke down between the center and the republics. Russia is desperately trying to avoid a similar fate and has been forced to take measures, as necessary, to maintain unity. For example, in 1992 the federal government struck a deal with Yakutia. The region was permitted to retain 20 percent of the diamonds and minerals it produced as well as 45 percent of hard currency earnings from foreign diamond sales. Later that year, Yakutia received further concessions when it formed a joint company with the Russian government, sharing equally in the whole Yakutian diamond industry, from extraction to sale (*New York Times,* October 8, 1992, "Siberian Frontier Covets Its Riches," and November 1, 1992, "Poor Region in Russia Lays Claim to Its Diamonds"). So, less than 1 percent of the Russian population now has access to half of the country's diamond wealth—a dramatic example of the central concessions currently being negotiated. Although the central government has so far been able to firefight each crisis as it arrives and to negotiate a settlement that keeps Russia together, the requests for special arrangements keep expanding.

On July 9, 1993, the Pacific Maritime Territory claimed control of its resources and seized a new measure of autonomy from the Russian federal government. The Maritime Territory, a region of more than 2 million people on Russia's southern Pacific coast, declared its new authority only a week after a similar declaration by the industrial province of Sverdlovsk. The oblast of Vologda, northeast of Moscow, declared itself a republic in

May 1992 (*The Washington Post,* July 9, 1993, "Russian Regions Seek Autonomy").

Perhaps the extreme nationalistic passions seen in the North Caucasus and Tatarstan can only be mollified by a confederation. But it might be possible to reach compromise solutions in other regions where demands can be addressed through the budgetary process—by strengthening and expanding linkages through redistribution; that is, through spending policies that favor these areas or grant greater autonomy on the revenue side.

Any system of intergovernmental fiscal relations requires careful design to meet the primary objectives of efficiency, equity, stabilization, and political legitimacy. In a federation the need to balance central and regional needs is particularly compelling, given that constitutional rights afforded to regions within a federation often lead to greater, and more disparate, regional demands. These demands become more vociferous when great economic resources are at stake, as in the case of oil and other natural resources. In Russia the Federation Treaty of April 1992 defined center-state relations. Whether details of the intergovernmental federal arrangements will be codified in the constitution is a major contentious issue surrounding the ongoing constitutional debate.

Balancing regional demands with central objectives has been handled differently throughout the world. Given the clamor for more political autonomy in Russia, greater devolution of responsibility for expenditures, and special tax regimes, international experience offers some valuable lessons.

Addressing regional demands in other countries

There are three ways that governments have approached regional demands for special treatment. The first is *ad hocery* (individually negotiated payments or other arrangements between the center and regions). The second is *special fiscal regimes,* which grant special rights on taxation and expenditures to certain regions. The third is a *formula-based system,* normally designed with (at least partial) equalization objectives. Although most countries use some kind of formula distribution to address regional issues, only a few include components in their formulas for dealing with demands made by a specific region.

Countries with unitary and federal governments face different constraints and opportunities in intergovernmental relations. An important distinction should be made between unitary government structures and fiscal systems and federal government structures and fiscal systems. Government structures refer to the relationship between center and state and the legal responsibilities of each. Although the extent of decentralization can vary greatly in both unitary and federal countries, federal governments differ fundamentally from unitary systems. They have constitutionally guaranteed rights for subnational as well as national governments. In theory, their re- lationships are not hierarchical but complementary, with each level assigned specific responsibilities and rights. The degree of decentralization of the federal or unitary structure of the fiscal system depends on the extent of state participation in revenue raising and the degree of expenditure author- ity granted, both of which indicate the respective leverage of central and subnational governments.

Some countries with unitary governments (France, the Philippines, China, Indonesia, the United Kingdom, and Spain) offer useful lessons to Russia regarding different strategies adopted to balance regional demands with central concerns. So, too, do the experiences of some with federal gov- ernments (Switzerland, Australia, Canada, India, Nigeria, and Malaysia).

Unitary governments

France is an interesting example of how strategies for equalization can change to accommodate greater decentralization and transparency, while retain- ing discretionary funds to use when politically expedient. Until the early 1970s France was one of the most centralized countries in the industrial world (Prud'homme 1977). It became increasingly decentralized after 1982, when greater fiscal and administrative autonomy was devolved to the subnational governments.

The most significant change was in expenditures. Local governments now have almost full discretion over use of revenues. Instead of central funds to finance specific projects, subnational governments now receive revenues from block transfers and local taxes. Block transfers are determined by a formula designed to compensate for unique tax bases and includes needs- related criteria (such as number of school children and kilometers of road, population, tax effort, and a factor that helps ease the transition from the previous system to the formula-based system). Thus, France continues to emphasize equalization but through different mechanisms. Formula-based transfers increase transparency. Channeling additional resources to a re- gion for political reasons can no longer occur through ad hoc transfers. The center, however, which still controls many sectors, can invest more in a region if it is economically *or* politically expedient.

The Philippines, which emphasizes decentralization but remains fiscally centralized, faced a situation where one region demanded greater au- tonomy. Its experience is a clear lesson in how some groups can force their will on central governments through rebellion. Why the violence? Perhaps because the Philippines is a unitary nation, without any formal channels for expressing local dissatisfaction or devolving more regional autonomy.

In the case of the Philippines the center attempted to resolve the issues by granting special rights.

In the 1980s the Muslim regions of Mindanao and Cordillera demanded greater autonomy from the central government in the Philippines because of their different religion and cultural heritage. This eventually led to insurrection and inspired antigovernment terrorist actions. Greater autonomy was granted in 1989 with the Organic Act for Muslim Mindanao, which provided a new financial structure for the region. Most spending was devolved to local governments, and central approval of expenditure composition was eliminated. The regional government was also given broad taxing powers.

China, despite its size and diversity, has a unitary system of government where the constitution does not expressly delineate the powers and responsibilities of various levels of government. Yet central, provincial, and local governments do have distinct powers and responsibilities and, in many ways, the system functions as in a federation. It provides an interesting case of how bottom-up tax collection—as in Russia—can threaten the fiscal viability of the central government because it is dependent on compliance from the periphery. Provincial tax contracting (or single channel regimes) is a system that relies on collecting revenues subnationally and remitting a share to the center: this can serve as an engine of economic development by permitting productive areas to reinvest their income directly. But the central government relinquishes much fiscal authority.

As in Russia, tax sharing between the center and provinces in China is an ad hoc affair, with much negotiation and special treatment. Like Russia, China has a tax administration that relies on bottom-up tax collection, and revenue sharing is designed to increase provincial incentives to collect more taxes. Since 1988, tax contracting (the delivery of a fixed tax quota to the center that differs by province) has been applied in most of China's prosperous (and high-tax-yield) provinces. Under this system the province may keep all revenues collected above a basic amount (quota) that must be transferred to the central government (Bahl and Wallich 1992).

Since 1988, however, most provinces have "bargained down" the center and reduced their obligations to share and transfer funds. The provincial contracting system has had some negative revenue consequences for the center. For example, contracts are fixed in nominal terms, which has left an increased share of fiscal resources with richer local governments. This reduces the growth (and, potentially, the real volume) of resources in the hands of central government. Moreover, the system introduces a procyclical bias to the fiscal system. The revenue (and, by implication, the expenditures) received by the provincial government under a fixed nominal contract booms or shrinks as the economy changes, while the center receives the same amount, regardless of the underlying growth of economic activity. The subnational level thus adds to demand pressures or shortfalls, while the center has no resources to play its countercyclical stabilizing role. If there must be contracts, they should be set in real, not nominal, terms (Bahl and Wallich 1992).

While the provincial contracting arrangements can increase incentives to collect revenue, they do not eliminate the potential conflict of interest between provincial and central governments. Neither do they ease a crucial problem of decentralization—the loss of control and flexibility by the center over the use of tax policy for macroeconomic purposes. Once the power of the purse was in the provinces' hands, the central government lost much of its financial muscle and could not "claw back" its special arrangements to share more fully in the benefits (Bahl and Wallich 1992). It is this feature that lies behind China's current efforts to reform its revenue system.

Indonesia is a unitary nation of twenty-seven provinces. Each provincial budget must be approved by the central government, although provinces are responsible for spending in many sectors. Indonesia uses a formula distribution system for fiscal revenues; its operation suggests that an inherent tradeoff exists between growth and equalization. The present grant formula to distribute funds to the provinces is based on population, which assumes equal per capita needs. Regional governments retain 70 percent of license fees and royalties from their natural resources. This has helped regional development in resource-endowed areas but has sharpened the line between regional haves and have-nots (Hutabarat 1991).

The central government is now trying to narrow per capita income differentials between provinces, as well as give them more autonomy, to reduce the central burden. Nevertheless, the provincial governments, beholden to a strong central government, have little power to speed or strengthen this effort.

The United Kingdom is four regions under a central government—England, Wales, Northern Ireland, and Scotland. It has devolved some political autonomy yet has kept a firm grip on fiscal affairs. While Wales and Scotland particularly want greater fiscal autonomy, they have accepted the outcome of the political process. The relationship between the United Kingdom and Scotland demonstrates the sensitive link between political and economic autonomy. Its experience suggests that if the population is willing, devolution of political autonomy does not have to mean devolution of fiscal autonomy.

Demands for greater autonomy, and even independence, arose in Scotland in the 1970s with the discovery of North Sea oil. Opponents warned that devolving much fiscal authority to Scotland, particularly on oil taxation, would lead to the political and economic breakup of the United Kingdom. In 1978 Scotland was granted its own elected assembly (as well as continued representation at Westminster) and specific expenditures were devolved. The most contentious aspect was that all revenues would come from central government as "block grants," distributed using a formula based on spending needs (Heald 1980)—not from natural resources. Many Scots were dissatisfied with the outcome, yet their recourse, short of secession, was minimal. The Scottish National Party tried to press these concerns on the national agenda but failed to make much impact, and, ultimately, was forced to accept the outcome—at least for the time being.

In *Spain* the special status of four regions with strong, historical local nationalism (the Basque country, Navarre, Catalonia, and Galicia) was assured through the Constitution of 1978. Each was granted special legal and fiscal regimes. The fast switch from a strongly unitary state to a semifederal government in the late 1970s was partly in response to deep-seated cultural differences among various regions. As the government changed from authoritarian to democratic, considerable power was devolved to many regions as a way of strengthening the return to democratic rule. As in Russia today, regional autonomy was the toughest issue for drafters of the new constitution. In part this was because two of the nationalistic regions, the Basque country and Catalonia, were among the most developed areas of Spain, with the highest per capita income (Lopez 1990).

The Spanish experience shows how a nonuniform approach to intergovernmental fiscal relations can work. In Spain two types of intergovernmental fiscal system exist: a "common regime" for fifteen autonomous communities and a "special regime" for two autonomous communities with historically stronger local nationalism. The sharing of tax revenue is the major source of finance for the common regime, while the Basque country and Navarre can levy and collect all taxes except customs taxes and excises on petroleum products and tobacco. In turn the regional authorities in the Basque country and Navarre are required to make an annual lump-sum payment to the central government for services. These payments are agreed for five years, with annual adjustments for inflation.

Federal countries

The acid test of a federal political system is whether regional governments have "consequential power" (Nathan and Balmaceda 1990). The test can be applied by looking at:

- Legal powers (the constitutional right to legislate and elect representatives; the basis on which state boundaries are determined; the role of regional governments in central decisionmaking, including settling disputes between the two).

- Revenue powers (the degree to which regional governments can determine the type and amount of regional revenue raised and the ability to influence revenue sharing between central and regional governments).
- Functional-area authority and responsibilities (the extent to which regional governments control financing, policymaking, and administration).
- The role of regional governments in the affairs of central government
- Historical, social, and cultural identification.
- The authority that regional governments have over local ones.

Although subnational governments differ greatly by country in responsibilities, interaction between national and subnational government in most federations is a two-way street. The rights and responsibilities of each are clearly stated and, in theory, protected by the constitution. Should conflict arise there are channels for resolving it. But these channels can also be used to exert pressure in times of discontent. In general, regional demands must be addressed more delicately in a federal than in a unitary system.

When Russia is subjected to this acid test, it lacks the characteristics of a federal country, except for historical, social, and cultural identification and, in most cases, power over local units. That regions have strong identities, in the absence of other federal features, suggests that the forces separating the regions are stronger than those unifying them—a powerful warning that regional issues must be addressed with extreme care. So how do other federal nations address regional demands? And what issues are important in the design of intergovernmental fiscal relations?

Switzerland is the archetypical federal country that is also regionally diverse. Income disparities between regions (cantons) widened in the 1950s and 1960s, and there was pressure from the regions to reverse this. The Swiss experience is a lesson in how interregional equalization can come about through changed public attitudes in a country with a strong democratic system. Institutional factors explain the shift. As high incomes became more regionally concentrated and the number of cantons with above-average income fell, their representation in the lower chamber of government fell. With this change, redistribution could be successfully advocated by representatives from other cantons (Frey 1977).

The political process in Switzerland makes the federal government responsive to local demands, which, in this case, led to greater equalization. Although the wealthier cantons were surely "losers," both the democratic process and common ties within the country were sufficiently strong, and the country small enough, to serve as a binding mechanism.

Australia has a long tradition of interstate equalization. Its experience demonstrates how a country that emphasizes interstate equalization can provide special benefits to destitute areas, allowing their service levels to catch up with the rest of the country: the distribution formula, as well as ad hoc funds allocated by the Australian "Grants Commission," result in disproportionate assistance to the Northern Territory, home to a high proportion of aboriginal peoples and their special problems.

The grant for the Northern Territory is calculated in the same way as all regional grants: regional revenue is deducted from explicitly calculated spending needs, and a grant makes up the difference. For the Northern Territory many additional components were included in calculating expenditure needs (for example, remoteness, dispersion, physical environment, and population characteristics). The territory's remoteness and scattered population means high transport and fuel costs, long delays in delivering supplies, higher costs of communication, and costlier recruitment of public service staff. A particularly young population (bimodal, with peaks in the age groups 0–9 and 24–35) requires high funding for maternal and child care and for education. Special consideration is also provided to the Northern Territory on the revenue side because of its minimal industry and small tax base. When this grant formula was first established, the Northern Territory had not begun to tap its mineral wealth. As revenues from natural resources increase, the grant is adjusted (Commonwealth Grants Commission 1979; Bird 1984).

Canada is a large and diverse federal country that is highly decentralized. Canada's provinces, like those in some other countries, have a long list of expenditure responsibilities; but, unlike those others, the provinces have legal and significant revenue-raising capacity. The central government provides fiscal transfers to lower-income provinces so that all have resources available to fund public services at similar tax levels. Canada's federal pool of tax revenues is distributed to provinces using an equalization formula. This ensures that all provinces receive the equivalent of at least the national average tax rate applied to the national average revenue base. This system was designed specifically because Canada is both geographically large, with widely differing natural resource endowments, and socially diverse (Graham 1982).

Canada's continuing constitutional debate highlights the problems of special regimes, rather than uniform devolution of authority to allow different regional policies. Indeed, it is a cautionary tale about how a large, diverse country, well-suited to a highly decentralized federal government and fiscal structure, should proceed. Whether or not Quebec should be granted status as a "distinct society" (and so be able to claim special rights in the future) has been the major hurdle to ratifying a constitution. Although Quebec's demand for greater autonomy is political (different language, religion, and culture) rather than fiscal, its demand for special status has led many Canadians who consider themselves distinct (for example, the native population, the oil-rich western provinces, and women) to demand special treatment. Attempts were made to resolve this issue by strengthening the authority of Canada's second legislative chamber (the Senate), which has equal representation by province, and thus giving the oil-rich areas more say in natural resource taxation. The demands of the native population, on the other hand, have been explicitly addressed in the constitution. A draft constitution, however, was rejected in a nationwide referendum, and the constitutional crisis remains unresolved.

India is a vast country with wide interregional differences in economic endowments, income, and culture. It has been a challenge to reduce interregional disparities while meeting diverse demands. Its fiscal system is an interesting example of how many economic and political regional issues can be addressed through a combination of formula-based and ad hoc grants.

The Constitution in India lays out in detail the country's political and governmental structure, including responsibilities and powers assigned to national and subnational governments. It also recognizes that the taxing powers of states give them insufficient revenues to match spending needs. Thus, a vertical imbalance is a built-in feature of the Indian union. Formula-based transfers play an important role in supplementing state revenues and filling gaps. For example, some capital investment transfers are distributed to the states according to a series of weights: population (60 percent); tax effort (10 percent); "backwardness," measured by per capita income compared to the all-India average (20 percent); and "special problem states" (10 percent) (Bagchi 1991; Bagchi, Bajaj, and Byrd 1992; Rao 1991; Wallich 1982). In addition, components in the formula for backward regions (defined by the center), as well as for special states (for example, the politically sensitive Punjab), help to address problems in a transparent way, and the fiscal system is to some extent removed from continuing political negotiations.

Nigeria has 30 states and 600 local governments. It too is a country that has tried to use formula-based fiscal distribution to address regional concerns, while limiting political pressure for patronage. It has met with some success, but the system has continued to be vulnerable to political pressures. Indeed, it is an example of the need to insulate intergovernmental fiscal relations from political pressures for patronage by establishing objective institutional structures to address fiscal issues. While statutory transfers posed few problems, by the late 1970s it was commonly perceived that nonstatutory funds allocated in a strongly ad hoc fashion benefited some politically privileged states more than others (Baker 1984). At that time there was no institutional body to review intergovernmental fiscal relations, only ad hoc commissions or irregular meetings with ministers or governors.

In 1988 the Revenue Mobilization and Fiscal Commission was established (similar to the Grants Commissions in Australia and India) and was made responsible for reviewing the revenue allocation formula and principles to ensure "conformity with changing realities." It was hoped that intergovernmental fiscal relations would thus be executed in a more transparent, consistent manner (Mohammadu 1985). Between 1988 and 1992, however, the allocation formula was changed five times, which partially defeats its objectives. Even so, the commission's formal structure may limit political influences that can color allocation decisions.

Malaysia is a federation of thirteen states with diverse ethnic groups in regions of different sizes and resources at differing stages of development. Since independence in 1963 the primary national goal has been economic growth. By permitting significant regional revenue retention (including of natural resource taxes), regions have developed at different paces, and more productive areas have thrived.

Two resource-rich states, Sabah and Sarawak, were attracted into the federation by "special fiscal regimes." Unlike other states, they can levy customs and excise duties and retain all revenues. In 1977–79, per capita revenues in Sarawak were five to six times those of the states with the next highest figures, which were themselves well above the national average. Sarawak's special regime was justified by its geographic separation from the Malayan peninsula and its distinct economic and cultural attributes (Ariff 1991). Indeed, Malaysia is an interesting case of how, if it is politically acceptable, a successful approach to national development is to deemphasize interregional equalization until the national economy is growing. It also demonstrates how special regimes can be granted to attract well-endowed areas into the national fold.

Common lessons of unitary and federal systems

In *unitary* nations power of the purse determines authority. Whoever has the ability to raise revenues has the upper hand in later negotiations between national and subnational governments. Although this may also be true in a federation, legal rights are not explicit in unitary countries. In France, Indonesia, and the United Kingdom regions not pleased with central decisions have few strings to pull short of insurrection or secession. Still, in democratic countries regional demands can be expressed through the political process by forming a political party, as in Scotland. In Spain a dramatic change from an authoritarian to a democratic government resulted in some autonomous communities being guaranteed constitutional rights, much like a federation. Two regions that voiced the loudest demands for separatism were given advantageous special fiscal regimes. Short of a major change of government, however, new political parties successfully able to achieve regional demands would be rare. More likely, regional demands would be realized through the measure of last resort—rebellion—as in the Philippines, where one ethnically different region secured a special fiscal regime. In China, once some provinces were given special privileges and were no longer financially dependent on national government, the center had few strings to pull, short of military might. Although it could (and did) appoint political representatives in the provinces to strongly represent central interests, bottom-up tax collection has left the center dependent on the provinces—and vulnerable.

Federal countries address the issue of revenue sharing and regional demands in many ways, depending on the degree of decentralization of the country and the nature of government. In a strong democracy regional equalization reflects popular will, as expressed by elected representatives; in weaker democracies regional equalization is determined more by the central government according to its development strategy.

With center-subnational rights and responsibilities legally outlined in a federation, regional demands are usually handled with less "ad hocery" than in unitary countries. Canada negotiated over the rights of the province of Quebec, the oil-rich western provinces, and the native population and sought to incorporate these rights in the Constitution. Malaysia attracted mineral-rich Sabah and Sarawak into its federation by Constitutionally guaranteeing them special tax privileges. India still attempts to reach consensus among diverse states by incorporating special treatment for some areas into its transparent distribution formula.

In federal, as in unitary countries, it is hard to avoid "ad hocery." In addition to its use of a transparent distribution formula, India allocates funds through discretionary transfers. Nigeria has attempted to limit ad hoc revenue distribution and insulate intergovernmental fiscal relations from political pressures for patronage by establishing an objective commission to address grant formulas. The strong history of individually negotiated sharing arrangements between regions and the center, however, has placed great pressure on the commission, which has been forced to reconvene annually (instead of every five years as designed). Nevertheless, by trying to minimize "ad hocery," transparency did improve and led regions to perceive a greater sense of justice. In countries with strong centrifugal forces the need for "perceived justice" should not be underestimated.

Lessons from intergovernmental systems and their relevance for Russia

Although Russia is in a unique situation, other countries' experiences can help the Federation as it seeks to design a system of intergovernmental fiscal relations. The highly charged political atmosphere in Russia means that all aspects of the system must be considered with special care. In the end the design of an intergovernmental fiscal system will ultimately reflect the extent of a country's decentralization, which is not necessarily related to its unitary or federal nature (Bird 1986). Nonetheless, all the unitary and federal nations discussed have confronted questions that Russia, as a federation, must face and answer.

Russia is changing radically. First, from authoritarian rule to democratic government; and second, from a centrally planned unitary regime camouflaged as a "federation" to a de facto federation, where some powers are actually devolved to subnational government. Policymakers are striving to design and create institutions and systems for a democratic, federal country. The dramatic transformation from the old to the new is difficult, particularly when actions, reactions, and thinking throughout the country often reflect the "old way."

Federal center-subnational relations are more sensitive in Russia today because of its fragile democracy. Skepticism about the democratic process's ability to faithfully represent subnational interests result in dramatic conflicts, as occurred in Tatarstan. Because Russia's system has, de facto, been unitary, lessons from such countries elsewhere should be taken seriously. These lessons show that there are fewer channels available to resolve conflicts between the center and states under unitary governments. So when problems escalate, subnational reactions can be extreme.

A critical issue for Russian policymakers is regional equalization. International experience provides a wealth of experience. Australia and Canada, two large, rich federations, place a high priority on equalization and strive to achieve similar services throughout the country. Democratically elected governments confirm the population's willingness to redistribute wealth. In contrast, Malaysia has not emphasized regional equalization; rather, it has seen a great need for economic growth and has allowed regions that are economically strongest to reinvest revenues and thrive. Democratic institutions in Malaysia have not been as strong as in some other countries, and the central government has not had to respond to popular pressure from less-wealthy areas. India is in the middle ground. It has tried to consider many factors in revenue distribution but has not had the redistribution success of Australia and Canada or the economic growth of Malaysia. But even with the multiple challenges of a diverse population, India has persisted—and succeeded remarkably well. Except in rare cases, there does appear to be a tradeoff between growth and fiscal equalization (Zimmermann 1992; Bookman 1991). And, ultimately, priorities are determined politically.

Regionalism and Russia

As Russia searches for national definition, the need for political unity may, for now, be greater than the need for equity. Rather than have states negotiate individually for special fiscal regimes or unilaterally decide to opt out of the federal system, widespread participation should be encouraged through a fiscal system that does not overemphasize regional equalization and that incorporates special circumstances within its distribution formula. Such a formula can, with luck, promote democracy and patience for economic reforms through its transparency. It can also pacify restless areas and keep them in the equalization pool as the notion of "we" becomes more solidly grounded in the nation. Moreover, such a formula can adapt to the times, a very relevant attribute given the pace of economic and institutional change in Russia.

Indeed, too much emphasis on equalization in Russia may not be appropriate right now. In the past, one of Russia's goals was that all citizens should be entitled to the same facilities and services. In practice, individually negotiated arrangements resulted in regional disparities, often with militarily important areas benefiting most. Today, Russians are left with the rhetoric of equity and the reality of disparities. As the country seeks to make decisionmaking more transparent in its transition to a democratic government and a capitalist economy, realities and priorities must be clearly identified. Whether or not the full regional equalization of past communist philosophy currently reflects the wishes of the Russian population is as yet unknown, since the democratic system is nascent. However, in some areas, there appears to be great dissatisfaction with redistribution. Even if all revenues are legally central government taxes, subnational governments that collect them think of them as theirs, as in China. The "aggravation" factor, arising from a perception of negative net regional flows, leads to cries for secession in many countries (Bookman 1991, ch. 11). In a country like Russia, which is struggling with nation building among a regionally and ethnically diverse population lacking a central thread, such aggravation should be kept to a minimum.

The priorities for Russia in the short and medium term are political cohesion, stabilization, and economic growth. Equalization was achieved in countries such as Australia and Canada, but further down the road. China, Malaysia, and India also offer valuable lessons for Russia. Less emphasis on equalization would enable reinvestment in prosperous regions, which could serve as engines of economic growth for the whole country, even though this would hurt economically weak regions in the short and medium term. Since maintaining political cohesion should be a major goal, the reality that wealthier areas have more bargaining muscle than poorer ones must be recognized. Wealthier discontented areas can more easily foment political dissolution than disgruntled poorer areas, especially if there is a well-targeted social safety net. Russia is in a dire economic state. It must be turned around to create the wealth that could allow equalization in poorer areas in the longer term. Using a formula-based distribution system, while also emphasizing "derivation-based sharing" (keeping a fixed part of revenues raised within the local area) should play an important role in revenue distribution at this time.

Also, given Russia's political fragility, demands for special treatment by some regions must be handled carefully. In some cases problems will be resolved by simply putting more weight on derivation sharing. In others, such as in ethnically distinct regions like Tatarstan, the situation must be rethought. Maybe these regions will not be content with greater retention of revenues; they may insist on more expenditure rights. If so, and if the areas can be narrowly defined to limit setting precedents for other places (as in Malaysia), they may receive special treatment. This could be in the form of additional government transfers through a distribution formula, which includes weights for such factors as ethnic differences. India is a useful example: it has included such special cases as "backward states" and "tribal and hilly areas" in its formula. Although it is critical to address the concerns of seriously aggrieved regions, this should be done transparently. Since people are "testing out" democracy in Russia, this should be done by including special factors in the formula, not by making ad hoc decisions.

What formula should be used in Russia? Given the weak data at the present time, a detailed needs-based approach is too complicated (and impossible) for now. A simple formula would be best (chapter 5). However, as Indonesia shows, a formula that is based solely on population (or any other basic per capita indicator) and therefore implicitly assumes equal expenditure needs will lead to regional disparities because of the different costs of services. Thus, per capita allocations should be weighted by a factor that includes some cost differential (and maybe a "catching up" factor) for that area.

Nigeria's experience holds another important lesson for Russia: institutionalize revenue distribution through an objective "grants commission." This is crucial to insulate the process from political pressures. And Russia's oblasts are in no mood for more central, unilateral executive-branch decisionmaking. But any commission needs a mandate and authority to complete its task effectively. This is especially so in Russia, where a system of ad hoc negotiations is deeply ingrained.

The catalyst that binds—a formula and special needs

In the past the Russian federal government has dealt with the discontented in a makeshift fashion, through intergovernmental negotiated subventions and ad hoc changes in tax retentions. Such make-do is not transparent. Some oblasts perceive that others are striking better deals with the central government, and a sense of injustice arises. The need for transparency is particularly great in Russia when many (skeptical) people are testing out democracy. When twenty of Russia's oblasts experimented with a single channel tax system in the fall of 1992, the financial (and political) future of the Russian Federation was threatened. Just such an approach contributed to the financial bankruptcy of the U.S.S.R. and hastened its political demise. That the central government of the Federation was able to force some compliance with the established tax laws, however, is a hopeful sign that regional demands can be met through a mixture of central leverage and concessions. But increasing demands for greater retention of natural resource taxes and more autonomy for ethnic regions raise the question of whether to grant special fiscal status to some territories within the Russian Federation. A few countries (for example, Australia, the Philippines, and Spain) do provide special regimes within otherwise uniform systems. Yet Canada clearly shows that the Pandora's box can open wide once such demands are expressed by any group.

Individually negotiated arrangements could still threaten the future of the Federation if the center concedes too much to each region. But so, too, could the insistence on totally uniform fiscal treatment, if disgruntled groups decide to opt out. Demands for special treatment should not be taken lightly, but great care should be exercised in granting it. Once given, special regimes are virtually impossible to "claw back." And given once, they will surely prompt similar demands from other groups.

Since special regimes are not an ideal solution, the challenge becomes how to meet these needs in the context of the sharing-cum-transfer system—how much should be allocated on a formula basis, and how much by derivation. Many oblasts (those rich in natural and industrial resources, for example) resent the perceived cross-subsidies inherent in the present system and would like to opt out. However, if one oblast is permitted a special regime, the others with above-average economic strength might demand similar treatment, leaving only the poorer oblasts in the system. Ironically then, overemphasis on equalization at this stage may prompt the wealthier oblasts to withdraw from the pool, which would reduce the possibility of implementing *any* equalization. A new intergovernmental system can help relieve this tension through transparent division of revenue-sharing monies between equalizing transfers (or equalization-based sharing) and derivation-based sharing (chapter 5). An independent, objective "grants commission" could decide on distributions and could reflect national participation in determining the size of the two suggested components— the formula grant and the derivation-based shares.

Other demands for special treatment also can be dealt with through the distribution formula. The Punjab in India receives extra government funding through the Indian tax devolution formula, which recognizes the difficulty of being a border state. Also, as part of India's grant formula, "backward" areas are given an extra weight, which means more compensation for them. In Russia, areas with a concentration of ethnic minorities might be assigned a higher weight in the distribution formula, giving them more revenues. Then, perhaps, these areas could be given greater expenditure responsibilities and more autonomy in spending than other areas. This would result in their having greater autonomy than other oblasts but would retain their participation in the common system. Resource-rich areas, which have suffered from underdevelopment and environmental degradation, could also be compensated through the formula.

Meeting special needs through the formula is appealing for several reasons. A formula represents an objective distribution method: however, once established, its components allow special treatment where deemed appropriate by policymakers. It appeases disgruntled groups while maintaining the transparency so necessary to prevent even a sense of injustice. A greater sense of justice will encourage areas to stay within the system rather than opt out and reduce the common resource pool. Moreover, although discontented regions might still demand special treatment (even in the formula), decisions would be made by an objective commission for about five years and thus would in principle be well insulated from political pressure.

Conclusion

The intergovernmental system has a crucial part to play in defusing the potentially explosive situation in ethnic and resource-rich regions by containing them within an agreed framework. Unless a transparent system is developed, based on consensus, the Federation will probably continue to run the risks inherent in a negotiated system. With no rules, subnational governments will drive hard bargains for the best they can get; they will create an "asymmetrical federalism" and special regimes. If, however, localities feel they are being treated fairly in uniform intergovernmental fiscal arrangements and that allocation is based on fair and objective criteria, they may give up demands for asymmetrical federalism. In particular, any special needs will be addressed within the formula more or less objectively—by virtue of the formula, not "ad hocery." A flexible formula serves shorter-term fiscal goals, while promoting the nation building that is necessary for longer-term fiscal health. More generally, any system that is seen to be fair and transparent and that is developed through an institutional process in which all oblasts take part is likely to contribute to a consensus on revenue sharing, to improve fiscal federalism, and to advance the prospects for Russia's future.

Note

1. On December 29, 1992, the president of Chechenya, Dzhorkhar Dudayev, wrote U.S. President-elect Clinton announcing his country's determination to use all means necessary to defend its freedom. The president of Tatarstan, Mintimer Shaymiyev, has made several visits to the United States and attended the inauguration of President Clinton in an attempt to forge close relations with the United States.

8

Making—or breaking—Russia

Christine I. Wallich

Intergovernmental finance in Russia is not a "local matter."[1] Fiscal federalism is at the heart of the future of the Russian Federation. Decisions on how services and goods are provided by subnational governments and who pays for them will have consequences that extend far beyond local areas. In Russia and other economies in transition the design of fiscal federalism is crucial, since it can affect most key aims of reform—including macroeconomic stabilization, the establishment of an effective safety net, private sector development, and nation building.

Russia is facing a difficult period of economic and political transition. It is attempting, simultaneously, to restructure its economic system, protect the well-being of citizens, stabilize prices and external balance, provide public services to support social and economic development, and establish a system of governance acceptable to regions whose cultural identity, natural resource endowments, and economic development differ widely.

Intergovernmental fiscal reform is crucial for the success of Russia's reform effort, and its future direction. Because Russia's subnational governments account for almost half of all budgetary outlays, sound intergovernmental fiscal policies are critical to successful stabilization. With various regional forces pulling at the Federation, *how* revenues and resources are divided across subnational governments is also crucial for creating a cohesive federation in the present period of nation building. Moreover, the ownership role of subnational governments makes them key players in (or impediments to) privatization efforts. Finally, expenditure reform has given subnational governments important new responsibilities for the social safety net, which will take on a new shape, shifting away from subsidies toward targeted programs. Failure to design an appropriate system of intergovernmental fiscal relations can jeopardize all these goals; a well-designed system can help greatly to achieve them.

Intergovernmental finance in traditional federations

In a traditional federation, the design of intergovernmental relations raises few issues. The first step in designing a good system of intergovernmental finance is determining clearly the role of government and the private sector (chapter 3). During transition from a centrally planned to a market economy, the pervasive role of government must be significantly reduced. In countries as diverse as China and Romania budgetary outlays (as a percentage of GDP) have been halved as reforms bite and as government changes from owner, entrepreneur, provider of private services, and "employer of first resort" to provider only of goods and services that cannot be left to market forces. Governments in market economies focus mostly on purely public goods whose benefits extend beyond individual households and are nonexclusionary. Russia has begun this process, but reducing the size of government and redirecting it are still distant goals for the Federation. Even so, over the long run in Russia, too, the private sector will eventually dominate production.

Expenditure assignment and subnational governments

The traditional question of expenditure assignment in a federation is, which services should be provided by which level of government? Public finance theory suggests that an "efficient" expenditure assignment relates to the geographic dimension of benefits (chapter 4) (Oates 1972). Services whose benefits do not go beyond the boundaries of municipalities should be provided by municipal government. Services whose benefits accrue to several communities (for example, intercity highways) should be provided by subnational government, and benefits affecting the entire country should be provided by central government. Expenditures related to macroeconomic stabilization and income distribution (such as the social safety net) are typically "assigned" to central government, since it is best equipped to pursue stabilization policy—labor and capital mobility often interfere with any serious attempt by local governments to affect income distribution. In Russia's system of intergovernmental finance these basic principles of expenditure assignment were until recently generally observed.

Revenue assignment and subnational governments

There are many models for providing subnational governments with revenues (chapter 5). Taxes can be assigned to, or shared between, levels of government. Some countries allow "concurrent" tax powers or share some *tax bases,* allowing, for example, local governments to surcharge federal taxes, such as the personal income tax. In unitary fiscal systems, including Russia and most economies in transition, the tax base and tax rates are usually decided by the center and defined for the whole nation. In some highly federal fiscal systems (for example, Canada, India, and the United States) subnational government has a strong voice in determining the nature of its taxes. In most countries, regardless of how the tax side is decided and allocated, subnational tax receipts are supplemented by transfers, since central government takes the best revenues and then assigns to the subnational level more expenditures than can be financed by assigned revenues or tax bases. Because of this "vertical imbalance," transfers and their design become crucial.

Designing the transfer system is complex, partly because there are usually so many objectives—for example, avoiding disincentives to subnational revenue collection, ensuring that central macroeconomic management is not compromised, and achieving some degree of equalization. The first step is to determine the aggregate *volume* of revenue transfers, the second to determine their *distribution* across subnational governments. Transfers can be ad hoc and negotiated or, more desirably, based on a formula and an ex ante agreed volume for subnational governments. This distribution formula can incorporate many factors. These typically include an estimate of subnational spending "needs" (often determined by population and per capita income or social development and the cost of delivering services in that area) and an assessment of the local revenues available for financing these needs, often adjusted by local "tax effort." There also needs to be a decision on how much of the resulting "gap" should be filled—that is, how far equalization should reach.

The complications for fiscal federalism in Russia

Transition from a centralized to a market economy necessarily means a dramatic change in the responsibilities of enterprises and government. Enterprises in Russia and other economies in transition provide social services that are the responsibility of the state in market economies. Schools, health clinics, housing, and urban infrastructure (including roads and sewerage) were all part of the enterprises' "social assets" and outlays. As "marketization" proceeds in Russia, enterprise spending not directly related to production must be shed. Spinning off social expenditure will reduce the need for government subsidies to enterprises and increase their after-tax profits. It is not certain, however, that the tax benefit will accrue to the same level of government that must pick up the expenditure tab. Some divested social assets (sports facilities and guesthouses) can be privatized as fee-earners.

But what level of government should take on the rest? Subnational governments are likely to be saddled with quite a few of them, since many of these social assets—in health and education, for example—are in traditional areas of subnational responsibility.

Looking ahead to a more appropriate system of tax sharing, tax assignment, or transfers in Russia, the first stage is an assessment of the expenditure responsibilities of subnational governments. One would begin by deciding those functions that will remain the responsibility of government. Then, there must follow concrete quantitative analysis of functions to be given up by enterprises and assumed by subnational government. Finally, a list must be drawn up of functions that should no longer be the responsibility of *any* government and that must be shed. The resulting size of subnational governments' budgets is difficult to judge, but their expenditure responsibilities may well increase. The future will likely mean stronger, more broadly responsible oblasts. However, *how* revenues are shared is perhaps more important for the shape of the Federation than actual assignment of expenditure responsibilities. The how of it will include the degree of revenue dependence or independence of oblast governments (so-called vertical balance); the degree of federal conditionality over use of oblast resources; the scope of the intergovernmental system; and above all, how, de facto, the system is implemented.

The critical task in designing Russia's revenue and transfer system is ensuring that each level of government has enough revenue (from all sources combined) to deliver assigned services. In most market economies, when expenditure needs and revenue assignments are ill-matched, one level of government (usually subnational) is left without enough to provide needed services, leading to a fiscal squeeze on local economies. In an economy in transition the nature of the "soft budget constraint" can lead to a fundamentally different outcome. Searching for ways to finance service delivery, Russia's subnational governments can revert to "coping mechanisms" that allow services to be delivered where otherwise they could not be (chapter 3). But the cost can be measured in many other important national objectives forgone. Such coping mechanisms can include shifting public budgetary outlays to enterprises still owned by local governments, resisting privatization of firms that provide extensive public services and, in the peculiar soft budget environment still prevailing in Russia, encouraging enterprises to borrow (or accrue arrears) to continue to provide services. Subnational governments may also establish extrabudgetary accounts and other sources of funds that reduce budgetary transparency. Finally, they may suspend or reduce tax remittances to the center. These coping mechanisms are particularly dangerous in Russia today because they threaten macroeconomic stability, privatization, social safety nets, and, not least, national cohesion.

Promoting macroeconomic stabilization

The main aim of Russia's macroeconomic stabilization policy is to stem inflation, implying austerity by central and subnational governments. How restrictive budgetary measures affect each level of government depends on how governmental functions are reassigned between federal and oblast levels.

The absence of revenue-expenditure correspondence is a striking reality of the current stabilization effort. In fiscal 1992 most major cuts were made in central government expenditures—enterprise investment, producer and consumer subsidies, and defense. This was followed by the delegation to subnational government of an important part of social expenditures and, later, of almost *all* investment outlays (including airports and military housing). Given the severity and duration of unemployment likely to accompany structural adjustment and the impact of inflation on fixed incomes, pressures will increase on subnational governments to help the most vulnerable groups of society. Subnational governments must also assume much social spending that has, until now, been carried by their state-owned enterprises. On the tax side the budget envisaged a marked increase in taxes (mainly on petroleum products and foreign trade), much of which accrues to the federal government, while most additional spending will be borne by the subnational governments. A "mismatching" of revenues and expenditures can be expected, which may be severe, especially in some of Russia's poorer oblasts.

The present intergovernmental system has not focused on these new responsibilities—or on the budgetary pressures on subnational governments. Pushing the deficit downward, by shifting unfunded expenditure responsibilities to subnational governments in the hope that they will do the cost-cutting, has alienated oblast governments. It has also pitted them against each other, at a time when forces within oblasts are pulling for greater participatory democracy and local control. Superficially, this has reduced the federal budget deficit; in fact, the central government is merely pushing its headaches down to subnational governments, suppressing the deficit but not necessarily reducing it. This is politically provocative at a time when nation building is a major concern. Political cohesion cannot be taken for granted. Skeptical oblasts ask, what expenditure functions remain for the center to fulfill? At the time of the dissolution of the Soviet Union, little more than defense, higher research, and administration of government remained with the center—not enough to justify its continued existence.

Subnational governments, caught without enough revenue to cover spending and new mandates, have been forced to cope. They accumulated expenditure arrears and, in some cases, delayed federal tax remittances. Some have borrowed from banks and from "their" enterprises (which have easier access to credit), adding to pressure for credit creation. They have also sought out extrabudgetary resources and funds and retained ownership of local enterprises so that they can continue providing social and other local services. All these coping mechanisms, deployed in response to misaligned expenditure responsibilities and revenue flows, threaten macroeconomic stability. Ironically, focusing economic stabilization policy on reducing the federal budget deficit—in essence, misspecifying the stabilization objective—may be leading to actions that will further destabilize the economy. It will also reduce the transparency of budgetary accounts and, if oblasts are "successful" in obtaining credit, subvert monetary objectives. Ironically, this too threatens Russia and its national cohesiveness, in that skeptical oblasts can lose faith in a central government that is not even up to a main task of government—providing price stability.

Privatization

The failed intergovernmental policy, which seeks to reduce the budget deficit by squeezing the subnational sector, also threatens privatization and the future economic direction of Russia. After the dissolution of the U.S.S.R. and the emergence of the Russian Federation, a broad agreement was reached that ownership of enterprises should be reassigned to the different levels of government. Most union property was transferred to the Russian Federation, and each enterprise was assigned to the level of government to which it was subordinated (mainly oblasts and rayons). Indeed, an important aspect of fiscal decentralization in Russia has been the transfer of assets from central ownership to subnational governments. Thus, unlike market economies, subnational governments in Russia's transition economy continue to see their role very much in terms of "ownership" and direct economic interventions, rather than service provision. They derive significant funds from enterprises they own and have a major stake in the assets and enterprises transferred to them during decentralization. Hard-pressed oblasts may therefore oppose privatization and seek to reinforce their revenue base by holding onto the enterprises they still own and control to ensure the continued provision of many needed (but now increasingly unaffordable) public services. Alternatively, they may encourage enterprises to directly provide such public services, making them harder still to privatize. The intergovernmental policy thus has implications for the economic shape Russia will take. Will it become commercial, capitalist, and market-oriented, or will it remain statist and publicly controlled?

Spurring economic growth

A fiscal squeeze on subnational governments can also worsen resource allocation and put Russia on a path of less efficient and lower growth. Subnational governments' vested interests in shares of enterprise revenues and local service provision could—in an economy as regionalized and with as few antimonopoly policies as Russia—encourage domestic protectionism and interoblast trade barriers to protect local monopolies (chapter 3). Such interregional trade barriers will ultimately reduce economic growth, as has impeding trade among the U.S.S.R.'s former republics. As a result, subnational governments play a crucial role in determining the future efficiency with which the Russian economy performs. Both incentives in the budgetary system and the potential responses of subnational governments need to be "right," if Russia's stabilization and privatization reforms are to succeed and if growth is to materialize. A failed intergovernmental policy can deepen regionalism and, if it succeeds in deepening protectionism, almost certainly reduce growth.

Providing a social safety net

The design of the intergovernmental fiscal system will also influence the differentiation (regional and interpersonal) that emerges in the Russian Federation. In 1992, in an apparent effort to balance the budget, Russia's central government transferred responsibility for social protection and price subsidies (previously financed with direct transfers from the federal government) to subnational governments. The government has not, it seems, estimated the cost of financing this social protection or considered whether it can be met with available revenues in each oblast. If the adequacy of the social safety net becomes an issue of *national* priority in the difficult transition ahead, it should not be a major responsibility of subnational governments alone. If it is, some will be able to provide, others will not, and regional differences in well-being will be accentuated. Moreover, the derivation-based approach to revenue sharing, so relied on in Russia, is strongly counterequalizing, with richer oblasts benefiting more than poorer ones. Service levels will inevitably vary across regions. The intergovernmental system will thus influence the future economic differentiation of Russia, depending on its commitment to equalization, or lack thereof.

Building the nation

The ad hoc shifts in expenditures from central to subnational governments (such as social outlays and capital investment) have made it difficult for

Russia to move away from the system inherited from the old Soviet regime. More important, it has led skeptical oblasts to ask, what functions are left to justify the center? Already the center is, in their eyes, failing to provide macroeconomic stability. Its lack of concreteness in assigning expenditures and its jettisoning of federal outlays onto subnational governments could contribute to the worst fear of the federal government—disintegration of the Russian Federation. The sense of injustice at the subnational level has risen as oblasts have been left struggling with inadequate resources and an untransparent revenue-sharing system.

Nation building is threatened in two ways by the lack of transparency. First, it has led wealthier oblasts to complain that the present negotiated intergovernmental fiscal system is overequalizing (that is, that they are subsidizing the poorer oblasts)—although statistical analysis suggests this is not so. Second, the system of tax administration, in which all revenues are collected by oblasts and below and remitted to the federal government, makes the center dependent on oblast compliance and, thus, vulnerable. Indeed, in the fall of 1992 about twenty disgruntled oblasts (by 1993, the number had reportedly reached thirty), concerned about overequalization, unilaterally decided to halt full payments to the center. Such behavior, if it continues or spreads, could lead to the fiscal dissolution of the Russian Federation, just as the republics' failure to contribute to the union budget hurried the dissolution of the U.S.S.R. in 1991.

Discontent among oblasts is heightened by ethnic tensions and disagreements over sharing natural resource revenues. Areas inhabited by non–Russian peoples claim the right to greater autonomy because of *their* different history and culture. And some resource-rich areas want special financial arrangements that give them greater benefits from what they see as *their* natural resource revenue and command over their resource heritage. These regions say that development in their area has not benefited from their natural resources and that, instead, they have sustained severe environmental damage because of past resource exploitation. The problem is compounded when the two overlap—that is, resource-rich territories inhabited by ethnic minorities. For example, Yakutia, with less than 1 percent of Russia's population, is home to an ethnic minority, as well as to 99 percent of Russia's (and 25 percent of the world's) diamonds; it is demanding greater autonomy and retention of natural wealth and has threatened to break away from the rest of Russia if these demands are not met. And Tatarstan has yet to sign Russia's Federation Agreement.

The danger of intergovernmental conflict seems to be well understood by Russian authorities at this critical time, when the importance of nation building is paramount. Given the extreme political tensions between federal and oblast governments, a carefully designed system of fiscal federalism can serve to bind the country when centrifugal forces threaten to tear it apart. In this context, the importance of developing a transparent intergovernmental system that is based on criteria which are agreed to be fair and that provides revenue-expenditure correspondence is crucial.

What about the tradeoff between regional equity and growth? If the new intergovernmental fiscal system overemphasizes equalization, wealthier oblasts (including the resource-rich) may be less willing to take part in the Federation. At this sensitive point in Russia's history the need for political unity may be greater than the need for equality. If this is so, it suggests more weight should be given to revenue sharing that emphasizes growth over redistribution, allowing the better-off oblasts to move ahead and reap the benefits of their larger fiscal capacity.

Whither Russia?

The future cohesion of the Russian Federation depends on a well-designed intergovernmental system that matches expenditures and revenues, while incorporating the interests of diverse regional entities. Whether it is economic or political differences that inspire demands for greater autonomy, the fiscal system is at the heart of any solution.

The critical linkages between intergovernmental fiscal relations and other key aims of reform (such as macroeconomic stability, privatization, the social safety net, and nation building) are not unique to Russia. They are found in most European economies in transition, and some aspects are found in countries throughout the world. Canada, India, Malaysia, and the United Kingdom have tried, with varying success, to buy the cooperation of subnational governments through the intergovernmental fiscal system. In economies in transition as diverse as Hungary, Romania, and Bulgaria, the fiscal squeeze on local governments seems to be turning them somewhat into barriers to (not partners in) privatization. Nor is it only in Russia that the social safety net and other outlays have been shifted downstairs, threatening services and provoking coping mechanisms that contribute to more instability. But the linkages are particularly striking in Russia, where both the economic and political systems are in flux.

The speed of change in Russia and the immediacy of issues now facing its policymakers make it hard to implement policies that require a *long-term* view. Nonetheless, unless the issue of an intergovernmental financing system is addressed quickly and comprehensively, it can jeopardize Russia's entire reform program. The major challenge is to create an integrated framework for change that will be compatible with short-term stabilization, combine "rules with discretion," and be flexible enough to accommodate the major structural shifts in the economy, while also providing stability to subnational governments.

The present time is a critical window of opportunity for introducing such refinements because the overall design of the intergovernmental system, like much else in Russia, is still in transition. Policymakers must change their view toward public finance issues. Issues that are traditionally viewed in isolation—expenditure assignment and spending mandates, tax sharing and assignment, subsidies and transfers, and tax and deficit reduction policies at the macroeconomic level—must be taken together and incorporated into the new intergovernmental system. A new system of laws on fiscal decentralization was introduced between 1991 and 1993 in an attempt to introduce greater transparency and to address some of these concerns. But the program is incomplete, and new laws may be needed. The next step for Russia is a careful, empirical study of all options. This is a complex, but essential, technical exercise to start defining the future intergovernmental system. And a "blue-ribbon commission" to establish consensus on the basic principles and directions of the system (and on the rights of resource producers) must be established also.

Russia is at a crossroads. It is searching for a new identity since the breakup of the Union, while struggling to introduce democracy and at the same time accommodate clashing economic demands from various groups. All this, when most immediately it is seeking to stabilize and privatize the economy. The stakes are high. Will Russia transform itself into a market economy and shake off the shackles of state ownership? Or will it remain burdened by ineffectual government? Will it become a nationally integrated market, in which enterprises compete on price and quality? Or will it remain regionalized and parochial, with protectionist local fiefdoms stifling integration of economic activity? Will Russia's oblasts see benefits from a close federation? Or will they see more benefits in confederation and greater independence? The incentives of the intergovernmental system will influence all three of these issues.

With all eyes on Russia's simultaneous transformation to a market economy and a democratic political system, it is easy to see intergovernmental fiscal relations as yet another technical area that needs to be tackled. However, subnational fiscal reforms and fiscal balance are key to most of Russia's major reform goals. And intergovernmental finance will have a major impact on Russia's macroeconomic performance, the safety net, and privatization. Fiscal federalism must be woven into the analysis of experts and policymakers studying privatization, stabilization, and growth. There is great danger in studying these subjects independently of the intergovernmental dimension. With Russia striving to reach so many ambitious objectives simultaneously, intergovernmental fiscal relations should not stand in the way. Local finance in Russia is not a "local matter." It could make Russia—or break it.

Note

1. This chapter draws on Litvack and Wallich (1993).

Appendixes

A. List of laws mentioned in the text
B. Decree by the Supreme Soviet of the Russian Federation: Law on the Basic Principles of the Tax System of the Russian Federation
C. Consolidated budget of the Russian Federation, 1992
D. Oblast revenues and expenditures, Russian Federation, 1991
E. Oblast revenues and expenditures, Russian Federation, 1992

Appendix A List of laws mentioned in the text

Law on the Basic Principles of Taxation

Passed December 1991, for implementation January 1, 1992. It was only partially implemented. See appendix B for text of the law, in unofficial translation.

Law on the Rights of Local Self-Governments

Passed 1992. This law on local self-government describes in great detail the rights and responsibilities of subnational governments. It includes a description of municipal property (Art.37) and confirms the right of subnational governments to grant tax benefits and give other forms of preferential treatment to local enterprises (Art.39). Furthermore, subnational governments can determine the enterprise profit tax rate in accordance with the applicable legislation. The law also endorses budget balance and includes the right of subnational governments to borrow and to set up extrabudgetary funds (Art.46).

Law on the Budgetary Rights of Local Self-Governments

Passed June 1993. This law has five parts. The first describes general provisions of the budgets of subnational levels. The second describes the division of budget revenues at the subnational level. Each level shares certain taxes with other levels of subnational government, but the sharing rates are negotiable among the subnational governments. Examples of shared ("regulating") taxes are the personal income tax, corporate income tax, payments for natural resources and water, and the land tax. In a second category are revenues that accrue 100 percent to one level of subnational government, such as stamp duties (districts), the tax on inherited property (district and city budgets), timber revenues and revenues from state-owned property (level of government that is the owner). The law calls for oblasts' fixed revenues and regulating revenues (those shared between levels) to provide for at least 70 percent of each oblast's "minimum budget." If the fixed revenues alone are not sufficient to provide this, shares in the regulating revenues must be provided. The third part of the law addresses the expenditure side of the budget and discusses the "minimum budget," but does not define it. The budget process is addressed in part four. The fifth part describes the budget rights of subnational governments. These guaranteed rights explicitly state that budget surpluses at the subnational level cannot be extracted and can be used at the discretion of the respective subnational government.

It also includes a detailed description of extrabudgetary funds and currency funds at the subnational level. Finally, the law "guarantees" rayons a minimum expenditure level.

Law on Property Tax

Passed 1992. A local mandatory tax levied anually on the value of buildings, premises, and structures, including apartments, residential houses, dachas, and garages owned by individuals. Regional and local councils may reduce the rates and establish tax benefits. The tax proceeds belong to the budget of the local council where the property is located.

Law on Payments for Natural Resources

Passed 1992. A two-tiered payment, consisting of an initial payment and periodic payments starting at the beginning of extraction. Payments are fixed on the basis of the quantity and quality of the mineral in the deposit and of the geographical, technological, and economic conditions of the exploration (and the risk involved). For energy carriers (petroleum, natural gas, and coal) the rate is 8 percent of the official wholesale price.

Natural resource revenue share of federal, regional, and local budgets
(percent)

	Federal	Regional	Local
Hydrocarbons	40	30	30
General-use minerals	0	0	100
Other onshore minerals	25	25	50
Continental shelf	40	60	0
High seas	0	0	100

Half the federal take goes to the krai or oblast where exploitation occurs. Governments may agree on different sharing in special cases. Proceeds from the payments belong to the budgets of rayons and cities.

Law on Land Tax

Passed 1992. A local mandatory tax on arable land assessed on the basis of the quality of land area and its location. This is to be the only tax paid by collective farms, state farms, peasant farms, agroeconomic entities and organizations, cooperatives, and other agricultural enterprises (but not by agroindustrial enterprises). They are liable to other taxes, however, if nonagricultural income exceeds 25 percent of total income.

The tax proceeds are earmarked for land development. Basic rates for the land tax vary among oblasts (regions) from R 10 (minimum rate) to R 176 per hectare. Coefficients are applied for historical sites, certain cities, and resort areas. The proceeds of the tax belong to the budgets of the rural, town, and district councils, depending on the location of the land.

Draft Law on Subventions to Local Governments

Passed June 1992, for implementation January 1, 1993. This law has not been implemented. To regulate federal transfers and therefore make them more transparent, the Supreme Soviet in June 1992 adopted the Law on Subventions to the Republics constituting the Russian Federation, its Territories, Regions, Autonomous Regions, Autonomous Districts, and the cities of Moscow and St. Petersburg. This law provides a framework for allocating and monitoring the use of federal grants. The general provisions of the law clearly establish that the objective of the federal grants to regions (called "subventions" in the law) is to equalize the levels of socioeconomic development throughout the country. Furthermore, federal transfers will take the form of conditional matching grants for specific purposes. Finally, federal transfers will systematically be subject to monitoring by the Supreme Soviet and the Ministry of Finance.

The specific conditions governing the allocation and use of federal transfers differ according to their budgetary or extrabudgetary origin. Budgetary resources are allocated by the Ministry of Finance and targeted at priority budget expenditures. These are (1) current expenditures for social and cultural measures, the maintenance of budget-funded organizations, and the social protection of the population; (2) capital investments for the development of the social infrastructure, the protection of the environment, and comprehensive area development; and (3) natural disasters, epidemics, mass riots, and other emergency situations. To qualify for federal grants for current expenditures, the share of the recipient regional government's revenue allocated to social expenditure should exceed the national average. Capital grants are subject to technical screening as regional investment projects by the Ministry of Economy.

In contrast to budgetary grants, extrabudgetary federal transfers are not intended to cover current budget expenditures of subnational governments but "to attract additional resources for the financing of local investment projects and programs." Federal transfers from extrabudgetary funds are also decided by the Supreme Soviet. Domestic and foreign credits and loans, as well as "other receipts," are cited as extrabudgetary resources. The share of federal extrabudgetary transfers is limited to 80 percent of the recipient's own investment in the given project.

Although the equalization principle is stated up front, the Law on Subventions does not provide objective criteria to meet the goal of equity. In practice the allocation may not be equitable. Transfers would only be allocated to those oblasts whose social expenditures as a share of total expenditures exceed the national average share. The per capita social outlay may be low in absolute terms in a low-income oblast, and if its share of social expenditure were also less than the average, it would be ineligible for transfers.

Although still far from perfect, this draft law was a first attempt to rationalize the existing practice of negotiated federal transfers (i.e., "subventions") to the oblasts (regions). The present grant system therefore remains without transparent criteria for allocating federal transfers to lower levels of government. At this stage, it seems that the reform of intergovernmental fiscal relations in the Russian Federation will have to await the outcome of the ongoing constitutional debate.

Decree on the Division of State Property

Passed 1992. This law decrees how the U.S.S.R. state property is transferred to ownership by the Russian Federation and its oblasts and rayons.

Law on the Basic Principles of the Budget System and Budgetary Process in the Russian Federation

Passed 1992. The Law on the Basic Principles of the Budget System divides the budget into current and capital outlays (Art.11) and states that the capital budget (deficit) may be financed through government bond issues or "credit resources" (Art.13). It also defines procedures for budget accounting and budget balance and defines procedures by which budget balance must be achieved, that is, capital expenditures are cut first, followed by 5,10, or 15 percent (or whatever is needed) across-the-board expenditure cuts of recurrent outlays.

Appendix B Decree by the Supreme Soviet of the Russian Federation: Law on the Basic Principles of the Tax System of the Russian Federation, "Basic Principles of Taxation"

Decree by the Supreme Soviet of the Russian Federation on the procedure to enact the Law of the Russian Federation, entitled Basic Principles of the Tax System of the Russian Federation (unofficial translation)

The Supreme Soviet of the Russian Federation decides:

1. To enact the law of the Russian Federation, entitled Basic Principles of the Tax System of the Russian Federation, as of January 1, 1992, with the exception of provisions concerning distribution within the budgetary system of the value-added taxes and taxes levied on profits of enterprises and organizations.

2. To invite the Committee of the Supreme Soviet of the Russian Federation on Legislation to propose, by February 1, 1992, to the Supreme Soviet of the Russian Federation measures to bring the existing legislation of the Russian Federation in line with the above-mentioned law.

3. To invite the government of the Russian Federation to:

a) bring by January 15, 1992, its decisions in line with the above-mentioned law;

b) establish by April 1, 1992, the list of levies and other nontax payments together with corresponding procedures and deadlines. Until that date the above-mentioned payments shall be collected in accordance with the procedure established for 1991;

c) prepare and include, as of the 1992/93 school year, a course on tax legislation to be includedin the secondary school curriculum;

d) negotiate with foreign governments agreements to avoid double taxation of income (profits) and property of legal and natural persons;

e) solve, within two weeks' time, the following issues:

• provide the State Tax Service of the Russian Federation with necessary means and facilities, including premises, printing facilities, vehicles, computers, offices, and communication equipment, with separate allocation of funds for these purposes in the 1992 federal budget;

• staff tax authorities, including the central office of the State Tax Service of the Russian Federation, with necessary personnel and provide the latter with housing, child care, and the like.

Ruslan Khasbulatov
Chairman of the Supreme Soviet of the Russian Federation

Law of the Basic Principles of the Tax System of the Russian Federation

This law defines general principles of the tax system of the Russian Federation, taxes, levies, duties, and other payments, as well as rights and obligations of taxpayers and tax authorities.

CHAPTER 1. GENERAL PROVISIONS

Article 1. Establishment and abolition of taxes and other payments

Taxes, levies, duties, and other payments as well as tax benefits shall be established and abolished by the Supreme Soviet of the Russian Federation and other authorities in accordance with this law.

Laws that entail changes in tax payments shall not apply retroactively.

Article 2. Concept of taxes, other payments, and tax system

Taxes, levies, duties, and other payments are compulsory contributions to corresponding budgets or extrabudgetary funds made by payers in accordance with legislative acts.

Tax system is a totality of taxes, levies, duties, and other payments (referred hereafter as taxes) collected in accordance with the established procedure.

Article 3. Payers of taxes

Payers of taxes are legal persons, other categories of payers, and natural persons who, in accordance with legislative acts, have an obligation to pay taxes.

Payers of taxes defined in this article are referred to hereafter as taxpayers.

Article 4. Compulsory registration of taxpayers

Taxpayers shall be subject to compulsory registration with bodies of the State Tax Service of the Russian Federation (referred hereafter as tax authorities). Banks and other credit and loan institutions shall open current and other accounts for taxpayers only after the taxpayers produce a document confirming their registration with a tax authority; the banks and credit and loan institutions shall, within five days, inform the tax authority of such accounts being opened.

Article 5. Objects of taxation

Objects of taxation are income (profits), value of certain articles, certain kinds of income-generating activities, operations with securities, use of natural resources, property of legal and natural persons, transfer of property, value added of goods, works, and services, as well as other objects established by legislative acts.

Article 6. Nonrecurrence of taxation

A tax of a particular type shall be levied on the same object only once for a taxation period established by law.

Article 7. Establishment of tax rates

Tax rates, with the exception of excise tax rates, shall be established by the Supreme Soviet of the Russian Federation and other authorities in accordance with this law.

Article 8. Establishment of excise tax rates

Excise tax rates for certain types and categories of goods defined by the Supreme Soviet of the Russian Federation shall be established by the government of the Russian Federation.

Article 9. Distribution of tax revenues among budgets of different levels

Tax revenues shall be distributed among budgets of different levels and extrabudgetary funds following the procedure and terms established by the Supreme Soviet of the Russian Federation and other authorities in accordance with this law and other legislative acts.

Article 10. Tax benefits

The following tax benefits may be established in accordance with the procedure and terms defined by legislative acts:
- nontaxable minimum of the subject of taxation;
- exemption from taxation of certain elements of the subject of taxation;
- exemption from taxation of certain persons or categories of payers;
- reduced tax rates;
- deductions from the amount of the tax due for the reported period;

- target tax benefits, including tax credits (postponement of tax payments);
- other tax benefits.

Article 11. Obligations of taxpayers

1. The taxpayer shall be obliged to:
   - pay taxes;
   - keep books and prepare financial reports to be retained for at least five years;
   - provide tax authorities with documents and data necessary to calculate and collect taxes;
   - make amendments to the books to account for the amounts of hidden or understated income (profit) exposed by tax authorities;
   - explain in writing, in case of disagreement with the verification report of a tax authority, motives for not signing the report;
   - follow orders by tax authorities to rectify violations of the tax legislation;
   - fulfill other obligations.

The aforementioned obligations shall arise from the possession by a taxpayer of an object of taxation and on other grounds established by legislative acts.

In order to establish obligations of taxpayers the legislative acts shall determine:
   - the taxpayer (subject of taxation);
   - the unit of small taxation;
   - the tax;
   - deadlines for tax payments;
   - the budget or extrabudgetary fund to be credited.

2. The obligation of a natural person to pay taxes shall be terminated upon payment or abolition of the tax or upon death of the taxpayer when it is impossible to pay the tax without the deceased's personal participation, unless otherwise provided by legislative acts.

3. The obligation of a legal person to pay taxes shall be terminated upon payment or abolition of the tax. The inability to pay taxes shall be a reason to declare, in accordance with the established procedure, the legal person engaged in business activities bankrupt. In case of liquidation of a business of a legal person by a court order or by the owner on his own initiative the obligation to pay taxes due shall rest with the liquidation commission.

4. Should the taxpayer fail to carry out his obligations, their fulfillment shall be ensured through administrative, criminal, or tax sanctions imposed in accordance with this law as well by depositing a security in the form of

money or inventories or by obtaining a guarantee from the taxpayer's creditors.

Article 12. Rights of taxpayers

The taxpayer shall have the right to:
- submit to tax authorities documents confirming his right to tax benefits;
- read verification reports compiled by tax authorities;
- submit to tax authorities explanations with regard to calculation and payment of taxes as well as verification reports;
- appeal, in accordance with the established procedure, against decisions and actions by tax authorities and their officers; and other rights established by legislative acts.

Article 13. Sanctions for violations of tax legislation

1. The taxpayer who violated the tax legislation shall be liable, when it is stipulated by the law, to the following sanctions:

a) recovery of the whole amount of the hidden or understated income (profit) or of the amount of the tax due for any other hidden or unaccounted object of taxation and a penalty equal to that amount or, in case of a repeated violation, a penalty twice that amount. When the fact of the deliberate hiding or understating of income (profit) is established by the court of law acting upon the suit brought by a tax authority or a public procurator, it may impose on a taxpayer a fine, payable to the federal budget, five times the amount of the hidden or understated income (profit);

b) a penalty of 10 percent of the tax due for the last reporting quarter preceding the date of the verification, for each of the following types of violations:
- failure to account for an object of taxation;
- gross violation of the established procedure in the process of accounting for an object of taxation leading to concealment or understatement of the tax due for the period under verification by at least 5 percent of the amount of the tax payable for the last reporting quarter;
- failure to submit documents necessary to calculate and collect taxes or late submission of such documents;

c) a penalty for a delay in tax payments in the amount of 0.2 percent of the overdue payment for each day of the delay starting from the date when the payment became due, unless the law provides otherwise in respect of the amount of the penalty;

d) other sanctions provided for by legislative acts.

The overdue amounts of taxes and other mandatory payments as well as penalties and other sanctions provided for by the law shall be recovered, in case of a legal person, through an administrative action and, in case of a natural person, by a court order. In the latter case the amount overdue shall be levied on the income of the taxpayer or, in the absence of such income, on his property.

2. Officials and private persons guilty of violations of the tax legislation shall be liable to administrative, criminal, and disciplinary sanctions.

Article 14. Rights of tax authorities and their officers

1. Tax authorities shall have the right to:

a) solicit, in accordance with the established procedure, the prohibition of business activities of a taxpayer;

b) initiate actions in courts or arbitration tribunals with a view to:

- liquidate enterprises on the grounds established by law;
- nullify transactions and confiscate proceeds under such transactions;
- confiscate proceeds of unlawful activities;

c) other rights in accordance with the law.

2. Subject to the procedure established by law, officers of the tax authorities shall have the right to:

a) verify all documents concerning calculation and payment of taxes and request necessary explanations, information, and data on issues arising from the verification;

b) inspect any production, storage, trading, and other facilities used by taxpayers to generate income (profits), regardless of their location. In case of a refusal by a natural person to allow such officers to inspect premises used to generate income (profits) or in case of his failure to submit documents necessary to calculate taxes, the taxable income shall be determined on the basis of income generated by similar types of businesses;

c) freeze taxpayers' accounts with banks and credit and loan institutions in case of their failure to submit documents concerning calculation and payment of taxes;

d) impose fines on executive heads of banks, credit and loan institutions, and financial bodies in case of their failure to fulfill orders by tax authorities;

e) confiscate, upon their examination and certification, documents that could serve as evidence of a concealment or understatement of income (profits) or of a concealment of other objects of taxation;

f) request all legal persons to submit free of charge information necessary to calculate tax payments;

g) other rights provided for by legislative acts.

Article 15. Obligations of banks, credit and loan institutions, and enterprises

Banks, credit and loan institutions, commodity and stock exchanges, and other enterprises shall be required to submit, in accordance with the procedure established by the Ministry of Economy and Finance of the Russian Federation, to the corresponding tax authorities information on the financial and business operations of their clients for the last financial year.

In case of failure to submit such information executive heads of the above-mentioned institutions and enterprises shall be liable to an administrative fine five times the amount of the minimum monthly salary established by law, for every week of the delay.

Banks and credit and loan institutions shall not be allowed to delay execution of the taxpayers' orders to transfer the amounts of taxes to the budget or to an extrabudgetary fund and to use such amounts as their credit resources. In case such a delay is established the tax authority shall confiscate the profit received, crediting it to the federal budget, and the executive heads of such institutions shall be liable to an administrative fine five times the amount of the minimum monthly salary established by law.

In the case of failure to fulfill (or delay in fulfillment), through the fault of a bank or a credit institution, the payment order of a taxpayer, a fine of 0.2 percent of the unpaid amount of tax for each day of nonpayment starting from the fixed date of payment shall be collected from this institution. Collection of fine shall not release the bank or credit institution from other forms of liability.

Enterprises shall be obliged to deduct correctly the income tax from income paid by them to natural persons and promptly transfer the deducted amounts to the budget. In the case of a failure to fulfill the indicated obligations, these enterprises shall be prosecuted in accordance with the procedure established by legislative acts of the Russian Federation.

Article 16. Obligations and responsibilities of tax authorities

Tax authorities and their staff shall be obliged to keep commercial secrets, safeguard confidentiality concerning deposits of natural persons, and fulfill other obligations provided for under the Russian Federation law entitled State Tax Service of the Russian Soviet Federal Socialist Republic (RSFSR).

The damage caused to taxpayers due to improper implementation by tax authorities and their staff of their obligations shall be subject to restitution according to the established procedure. In addition, other sanctions provided by legislative acts of the Russian Federation may be applied to tax authorities and their staff.

Article 17. Protection of rights and interests of taxpayers and the State

The protection of rights and interests of taxpayers and the State shall be effected in accordance with judicial or other procedure provided by legislative acts of the Russian Federation.

CHAPTER 2. TYPES OF TAXES AND COMPETENCE OF GOVERNMENT AUTHORITIES

Article 18. Types of taxes levied on the territory of the Russian Federation

1. In the Russian Federation the following taxes shall be levied:
    a) federal taxes;
    b) taxes of republics within the Russian Federation and taxes of territories, regions, autonomous regions, and autonomous districts;
    c) local taxes.
    2. The competence of government authorities in resolving the questions concerning taxes shall be defined in accordance with the present law and other legislative acts.

Article 19. Federal taxes

1. The federal taxes shall include the following:
    a) value-added tax;
    b) excises on separate groups and types of goods;
    c) tax on bank profits;
    d) tax on profits from insurance activities;
    e) tax on exchange activities (exchange tax);
    f) tax on operations with securities;
    g) custom duty;
    h) allocations for reproduction of raw materials base transferred to the special extrabudgetary fund of the Russian Federation;
    i) payments for the use of natural resources transferred to the federal budget, republican budget of a republic within the Russian Federation, territorial and regional budgets of territories and regions, regional budget of an autonomous region, district budgets of autonomous districts, and local budgets of areas according to the procedure and conditions provided by legislative acts of the Russian Federation;
    j) income tax (profit levy) from enterprises;
    k) income tax from natural persons;
    l) taxes that serve as sources for formation of road funds transferred to these funds in accordance with the procedure established by legislative acts concerning road funds in the Russian Federation;

m) stamp duty;

n) state duty;

o) tax on property transferred as legacy or gift.

2. All amounts of receipts from taxes indicated in subparagraphs a) to g) of paragraph 1 of the present article shall be transferred to the federal budget.

3. The taxes indicated in subparagraphs j) and k) of paragraph 1 of the present article shall be regulating sources of profit, and amounts of allocations from these taxes transferred directly to the republican budget of a republic within the Russian Federation, territorial and regional budgets of territories and regions, regional budget of an autonomous region, district budgets of autonomous districts, and budgets of other levels shall be defined at the moment of approval of said budgets.

4. All amounts of receipts from taxes indicated in subparagraphs m) to o) of paragraph 1 of the present article are transferred to the local budget in accordance with the procedure established at the moment of approval of appropriate budgets unless otherwise provided by law.

5. The federal taxes (including determination of rates, objects of taxation, and taxpayers) and the procedure of their transfer to the budget or to the extrabudgetary fund shall be established by legislative acts of the Russian Federation and leveled on its entire territory.

Article 20. Taxes of republics within the Russian Federation and taxes of territories, regions, autonomous regions, and autonomous districts

1. The taxes of republics within the Russian Federation, territories, regions, autonomous regions, and autonomous districts shall include the following:

a) tax on property of enterprises. The amount of tax payments shall be transferred, in equal parts, to the republican budget of a republic within the Russian Federation, territorial and regional budgets of territories and regions, regional budget of an autonomous region, district budgets of autonomous districts and local budgets of areas, municipal budgets of cities according to the location of the taxpayer;

b) forest tax;

c) payment for water taken by industrial enterprises from water management systems.

2. The taxes indicated in paragraph 1 of the present article shall be established by legislative acts of the Russian Federation and levied on its entire territory. Specific rates of these taxes shall be defined by laws of *republics within* the Russian Federation or by decisions of government authori-

ties of territories, regions, autonomous regions, and autonomous districts, unless otherwise established by legislative acts of the Russian Federation.

Article 21. Local taxes

1. The local taxes shall include the following:

a) tax on property of natural persons. The amount of tax payments shall be transferred to the local budget according to the location of an object of small taxation;

b) land tax. The procedure of the transfer of tax receipts to the appropriate budget shall be defined by land legislation;

c) registration fee from natural persons involved in business activities. The amount of the fee shall be transferred to the budget according to the place of registration;

d) tax on construction of industrial facilities in resort areas;

e) resort fee;

f) fee for the right to trade. The fee shall be established by local, municipal (in absence of local division), area (in urban areas), settlement, or village authorities. The fee shall be paid in the form of acquisition of disposable ticket or temporary patent and shall be entirely transferred to the appropriate budget;

g) target fees from persons and enterprises, institutions, and organizations, irrespective of their institutional and legal forms, for the maintenance of militia, improvement of territory, and other purposes.

The annual rate of fees cannot exceed one percent of the established-by-law rates of the lowest monthly salary for a natural person and one percent of the annual payroll amount calculated on the basis of the established-by-law lowest monthly salary for a legal person.

The rates in cities and areas shall be established by appropriate government authorities, and in settlements and villages at the meetings and gatherings of residents;

h) tax on advertising. The tax shall be paid by legal and natural persons advertising their products at a rate not exceeding 5 percent of the value of advertising services;

i) tax on resale of cars, calculators, and personal computers. The tax shall be paid by legal and natural persons that sell the merchandise, at a rate not exceeding 10 percent of the amount of transaction;

j) fee from dog owners. The fee shall be paid annually by natural persons possessing dogs (excluding specially trained dogs) in urban areas in an amount not exceeding one-seventh of the established-by-law lowest monthly salary;

k) license fee for the right to sell wines and liquors. The annual fee shall be paid by legal and natural persons selling wines and liquors to the public in the following amounts: fifty established-by-law lowest monthly salaries from legal persons and twenty-five established-by-law lowest monthly salaries from natural persons. If these persons are trading from temporary stalls servicing parties, balls, festivities, and other activities the fee shall amount to half of the established-by-law lowest monthly salary for each day of trading;

l) license fee for the right to hold local auctions and lotteries. The fee shall be paid by organizers in an amount not exceeding 10 percent of the value of the goods declared for auction or the value of the issued lottery tickets;

m) fee for the issuing of order for an apartment. The fee shall be paid by natural persons upon obtaining the right to move into a separate apartment in an amount not exceeding three-fourths of the established-by-law lowest monthly salary (with level of fee depending on the total area and quality of dwelling);

n) fee for car parking. The fee shall be paid by legal and natural persons for car parking in areas especially equipped for these purposes in amounts established by local government authorities;

o) fee for the right to use local symbols. The fee shall be paid by manufacturers of products carrying local symbols (coats of arms; views of cities, localities, historical monuments; and the like) in an amount not exceeding 0.5 percent of the value of sold items;

p) fee for participation in the horse races at the hippodrome. The fee shall be paid by legal and natural persons whose horses participate in commercial races in the amounts established by local authorities of the area where the hippodrome is located;

q) fee for winnings at horse races. The fee shall be paid by persons who win at the hippodrome in an amount not exceeding 5 percent of winnings;

r) fee from persons participating in the totalizer game at the hippodrome. The fee shall be paid in the form of a percentage addition to the price established for the participation in the game in an amount not exceeding 5 percent of this price;

s) fee from transactions effected at commodity exchanges and from sale and purchase of currency. The fee shall be paid by participants of transactions in an amount not exceeding 0.1 percent of the amount of transaction;

t) fee for the right of cinematic and television filming. The fee shall be paid by commercial cinematic and television organizations conducting filming that requires local government authorities to implement organizational activities (detachment of militia details, organizing cordons around the filming area, and the like) in the amounts established by local government authorities;

u) fee for the cleaning of settlement territory. The fee shall be paid by legal and natural persons (owners of buildings) in the amount established by local government authorities.

2. The taxes indicated in subparagraphs a) to c) of paragraph 1 of the present article shall be established by legislative acts of the Russian Federation and shall be levied on its entire territory. Specific rates of these taxes shall be defined by legislative acts of republics within the Russian Federation or by decisions of government authorities of territories, regions, autonomous regions, autonomous districts, areas, cities, and other administrative units, unless otherwise provided by a legislative act of the Russian Federation.

3. The taxes indicated in subparagraphs d) and e) of paragraph 1 of the present article may be imposed by local and municipal government authorities that have jurisdiction over resort areas. The tax payments shall be transferred to local budgets of areas and municipal budgets of cities.

In the rural areas the amount of tax payments in equal parts shall be transferred to budgets of rural settlements, villages, and towns under local jurisdiction and to budgets of territories and regions that have jurisdiction over resort areas.

4. The taxes and fees indicated in subparagraphs a) to u) of paragraph 1 of the present article may be established by decisions of local and to municipal government authorities.

The amounts of tax and fee payments shall be transferred to local budgets of areas, to municipal budgets of cities or, following the decision of local and municipal government authorities, to local budgets of urban areas, villages, and rural settlements.

CHAPTER 3. CONCLUDING PROVISIONS

Article 22. Procedure of tax payment

The procedure for paying tax on income (profit levy) of a legal person who is, according to legislation, subject to several taxes shall be the following:
- all property taxes, duties, and other levies shall be paid in accordance with legislative acts;
- taxable income (profit) of taxpayer shall be reduced by the amount of taxes paid in accordance with the second paragraph of the present article, and then local taxes on income (profit), if any, shall be paid;
- taxable income (profit) of taxpayer shall be reduced by the amount of the paid local taxes indicated in the third paragraph of the present

article, and then all remaining taxes transferred to the account of income (profit) shall be paid in accordance with the established procedure;

- income tax (profit levy) shall be transferred to the account of income (profit) remaining after the payment of taxes indicated in the present article.

The payment of taxes by natural persons shall be effected in accordance with the procedure established by legislation of the Russian Federation.

Article 23. International agreements

1. The government of the Russian Federation shall participate in coordination of taxation policy with other members of the Commonwealth of Independent States and shall conclude international taxation agreements on prevention (elimination) of double taxation with subsequent ratification of these agreements by the Supreme Council of the Russian Federation.

2. If international treaties of the Russian Federation or the former U.S.S.R. establish rules other than those contained in the tax legislation of the Russian Federation the rules of international treaty shall apply.

Article 24. Control over tax collection

Control over accuracy and promptness of tax collection for the budget shall be implemented by tax authorities in accordance with the Russian Federation law, State Tax Service of the RSFSR, and other legislative acts.

The statutory limitation for claims made against natural persons in connection with tax collection for the budget shall be three years. Indisputable procedures for collecting the arrears in connection with taxes from legal persons may be applied within six years from the date of the emergence of the said arrear.

Article 25. Publication of methodological instructions

Instructions and methodological guidelines concerning application of tax legislation shall be published by the State Tax Service of the Russian Federation in consultation with the Ministry of Economy and Finance of the Russian Federation.

Article 26. Taxation reform

The taxation system shall stay in effect without changes until the adoption by the Supreme Council of the Russian Federation of decisions concerning taxation reform in accordance with the Russian Federation law entitled Basic Principles of the Budget System and Budgetary Process.

Boris Yeltsin
President of the Russian Federation

Appendix C Consolidated budget of the Russian Federation, 1992

(in billions of rubles; as a percentage of GDP)

Budget item	Central	Subnational	Consolidated	Share of GDP
Revenues	**2,951.3**	**2,280.3**	**5,231.6**	**30.0**
Profit taxes	645.9	921.5	1,567.4	9.0
Value-added taxes	1,500.7	498.2	1,998.9	11.5
Excises	100.5	111.0	211.5	1.2
Sales tax	0.0	4.7	4.7	0.0
Personal income tax	0.0	431.3	431.3	2.5
Property tax	0.0	54.7	54.7	0.3
Timber tax	0.0	31.8	31.8	0.2
Foreign economic activity	459.4	8.0	467.4	2.7
Geological exploration	73.4	0.0	73.4	0.4
Other tax and nontax revenue	171.4	219.1	390.5	2.2
Of which:				
Payment for land	17.0	54.0	71.0	0.4
Reevaluation of stock	33.7	10.1	43.8	0.3
Expenditures	**3,590.2**	**2,253.3**	**5,843.5**	**33.6**
National economy	1,095.2	963.5	2,058.7	11.8
Social and cultural activities	411.4	971.6	1,383.0	7.9
Of which:				
Education	229.7	449.8	679.5	3.9
Health and physical culture	52.8	415.0	467.8	2.7
Culture and mass media	59.4	56.8	116.2	0.7
Allowances to single mothers	—	—	—	n.a.
Poor families	3.4	0.0	3.4	0.0
Social security	15.0	50.0	65.1	0.4
Transfers to Pension Fund	51.2	0.0	51.2	0.3
Science	104.2	3.4	107.6	0.6
Foreign economic activities	416.5	0.2	416.7	2.4
Law enforcement and state administration	282.4	68.8	351.2	2.0
Defense	855.3	0.0	855.3	4.9
Other	425.1	245.8	670.9	3.9
Chernobyl	77.7	0.5	78.2	0.4
Budget balance	**(638.8)**	**26.9**	**(611.9)**	**-3.5**
Privatization receipts	18.9	43.4	62.3	0.4
Balance, including privatization receipts	**(619.9)**	**70.3**	**(549.6)**	**-3.1**
Intergovernmental financial transfers (net)	(267.4)	267.4	0.0	-1.5
Federal subventions to oblasts	(142.5)	142.5	0.0	-0.8
Net mutual settlements	(107.6)	107.6	0.0	-0.6
Short-term loans	(17.3)	17.3	0.0	-0.1
Balance, including transfers	**(887.3)**	**337.7**	**(549.6)**	**-5.1**
(as a percentage of GDP)	-5.1	1.9	-3.2	n.a.
Budgetary loans	(72.3)	(34.1)	(106.4)	-0.6
Balance, including loans	**(959.6)**	**303.6**	**(656.0)**	**-3.8**
(as a percentage of GDP)	-5.5	1.7	-3.8	n.a.

Budget item	Central	Subnational	Consolidated	Share of GDP
Memo items (in billions of rubles):				
Total wages	922.9	323.3	1,246.2	7.2
Total investment	315.4	363.4	678.8	3.9
GDP	—	—	17,410.0	n.a.

— Not available.
n.a. Not applicable.
Note: Data presented in tables have been made available to the authors by the Ministry of Finance of the Russian Federation (unless another source is noted) and have not hitherto been published. Data may not correspond fully to other sources or to data from the same source obtained at a different time as revisions are ongoing (dates have been specified whenever possible). This is especially so for oblast-level data. Furthermore, categories undergo definitional changes and may not correspond from source to source.
Source: Ministry of Finance of the Russian Federation.

Appendix D   Oblast revenues and expenditures, Russian Federation, 1991

(in thousands of rubles)

Oblast	Population (thousands)	Revenue	Per capita revenue	Expenditure	Per capita expenditure	Balance	Per capita balance
Republic of Adygeya	437	295,802	676.9	392,859	899.0	(97,057)	(222.1)
Aginskii-Buryatskii AO	78	74,303	952.6	108,960	1,396.9	(34,657)	(444.3)
Republic of Altai	196	142,326	726.2	222,559	1,135.5	(80,233)	(409.4)
Altaiskii krai	2,655	1,940,107	730.7	2,633,866	992.0	(693,759)	(261.3)
Amurskaia oblast	1,074	1,562,947	1,455.3	1,674,043	1,558.7	(111,096)	(103.4)
Arkhangelskaia oblast	1,522	1,501,173	986.3	1,902,643	1,250.1	(401,470)	(263.8)
Astrakhanskaia oblast	1,007	1,186,563	1,178.3	1,194,056	1,185.8	(7,493)	(7.4)
Republic of Bashkortostan	3,984	4,378,923	1,099.1	4,086,550	1,025.7	292,373	73.4
Belgorodskaia oblast	1,401	1,240,939	885.8	1,350,950	964.3	(110,011)	(78.5)
Brianskaia oblast	1,464	1,482,751	1,012.8	1,574,356	1,075.4	(91,605)	(62.6)
Republic of Buryatiia	1,056	1,072,213	1,015.4	1,517,389	1,436.9	(445,176)	(421.6)
Chechen Republic and Ingush Republic	1,307	479,310	366.7	866,978	663.3	(387,668)	(296.6)
Cheliabinskaia oblast	3,641	3,758,480	1,032.3	3,810,969	1,046.7	(52,489)	(14.4)
Chitinskaia oblast	1,314	927,525	705.9	1,440,004	1,095.9	(512,479)	(390.0)
Chukotskii AO	154	654,141	4,247.7	691,148	4,488.0	(37,007)	(240.3)
Republic of Chuvash	1,346	1,281,726	952.2	1,437,693	1,068.1	(155,967)	(115.9)
Republic of Dagestan	1,854	1,259,961	679.6	1,569,272	846.4	(309,311)	(166.8)
Evenkiiskii AO	25	52,001	2,080.0	71,289	2,851.6	(19,288)	(771.5)
Evreyskaia AO (Jewish)	220	318,663	1,448.5	356,799	1,621.8	(38,136)	(173.3)
Ivanovskaia oblast	1,317	—	—	—	—	—	—
Irkutskaia oblast	2,863	3,171,543	1,107.8	3,606,921	1,259.8	(435,378)	(152.1)
Kabardino-Balkar Republic	777	696,876	896.9	817,236	1,051.8	(120,360)	(154.9)
Kaliningradskaia oblast	887	839,398	946.3	900,772	1,015.5	(61,374)	(69.2)
Republic of Kalmykia	328	345,937	1,054.7	525,813	1,603.1	(179,876)	(548.4)
Kaluzhskaia oblast	1,080	843,997	781.5	967,380	895.7	(123,383)	(114.2)
Kamchatskaia oblast	433	800,892	1,849.6	909,213	2,099.8	(108,321)	(250.2)
Karachai-Cherkess Republic	427	272,591	638.4	363,836	852.1	(91,245)	(213.7)
Republic of Karelia	799	1,088,531	1,362.4	1,157,291	1,448.4	(68,760)	(86.1)
Kemerovskaia oblast	3,180	3,790,760	1,192.1	3,956,361	1,244.1	(165,601)	(52.1)
Khabarovskii krai	1851	2,341,563	1,265.0	2,537,008	1,370.6	(195,445)	(105.6)
Republic of Khakasia	577	723,447	1,253.8	627,975	1,088.3	95,472	165.5
Khanty-Mansiiskii AO	1,314	2,834,674	2,157.3	2,406,429	1,831.4	428,245	325.9
Kirovskaia oblast	1,700	1,622,485	954.4	1,824,946	1,073.5	(202,461)	(119.1)
Republic of Komi	1,265	1,904,292	1,505.4	1,975,659	1,561.8	((71,367)	(56.4)
Komi-Permyatskaia AO	160	113,128	707.1	154,163	963.5	(41,035)	(256.5)
Koriakii AO	40	82,265	2,056.6	133,369	3,334.2	(51,104)	(1,277.6)
Kostromskaia oblast	813	661,370	813.5	749,784	922.2	(88,414)	(108.8)
Krasnodarskii krai	4,738	3,921,575	827.7	4,345,726	917.2	(424,151)	(89.5)
Krasnoiarskii krai	2,969	3,381,520	1,138.9	3,432,315	1,156.1	(50,795)	(17.1)
Kurganskaia oblast	1,110	839,979	756.7	1,167,193	1,051.5	(327,214)	(294.8)
Kurskaia oblast	1,336	1,234,061	923.7	1,375,865	1,029.8	(141,804)	(106.1)
Leningradskaia oblast	1,670	1,168,433	699.7	1,504,332	900.8	(335,899)	(201.1)

Oblast	Population (thousands)	Revenue	Per capita revenue	Expenditure	Per capita expenditure	Balance	Per capita balance
Lipetskaia oblast	1,234	1,094,250	886.8	1,246,369	1,010.0	(152,119)	(123.3)
Magadanskaia oblast	380	1,595,209	4,197.9	1,415,568	3,725.2	179,641	472.7
Republic of Marii-El	758	489,252	645.5	810,936	1,069.8	(321,684)	(424.4)
Mordovian Republic	964	887,711	920.9	1,013,439	1,051.3	(125,728)	(130.4)
Moscow City	9,003	13,429,366	1,491.7	12,601,794	1,399.7	827,572	91.9
Moskovskaia oblast	6,718	4,684,804	697.4	5,075,426	755.5	(390,622)	(58.1)
Murmanskaia oblast	1,159	2,001,440	1,726.9	1,868,415	1,612.1	133,025	114.8
Nenetskii AO	55	126,207	2,294.7	142,631	2,593.3	(16,424)	(298.6)
Nizhniy Novgorod oblast	3,712	3,469,154	934.6	2,753,034	741.7	716,120	192.9
North-Osetien Republic	643	620,358	964.8	713,938	1,110.3	(93,580)	(145.5)
Novgorodskaia oblast	755	744,650	986.3	910,800	1,206.4	(166,150)	(220.1)
Novosibirskaia oblast	2,796	2,400,519	858.6	2,690,377	962.2	(289,858)	(103.7)
Omskaia oblast	2,163	1,731,030	800.3	2,103,188	972.3	(372,158)	(172.1)
Orenburgskaia oblast	2,194	2,018,452	920.0	2,069,082	943.1	(50,630)	(23.1)
Orlovskaia oblast	901	863,623	958.5	1,029,582	1,142.7	(165,959)	(184.2)
Penzenskaia oblast	1,512	1,157,062	765.3	1,264,334	836.2	(107,272)	(70.9)
Permskaia oblast	2,950	2,666,052	903.7	2,697,104	914.3	(31,052)	(10.5)
Primorskii krai	2,299	1,929,181	839.1	2,414,338	1,050.2	(485,157)	(211.0)
Pskovskaia oblast	845	909,470	1,076.3	1,006,498	1,191.1	(97,028)	(114.8)
Riazanskaia oblast	1,349	1,288,963	955.3	1,287,502	954.4	1,191	0.9
Rostovskaia oblast	4,348	3,058,865	703.5	3,348,207	770.1	(289,342)	(66.5)
Republic of Sakha (Yakutia)	1,109	4,377,041	3,946.8	4,627,240	4,172.4	(250,199)	(225.6)
Sakhalinskaia oblast	717	1,604,295	2,237.5	1,711,384	2,386.9	(107,089)	(149.4)
Samarskaia oblast	3,290	3,121,033	948.6	3,116,433	947.2	4,600	1.4
Saratovskaia oblast	2,708	1,770,692	653.9	2,262,589	835.5	(491,897)	(181.6)
Smolenskaia oblast	1,166	1,078,891	925.3	1,170,854	1,004.2	(91,963)	(78.9)
St. Petersburg	5,035	8,103,287	1,609.4	7,830,120	1,555.1	273,167	54.3
Stravropolskii krai	2,499	2,333,168	933.6	2,407,597	963.4	(74,429)	(29.8)
Sverdlovskaia oblast	4,730	4,890,558	1,033.9	5,172,310	1,093.5	(281,752)	(59.6)
Taimyrskii (Dolgano-Nenetskii) AO	54	111,797	2,070.3	127,827	2,367.2	(16,030)	(296.9)
Tambovskaia oblast	1,315	861,350	655.0	1,192,837	907.1	(331,487)	(252.1)
Republic of Tatarstan	3,679	3,452,733	938.5	3,832,670	1,041.8	(379,937)	(103.3)
Tomskaia oblast	1,012	1,271,413	1,256.3	1,445,907	1,428.8	(174,494)	(172.4)
Tul' skaia oblast	1,855	1,743,261	939.8	1,686,312	909.1	56,949	30.7
Republic of Tuva	307	379,600	1,236.5	606,579	1,975.8	(226,979)	(739.3)
Tverskaia oblast	1,676	1,612,380	962.0	1,506,627	898.9	105,753	63.1
Tyumenskaia oblast	1,349	2,358,208	1,748.1	2,316,825	1,717.4	41,383	30.7
Udmurt Republic	1,628	1,873,250	1,150.6	1,782,566	1,094.9	90,684	55.7
Ulianovskaia oblast	1,430	1,386,572	969.6	1,740,241	1,217.0	(353,669)	(247.3)
Ust'-Ordynskii Buryatskii AO	138	116,613	845.0	176,706	1,280.5	(60,093)	(435.5)
Vladimirskaia oblast	1,660	1,558,874	939.1	1,508,961	909.0	49,913	30.1
Volgogradskaia oblast	2,632	1,619,192	615.2	1,958,852	744.2	(339,660)	(129.1)
Vologodskaia oblast	1,361	1,469,141	1,079.5	1,539,260	1,131.0	(70,119)	(51.5)
Voronezhskaia oblast	2,475	1,323,837	534.9	1,842,649	744.5	(518,812)	(209.6)
Yamal-Nenets AO	493	1,540,226	3,124.2	1,423,859	2,888.2	116,367	236.0
Yaroslavskaia oblast	1,476	1,432,820	970.7	1,290,251	874.2	142,569	96.6

(Table continues on the following page.)

Appendix D (continued)

Oblast	Population (thousands)	Revenue	Per capita revenue	Expenditure	Per capita expenditure	Balance	Per capita balance
Standard deviation		1,837,858	717	1,764,762	729	237,362	228
Maximum		13,429,366	4,248	12,601,794	4,488	827,572	473
Minimum		52,001	367	71,289	663	(693,759)	(1,278)
Range		13,377,365	3,881	12,530,505	3,825	1,521,331	1,750
Average		1,779,825	1,195	1,897,494	1,338	(117,669)	(143)
Coefficient of variation		1.0	0.6	0.9	0.5	(2.0)	(1.6)

— Not available.
AO Autonomous okrug.
AR Autonomous republic.
Note: Figures in parentheses are deficits.
Source: Ministry of Finance of the Russian Federation.

Appendix E Oblast revenues and expenditures, Russian Federation, 1992

(in thousands of rubles)

Oblast	Population (thousands)	Revenue	Per capita revenue	Expenditure	Per capita expenditure	Privatization revenue	Subventions	Per capita subventions
Republic of Adygeya	442	3,543,956	8,018	4,828,348	10,924	54,653	1,285,964	2,909.4
Aginskii-Buryatskii AO	79	210,434	2,664	1,679,888	21,264	2,766	1,357,481	17,183.3
Republic of Altai	198	973,262	4,915	3,055,390	15,431	48,359	2,058,106	10,394.5
Altaiskii krai	2,666	23,616,360	8,858	30,607,228	11,481	517,670	5,134,512	1,925.9
Amurskaia oblast	1,075	12,428,275	11,561	14,471,248	13,462	331,141	2,536,178	2,359.2
Arkhangelskaia oblast	1,517	18,381,816	12117.2	19,358,917	12,761	407,298	263,454	173.7
Astrakhanskaia oblast	1,010	7,930,499	7,852	10,761,646	10,655	196,306	2,669,678	2,643.2
Republic of Bashkortostan	4,008	142,239,692	35,489	86,178,208	21,502	523,998	—	—
Belgorodskaia oblast	1,408	20,992,327	14,909	20,675,046	14,684	506,970	503,272	357.4
Brianskaia oblast	1,464	12,049,196	8,230	13,529,054	9,241	446,710	1,633,381	1,115.7
Republic of Buryatiia	1,059	9,112,282	8,605	16,198,921	15,296	5,395	6,539,462	6,175.1
Chechen Republic and Ingush Republic	1,308	4,976,995	3,805	6,640,354	5,077	6,750	2,889,534	2,209.1
Cheliabinskaia oblast	3,638	60,459,909	16,619	66,560,604	18,296	1,064,655	—	—
Chitinskaia oblast	1,312	11,878,942	9,054	16,168,564	12,324	552,616	3,670,083	2,797.3
Chukotskii AO	146	4,461,060	30,555	9,954,633	68,182	11,824	2,045,517	14,010.4
Republic of Chuvash	1,353	10,717,053	7,921	15,888,734	11,743	348,106	4,657,861	3,442.6
Republic of Dagestan	1,890	4,795,013	2,537	21,239,210	11,238	16,812	14,425,572	7,632.6
Evenkiiskii AO	25	330,314	13,213	1,018,445	40,738	30,326	597,350	23,894.0
Evreyskaia AO (Jewish)	221	1,867,083	8,448	3,299,664	14,931	30,382	1,515,480	6,857.4
Ivanovskaia oblast	1,312	14,316,661	10,912	14,131,299	10,771	399,812	—	—
Irkutskaia oblast	2,732	50,223,094	18,383	50,418,349	18,455	596,563	—	—
Kabardino-Balkar Republic	784	4,610,216	5,880	7,790,019	9,936	6,592	3,042,519	3,880.8
Kaliningradskaia oblast	894	9,311,347	10,415	10,130,242	11,331	589,731	40,727	45.6
Republic of Kalmykia	327	1,952,865	5,972	5,619,094	17,184	14,858	3,484,637	10,656.4
Kaluzhskaia oblast	1,081	8,887,122	8,221	9,905,140	9,163	254,516	485,570	449.2

(Table continues on the following page.)

Appendix E (continued)

Oblast	Population (thousands)	Revenue	Per capita revenue	Expenditure	Per capita expenditure	Privatization revenue	Subventions	Per capita subventions
Kamchatskaia oblast	433	6,798,134	15,700	11,565,719	26,711	—	4,298,216	9,926.6
Karachai-Cherkess Republic	431	2,774,613	6,438	4,217,158	9,785	198,141	1,249,811	2,899.8
Republic of Karelia	800	15,027,547	18,784	21,150,326	26,438	258,472	—	—
Kemerovskaia oblast	3,181	61,925,004	19,467	63,719,325	20,031	803,216	10,201,831	3,207.1
Khabarovskii krai	1,634	28,407,400	17,385	30,296,419	18,541	645,027	479,708	293.6
Republic of Khakasia	581	7,530,133	12,961	7,460,473	12,841	466,706	—	—
Khanty-Mansiiskii AO	1,305	87,395,792	66,970	66,787,953	51,179	810,061	—	—
Kirovskaia oblast	1,700	18,903,584	11,120	19,088,408	11,228	320,872	774,069	455.3
Republic of Komi	1,255	26,905,827	21,439	26,402,525	21,038	337,728	974,806	776.7
Komi-Permyatskaia AO	160	799,648	4,998	1,907,029	11,919	14,545	999,075	6,244.2
Koriakii AO	39	438,917	11,254	3,156,960	80,948	—	1,955,500	50,141.0
Kostromskaia oblast	812	8,895,526	10,955	10,338,768	12,732	195,024	1,856,522	2,286.4
Krasnodarskii krai	4,797	47,389,207	9,879	45,625,810	9,511	1,116,773	892,672	186.1
Krasnoiarskii krai	2,973	59,401,466	19,980	53,000,160	17,827	596,110	—	—
Kurganskaia oblast	1,115	10,595,683	9,503	12,758,761	11,443	318,361	3,125,785	2,803.4
Kurskaia oblast	1,335	17,520,577	13,124	15,225,220	11,405	472,684	383,293	287.1
Leningradskaia oblast	1,673	20,487,173	12,246	19,934,493	11,915	509,914	123,413	73.8
Lipetskaia oblast	1,234	18,385,753	14,899	16,403,115	13,293	283,330	—	—
Magadanskaia oblast	363	12,940,699	35,649	14,378,116	39,609	56,374	1,896,893	5,225.6
Republic of Marii-El	762	5,018,805	6,586	10,250,462	13,452	171,985	4,517,005	5,927.8
Mordovian Republic	964	7,675,552	7,962	13,279,758	13,776	132,451	5,869,847	6,089.1
Moscow City	8,957	183,386,937	20,474	178,164,972	19,891	4,077,545	—	—
Moskovskaia oblast	6,707	74,632,255	11,128	61,206,391	9,126	1,831,935	—	—
Murmanskaia oblast	1,148	25,676,874	22,367	24,933,420	21,719	682,612	1,351,567	1,177.3
Nenetskii AO	54	641,604	11,882	2,656,126	49,188	118	1,048,436	19,415.5

Nizhniy Novgorod oblast	3,704	56,246,635	15,185	49,339,206	13,321	1,467,282	—	—
North-Osetien Republic	695	5,160,436	7,425	9,689,883	13,942	—	2,847,080	4,096.5
Novgorodskaia oblast	752	8,683,875	11,548	11,559,795	15,372	225,494	3,029,041	4,028.0
Novosibirskaia oblast	2,803	26,034,143	9,288	28,949,745	10,328	1,225,177	270,986	96.7
Omskaia oblast	2,170	28,223,413	13,006	31,528,589	14,529	1,187,202	2,885,341	1,329.7
Orenburgskaia oblast	2,204	28,623,651	12,987	25,885,130	11,745	504,669	363,261	164.8
Orlovskaia oblast	903	9,019,448	9,988	11,349,342	12,568	557,229	1,876,217	2,077.8
Penzenskaia oblast	1,514	11,341,103	7,491	12,901,945	8,522	381,141	988,001	652.6
Permskaia oblast	2,949	46,645,430	15,817	43,690,925	14,816	361,711	—	—
Primorskii krai	2,309	29,268,971	12,676	31,790,386	13,768	1,637,857	700,000	303.2
Pskovskaia oblast	841	7,220,388	8,585	11,967,065	14,230	168,887	3,644,014	4,333.0
Riazanskaia oblast	1,344	15,801,810	11,757	14,392,811	10,709	199,874	—	—
Rostovskaia oblast	4,363	47,449,860	10,876	43,877,993	10,057	922,166	—	—
Republic of Sakha (Yakutia)	1,093	96,578,853	88,361	91,446,319	83,665	156,147	—	—
Sakhalinskaia oblast	719	12,706,122	17,672	19,157,221	26,644	476,917	5,015,952	6,976.3
Samarskaia oblast	3,296	69,518,995	21,092	58,667,629	17,800	791,006	—	—
Saratovskaia oblast	2,711	28,148,709	10,383	26,564,129	9,799	360,770	377,096	139.1
Smolenskaia oblast	1,163	13,004,901	11,182	12,693,548	10,914	430,845	164,803	141.7
St. Petersburg	5,004	60,240,381	12,038	62,953,201	12,581	1,827,700	1,475,411	294.8
Stravropolskii krai	2,536	18,520,053	7,303	18,467,774	7,282	858,983	271,829	107.2
Sverdlovskaia oblast	4,719	79,423,665	16,831	73,911,170	15,662	1,051,991	—	—
Taimyrskii (Dolgano-Nenetskii) AO	53	1,167,916	22,036	1,970,854	37,186	7,257	665,746	12,561.2
Tambovskaia oblast	1,310	11,536,667	8,807	13,518,091	10,319	368,798	450,670	344.0
Republic of Tatarstan	3,696	104,649,382	28,314	82,187,484	22,237	9,538	—	—
Tomskaia oblast	1,012	13,806,067	13,642	13,969,768	13,804	308,299	503,009	497.0
Tul'skaia oblast	1,844	22,058,959	11,963	19,050,090	10,331	384,672	—	—
Republic of Tuva	306	1,083,441	3,541	6,574,946	21,487	13,875	4,650,876	15,198.9
Tverskaia oblast	1,668	15,891,702	9,527	15,184,758	9,104	799,189	—	—
Tyumenskaia oblast	1,353	23,703,942	17,520	27,761,269	20,518	620,010	4,685,551	3,463.1
Udmurt Republic	1,637	20,629,990	12,602	20,761,620	12,683	609,311	213,008	130.1
Ulianovskaia oblast	1,444	18,384,494	12,732	17,938,497	12,423	205,888	790,667	547.6

(Table continues on the following page.)

Appendix E (continued)

Oblast	Population (thousands)	Revenue	Per capita revenue	Expenditure	Per capita expenditure	Privatization revenue	Subventions	Per capita subventions
Ust-Ordynskii Buryatskii AO	140	508,959	3,635	2,029,217	14,494	3,803	1,491,170	10,651.2
Vladimirskaia oblast	1,656	21,085,654	12,733	17,932,744	10,829	1,203,298	—	—
Volgogradskaia oblast	2,643	35,585,719	13,464	33,098,850	12,523	1,244,188	—	—
Vologodskaia oblast	1,362	20,305,266	14,908	20,463,576	15,025	315,181	—	—
Voronezhskaia oblast	2,475	23,000,244	9,293	23,045,634	9,311	535,265	2,325,915	939.8
Yamal-Nenets AO	479	32,950,735	68,791	29,696,956	61,998	14,614	—	—
Yaroslavskaia oblast	1,472	26,336,213	17,891	23,397,861	15,895	650,253	—	—
Total	148,704	2,280,366,675	n.a.	2,253,382,133	n.a.	43,351,280	142,520,431	n.a.
Standard deviation		31,682,152	11,855	26,837,963	14,164	584,893	2,484,713	7,843
Maximum		183,386,937	88,361	178,164,972	83,665	4,077,545	14,425,572	50,141
Minimum		210,434	2,537	1,018,445	5,077	118	40,727	46
Range		183,176,503	85,824	177,146,527	78,588	4,077,427	14,384,845	50,095
Average		25,826,508	14,122	25,584,736	17,932	514,294	2,298,717	4,961
Coefficient of variation		1.23	0.84	1.05	0.79	1.14	1.08	1.58

— Not available.
n.a. Not applicable.
AO Autonomous okrug.
AR Autonomous republic.
Source: Ministry of Finance of the Russian Federation, State Tax Service; staff estimates.

Bibliography

ACIR (Advisory Commission on Intergovernmental Relations). 1992. *Significant Features of Fiscal Federalism.* Vol. 1, *Budget Processes and Tax Systems.* Washington, D.C.

Antolio, Bomfim N., and Anwar Shah. 1991. "Macroeconomic Management and the Division of Powers in Brazil: Perspectives for the Nineties." PRE Working Paper 567. World Bank, Policy Research Department, Washington, D.C.

Ariff, Mohamed. 1991. "Case Study: Malaysia." In ESCAP (Economic and Social Commission for Asia and the Pacific), ed., *Fiscal Decentralization and the Mobilization and Use of National Resources for Development: Issues, Experience, and Policies in the ESCAP Region,* 193–231. Bangkok: United Nations.

Ashwe, Chiichii. 1986a. *A Critique of Nigeria's Existing Revenue Sharing Scheme.* Center for Research on Federal Financial Relations Occasional Paper 39. Canberra: Australian National University.

———. 1986b. *Fiscal Federalism in Nigeria.* Research Monograph 46. Canberra: Australian National University, Center for Research on Federal Financial Relations.

Auerbach, Alan, and Martin Feldstein, eds. 1985. *Handbook of Public Economics.* Vol. 1. Amsterdam: North Holland.

Bagchi, Amaresh. 1991. "Case Study: India." In ESCAP (Economic and Social Commission for Asia and the Pacific), ed., *Fiscal Decentralization and the Mobilization and Use of National Resources for Development: Issues, Experience, and Policies in the ESCAP Region,* 97–129. Bangkok: United Nations.

Bagchi, Amaresh, J. L. Bajaj, and William A. Byrd. 1992. *State Finances in India.* New Delhi: National Institute of Public Finance and Policy.

Bahl, Roy. 1971. "A Regression Approach to Tax Effort and Tax Ratio Analysis." *IMF (International Monetary Fund) Staff Papers* 18(3): 570–612. Washington, D.C.

———. 1986. "The Design of Intergovernmental Transfers in Industrialized Countries." *Public Budgeting and Finance* 6(4): 3–22.

Bahl, Roy W., and Johannes F. Linn. 1992. *Urban Public Finance in Developing Countries.* New York: Oxford University Press.

Bahl, Roy W., and Christine I. Wallich. 1992. "Intergovernmental Fiscal Relations in China." PRE Working Paper 863. World Bank, Policy Research Department, Washington, D.C.

Bahry, Donna. 1987. *Outside Moscow: Power, Politics, and Budgetary Policy in the Soviet Republics.* New York: Columbia University Press.

Baker, Pauline H. 1984. "The Economics of Nigerian Federalism." Prepared for the Bureau of Intelligence and Research, U.S. Department of State, Washington, D.C.

Barr, Nicholas. 1992. *Income Transfers and the Social Safety Net in Russia.* World Bank Studies of Economies in Transformation, no. 4. Washington, D.C.

Barsh, Russell Lawrence, and James Youngblood Henderson. 1980. *The Road: Indian Tribes and Political Liberty.* Berkeley, Calif.: University of California Press.

Bartlett, Richard H. 1978. "The Indian Act of Canada." *Buffalo Law Review* 27 (summer): 581–615.

Bausk, Olga, ed. 1991. *Ways of Political Development of Indigenous Peoples of the North.* Institute of Philosophy and Law, Laval University, Quebec, and Novosibirsk Architecture Technology Center for Traditional Arctic Cultural Ecology Fund. Second Scientific Colloquium, "Russia-Quebec."

Bird, Richard M. 1978. *Intergovernmental Fiscal Relations in Developing Countries.* World Bank Staff Working Paper 304. Washington, D.C.

———, ed. 1980. *Fiscal Dimensions of Canadian Federalism.* Toronto: Canadian Tax Foundation.

———. 1984. *Intergovernmental Finance in Colombia.* Cambridge, Mass.: Harvard University International Tax Program.

———. 1986. *Federal Finance in Comparative Perspective.* Toronto: Canadian Tax Foundation.

Bird, Richard M., and Christine I. Wallich. 1992. "Financing Local Governments in Hungary." PRE Working Paper 869. World Bank, Policy Research Department, Washington, D.C.

———. 1993a. "Fiscal Decentralization and Intergovernmental Relations in Transition Economies: Towards a Systemic Framework of Analysis." PRE Working Paper 1122. World Bank, Policy Research Department, Washington, D.C.

———. 1993b. "Moving from Command to Market Economies." In Colin Farringdon, ed., *Local Government Taxation.* Proceedings of the Second International Conference of the Institute of Revenues, Rating, and Valuation, Budapest.

———. Forthcoming (1994). "Subnational Finance in Transitional Economies: Towards a Systemic Approach. *National Tax Journal.*

Blejer, Mario I., and Gyorgy Szapary. 1989. "The Evolving Role of Fiscal Policy in Centrally Planned Economies under Reform: The Case of China." IMF (International Monetary Fund) Working Paper WP/89/26. Washington, D.C.

Boadway, Robin. 1992. *The Constitutional Division of Powers: An Economic Perspective.* Ottawa: Economic Council of Canada.

Boadway, Robin, and Frank Flatters. 1983. "Efficiency, Equity, and the Allocation of Resource Rents." In Charles E. McLure, Jr., and Peter Mieszkowski, eds., *Fiscal Federalism and the Taxation of Natural Resources,* 99–133. Lexington, Mass.: Lexington Books.

———. 1991. "The Taxation of Natural Resources: Principles and Policy Issues." Consultants' report. Prepared for the World Bank, Country Economics Department, Washington, D.C.

Bomfin, Antulio, and Anwar Shah. 1991. "Macroeconomic Management and the Division of Powers in Brazil." PRE Working Paper 567. World Bank, Policy Research Department, Washington, D.C.

Bookman, Milica Z. 1991. *The Political Economy of Discontinuous Development: Regional Disparities and Inter-Regional Conflict.* New York: Praeger Press.

Bradford, David F. 1986. *Untangling the Income Tax.* Cambridge, Mass.: Harvard University Press.

Break, George. 1980. *Financing Government in a Federal System.* Washington, D.C.: The Brookings Institution.

Brean, D. J. S., and Richard M. Bird. 1984. "Fiscal Risk of State-owned Enterprise." In Bernard P. Herber, ed., *Public Finance and Public Debt.* Proceedings of the 40th Congress of the International Institute of Public Finance, Innsbruck.

Brown, Robert D. 1982. "Comment" on Robert D. Cairns, "Extractive Resource Taxation in Canada." In Wayne Thirsk and John Whalley, eds., *Tax Policy Options in the 1980s.* Toronto: Canadian Tax Foundation.

Cagan, Phillip. 1956. "The Monetary Dynamics of Hyperinflation." In Milton Friedman, ed., *Studies in the Quantity Theory of Money.* Chicago, Ill.: University of Chicago Press.

Cairns, Robert D. 1982. "Extractive Resource Taxation in Canada." In Wayne Thirsk and John Whalley, eds., *Tax Policy Options in the 1980s.* Toronto: Canadian Tax Foundation.

Calvo, Guillermo, and Fabrizio Coricelli. 1992. "Output Collapse in Eastern Europe: The Role of Credit." IMF (International Monetary Fund) Working Paper WP/92/64. Washington, D.C.

Chelliah, R. 1990. "Issues in Fiscal Policy and Fiscal Federalism." In "World Bank Asia Region Seminar on Policy Challenges in India," 9–15. Discussion Paper 88. World Bank, East Asia Region, Washington, D.C.

Church, Albert M. 1978. "Conflicting Federal, State and Local Interest Trends in State and Local Energy Taxation: Coal and Copper—A Case in Point." *National Tax Journal* 31(3): 269–83.

Collins, A. F. 1980. "The Alberta Heritage Savings Trust Fund: An Overview of the Issues." *Canadian Public Policy* 6 (February): 158–65.

Commonwealth Grants Commission. 1979. *First Report on Special Assistance for the Northern Territories.* Canberra: Commonwealth Government Printer.

Conrad, Robert, Zmarak Shalizi, and Janet Syme. 1990. "Issues in Evaluating Tax and Payment Arrangements for Publicly Owned Minerals." PRE Working Paper 496. World Bank, Policy Research Department, Washington, D.C.

Courchene, Thomas J. 1976. "Equalization Payments and Energy Royalties." In Anthony Scott, ed., *Natural Resource Revenues: A Test of Federalism.* Vancouver: University of British Columbia Press.

Courchene, Thomas J., and James R. Melvin. 1980. "Energy Revenues: Consequences for the Rest of Canada." *Canadian Public Policy* 6 (February): 193–204.

Courchene, Thomas J., and Lisa M. Powell. 1992. *The First Nations Province.* Kingston, Ontario: Institute of Intergovernmental Relations, Queen's University.

Craig, Jon, and George Kopits. Forthcoming (1994). "International Fiscal Relations in Transition: The Case of Russia." *Government and Policy.*

Cuciti, Peggy, Harvey Galper, and Robert Lucke. 1983. "State Energy Revenues." In Charles E. McLure, Jr., and Peter Mieszkowski, eds., *Fiscal Federalism and the Taxation of Natural Resources.* Lexington, Mass.: Lexington Books.

Dahlby, Bev. 1988. "Taxation under Alternative Constitutional Arrangements." In Paul Boothe, ed., *Alberta and the Economics of Constitutional Change.* Edmonton, Alberta: Western Center for Economic Research.

Davey, Kenneth. 1988. "Municipal Development Funds and Intermediaries." PRE Working Paper 32. World Bank, Office of the Vice President, Development Economics, Washington, D.C.

Dornbusch, Rudiger, and Stanley Fischer. 1987. *Macroeconomics.* 4th ed. New York: McGraw-Hill.

Economist. 1993. "Russia: Things Fall Apart." Vol. 326, no. 7796 (January 30–February 5): 47.

Fisher, Ronald C. 1989. *State and Local Public Finance.* Glenview, Ill.: Scott, Foresman and Company.

Flatters, Frank, Vernon Henderson, and Peter Mieszkowski. 1974. "Public Goods, Efficiency, and Regional Fiscal Equalization." *Journal of Public Economics* 3(2): 99–112.

Floyd, Robert H., Clive S. Gray, and R. P. Short. 1984. "Public Enterprises in Mixed Economies: Some Macroeconomic Aspects." International Monetary Fund, Washington, D.C.

Frey, Rene L. 1977. "The Interregional Income Gap as a Problem of Swiss Federalism." In Wallace E. Oates, ed., *The Political Economy of Fiscal Federalism,* 93–105. Lexington, Mass.: Lexington Books.

Gandhi, Ved P. 1983. "Tax Assignment and Revenue Sharing in Brazil, India, Malaysia, and Nigeria." In Charles E. McLure, Jr., ed., *Tax Assignment in Federal Countries.* Canberra: Australian National University Press.

Garnaut, Ross, and Anthony Clunies Ross. 1975. "Uncertainty, Risk Aversion, and the Taxing of Natural Resource Projects." *Economic Journal* 85 (June): 272–87.

Gelb, Alan, and associates. 1988. *Oil Windfalls: Blessing or Curse?* New York: Oxford University Press.

Gleason, Gregory. 1990. *Federalism and Nationalism: The Struggle for Republican Rights in the USSR,* 61–90. Boulder, Colo.: Westview Press.

Gordon, Roger H. 1983. "Taxation in Federal Systems: An Optimal Taxation Approach." In Charles E. McLure, Jr., ed., *Tax Assignment in Federal Countries.* Canberra: Australian National University Press.

Graham, John F. 1982. "Equalization and Canadian Federalism." *Public Finance* 37(2): 247–62.

Gramlich, Edward M. 1984. " 'A Fair Go': Fiscal Federalism Arrangements." In Richard E. Caves and Lawrence Krause, eds., *The Australian Economy: A View from the North.* Washington, D.C.: The Brookings Institution.

Gray, Cheryl W. 1990. "Tax Systems in the Reforming Socialist Economies of Europe." PRE Working Paper 501. World Bank, Policy Research Department, Washington, D.C.

Grewal, Bhajan S., Geoffrey Brennan, and Russell L. Mathews, eds. 1980. *The Economics of Federalism.* Canberra: Australian National University Press.

Groenewegen, Peter. 1983. "Tax Assignment and Revenue Sharing in Australia." In Charles E. McLure, Jr., ed., *Tax Assignment in Federal Countries,* 293–318. Canberra: Australian National University Press.

Hall, Robert E., and Alvin Rabushka. 1983. *Low Tax, Simple Tax, Flat Tax.* New York: McGraw-Hill.

———. 1985. *The Flat Tax.* Stanford, Calif.: Hoover Institution Press.

Hardy, Daniel, and Dubravko Mihaljek. 1992. "Economic Policymaking in a Federation." *Finance and Development* 29 (June): 14–17.

Heald, David. 1980. *Financing Devolution within the United Kingdom: A Study of the Lessons.* Research Monograph 32. Canberra: Australian National University Press, Center for Research on Federal Financial Relations.

Heaps, Terry, and John F. Helliwell. 1985. "The Taxation of Natural Resources." In Alan J. Auerbach and Martin Feldstein, eds., *Handbook of Public Economics*. Vol. 1, 420–72. Amsterdam: North Holland.

Hellerstein, Walter. 1978. "Constitutional Constraints on State and Local Taxation of Energy Resources." *National Tax Journal* 31(3): 245–56.

———. 1983. "Legal Constraints on State Taxation of Natural Resources." In Charles E. McLure, Jr., and Peter Mieszkowski, eds., *Fiscal Federalism and the Taxation of Natural Resources*. Lexington, Mass.: Lexington Books.

———. 1986. *State and Local Taxation of Natural Resources in the Federal System: Legal, Economic, and Political Perspectives*. Washington D.C.: American Bar Association, Section of Taxation.

Helliwell, John F. 1982. "Comment" on Robert D. Cairns, "Extractive Resource Taxation in Canada." In Wayne Thirsk and John Whalley, eds., *Tax Policy Options in the 1980s*. Toronto: Canadian Tax Foundation.

———. 1984. "Natural Resources and the Australian Economy." In Richard E. Caves and Lawrence Krause, eds., *The Australian Economy: A View from the North*. Washington, D.C.: The Brookings Institution.

Helliwell, John F., Mary E. MacGregor, Robert N. McRae, and Andre Plourde. 1989. *Oil and Gas in Canada: The Effects of Domestic Policies and World Events*. Toronto: Canadian Tax Foundation.

Helliwell, John F., and Anthony Scott. 1981. *Canada in Fiscal Conflict: Resources and the West*. Vancouver: Pemberton Securities.

Hewitt, Daniel, and Dubravko Mihaljek. 1992. "Fiscal Federalism." In Vito Tanzi, ed., *Fiscal Policies in Economies in Transition*, 330–49. Washington, D.C.: International Monetary Fund.

Hinds, Manuel, and Gerhard Pohl. 1991. "Going to Market: Privatization in Central and Eastern Europe." PRE Working Paper 768. World Bank, Technical Department, Europe, Middle East, and North Africa Regional Office, Washington, D.C.

Holzmann, Robert. 1989. "The Welfare Effects of Public Expenditure Programs Reconsidered." IMF (International Monetary Fund) Working Paper WP/89/62. Washington, D.C.

Hutabarat, H. 1991. "Case Study: Indonesia." In ESCAP (Economic and Social Commission for Asia and the Pacific), ed., *Fiscal Decentralization and the Mobilization and Use of National Resources for Development: Issues, Experience, and Policies in the ESCAP Region*, 129–63. Bangkok: United Nations.

IMF (International Monetary Fund). 1986. *A Manual of Government Finance Statistics*. Washington, D.C.

———. 1992a. *The Economy of the Former USSR in 1991*. Washington, D.C.

———. 1992b. *Russian Federation Economic Review*. Washington, D.C.

IMF (International Monetary Fund), IBRD (International Bank for Reconstruction and Development), OECD (Organization for Economic Co-operation and Development), and EBRD (European Bank for Reconstruction and Development). 1991. *A Study of the Soviet Economy*. Volumes 1-3. Washington, D.C.

Institute for Fiscal Studies. 1978. *The Structure and Reform of Direct Taxation*. London: George Allen & Unwin.

Ip, Irene K., and Jack M. Mintz. 1992. *Dividing the Spoils: The Federal-Provincial Allocation of Taxing Powers*. Toronto: C. D. Howe Institute.

James, Dennis W. 1992. *Intergovernmental Financial Relations in Australia*. Sydney: Australian Tax Research Foundation.

Kikeri, Sunita, John Nellis, and Mary Shirley. 1992. *Privatization: The Lessons of Experience.* Washington, D.C.: World Bank.

King, David N. 1984. *Fiscal Tiers: The Economics of Multi-Level Government.* London: George Allen & Unwin.

Kornai, Janos. 1986. "The Soft Budget Constraint." *Kyklos* 39(1): 3–30.

———. 1992. *The Socialist System: The Political Economy of Communism.* Princeton, N.J.: Princeton University Press.

Krutilla, John V., Anthony C. Fisher, and Richard E. Rice. 1978. *Economic and Fiscal Impacts of Coal Development: Northern Great Plains.* Baltimore, Md.: Johns Hopkins University Press.

Kumar, Manmohan S., and Kent Osband. 1991. "Energy Pricing in the Soviet Union." IMF (International Monetary Fund) Working Paper WP/91/125. Washington, D.C.

Law of the Russian Federation on the Subsoil. 1992. Vedomosti SND RSFSR, no. 16 (February 21), item 834. Translated by W. E. Butler.

Le Houerou, Philippe. 1993. "Fiscal Management in Yaroslav." Discussion paper. World Bank, Europe and Central Asia Region, Washington, D.C.

Leman, Christopher K. 1981. "Comparing Canadian and U.S. Regional Energy Conflicts: Beyond Greed and Envy." In Christopher K. Leman, ed., *Regional Issues in Energy Development: A Dialogue of East and West.* Report of a symposium held April 10–11, Harvard University Center for International Affairs, Cambridge, Mass.

Link, Arthur A. 1978. "Political Constraint and North Dakota's Coal Severance Tax." *National Tax Journal* 31(3): 263–68.

Litvack, Jennie I., and Christine I. Wallich. 1993. "Fiscal Federalism: A Facilitator or Impediment to the Socialist Tradition? The Case of Russia." *Finance and Development* 30(2): 6–9.

Litwack, John M. 1991. "Discretionary Behavior and Soviet Economic Reform." *Soviet Studies* 43(2): 255–79.

Long, Millard, and Silvia B. Sagari. 1991. "Financial Reforms in Socialist Economies in Transition." PRE Working Paper 711. World Bank, Policy Research Department, Washington, D.C.

Longo, Carlos. 1982. "Restricted Origin Principle under Triangular Trade Flows: Implications for Trade and Tax Revenues." *Journal of Development Economics* 10:103–12.

Lopez, Cesar Diaz. 1990. "Center-Periphery Structures in Spain: From Historical Conflict to Territorial Constitutional Accommodation." In Yves Meny and Vincent Wright, eds., *Center-Periphery Relations in Western Europe,* 237–69. London: George Allen & Unwin.

Martin, E. Douglas K. 1978. "Taxation of Petroleum Production: The Canadian Experience, 1972 to Date." *National Tax Journal* 31(3): 291–307.

Mathews, R. L., ed. 1980. *Federalism in Australia and the Federal Republic of Germany: A Comparative Study.* Canberra: Australian National University Press, Center for Research on Federal Financial Relations.

McCleary, William. 1989. "Earmarking Government Revenues: Does It Work?" PRE Working Paper 322. World Bank, Policy Research Department, Washington, D.C.

McLure, Charles E., Jr. 1978. "Economic Constraints on State and Local Taxation of Energy Resources." *National Tax Journal* 31(3): 257–62.

———. 1979. "Severance Taxes on Energy Resources in the United States: Comment." *Growth and Change* 10(1): 72–74.

———. 1980. "Economic Effects of a Texas Tax on the Refining of Petroleum Products." *Growth and Change* 11(3): 2–8.

————. 1981. "Incidence Analysis and the Courts: An Examination of Four Cases." *Supreme Court Economic Review: The 1980 Term* 1: 69–112.

————. 1983a. "Assignment of Corporate Income Taxes in a Federal System." In Charles E. McLure, Jr., ed., *Tax Assignment in Federal Countries*. Canberra: Australian National University Press.

————. 1983b. "Introduction: The Revenue Side of the Assignment Problem." In Charles E. McLure, Jr., ed., *Tax Assignment in Federal Countries*. Canberra: Australian National University Press.

————, ed. 1983c. *Tax Assignment in Federal Countries*. Canberra: Australian National University Press.

————. 1983d. "Tax Exporting and the Commerce Clause." In Charles E. McLure, Jr., and Peter Mieszkowski, eds., *Fiscal Federalism and the Taxation of Natural Resources*. Lexington, Mass.: Lexington Books.

————. 1984. "Fiscal Federalism and the Taxation of Economic Rents." In George Break, ed., *State and Local Finance: The Pressures of the 1980s*. Madison: University of Wisconsin Press.

————. 1992a. "A Consumption-based Direct Tax for Countries in Transition from Socialism." *Wayne Law Review* 38(4): 1697–756.

————. 1992b. "A North American View of Vertical Fiscal Imbalance and the Assignment of Taxing Powers." Paper presented at a conference of the Australian Tax Research Foundation, November 4-5. Canberra.

McLure, Charles E., Jr., and Peter Mieszkowski, eds. 1983. *Fiscal Federalism and the Taxation of Natural Resources*. Lexington, Mass.: Lexington Books.

McMillan, M. L., and K. H. Norrie. 1980. "Province-building vs. A Rentier Society." *Canadian Public Policy* 6 (February): 213–20.

McPherson, Charles P., and Keith Palmer. 1984. "New Approaches to Profit Sharing in Developing Countries." *Oil and Gas Journal* (June): 119–28.

McRae, Robert N. 1985. "A Survey of Canadian Energy Policy: 1974–1983." *Energy Journal* 6(4): 49–64.

Mieszkowski, Peter. 1983. "Energy Policy, Taxation of Natural Resources, and Fiscal Federalism." In Charles E. McLure, Jr., ed., *Tax Assignment in Federal Countries*. Canberra: Australian National University Press.

Mieszkowski, Peter, and Eric Toder. 1983. "Taxation of Energy Resources." In Charles E. McLure, Jr., and Peter Mieszkowski, eds., *Fiscal Federalism and the Taxation of Natural Resources*. Lexington, Mass.: Lexington Books.

Milanovic, Branko. 1992a. "Distributional Impact of Cash and In-Kind Social Transfers in Eastern Europe and Russia." PRE Working Paper 1054. World Bank, Policy Research Department, Washington, D.C.

————. 1992b. "Privatization Options and Procedures." In Arye L. Hillman and Branko Milanovic, eds., *The Transition from Socialism in Eastern Europe: Domestic Restructuring and Foreign Trade*. Washington, D.C.: The World Bank.

————. 1993. "The Collapse of Communist Federations." World Bank, Policy Research Department, Washington, D.C.

Mohammadu, Turi. 1985. "Getting the Formula Right." *West Africa* 18 (March): 516–17.

Moore, A. Milton. 1976. "The Concept of a Nation and Entitlements to Economic Rents." In Anthony Scott, ed., *Natural Resource Revenues: A Test of Federalism*. Vancouver: University of British Columbia Press.

Musgrave, Peggy B. 1984. "Principles for Dividing the State Corporate Tax Base." In Charles E. McLure, Jr., ed., *The State Corporation Income Tax: Issues in Worldwide Unitary Combination*. Stanford, Calif.: Hoover Institution Press.

Musgrave, Richard A. 1959. *The Theory of Public Finance.* New York: McGraw-Hill.
———. 1961. "Approaches to a Fiscal Theory of Political Federalism." In *Public Finances: Needs, Sources, and Utilization* (National Bureau of Economic Research Special Conference Series), 97–122. Princeton, N.J.: Princeton University Press.
———. 1983. "Who Should Tax, Where, and What?" In Charles E. McLure, Jr., ed., *Tax Assignment in Federal Countries.* Canberra: Australian National University Press.
Musgrave, Richard A., and Peggy B. Musgrave. 1989. *Public Finance in Theory and Practice.* 5th ed. New York: McGraw-Hill.
Muzondo, Timothy R. 1992. "Alternative Forms of Mineral Taxation, Market Failure, and the Environment." IMF (International Monetary Fund) Working Paper WP/92/49. Washington, D.C.
Nathan, Richard P., and Margarita M. Balmaceda. 1990. "Comparing Federal Systems of Government." In Robert J. Bennett, ed., *Decentralization, Local Governments and Markets: Towards a Post-Welfare Agenda,* 60–77. Oxford: Clarendon Press.
Nellor, David. 1983. "Taxation of Australia's Natural Resources." In John G. Head, ed., *Taxation Issues of the 1980s.* Sydney: Australian Tax Research Foundation.
Newbery, David. 1991. "Reform in Hungary: Sequencing and Privatization." *European Economic Review* 35:571–80.
Oates, Wallace E. 1968. "The Theory of Public Finance in a Federal System." *Canadian Journal of Economics* (February): 37–54.
———. 1972. *Fiscal Federalism.* New York: Harcourt Brace Jovanovich.
———. 1977. "An Economist's Perspective on Fiscal Federalism." In Wallace E. Oates, ed., *The Political Economy of Fiscal Federalism.* Lexington, Mass.: Lexington Books.
———. 1990. "Decentralization of the Public Sector: An Overview." In Robert J. Bennett, ed., *Decentralization, Local Governments and Markets: Towards a Post-Welfare Agenda,* 43–58. Oxford: Clarendon Press.
———. Forthcoming. *Federalism and Government Finance.* Cambridge, Mass.: Harvard University Press.
Olowa, Bola. 1992. "Sharing the Cake: The Politics of Revenue Allocation." *West Africa* (August 24–30): 1434–35.
Palmer, Keith E. 1980. "Mineral Taxation Policies in Developing Countries." *IMF (International Monetary Fund) Staff Papers* 27(3): 517–42. Washington, D.C.
Plourde, Andre. 1991. "The NEP Meets the FTA." *Canadian Public Policy* 17(1): 14–24.
Pretes, Michael, and Michael Robinson. 1989. "Beyond Boom and Bust: A Strategy for Creating Sustainable Development in the North." *Polar Record* 25 (April): 115.
———. 1990. "Alaskan and Canadian Trust Funds as Agents of Sustainable Development." In J. Owen Saunders, ed., *The Legal Challenge of Sustainable Development.* Calgary: Canadian Institute of Resources Law.
Prud'homme, Remy. 1977. "France: Central Government Control over Public Investment Expenditures." In Wallace E. Oates, ed., *The Political Economy of Fiscal Federalism,* 65–75. Lexington, Mass.: Lexington Books.
Rao, M. Govinda. 1991. "Central Transfers to Offset Fiscal Disadvantages of the States: Measurement of Cost Disabilities and Expenditure Needs." *Indian Economic Review* 26(1): 12–34.
Redhorse, David, and Theodore Reynolds Smith. 1982. "American Indian Tribal Taxation of Energy Resources." *Natural Resources Journal* 22(3): 659–71.
Renaud, Bertrand. 1991. *Housing Reform in Socialist Economies.* World Bank Discussion Paper 125. Washington, D.C.

Roback, Jennifer. 1992. "Exchange, Sovereignty, and Indian-Anglo Relations." In Terry L. Anderson, ed., *Property Rights and Indian Economies.* Boston, Mass.: Rowman and Littlefield.

Robinson, Michael, Mark Dickerson, Jack Van Camp, Wanda Wuttunee, Michael Pretes, and Lloyd Binder. 1989. *Coping with the Cash.* Calgary: Arctic Institute of North America, Sustainable Development Research Group.

Robinson, Michael, Michael Pretes, and Wanda Wuttunee. 1989. "Investment Strategies for Northern Cash Windfalls: Learning from the Alaskan Experience." *Arctic* 42(3): 265–76.

Rosen, Harvey S. 1988. *Public Finance.* 2nd ed. Homewood, Ill.: Irwin Publications in Economics.

Scott, Anthony. 1978. *Central Government Claims to Mineral Revenues.* Canberra: Australian National University Press, Center for Research on Federal Financial Relations.

Shah, Anwar. 1990. "The New Fiscal Federalism in Brazil." PRE Working Paper 557. World Bank, Policy Research Department, Washington, D.C.

———. 1991. "Perspectives on the Design of Intergovernmental Relations." PRE Working Paper 726. World Bank, Policy Research Department, Washington, D.C.

Shannon, Francis J. 1972. *Business Taxes in State and Local Governments.* Lexington, Mass.: Lexington Books.

Smith, Ernest H. 1976. "Allocating to Provinces the Taxable Income of Corporations: How the Federal-Provincial Allocation Rules Evolved." Paper presented to members of the Federal-Provincial Subcommittee on Income Allocation, September 24. *Canadian Tax Journal* (September-October): 545–71.

Smith, Roger S. 1980. "The Alberta Heritage Savings Trust Fund." *Canadian Public Policy* 6 (special issue, February).

Sole-Vilanova, Joaquim. 1990. "Regional and Local Finance in Spain: Is Fiscal Responsibility the Missing Element?" In Robert J. Bennett, ed., *Decentralization, Local Governments and Markets: Towards a Post-Welfare Agenda,* 333–53. Oxford: Clarendon Press.

Stevenson, Garth. 1976. *Mineral Resources and Australian Federalism.* Canberra: Australian National University Press, Center for Research on Federal Financial Relations.

Strother, Robert C., and Robert A. Brown. 1991. "Self-Government and the Taxation of Aboriginal People in Canada." Paper prepared for a conference on Indian Governments and Tax, Whistler, British Columbia, November 12-15.

Tait, Alan. 1988. *Value Added Tax: International Experiences and Problems.* Washington, D.C.: International Monetary Fund.

Tanzi, Vito, ed. 1992. *Fiscal Policies in Economies in Transition.* Washington, D.C.: International Monetary Fund.

———. 1993a. "Fiscal Policy and the Economic Restructuring of Economies in Transition." IMF (International Monetary Fund) WP/93/22, Washington, D.C.

———, ed. 1993b. *Transition to Market: Studies in Fiscal Reform.* Washington, D.C.: International Monetary Fund.

Thirsk, Wayne R. 1983a. "Tax Assignment and Revenue Sharing in Canada." In Charles E. McLure, Jr., ed., *Tax Assignment in Federal Countries.* Canberra: Australian National University Press.

———. 1983b. "Tax Harmonization in Canada." In George Break, ed., *State and Local Finance: The Pressures of the 1980s.* Madison: University of Wisconsin Press.

Van Wijnbergen, Sweder. 1992. "Enterprise Reform in Eastern Europe." PRE Working Paper 1068. World Bank, Central Europe Department, Washington, D.C.

Vickers, J., and G. Yarrow. 1988. *Privatization: An Economic Analysis.* Cambridge, Mass.: MIT Press.

Wallich, Christine I. 1982. *State Finances in India.* Vol. 1, *Revenue Sharing.* World Bank Staff Working Paper No. 523. Washington, D.C.

Wallich, Christine I. 1992a. *Fiscal Decentralization: Intergovernmental Relations in Russia.* Studies of Economies in Transformation No. 6. Washington, D.C.: World Bank.

———. 1992b. "Local Finance in Developing Countries." Paper prepared for EDI (Economic Development Institute) conference, "Urban Policy Seminar," Hanoi, Viet Nam, June 1992. World Bank, East Asia and Pacific Region, Washington, D.C.

Wallich, Christine I., and Ritu Nayyar. 1993. "Russia's Intergovernmental Relations: A Key to National Cohesion." *Challenge* (November-December): 46–52.

Whyte, John D. 1983. "A Constitutional Perspective on Federal-Provincial Sharing of Revenues from Natural Resources." In Charles E. McLure, Jr., and Peter Mieszkowski, eds., *Fiscal Federalism and the Taxation of Natural Resources.* Lexington, Mass.: Lexington Books.

Wilson, Thomas. 1984. *Fiscal Decentralization.* London: Anglo-German Foundation for the Study of Industrial Society.

World Bank. 1988. *World Development Report 1988.* New York: Oxford University Press.

———. 1990a. *Argentina: Provincial Government Finances.* World Bank Country Study, Washington, D.C.

———. 1990b. *China: Revenue Mobilization and Tax Policy.* World Bank Country Study, Washington, D.C.

———. 1990c. *Transitions: The Newsletter about Reforming Economies* 3(10) (World Bank, Policy Research Department, Washington, D.C.)

———. 1992a. "Privatization: The Lessons of Experience." Private Sector Development Department, Washington, D.C.

———. 1992b. *Russian Economic Reform: Crossing the Threshold of Structural Change.* World Bank Country Study, Washington, D.C.

———. 1992c. "Taxation Reform for the Upstream Petroleum Sector." Europe and Central Asia Region. Washington, D.C.

Zimmermann, Horst. 1992. "Intergovernmental Transfers in Russia." Consultant's report. World Bank, Country Economics Department, Washington, D.C.

Zodrow, George R., and Charles E. McLure, Jr. 1991. "Implementing Direct Consumption Taxes in Developing Countries." *Tax Law Review* 46(4): 405–87.

Index

Accountability of public officials, 3, 99, 101–02, 146, 163, 167

Ad hoc approaches to revenue sharing, 4, 14, 78–80, 136, 157, 162, 225, 234. *See also* Negotiated revenue sharing

Agriculture, 122–23

Alaska, 182, 196–97, 201, 207

Alaska Native Claims Settlement Act corporations, 212

Alaska Permanent Fund, 210, 211, 215 n24

Alberta, 182, 196–97, 202, 216 n36

Alberta Heritage Savings Trust Fund, 210, 211, 215 n24

Argentina, 69, 87

Arrears, payment, 6, 72, 74, 78, 94 n2, 114, 245

Asset transfers, 6, 59–60, 87, 125–26, 246

Assignment of expenditures and taxes. *See* Expenditure assignment; Tax assignment

Australia, 139, 166, 171, 202, 214 n11, 230–31, 235

Autonomous regions (okrugs), 23–24

Autonomy: budget, 4, 26–27, 29, 43–46, 101, 108–14; for cities, 171; demands of ethnic minorities for, 100, 165, 207, 219–22, 248; demands of industrial regions for, 12, 57, 100, 139, 165, 219–22, 238; demands of natural resource–rich regions for, 221–22; and efficiency, 101, 151–52; and expenditure assignment, 43–46, 99–101, 104, 108–10; in Law on the Budgetary Rights of Local Self-Governments, 54–56, 104, 124, 176; in other countries, 226–34; political, 12, 24, 219–25; and tax sharing, 146

Bahry, Donna, 107, 128 n1

Banks, 7, 33, 80, 83–85, 92, 125

Barannikov, Viktor, 222

Bargaining for revenue shares. *See* Negotiated revenue sharing

Bashkortostan, 12, 21, 57, 79, 154, 220

Basic Principles of Taxation. *See* Law on the Basic Principles of Taxation

Benefit areas, 35–36, 99

Block grants, 229

Block transfers, 226

Blue-ribbon commission on intergovernmental fiscal strategies, 5, 139, 250

Bond issues, 84, 125

Borrowing by subnational governments, 6, 69, 71, 80–85, 120, 245. *See also* External debt

Branch principle of organization, 25, 26–27, 30–31

Brazil, 69, 167, 176